NOW AND FOREVER

Towards a Theory and History of the Loop

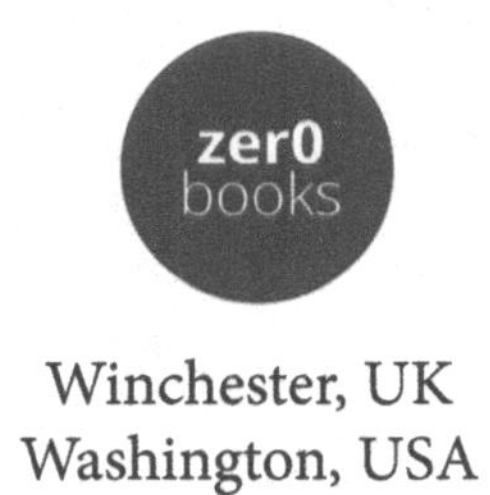

Winchester, UK
Washington, USA

NOW AND FOREVER

Towards a Theory and History of the Loop

Tilman Baumgärtel

Translated by Sabrina Stolfa

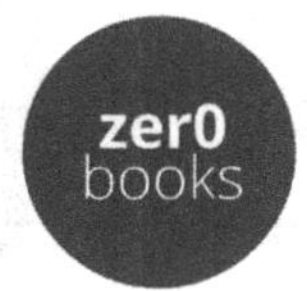

Winchester, UK
Washington, USA

JOHN HUNT PUBLISHING

First published in the Federal Republic of Germany
by Kulturverlag Kadmos Berlin, 2015
English edition by Zero Books, 2023
Zero Books is an imprint of John Hunt Publishing Ltd., No. 3 East St.,
Alresford,
Hampshire SO24 9EE, UK
office@jhpbooks.com
www.johnhuntpublishing.com
www.zero-books.net

For distributor details and how to order please visit the 'Ordering' section on
our website.

ISBN: 978 1 78904 151 4
978 1 78904 152 1 (ebook)
Library of Congress Control Number: 2021930334

Design: Stuart Davies

CONTENTS

THOU canst not end, and that doth make thee great,
Thou never dost begin that is thy fate.
Thy song wheels round as does the starry frame,
End and beginning evermore the same,
And what the middle brings we clearly see
Is what the opening was, the end shall be.
J. W. Goethe: Limitless, The West-Eastern Divan

It was Friday, and in the dining room the German clock maker wound up the clock.
Leo Tolstoy: Anna Karenina

Great things do not become dull when repeated. Only petty things need change and have to be replaced quickly by something else. The Great becomes greater, when we repeat it, and we our-self become richer and become quiet and become free.
Pope Benedict XVI

PREFACE

The alarm goes off at four o'clock on Sunday morning, but I've already been awake for half an hour. It's due to the excitement. We've been away from Berlin for a long time. And for a long time, we haven't been able to do what we are about to do – visit our favourite club.

The club has become so popular that on a Sunday night between one and six o'clock, you sometimes have to wait for 2 hours to get in. Yesterday, we went to bed at ten – probably just as the lights were being turned on over there for another non-stop night. We set the alarm so that when we get there, the queues at the entrance to the huge building have subsided. There's no such thing as being late. A cup of tea, a sandwich and we're on our bikes, riding through quiet side streets, then through Görlitzer Park. As we cycle across Oberbaum Bridge, S. comments on how beautiful it is to be out and about this early. "Only if you don't have to go to work the next day, of course", she adds. Well, we won't be going to work. And we're going dancing.

Berlin is bathed in a grey-blue twilight, the River Spree sparkles metallically. Past the Ostbahnhof, up the street of the Paris Commune, take a right into an unassuming cul-de-sac and ride through an industrial area, then past a long line of waiting taxis. And there it is in front of us, a dark mountainous shape – the former power station on Stalin Avenue.

We lock up our bikes and walk towards the building through a narrow passage between two fences. Here and there, an empty champagne bottle is lying on the ground. A torn T-shirt hangs on a pole and on another there's a headdress that someone fashioned from a coat hanger and some tinsel. The closer we get to the building, the louder the rhythmic thunder gets; it seems to make the entire building shake.

At the entrance, there are a few people who look like they've had a long night. Quick, get inside, before it gets light outside. The steel door swings open and a bouncer waves us through with a quick nod. Behind the cash register there's a huge staircase that looks like a backdrop to Fritz Lang's *Metropolis,* left behind after shooting. Up a steel staircase that reverberates in time to the music and we find ourselves on a dance floor in a high-ceilinged hall; about 500 people are moving to the monotonous electronic beats as if it wasn't already early morning; as if the city weren't slowly waking up to go to church or Sunday morning shift, or to get fresh bread rolls and a newspaper from the kiosk.

No, time has stopped here; it has dissolved into endless loops. Loops that never stop moving, never arrive anywhere, loops that just go on and on. My thoughts get entangled in them; my body, cocooned in them, begins to move to their beat. At some point, my shirt is drenched in sweat. I am dancing on a platform at the edge of the dance floor. Below me, all around me, others are heaving to the same rhythm. Screams. Red flickering lights. Arms shoot up in the air, dovetailing with the hands of the clock, and time stands still. Things begin to rotate. All things.

I'm standing in front of the main entrance to Shibuya Station in Tokyo, at an intersection thought to be the busiest in the world. It's six o'clock on an evening in November; it is almost dark and the city's offices are emptying onto the streets. From all directions, thousands of commuters are surging towards the intersection. Behind me is the train station from which passengers emerge in short successive bouts, as if pumped into the open by a great muscle. They stop by the side of the road; the traffic is flowing past them. As soon as the traffic lights turn green, the crowd starts to march hectically. Hundreds of people hurry across the street in less than a minute. Only I remain standing. I let the crowd wash around me and as if in a trance, wait for the traffic lights to change their signal again. Once. Twice. Ten times. A hundred times. Neon advertisements flicker above the crossing. The commercials run simultaneously on three giant screens. Below, the traffic lights set the beat. If I wait long enough, the commercials on the screens repeat, just like the phases of the traffic lights are doing. If I wait longer still, it will get dark, then turn into day again, night again, and eventually, autumn will turn into winter. Everything repeats, faster and faster. Day after day, night after night. It's light, then dark, light, dark, faster, faster, until there's just a flickering around me.

The stroboscope transforms the movements of the people on the dance floor into a series of snapshots. The music turns out loop after loop, repeating itself and vibrating, and now the hall is full of huge machines. They are working – gigantic steel wheels, cranks and connecting rods moving with the same staccato rhythm as the forging hammers that come down on the workpieces. Gears interlock, pistons move in and out. Everything rotates, turns, booms. Now and forever. A man is shovelling coal into a blazing furnace. It's Georg, No. 11811, the stoker from *Metropolis*. I can see around the globe now, where everywhere, slave-like, bent figures are working in semi-darkness, moving to the rhythm imposed on them by the machines. On a conveyor belt, thousands of hands assemble components to the beat. Once the devices are completed, they will be producing their own rhythm. In another corner, dark figures surround a large drum (or is it an oil barrel?), which they belabour, following the rhythm.

Everything is part of these infinite loops. Steam engines, centrifuges, drills, rotors, propellers, fans, crankshafts, two-stroke and four-stroke engines. Relays jangle, computer hard drives hum in time. All rotary machines, rhythm machines. They loop, tap, roll, oscillate and join loop to loop to loop to loop. Each a doppelganger of the previous one. *Déjà vu* after *déjà vu*.

The globe rotates, cells replicate, huge celestial bodies turn around each other, electrons rotate around the nucleus, matter vibrates. Endless vistas of space full of mirrors open up, one reflection reflecting the next, echoes reverberating through them, only to fade away and resound again, without end because every end is another beginning. Everything moves, all the time. Nothing begins, nothing ceases.

The big drum. Sometimes manic and demonic, sometimes infinite and exalted, sometimes merely annoying. I let the rhythms dance inside me and keep moving, my breath accelerating, my heart beating in time. The DJ's records on the turntables continue to turn when we leave the dance floor and go back down the reverberating steel staircase to the exit. While time had stopped inside that machine room, it has been continuing outside. When we step outside, it's already dark again. A gentle wind blows from the Spree; the street lights are on in Holzmarkt Street. In 8 hours' time it will get light again.

NOW AND FOREVER: INTRODUCTION

Everything remains the same, only the appearance changes.
Anton Webern

In 1983, I bought a Commodore 64 from my neighbour. The Commodore 64 remains the most-sold computer in history. My neighbour wanted a newer model, so I bought my first computer for 100 German Marks pocket money. It came with a manual for the BASIC programming language. At the time, computers had very rudimentary graphical user interfaces, and if you wanted to use them, you had to know a programming language. So, after playing a few rounds of *Donkey Kong* and *Scramble,* I set about entering my first BASIC commands into the computer.

According to the handbook, the first program to be tried was as follows:

```
100 PRINT "HELLO"
200 GOTO 100
RUN
```

BASIC, unlike other programming languages, has the advantage that its commands bear some resemblance to spoken English. The commands are arranged as a numbered list, which the computer processes one after the other. The PRINT "HELLO" command tells the computer to write the word "HELLO" on the display. The second command, GOTO 100, tells the program to jump back to the first command in the list, i.e. to PRINT "HELLO". The RUN command tells the computer to start executing the program. This little program did nothing but write the word "HELLO" on the monitor, over and over – in capital letters, one letter at a time.

Hello Hello Hello Hello Hello Hello Hello Hello Hello
Hello Hello Hello Hello Hello Hello Hello Hello Hello
Hello Hello Hello Hello Hello Hello Hello Hello Hello
Hello Hello Hello Hello Hello Hello Hello Hello Hello
Hello Hello Hello Hello Hello Hello Hello Hello Hello
Hello Hello Hello Hello Hello Hello Hello Hello Hello
Hello Hello Hello Hello Hello Hello Hello Hello Hello
Hello Hello Hello Hello Hello Hello Hello Hello Hello
Hello Hello Hello Hello Hello Hello Hello Hello Hello
Hello Hello Hello Hello Hello Hello Hello Hello Hello
Hello Hello Hello Hello Hello Hello Hello Hello Hello
Hello Hello Hello Hello Hello Hello Hello Hello Hello
Hello Hello Hello Hello Hello Hello Hello Hello Hello
Hello Hello Hello Hello Hello Hello Hello Hello Hello
Hello Hello Hello Hello

Although I was unaware of the term "loop" at the time, I had created a small loop on my computer – a program loop, which repeated the same thing over and over. The computer continued to write the same word on the monitor and did not stop until I turned it off.

I do not recall that this program, the first one I ever "wrote", made a big impression on me in any technical sense. But I still remember its *effect* – it had mesmerized me. As though hypnotized,

I had watched as the word "Hello" rolled over the screen, line after line in the clumsy BASIC font, white on a blue background. The slow, consecutive appearance of the words had been both soothing and stimulating.

Just like after the consumption of certain drugs, I felt completely focused and relaxed at the same time. I had lost any sense of time. I stared at the words, the blurred letters that appeared on the screen one after the other. I do not remember how long I continued watching the lines crawl across the screen. It might have been minutes, or as long as half an hour before I turned the machine off.

I never repeated this strange experiment. And I might as well admit that my BASIC programming skills progressed very little after that. But the computer's unceasing repetition, which would have continued to this day had I not turned it off, did leave a lasting impression on me.

Almost 30 years have passed since then. Along with the computer, loops have acquired a place in our daily life that is as far-reaching as it is largely unnoticed. It's not only in the computer programs we use daily that loops are continuously running. In the last decade, they have emerged from the background of life, and are now a part of our lives that cannot be ignored.

Repetitive animations tell us to put the debit card in the ATM, musical loops keep us hanging on while we wait for the call centre to answer. The ringing of mobile phones and the endlessly repeated commercials on the screens of large train stations are loops. On CNN, the news tape at the bottom of the screen shows stock market prices and newsflashes in a continuous loop. Spectacular news images are run as non-stop loops during special broadcasts while experts debate.

The data, the video images, seem to have taken on a life of their own. It is as though these recordings of life do not wish to exist only as inanimate information on hard disks, tapes or diskettes; it is as though they want to find a way back to the world of the living. And what repeats itself is not dead.

This book will attempt a reading of the "state of the human soul from the sundial of human technology" (Theodor W. Adorno) by telling the story of the loop. In doing so, it will try to elucidate the effect and the significance of the loop. However, the focus will not be on loops like the ones previously referred to, those that surround us in daily life. Instead, I will focus on the visual arts and music, fields in which loops have become an important design element in the second half of the twentieth century. Loops, for me, are part of a culture of repetition. They reflect the creative possibilities of repetition in digital media.

What, exactly, is a loop? The word has established itself as a technical term for short sound and image sequences that can be repeated indefinitely, both in the world of music and in the world of audio-visual media, whether analogue or digitally recorded. Anyone who can conjure up an image in connection with the term "loop" will probably be thinking of a strip of tape or film that is glued together to form a loop. Today, loops – both audio and visual – are usually generated on a computer.

Let us imagine such a loop. Imagine how a piece of recording tape, ends glued together, proceeds laboriously through the tape deck, again and again. Or imagine how a short sound file is repeated by a music program. Let us imagine how it reproduces a sound fragment, over and over. A few seconds of laughter, for example. "Ha, ha!", "Hahahaha. Hahahahahahahaha." The longer the laughter loop lasts, the more superhuman it comes across. Depending on the listener's state of mind, it may become funnier and funnier the longer it plays, and may even have a contagious effect. Or it can create an increasingly demonic and terrifying effect – as in the techno track *Do Not Laugh* by Josh Wink, which is based on looped laughter.

When a sound is looped, the loop can make time stand still. The immobilized sound embalms the moment. As the world-weary Faust closes his deal with the Devil, he imposes one condition – he will allow the Devil to take his soul if, at that moment, the Devil can get Faust to say, "please stay! You are so beautiful!" The tape loop fulfils such a wish, a wish that is blasphemous and deeply romantic at the same time. Loops promise that the beautiful (but also terrible) moment does not have to pass, but may linger, *now and forever.* That it can be repeated until desire is transformed into weariness. Or until *ennui* becomes transcendence.

Repetition *per se* has, of course, always been an important means of aesthetic expression in the arts. The charm of music is to be found precisely in the interplay between repetition and variation. Barely varied forms of repetition play an important role in such different styles of music as the Brazilian samba and the Javanese gamelan, in the Moroccan ganawi music and the Eastern European polka. Repetition is found in the percussion music of West Africa and in Indian *tabla* music, in the funk music of James Brown, in Ravel's *Bolero*, in the canon *Brother Jacob* and in *Sweet Home Alabama* by Lynyrd Skynyrd. And these "minimalist" forms of expression are not only normal in music, but also in the visual arts. The ancient Greek and Roman mosaics and the Moorish alicatado tile images on the walls of the Alhambra, Arabic calligraphy or Josef Albers' *Homage to the Square* are all based on repetitive structures. But this book is not about these forms of repetition.

It is about music and art forms that are shaped and characterized by repetition because they are produced using the machines of modern media, the computers. The optical toys of the eighteenth and nineteenth centuries, such as the wheel of life, the zoetrope or Ottomar Anschütz's "Schnellseher" [speed viewer] were all loops, albeit without making any decidedly artistic use of the special possibilities that their technological forms suggested. That is why this book is not about them either. Rather, it is about artists who have utilized the possibilities of repetition the technology offers to create an aesthetic concept.

Machines have been making sounds and images into loops for more than half a century. In the fields of music, film and the visual arts, this method has been used to achieve very different aesthetic objectives. In my story of the loop, the first artist who worked systematically with loops and their aesthetic possibilities was French composer Pierre Schaeffer, who created his first *musique concrète* compositions shortly after the Second World War, using "skipping" records.

The arrival of the new medium of magnetic tape made it easier to produce such sound loops. Schaeffer and, following him, an entire generation of composers started a thorough investigation of these new musical possibilities. Soon, in centres for experimental and electronic music, as well as in many recording studios where pop music was produced, long tape loops were coiled around tape reels, guide rollers, microphone stands – and even around ball point pens, beer bottles and wine glasses.

Loops became one of the most important new tools for producing electronic music. But those composers who were among the first to work with loops, for instance, Schaeffer, Karlheinz Stockhausen or Pierre Henry, generally tried to avoid drawing attention to the loop's repetitive qualities. It was the succeeding generation of post-war composers that focused on just that: the music of the American minimalists consisted of nothing other than uninterrupted, minimally varied repetitions, of *patterns*. This technique was developed by minimalists Terry Riley and Steve Reich in the mid-1960s and arose directly from their experiments with tape loops. Many other music genres were to adopt this approach and turn the repetitive possibilities of recorded media into a foundation for compositions.

From the 1970s onwards, popular music was increasingly shaped by loops and by the extremes of repetition made possible by technology. Entire genres like hip-hop, electro, house, techno or one Giorgio Moroder's electronic disco are based explicitly on repetition by means of media technology and they have developed original forms of expression based on loops. These, in turn, have become the basis of complex sub-and youth cultures, influencing whole generations with their own manners, fashions and codes of behaviour. And not infrequently, these loop-based art forms have also been the foundation of flourishing business endeavours.

In the visual arts and experimental cinema, artists and filmmakers like Bruce Connor, Nam June Paik, Peter Roehr and Lutz Mommartz began working with film strips that were continuously fed into the projector as loops. The same time frame saw the development of the Minimalist Music genre. Such works fit perfectly into an arts scene that had begun to develop an unexpected taste for repetition. Amazing enthusiasm for repetitions and series, for lists and arrays, is a characteristic of minimalist art, pop art, conceptual art and the performance arts of the 60s and 70s.

In 1965, video cameras and recorders appeared in the consumer marketplace and were discovered as a new medium by a number of artists. Soon after, artists like Nam June Paik, Klaus vom Bruch or Dara Birnbaum began to repeat themselves, over and over, in their video works, installations and performances. In video art, the loop became an important formal tool that has continued to shape the works of artists like Rodney Graham, Daniel Pflumm, Francis Alÿs, Paul Pfeiffer, Stan Douglas, Douglas Gordon, Carsten Höller, Safy Etiel and Matthias Müller to the present day.

In view of this, it is difficult not to wonder why loops have not been seen as one of the significant aesthetic elements of the last decades.[1] From a historical perspective, loops would seem to be one of the most important forces in the culture of the second half of the twentieth century. Today, they have become such an influential form of expression in so many fields that I think it is appropriate to refer to them as a "cultural form".

How did the loop become so popular in music and the visual arts? How could a style of music such as techno, which is based on continuous repetition, become a youth movement? And what was so dangerous about this music, which reminds many people of Chinese water torture, that the UK Parliament even passed a law in 1994 in the *Criminal Justice Act* to prohibit the playing of music "that totally or mainly consists of series of repetitive *beats*" outdoors?[2]

Especially in Western culture, repetition has traditionally been regarded as boring and soul-destroying. "You're repeating yourself!" is intended as a criticism. Or, "it's always the same story with you!" Or, as if someone had been able to see the triumph of loops coming, "can't you change the record?" In the intellectual history of the twentieth century, repetition has had a bad name, something that will be discussed in detail later. For the moment, it will suffice to recall Freud's idea of the pathological "compulsion to repeat". The Frankfurt School, and especially Theodor W. Adorno, were harsh critics of repetition in mass media and popular music, which they saw as regressive and soporific. Adorno declares,

> what repeats itself is healthy, like the natural or industrial cycle. The same babies grin eternally out of the magazines, the Jazz machine will pound away forever. In spite of all the progress in reproduction techniques, in controls and the specialities, and in spite of all the restless industry, the bread which the culture industry offers man is the stone of the stereotype.[3]

Contemporary Westerners have grown accustomed to looking at life as if it were moving forward in a linear progression. Repetitions were primarily regarded as an element of delay on a forward path. The idea of "circular time" (Jorge Luis Borges) seems strange and suspicious in Western culture. Peter Handke writes in his novel *Across* that it is striking "how the repetitions in current phrases usually impress me as something evil, pathological, or even criminal. Could one not, on the other hand, speak of refreshing repetition as opposed to wearisome repetition; voluntary repetition as opposed to forced repetition? The possibility of repetition as opposed to the danger of repetition?[4]

The loop contradicts the teleological directionality of the Western Christian world towards a better life after death as much as it contradicts the Modernist belief in progress. Those who work hard will achieve their objective. – Whoever is good in this life will go to heaven when he dies. – Whoever pays his social security taxes will get a pension later. – The course of history is a history of class struggle that "naturally" leads to revolution, the dictatorship of the proletariat and, finally, to a classless society. The Westerner's present has always moved towards such a future.

The loop, as a cultural form, contradicts such ideas. Art works and compositions based on loops often create a feeling of an "endless present" or "cyclical time" in their audience. These concepts are in direct opposition to the modern understanding of time and history as constant "progress". *Time's arrow* was the phrase used by Harvard professor Stephen Jay Gould in his influential book to describe the Western notion of history: time as an arrow shooting toward a target. In contrast to the concept of time as an "arrow" moving forward, *Time's Cycle*, for Gould, represents the cyclical, periodic concept of time, as it is perceived in many non-Western cultures. Insofar as loop-based art and culture contradict a linear understanding of time and history, they also represent a critique of, or alternative to, that understanding.[5]

The teleological-linear orientation of Western culture is also reflected in Western art. The traditional music of the West, whether folk songs, pop songs or Beethoven symphonies, as a rule has a narrative, teleological orientation. It is organized to follow a functional harmonic schematic of tension building towards a climax – in the process of movement, the music develops towards a goal, a resolution, a climax. Music based on loops, on the other hand, is non-narrative and non-teleological. The music just goes on and on, an evolution without direction, in which the listener no longer has to follow a strict musical development, but rather, is confronted with the cyclical, repetitive movement of short musical *patterns.*

Whether Minimalist Music or techno – this type of loop-based music refuses to fit in with the compositional development of motifs and the like. As in the famous dream of Friedrich August Kekulés, in which the molecular structure of benzene appeared to him as a snake biting its own tail, in techno, loop-based music is a "monkey's dance" of rhythmic sound events, one following the next, "long rows, often joined together densely...winding and rotating like a snake", as Kekulé described the molecular loop-structure of benzene that appeared to him in a dream vision after some glasses of punch.

Significantly, the triumph of repetition in the world of culture coincided with the very moment when the first cracks appeared in the euphoric belief in progress and the exaggerated optimism of the modern age – in the second half of the twentieth century. One of the maxims of the Enlightenment and the modern era was that humanity would follow a path of progressive (and progressing) development in which the rapid advances of science and technology would lead to more justice, humanity and self-determination.

However, the Second World War, the Holocaust and detonation of the first atomic bomb showed that the scientific and technical progress of the modern era had by no means led to a more just and enlightened global society, on the contrary, it had been a prerequisite for the most terrible barbarism in the history of mankind. That the "fully enlightened earth…" would come to radiate "disaster triumphant",[6] as expressed in *Dialectic of Enlightenment* by Horkheimer and Adorno, triggered increasing doubts in the post-war generation about the maxims of progress that had defined the modern era. This is the context in which the emergence of repetition-orientated artistic and musical schools, such as minimalist art and Minimalist Music, played out like an unexpected retarding moment in the modern era, a kind of pause or rejection of the "Western mobilization civilization" (Peter Sloterdijk).

This process culminated in a period marked by two symbolically charged dates – the simultaneous end of the second millennium and twentieth century. In this double "fin de siècle" mood, contemporary, postmodern philosophy proclaimed the "end of the grand narrative" (Jean-Francois Lyotard) while journalism proclaimed "the end of history" (Francis Fukuyama) after the fall of the Berlin Wall and collapse of the Warsaw Pact. The German historian Achim Landwehr has shown in his book *Geburt der Gegenwart* [The Birth of the Present] that our perception of time is a cultural construction.[7] The assumption borrowed from Newtonian physics of a homogeneous time flowing inexorably forward is a specifically modern concept that has dominated modern times. This concept of time was not, of course, suddenly overturned in the last years of the previous millennium, but the sudden success of loop-based music may be a sign that time might have appeared to some as arrested, jammed, compressed or even transformed into a closed loop. Loop-based culture was an appropriate reflection of the "timeless time" of the era. Because one of its most important characteristics was not to develop further, not to demonstrate progress. It seems fitting that the 1990s saw the coming together of techno-as-music and the youth culture phenomenon.

But this book is not a book about electronic dance music either. Numerous excellent studies have been published in recent years about its history and aesthetics, and it is not necessary for me to rework it.[8] Rather, I am concerned with the prehistory and early history of a development that ultimately led to styles based entirely on media repetition, such as techno and hip-hop.

Why did artists and composers from such widely varying backgrounds suddenly start working with loops in the second part of the twentieth century? How did music based on minimally varied repetitions catch on? Upon what aesthetic assumptions was the phenomenon based? I find it amazing that a musical style such as techno, which has so little to do with what we in the West are taught about music in school or instrumental lessons, was able to grow into a kind of mass movement at the end of the twentieth century. I was amazed when this music first appeared, and I am still amazed. My amazement is the reason for me to write this book – to answer these questions for myself.

The answer suggested in this book, in broad strokes, is this: the form of loop-based music and art is a direct result of the fact that these art forms are created with electronic devices, with machines. The artists have made the characteristic properties of these media machines into an art form. They were created with turntables, tape recorders and video equipment, with synthesizers, sequencers and computers. And these devices are – like all machines – repetitive creations. They reproduce and repeat.

The visual arts and music that make use of these devices used the technical imperative of reproduction and repetition in the loop as their subject matter and developed their specific forms from this. The development from the initial, tentative experiments with loops into musical styles that emerge out of loops took place in a constant interplay between the media technology that made such repetitions possible and a culture that was increasingly prepared to accept such repetition as an artistic method. The presentation of this interaction is the most important concern of this book. The artistic work with loops seems like an attempt to develop an element of difference from the mechanical repetitions of technological media (tape recorders, sequencers or computers), that is, from the immaculate and faultless expiration of machine time. What Gilles Deleuze writes in *Difference and Repetition* about the role of the imagination in repetition also applies to the artistic work with loops – "the role of the imagination, or the mind which contemplates in its multiple and fragmented states, is to draw something new from repetition, to draw difference from it."[9]

As I will show, the best artistic works with loops are always concerned with bringing their "complicated inner repetitions" (Gilles Deleuze) into view. Artistic work with loops is therefore also an attempt to curb or tame the seemingly overpowering technology by lending slightly irregular, "organic" traits to its precise, periodic pounding. Artists have either manipulated the technology they used to create loops, or they have prompted their audience's perception to produce such differences by playing with the mechanically perfect repetitions of the recording media. Loop-based art and music must therefore always have a phenomenological component. It is no longer primarily about what the artist or composer is trying to say or express. Instead, this type of music and art deals with the body of the listener or viewer and the conditions of their perception. This shift in the roles of the art-producer on the one hand, and the art-consumer on the other is the most radical aesthetic innovation that loops have introduced into the art and music of the postmodern era. Art and music using loops, therefore, are not "anti-progressive" *per se*, that is, they do not celebrate stasis and stagnation. They are neither a negation of progress, nor an aestheticization, nor even a celebration of compulsive repetition (Sigmund Freud), an eternal recurrence of the same (Friedrich Nietzsche) or a negative infinity (Georg Wilhelm Friedrich Hegel), for which a "Hauntology" in Mark Fisher's sense would be responsible.[10] As a surprisingly flexible artistic tool, loops are used by artists for widely differing purposes. If their repetitive features were at the centre of the artist's cognitive interest, then it was not on account of the paralyzing, but of the productive moment of repetition. Diedrich Diederichsen writes:

> anyone who has experienced something new in the sameness of the loop is dealing with a much harder "new" than those who experience it in a structure where the occurrence of the new is intended, as in conventional narration...If something that is the same becomes different, and something that is different becomes the same, then we know better where we stand. We are making progress. Well, you get ahead in the loop.[11]

Seen from a present-day perspective, working in loop-based art seems like a kind of grassroots movement in which artists, composers and musicians from very different backgrounds participated for very different reasons. Some of them did know of others who worked in the same way. But many came up with the idea of making art using technology-based repetitions without any knowledge of predecessors or contemporary practitioners; they did it because the media itself suggested these methods to them. In the following story of the loop, we will meet some very well-known, recognized artists, e.g. Andy Warhol, Ken Kesey and Karlheinz Stockhausen. But there will also be outsiders – like jazz composer and instrument maker Raymond Scott – who are probably known only to specialists.

This is therefore not a history book in the strict sense of the word. Although the chapters are arranged in roughly chronological order, it is not my intention to write a definitive narrative, and this book does not claim to be an exhaustive treatment of the subject.

It can't be about recounting all the artistic or musical experiments that have been done with loops; otherwise, its scope would have expanded into the infinite and it would be unreadable. Rather, I have tried to trace the aesthetics of the loop by concentrating on episodes and works that I regard as "key events" in the development of the loop as an artistic form of expression. Some of these key events involve artists like the minimalist composers Terry Riley and Steve Reich, whom one would expect to find in a history of the loop. Others, like Elvis, The Beatles or Ken Kesey, probably wouldn't be associated with loops in the minds of most people.

From the key events I will develop the historical and discursive framework in which they happened. The focus will be on music, because no other art form can handle repetition with more virtuosity than music. I will consider loops in the visual arts mainly in terms of their points of contact with music.

The book is divided into two parts. The first part is about loop-based works from the immediate post-war period until the end of the 1950s. In this period, loops in music were almost exclusively used to create sound effects (film and other visual loops played practically no role at that time). The repetitive characteristics of loops were, amazingly, almost never used to create rhythms and *patterns* – the explanation for this, I believe, lies in the still dominant, late modernist rejection of "soulless" repetition. Composers such as Karlheinz Stockhausen, who were working with loops at the time, did so in order to produce sounds that had not been heard before. Part I of the book is therefore called *Into the Sound*.

In the first chapter of Part I, I will – starting with the first films of Edison, which were presented as loops – introduce the modernist rejection of strict, technology-made repetition and some of the early critics of "mindless, regressive" repetition from the worlds of philosophy and culture. Thereafter I will describe some of the early stages in the development of the loop as a means of artistic expression. The early *Noise Etudes* by Pierre Schaeffer, which I consider to be the first example of a conscious use of loops as an aesthetic tool, will be the focus here. The third chapter deals with Karlheinz Stockhausen, whose own introduction to the use of loops was listening to Schaeffer, but who came to use loops for completely different purposes than Schaeffer. While Schaeffer was, above all, concerned with creating music out of common noises, using loops to structure these noises, Stockhausen used tape loops to expand the compositional methods of serial music, adding timbre to pitch in a bid to achieve complete control of the sound.

I will then go on to discuss an episode which, while generally considered a milestone in the history of pop music, was equally important in the popularization of tape loops: the Sun Sessions of Elvis Presley. Even in these first Elvis recordings, which were to catapult him to fame, loops were already in play. I will argue in this chapter that the tape recorder echo, which was used to alter Elvis' voice during these recordings, influenced both his singing style and artistic persona. At the same time, I will show that the Sun Sessions are also the beginning of a kind of pop music that is no longer the simple playback of live performances, but rather, the product of technical interventions, manipulations and production tricks, with the recording studio itself becoming an instrument.

The first part of the book ends with a chapter on an instrument maker who was working on new technical instruments based on the principle of loops: Raymond Scott. He is not the only one who worked on this project at that time, but his contribution is so important that it justifies dedicating an entire chapter to him.

Part II of the book is called *Into the Rhythm* because it deals with the development of loops from the early 1960s onward, a time when they were increasingly used for their repetitive and metrical qualities. The second part begins with a chapter on the German artist Peter Roehr, who, in the mid-60s, was one of the first to work with raw image and tone loops. In the 60s, technical repetitions irrevocably found their way into the canon of art and music. In terms of method, Roehr was close to American minimalism, and his relatively unknown work even precedes this movement in strict historical terms. I will use his example to discuss some of the intellectual foundations that led to repetitions being no longer regarded as soul-destroying and boring, but instead as legitimate aesthetic means. To this end, I will discuss the often underestimated influence of phenomenology, especially that of the French philosopher Maurice Merleau-Ponty, and of Fritz Perl's Gestalt therapy in the USA, on the art and music of this period. I will show that these two schools of thought influenced not only American minimalist art, but also the psychedelic movement, which was emerging at that time.

The first musical movement to emerge directly from the use of repetitive tape loops was American Minimalist Music. In the second and third chapters of Part II, I will therefore show how a musical style appeared from an engagement with tape loops which still has an influence on both serious music and pop music today. First, I will use the example of a unique collaboration between Andy Warhol and La Monte Young, the founder of Minimalist Music, to show how they, respectively, developed an art form and a musical form from a confrontation with stasis as an aesthetic principle, and what remarkable parallels existed between these seemingly so different artists.

While the minimalism of La Monte Young was one of stasis, of long, standing tones, or *drones*, the music of the other two important minimalists was characterized by repetitive *patterns*. In the chapters on Terry Riley and Steve Reich I will show how, in their early tape pieces, they developed their compositional techniques from their work with tape loops.

An example of how the tape loop from the electronic music of the post-war period infiltrated the pop culture of the Swinging Sixties can be found in the phenomenological experiments that the writer Ken Kesey (author of *One Flew Over the Cuckoo's Nest*) performed using tape loops with his group, the Merry Pranksters. From these, he developed a kind of "psychedelic heuristics". With Kesey and the Merry Pranksters, tape loops became an important part of the psychedelic culture of San Francisco in the late 1960s. Loops were used at many important events of this period – for example, the *Acid Test* and other Be-In events – as elements of multimedia spectacles with live music, projection images, light shows and performances. In their psychedelic phase, The Beatles experimented with tape loops. The fifth chapter shows how their experiments with loops inspired by Stockhausen and Riley led to one of the most unusual pop songs of the 1960s: *Tomorrow Never Knows.*

The culture of the collective musical spectacles, which decisively shaped the psychedelic period, was also one of the starting points for the disco culture of the 1970s – a repetitive, partly loop-based music that became the foundation of ecstatic dance marathons. As a final case study, I will examine *I Feel Love* by Donna Summer and Giorgio Moroder. Not only can this piece be considered the best example of the electronic variety of 70s disco that was based on sequencer loops, it is also an early precursor of the techno music of the 1980s and 1990s. The final chapter summarizes the book's insights.

My account begins with a filmed kiss, endlessly repeated by technological means, which provoked both amusement and stark horror in audiences. It concludes with the electronic robot sex of Donna Summers' *I Feel Love*, one of the most successful and momentous hits of the disco era, which, with its throbbing synthesizer riffs, took the theme of repetition and reproduction to new heights, making the repetitive theme a part of its aesthetic concept.

"It takes courage to want repetition", Kierkegaard writes in his essay *Repetition*. "He who wills repetition is a man, and the more expressly he knows how to make his purpose clear, the deeper he is as a man."[12] Kierkegaard was not thinking of the technical repetition of the loop. But his remarks were written at a time when revolutionary technological progress had led to a state in which men's lives were becoming more and more influenced by mechanical repetition – work in the factories, mass production, the appearance of mass media.

"In manufacture and handicrafts, the workman makes use of a tool; in the factory, the machine makes use of him. In manufacture, the motion of the implement proceeds from him; in the factory, he only follows the movements of the machine," writes Marx, for instance, in *Das Kapital*.[13] Elsewhere, he points out that "man is a very inadequate instrument when it comes to the performance of continuous, uniform movement". Continuous, uniform movements are what the machines in the factory force the worker to do. Marx condenses this observation into the concise phrase "the tools of production kill the worker". To make the workers into a willing "appendage of the machine", and to teach them to do work consisting of endless repetitions – these were among the most difficult tasks faced by early capitalists, as is well-known. "The imperative and behavioural demands of wage labour, sentenced, regardless of biological and climatic rhythms, to repeat the same monotonous motions every day, to arrive on time at the factory and not to leave before closing time, were absolutely alien to pre-industrial man," writes Götz Eisenberg. "Their lives followed a different rhythm and they did not yet know the strict separation of working and living."[14] To accustom workers to the repetitiveness of machine work and the linear time of capitalism effectively, some factory owners had lackeys fetch them from their homes and virtually drag them to work; at times they would impose draconian punishments for dawdling or for leaving the workplace.

Michel Foucault discusses this in *Discipline and Punishment*, his study of the emergence of "enclosed environments", such as prisons, schools and factories. These enclosures made possible the "dictatorship of punctuality" and the "micro-justice of time". He, too, emphasizes the enormity of the difference between division of time in pre-industrial and industrial work. For the people in Europe before the Industrial Revolution, writes Foucault, life was not primarily work, but "pleasure, unsteadiness, celebration, tranquillity, needs, coincidences, desires, acts of violence, robberies, etc", and "this quite explosive, momentary and discontinuous energy must be transformed by capital into labour-power, something which implies compulsion."[15]

With his focus on the emergence of anonymous power structures, Foucault pays little attention to the role that factory machines played in transforming workers into efficient cogs of the industrial process. But it is precisely the "worker's dependence on the continuous and uniform movements of the machine" (Karl Marx) that the labour movement of the nineteenth century saw as a drastic symptom of the "tyranny of technology". The dull monotony that characterizes factory work has, since this period, been one of the most important arguments against it.

The criticism of rigorous mechanical repetition is found not only in the political theories of the day, however, but also in the arts. The romantics, as intellectual contemporaries of both Marx and the Industrial Revolution, responded to these developments by celebrating the unique, the peculiar, the original. The art and culture of the modern era has inherited the dislike of the "unpleasantly correct, soulless rhythm of the singing machine" (ETA Hoffmann)[16] from the Romantics. The arts of classical modernism have almost obsessively presented themselves as the *Other* in relation to the eternal repetition of everyday life and technology. The avant-garde of the twentieth century saw itself as dedicated to continuous progress and celebrated shock, the unique, the entirely new.

Modernism, with its fixation on newness, seems almost to be a "grand movement to escape the curse of repetition".[17] This attitude has continued up to the present time, finding expression in the preference for craft products rather than factory-made, handmade things rather than machine-made, antiques instead of Ikea furniture, and homemade jam instead of Nutella. These are only some examples of the kinds of things in which the "movement to escape mechanical repetition" has sought refuge.

In high culture as much as pop culture, modernism has found impressive images for the horror of the inhuman repetition required by technology: from the Gothicism of the nineteenth century – with their homunculi, artificial humans, ETA Hoffmann's Olympia, Frankenstein's monster and others – to the cyberpunk of the 1990s with its cyborgs, humanoid robots and the repeatedly portrayed "Rise of the Machines", as in the *Terminator* and *Matrix* films. These scenarios can be read as a symbolic process of coping with the horrors found in the world of machines, unleashed in the modern era.

Cinema in particular has produced powerful iconic images to symbolize the fear of machines and their endless repetitions; for example, in Chaplin's *Modern Times*, the little tramp goes crazy doing the soul-destroying, repetitive work on the assembly line before he is literally devoured by a machine. Fritz Lang's *Metropolis* also portrays workers as dehumanized extensions of machines, as robotically shuffling, living corpses – Worker No. 11811 is shown as the kind of "appendage of a machine" which Marx referred to when he is compelled to push two indicators on a gigantic machine into the position that the machine indicates with light bulbs. In a brief vision, this machine finally appears as a man-eating Moloch. Films like *Metropolis* articulate the horror of a world dominated by machines, of their inhumanly precise capabilities and their ability to repeat, again and again, the same action with perfect indifference.

It is therefore ironic that the arts of classical modernism continually portray themselves as the antithesis of the endless repetitions found in modern daily life. One could actually regard modern art as an ongoing attempt to escape the "curse of repetition". The artistic avant-garde of the twentieth century has celebrated shock, the unique and the new. Mass culture, especially the media, has followed their lead. It was not until the postmodern age that the technical repetitions of factory machines were transferred to culture through the artistic work with loops.

In modernism, technology, the machines, are often portrayed as tyrannical, repressive and inhuman. This book tells a different story. It will use the example of loops to show how the dull, mindless beat of machines was turned into a dance beat. Loop-based art tames the shocks of the modern age and turns what was previously considered soulless or simply unbearably monotonous into the foundation of the most beautiful forms of human expression: art, music, dance.

AN AMERICAN KISS: THOMAS ALVA EDISON'S KISS LOOP AND THE FORMS OF TECHNOLOGICAL REPETITION

My dad always sits in the twelfth row in the middle of the twelfth row and always in the same seat.

Thomas Bernhard

The First Pair of Lovers in Film History

Technically, it's not even a real kiss. The ageing Victorian couple – he with highly waxed moustache, frock coat and bow tie, she with her hair in a bun and wearing a ruched dress – are talking out of the corner of their mouths for almost the entire length of the twenty-second film clip, their lips seemingly stuck together at the other end. Finally, right at the end, the gentleman escapes the embrace, twirls up the ends of his moustache one more time and determinedly presses a hearty kiss on his sweetheart's lips. Just as he does so, the clip ends. It is both the first on-screen kiss and the first close-up in film history. This kiss on celluloid makes the greying pair, who could hardly bear to tear themselves apart from each other, the first romantic heroes in film history. The *May Irwin Kiss*, named after its female protagonist, is one of the films that Thomas Alva Edison showed to a paying audience in New York in May 1896. It was the dawn of cinema, and film historians now refer to the novelty period. When Edison showed the clip as part of his film programme, it ended after 20 seconds – only to begin again. Once more, the two sweethearts embraced and inaudibly whispered sweet nothings to each other, their mouths stuck together. Once more, the gentleman tears himself away, twirls his moustache and resolutely presses a kiss on his partner's lips. Again. And again. And again. It is wonderfully ironic that something as sensuous and affectionate as a kiss was the subject of a mechanical repetition.

The audience thought it was hysterical. The *Los Angeles Times* published an article about the clip and its protagonist – "her smile, her glances, her gestures and the concluding, overwhelming, sensual kiss was repeated over and over, while the audience roared with laughter and cheered approvingly".[1] In Edison's film distribution catalogue, the comic aspect of the film is highlighted, too: "they get ready for the kiss, start kissing, and then they kiss and kiss and kiss in a way that makes the audience convulse with laughter every time." But not everyone was amused – the critic Herbert Stone wrote that "neither of them is physically attractive and the spectacle of their prolonged pasturing on each other's lips was hard to beat when only life size. Magnified to gargantuan proportions...it is absolutely disgusting!"[2]

The wonders of recording and reproducing moving pictures were still new at that time. The Lumière brothers had staged the first public film showing just under 6 months previously in Paris. In the USA, it was Thomas Alva Edison who showed the first-ever film clips projected onto canvas at the Koster and Bial's Music Hall on Herald Square in New York in April 1896. One month after this premiere, the kiss-on-canvas was adopted into the programme – that self-same *May Irwin Kiss* sequence which either amused or disgusted audiences. The lovers, immortalized on screen, had to kiss each other three times, wrote Herbert Stone. Other reports of the time mention even more repetitions.

Why was the kiss scene being shown over and over? One answer lies in the construction of Edison's vitascope, which differed fundamentally from the projector used by the Lumière brothers, as well as from all the other projectors that were to follow. The Lumières' original projector was designed to let the film strip run into a fabric bag after it was shown, and, once the entire film had been shown, it was wound onto a second spool – a method that continued to be in use until the advent of digital technology. Edison's projector, the vitascope, on the other hand, copied the operating principle of its predecessor, the kinetoscope, which had earned Edison a fortune during the preceding years. The kinetoscope was a box with an observation slit. Turning a crank at the side of the appliance made a short scene appear on celluloid and in order to enable the clip to run continuously, the ends of the film strips were glued together. The first films to be viewed in the USA at the end of the nineteenth century, therefore, were loops.[3]

Edison retained this construction method for his first film projector. While his method created a closed circle of time captured on film, the Lumière brothers let it run on. It's hardly necessary to point out that their method was the more effective in terms of media history. Cinema and all other reproduction processes for moving images that followed do not reproduce passing time as cyclical repetition, as Edison's films do. Instead, they proceed linearly, like the films of the Lumière brothers.

In Edison's kinetoscope films, the irreversibility and inexorability of time was abolished. The images shown in the early Edison films were quite literally captured – the people who kissed, danced, boxed or made dogs do tricks to entertain audiences were not just recorded on celluloid. When these films were shown in Edison's kinetoscope, they were repeating their actions in a continuous loop. For as long as the viewer turned the crank, the performers jumped and ran, sneezed and laughed, somersaulted or threw lassos, over and over.

Likewise, in screenings that used Edison's projector, the vitascope, the films were generally shown repeatedly. The *May Irwin Kiss* was a favourite of the projectionists, who were more than happy to let the images run through the projector several times to amuse the audience. The advertising slogan "once seen, never forgotten", used to advertise the vitascope screenings on posters, is, strictly speaking, wrong – the majority of films were projected repeatedly, rather than just once, and this would have contributed to their memorability ("never forgotten"). From the beginning of cinema and mass media history, then, the two fundamental characteristics of all recording media were already combined. They reproduce and repeat, and nowhere is this technical device more apparent than in the endless, mechanical repetition of the loop. André Bazin contends that film "embalms time", since:

> the guiding myth...inspiring the invention of cinema is
> the accomplishment of that which dominated in a more
> or less vague fashion all the techniques of the mechanical
> reproduction of reality in the nineteenth century, from
> photography to the phonograph, namely an integral
> realism, a recreation of the world in its own image, an image
> unburdened by the freedom of interpretation of the artist or
> the irreversibility of time.[4]

The Edison film loops demonstrated to their viewers particularly strikingly that the course of time could be stopped, "embalmed" as it were, through cinema – by repeating recorded time several times.

Since any film screening makes the past meet the present through the performance of cinematic documentation, film theorists like Noël Burch see cinema as a cultural technique that resonates with the nineteenth-century *Frankenstein* dream – that of the recreation of life, of the symbolic triumph over death. And Edison's loops are not limited to rendering the past as an instantaneous present just the once. They do so over and over, thereby making visible the process of recapturing "embalmed" time – each sequence of images repeats the previous one. This can (like Frankenstein's experiments with artificial life) have something uncanny about it – it's not without significance that cinema has dealt with uncanny doppelgangers, vampires, zombies and other undead people from the beginning. But it can also have a comic effect, as the description of the *May Irwin Kiss* in the Edison catalogue shows – they "kiss and kiss and kiss each other in a way that makes the audience convulse with laughter, every time".

Henri Bergson, in his essay *Laughter: An Essay on the Meaning of the Comic*,[5] which was published 4 years after the performance of the *May Irwin Kiss,* emphasizes that when a body is likened to an ordinary mechanism – when a person appears like a marionette – it is perceived as comical. In the case of the *May Irwin Kiss*, the two performers become puppets of the looped reproduction medium, and the public "screams with laughter and cheers appreciatively".[6] Bergson writes that "the more closely both images – man and mechanism – are meshed together, the more convulsive the comic effect".[7] It is significant that Bergson associates this effect with reproduction media – albeit from a time before photography and film – namely, with sealing and printing:

real life may never repeat. Where repetition does take place, where there is a complete reproduction, a mechanism is always assumed behind the living phenomenon. Analyse the impression you get from two faces that are too much alike, and you will find that you are thinking of two copies cast in the same mould, or two impressions of the same seal, or two reproductions of the same negative – in a word, of some manufacturing process or other. This deflection of life towards the mechanical is here the real cause of laughter.[8]

The fact that it was possible to screen a film clip like the *May Irwin Kiss* over and over was also the reason for the memorable reception story of this short film. Charles Musser has shown how film turned actors into movie stars, and indeed, into the first "romantic couple in film history".[9] May Irwin and her partner, John C. Rice, also appeared together in the comedy *The Widow Jones*, which was shown successfully as a touring play in various cities of the USA. But it was the Edison studio movie that made them into stars across the United States.

Modern mass media are responsible for the emergence of a star system, since they make it possible to show performances of actors and singers to a broad, international audience that could not be reached through live performances. Film and gramophone records, and later, radio and television, made it possible for a mass audience to admire artists they had never seen in the flesh. And just as Enrico Caruso only became an internationally acclaimed tenor through his phonograph recordings, the *May Irwin Kiss* from the Edison studio made its two actors so famous that they can be called the first-ever film stars in today's sense. The film kiss impacted May Irwin's career to such an extent that in 1922, she was able to retire as a millionaire to her own island on the St Lawrence River – even though she only ever appeared in one other film.

The film clip, capable of an unlimited number of repetitions, also caused the actors to compete with their own image; their stage kiss in the play *The Widow Jones* was suddenly perceived as a repetition of the film clip, which had quickly become known throughout America through screenings, which continued to be shown in the USA, and also through press coverage.

The screen kiss took on a life of its own and went far beyond its original intention, which had been to adapt a scene from the comedy *The Widow Jones* for cinema. The success of the film was such that after an initial discontinuation in September 1896, it was re-released using the original cast the following year. The film version of the screen kiss continued to be shown for several more years. It was so popular that 4 years later, Edison's production company produced one of the first remakes of film history, naming it simply *The Kiss*.

The film probably owed part of its impact to the fact that its initial screenings coincided with debates about what was to be permitted on the American stage. By the end of 1895, British actress Olga Nethersole had appeared in a Broadway production of *Carmen*, during which she had kissed various lovers so often and so indefatigably that the performances were considered offensive by many. A review appearing in *The Herald* stated that, "Miss Nethersole's kisses have given rise to comment throughout the city, and you either will or won't – depending on what kind of person you are – consider their intensity, their duration and the audible smooching sounds to be necessary for the artistic portrayal of Carmen's character. Most people, I think, will find this aspect of the portrayal exaggerated..."[10] By contrast, Musser found May Irwin and John C. Rice's stage kiss in *The Widow Jones*, which was being performed concurrently, to be a "beautiful, old-fashioned American kiss, one that distances itself from the filth imported by the English and French stage shows".[11]

The daily newspaper *New York World* was responsible for the fact that the *May Irwin Kiss* was captured on film in the first place. Aiming to convert the kiss controversy into circulation figures, it invited the two leading actors of *The Widow Jones* to Edison's film studio in Orange, New Jersey, where their kiss was "cinematographed" by cameraman William Heise. The following Sunday edition featured the film strip, with the headline "Widow Jones's Kiss Forty-Two Feet Long". If Nethersole's kisses had seemed interminable in *Carmen*, the new technology made sure that Irwin and Rice's caresses exceeded them in terms of duration.

Musser argues that when, to the amusement of audiences in New York and soon thereafter in cities across the USA, the kiss was shown as a loop, it also acted as an effective parody of Nethersole's tenacious stage embraces, which had so stirred up the New York press. The film, "repeated, duplicated and multiplied the repetition of their disembodied performance in many theatres. A closer analysis of *The May Irwin Kiss* would show that the repeated kiss resonated with Nethersole's lavish kissing in *Carmen*. The film pokes fun at her excess by mechanical means. One might say that this was an American kiss – using American technology."[12]

Excessive, machine-like repetition, whether produced as a loop or by other means, has often been used in modern art as a satirical or parodistic instrument intended to ridicule a phenomenon through endless repetition. The title of Erik Satie's infamous composition *Vexations*, which he had composed 3 years before Edison's film loops and in which a short piano figure was repeated 840 times, indicates what is to be expected from such a protracted repetition exercise – it is a torment. Satie, who was fascinated by the phenomenon of boredom, apparently composed the piece as a satire on the merciless instrumental drill at the Paris Conservatory.

Later, repetitions in the plays of Samuel Beckett and Thomas Bernhard or in the video works of Bruce Nauman, Dara Birnbaum and Paul Pfeiffer were to serve precisely the purpose of emphasizing the absurdity and senselessness of what was shown. In Beckett's piece *Krapp's Last Tape*, it is the repetitions on a tape that cause Krapp to lapse into drunken fits of despair. In Thomas Bernhard's plays and novels, too, repetition symbolizes the entanglements of a past that does not want to pass away, and from which there is no escape.

As though Bernhard had wanted to comment on the technical reproducibility of music, he often uses compositions that become empty and irrelevant through the use of ever-recurring repetitions. In his piece *Der Ignorant und der Wahnsinnige* [The Ignoramus and the Madman], a singer repeats her role as Queen of the Night for years, until her singing becomes machine-like and sterile. In *Die Macht der Gewohnheit* [The Power of Habit], a group of circus performers practise Schubert's *Trout Quintet* without ever going beyond the rehearsal phase. Through their increasingly manic repetition, they not only destroy the work, but ultimately also themselves.

In Nauman, Pfeiffer and Birnbaum's works, video tape loops turn their protagonists into lurching jumping jacks or helpless, dehumanized victims, that is to say, into a "mere mechanism" (Henri Bergson). Bruce Neumann cited Samuel Beckett's absurd theatre as an important influence, and in his video installation *Clown Torture* (1987), a clown shown on a monitor repeats the rhyme "Pete and Repeat were sitting on a fence. Pete fell off; who was left? Repeat. Pete and Repeat were sitting on a fence ...", and so on, *ad nauseam*, while on another monitor, clowns, akin to the ancient Sisyphus, are seen trying to balance aquariums and buckets of water that keep falling off. In the installation *Double No* (1988), two clowns are jumping up and down in a loop, and, like toddlers, they repeatedly shout "No no no no no" – like many of Nauman's works, this piece expresses helplessness in the face of a meaningless and endless existence that has become eternal.

Pfeiffer and Birnbaum combine found media images to form a gruelling *circulus vitiosus* in order to expose these images, taken from advertising and television, as stereotypical and mindless. Dara Birnbaum explains that in her videos, in which short segments from television series are repeated over and over, she wants to undermine "the expectations and the absorption [of the viewer by television]".[13] In an interview about clips that are monotonously repeated in his works, Paul Pfeiffer says that "in these images [from television and advertising] I see testimonies of a society that is in decline...desperately longing for everything to be all right...for everything to be and remain good...Everything will continue as it is now...no-one will die, and everything will remain beautiful and glamorous for all eternity".[14]

In modernist high culture, repetitions can only be regarded as boring, soul-destroying and regressive, for reasons that will be examined in more detail in the following section. At the beginning of the twentieth century, modernism had acquired a hostile attitude towards repetition. It was not until the end of the twentieth century that the modernist habitus changed into a far more positive attitude towards mechanical repetition, which began to foreground the loop as an aesthetic means.

As an aesthetic means, loops are paradoxical. They can lull, like counting sheep before falling asleep. But they can also be mind-numbing, like an artistic version of Chinese water torture. They can have a bludgeoning and levelling effect, a sense that many people get overwhelmed by on their first-ever visit to a techno party. But they can also enliven, engender a feeling of freedom, and enable a picture or a sound to be newly perceived. They can fascinate and captivate, draw the listener into their repetitions, or they can be colossally annoying. Repeated sentences, fragments of sentences, samples or image sequences can be stripped of their content, but they can also be charged with new meaning. They can prolong a beautiful moment. Or they can repeat *until* something pleasurable is found in the repetition.

The art of classical modernism has tended to look askance at repetition. Composers who worked with loops in the immediate post-war period usually disregarded the repetitive properties of tape loops and focused on the possibilities of sound processing that they also offer.[15] In the following chapters, I will introduce examples from the 1940s and 1950s to show how this type of sound generation and modification functioned. Further, I will explore why the first composers who worked with loops did not allow them to do what they do best – repeat, pulsate, knock, pound, hammer, drum.

This rejection of the repetitive properties of loops is deeply rooted in Western intellectual history of modernity. It combines specifically modern reservations about the allegedly blunting and regressive effects of repetitions, as formulated by Freud, with an – entirely justified – critique of industrial labour, which turned workers into "appendages of machines" (Adorno) and forced them to perform mindless and monotonous work. What seems to me to lie deeper still, however, is discomfort with notions of cyclical time in European intellectual history.

For Freud, the human psychic apparatus was characterized by two fundamental drives, the so-called basic instincts – the libido and the death drive. According to his psychoanalytic theory, organic life on the one hand tends towards the inorganic, a tendency he identified with the Greek personification of death, *Thanatos*. With this concept, Freud wanted to explain why, for instance, World War veterans repeatedly returned to the traumatic experiences of the war instead of processing them and leaving them behind. For him, this inclination stood in direct and paradoxical contrast to another instinct, which he also regarded as an immutable principle of human life – the instinct to preserve oneself and one's species, to survive, to reproduce the individual, and to avoid listlessness. Freud called this instinct the pleasure principle and identified it with another figure of Greek mythology, the god of love, *Eros*.

The modernist critique of repetition has tended to identify it with Thanatos and the death drive. From this perspective, repetitions can only appear as regressive, lifeless or deadly – if not quite representing a regression to the inorganic, then they are at any rate allied with a state preceding human consciousness and the development of subjectivity, and with infantile, schizoid or degenerate conditions. Yet for Freud, repetition was also an essential tool used by the human psyche to reduce tension. Undoubtedly, they also form the basis of organic life, of growth and sexuality, of pleasure and Eros.

The rejection of repetition – by modernist composers such as Stockhausen and Boulez or philosophers such as Adorno, for instance – becomes understandable when considered from a standpoint that views it as regressive, or even as the epitome of the death drive. It was not until the postmodern period that it became possible to recognize repetition as something capable of contributing to the pleasure principle. It is therefore ironic that at the beginning of the story of the loop there should be a kiss – a form of Eros, which in Edison's looped film was subjected to mechanical, "soulless" repetition, which turns the "body into an ordinary mechanism" (Bergson).

Edison and his film projectionists had no such thoughts when they sent the *May Irwin Kiss* through the projector, of course. They were interested in creating a quick laugh, not in modernistic ennui à la Beckett or Nauman, or Bergson's slapstick, in which "the mechanical obscures the living". They were merely subject to a technological limitation, one, moreover, that was quickly to become a thing of the past.

But the result they achieved bore a striking resemblance to the artistic work with media repetitions which found their way into different artistic disciplines during the second half of the twentieth century. From the mid-1960s onwards, artists and composers began to take an increasing interest in how technical repetitions – instead of expressing boredom and senselessness – could be used to create intensities, to prompt mind-altering states and be a general source of pleasure. For this to be possible, they had to learn to regard repetition, or loops, not as a technical-medial agent of Thanatos, the death drive. Instead, they needed to regard loops as a way of working towards the pleasure principle, Eros.

It was not until the postmodern era that it became possible to regard the repetitions created by loops in this way and to create music and art that foregrounds the "timeless time" of the loop. The composers and artists who worked in this way were concerned with eliciting an element of difference from mechanical repetitions and, at best, with triggering a state that Jacques Lacan referred to as *jouissance* – a term that Slavoj Žižek has translated as "obscene pleasure".

In an interview, German-Chilean DJ and producer Ricardo Villalobos formulated a more popular definition of the state that loop-based, repetitive music can trigger – "it is ideal for a totally strung-out state of mind in which you do not know anymore who you are or who your father is".[16] Freud's Thanatos, the law of the father, the ego – loop-based art can turn all that into a fount of joy through repetition.

CHAPTER 3

IF YOU REPEAT THE SAME THING, IT BECOMES MUSIC

Pierre Schaeffer and the French musique concrète

Standing before the turntables and magnetophones, we experienced moments of intense amazement.

Pierre Schaeffer

Musique concrète is a music of remembering...It's music that has to do with photography, with cinema, a little with literature, but not so much with music because the music is in you; you don't have to learn that, while you do have to learn the rest.

Pierre Henry

And then there's this Pierre Schaeffer, with his eagle face and his strict side parting. Contemporaries described him as stubborn and ambitious. He is said to have been a good organizer, but to use a colloquialism of the time, a bit of a "stalinist" as well. "His Parisian charm seemed to have been transformed into almost repulsive, fanatical perseverance," writes a contemporary.[1]

Perhaps it was this fanaticism that made him return to his workplace, the Parisian radio station *Office de Radiodiffusion-Télévision Française* (ORTF), on the eve of a business trip. He went there in order to listen.

It's the end of 1949 and French radio did not yet have a tape player. Recordings were made on thick gramophone records. Schaeffer rotates four of these on turntables, lowers the needles onto the grooves. Additional records are at the ready for mixing.

Ordinary records have grooves that lead from the outside to the inside in a long spiral. Not so the records that Schaeffer played that evening. Their grooves are closed, so that – just like a broken record, where the needle skips back and forth – they repeat short sound sequences over and over.

Pierre Schaeffer was a radio official, and after the Second World War even acted as director for ORTF for a while. The radio station was a subdivision of the French Post Office, which was financed by public funds at that time, so Schaeffer was a kind of civil servant. The following day he was supposed to travel to an international conference in Morocco to negotiate the redistribution of radio frequencies post-WWII. But that evening, he wanted nothing more than to let the records skip and to listen to them.

Let's imagine what Schaeffer heard – metallic rattling, crashing, grinding, buzzing, the whimpering of a harmonica, the fragment of a sentence, the chugging of a boat. A cough. If it were all merely strung together, it would make for a cacophonous din. But Schaeffer makes the sounds repeat. The repetitions give order to the chaos, they create structures in the random.

Schaeffer mixed the sounds with the aid of the volume controls, which in 1949 were still called "potentiometers", and recorded his mix live onto another gramophone record. After 4 minutes, a piece emerged that he would later call *Étude Pathétique*. Recording time is equal to playback time. He later annotated the recording with the phrase "the innocent shall be amply provided".[2]

The *Étude Pathétique* is one of five short pieces on the basis of which Schaeffer is today regarded as the founder of *musique concrète,* a type of music that uses found sounds to create compositions. Everyday noise like the sound of trains, the clattering of cooking pots, giggles or chirping birds, as well as recordings of classical instruments like the piano were the raw materials from which Schaeffer and, later, other *musique concrète* composers created their compositions. Schaeffer's technique with the skipping records was one of the tricks that allowed him to organize noise into music. Schaeffer called this technique *sillon fermé*, or closed groove. Nowadays, we refer to it as a loop.

Schaeffer didn't have to produce his loops with the aid of vinyl records for long. The more flexible and better-sounding magnetic tape had been developed in Germany during the Second World War by IG Farben and AEG, and its internationally successful history began after the end of the war. It was introduced as a recording medium at the beginning of the 1950s by French radio, and Schaeffer immediately began working with magnetic tape rather than with records.

Pierre Schaeffer was one of the first composers in Europe to deal with electronic (or media) forms of composition after the Second World War. His *musique concrète* compositions inspired people from all over the Western world to make music using tape as the recording medium. He influenced not only the experiments of the *Kölner Schule* [Cologne School] that gathered around Karlheinz Stockhausen and the Cologne Studio for Electronic Music at the West German radio station *Westdeutscher Rundfunk* [West German Radio] (WDR). The composers of American Music for Tape – such as Otto Luening and Vladimir Ussachevsky in New York – were also well aware of Schaeffer's activities. Likewise, American Jazz musician Raymond Scott, who will be the subject of a later chapter, was inspired by *musique concrète* in the development of his electronic instrument, the *Electronium*. Even contemporary producers working with sampled sounds in the genres of Hip-hop, House and Techno are ultimately Schaeffer's successors, even if many of them may never have heard of him.

Schaeffer was the first to create an institutional infrastructure for the production of electronic music when he founded *Club d'essai*.

The resulting music research group *Groupe de Recherche Musicales* (GRM), together with the Columbia-Princeton Electronic Music Center in the USA, the *Studio di Fonologia Musicale* in Milan and the Philips *Versuchslabor* in Eindhoven were important hubs for electronic music in the 1950s and 1960s.

At a time when the equipment for producing electronic music was still prohibitively expensive, almost all the academic composers who excelled in this field were associated with one of these studios. Even "non-electronic" avant-garde composers such as György Ligeti, Luciano Berio, Iannis Xenakis, Edgar Varèse or Pierre Boulez benefitted from this infrastructure and composed their own electronic works in these studios. This epoch is now regarded as the first golden age of electronic music.

And yet, the term "electronic music" is misleading, because it suggests that the music was made with electronic musical instruments. The first so-called "electronic" compositions were, in fact, rarely composed for the few electronic instruments that existed around 1950, before the first synthesizers like the *Theremin* or the *Ondes Martenot* were built.

The majority of these compositions were realized with magnetic tape. Tape that was played backwards, slowed down or speeded up. Tape that was cut and reassembled in accordance with elaborate plans. And tape that was glued together to produce loops. Loops were a central compositional technique of post-war electronic music – not just for Pierre Schaeffer, but for an entire generation of avant-garde composers who more often than not had learned this technique from him.

But as much as these composers' methods may have resembled each other, the musical results that they produced on their comparatively simple equipment were very different. These differences and their aesthetic value became the subject of debates that were so embittered that it is difficult to imagine today. There was intense competition, especially between the French *musique concrète* group around Schaeffer and the Cologne School around Karlheinz Stockhausen – even though Stockhausen had learned the general techniques of working with tape, and with loops in particular, during his stay with Schaeffer in Paris. A complicated mixture of artistic rivalry, nationalism and barely repressed resentment – a consequence of the Second World War, which had ended less than a decade previously – may have been among the reasons why "the Germans" and "the French" attacked each other so ruthlessly.[3]

It wasn't just the technology with which this music was produced that was a product of the Second World War. The terminology used in these debates also had militaristic traits. Pierre Schaeffer repeatedly depicted the competition between French *musique concrète* and German electronic music in terms of military metaphors. After the unsuccessful premiere of his opera *Orphée 53* at the *Donaueschinger Musiktage* [Donauesching music days] in 1953, which was torn to pieces in the German press, he referred to "*musique concrète's Waterloo*". He later wrote, "so we lost the battle of *Donaueschingen*, and for years were internationally discredited, while a rosy day dawned for the electronic arch-enemy under Cologne's skies". Even in 1987, he still described the conflicts of the post-war period in terms of a campaign. In an interview he commented that, "after the war, in the '45 to '48 period, we had driven back the German invasion, but we hadn't driven back the invasion of Austrian music, 12-tone music. We had liberated ourselves politically, but music was still under an occupying foreign power, the music of the Vienna School."[4]

Behind these nationalistically tinged barbs, however, there was a fundamental aesthetic conflict about how one should make music with magnetic tape. At the core of the conflict, it was not only the sound material to be used which was at stake – but also sine tones in Stockhausen and German electronic music, all manner of sounds and noises in Schaeffer and *musique concrète*. In essence, the controversy was about the extent to which composers claimed or relinquished the control which the new music machines enabled.

The composers of *musique concrète* opened their ears to the inaudible, surprising sounds that their tape manipulations often produced. The Germans, and Stockhausen in particular, subjected the sounds to a strict order – the order of serial composition techniques, which had been denounced by the National Socialists as "degenerate".

The studios which public broadcasters, conservertoires and universities set up for electronic music in post-war West Germany therefore encompassed an attempt to reconnect with the pre-war avant-garde. Fascism had interrupted important lines of tradition in avant-garde music. In Germany, the memory of artistic movements like Futurism, Dada and Surrealism, and of such figures as Russolo, Antheil and Satie, as well as Schönberg, Webern and Berg had been suppressed by National Socialism.

The group that gathered around the Cologne Studio for Electronic Music at the WDR revived Viennese School's serial composition methods with such fervour that it seemed as if they were trying to undo the Nazis' denunciation of this music as fast as they could. Schaeffer, on the other hand, had worked with surrealist poets such as Louis Aragon and Paul Eluard during the Second World War. The influence of such lines of tradition is clearly noticeable in his music.

Even if they worked with the same tools, and despite the fact that Stockhausen had first learned about these tools from Schaeffer, French *musique concrète* and German electronic music therefore achieved entirely different musical results. It is amazing how divergent the aesthetic and philosophical differences are that resulted from a handful of tape manipulation methods. While Schaeffer and Henry were concerned with developing compositions from recorded "found" sounds, which took into account the specific characteristics of these sounds, the Germans, and especially Stockhausen, wanted to exercise control in a way that was reminiscent of the methods of natural science. The clean and tidy studio for electronic music at the WDR therefore did not just look like a physics room. It was also perceived as a laboratory for sound production in controllable circumstances.

The schism between "concrete" and "abstract" music, which first emerged in serious music in the early 1950s, was to erupt time and again in different forms over the decades that followed, and it has impacted on approaches to loop-based music right up to the Hip-hop and Techno of the present day. Even though it never triggered debates as embittered as those of the 1950s again, the opposition of "abstract" and "concrete" has continued in the history of working with loops.

"The change of scenery makes me forget the weight on my mind", Pierre Schaeffer wrote during a skiing holiday in February 1948.

> Without memories, without worries, I can feel stirrings deep within me. Ideas are seeking outlets other than words: Ta ra ra boom – whistlings – the snow – gusts of perfect fullness of sound...On the windswept plateau, right at the top of the ski tow, iron hooks turn around the wheel, having scraped the frozen snow away. The whirligig of this mechanism injures the frost-crystal. Yet these things must, of necessity, be in harmony.[5]

Nature and technology, things that developed organically, and things created by man – "things [that] must, of necessity, be in harmony". This strange observation marks the beginning of Pierre Schaeffer's musical experiments at the end of the 1940s, which not only made him the inventor of *musique concrète,* but also the discoverer of the musical loop. Schaeffer describes the beginnings of his development as a composer in his book *A la recherche d'une musique concrète* and highlights his desire to establish a new symbolic balance for the relationship between technology and nature. In his compositions, Schaeffer was to attempt to transform natural sounds and noise produced by machines and technology into music by means of the new recording media, in an effort to fashion an acoustic unity out of nature and technology.

In his diary, Schaeffer keeps returning to the idea of reconciling nature with technology. "People today return to nature in bouts of ski tows, half-tracks, Kandahar ropes, super-light alloys. Thus, perfectly equipped, chrome-shod, asbestos-gloved, nylon-clad, they sample the immaculate mountain air...I must find a way to express this."[6]

Musique concrète emerged from Schaeffer's search for a form of artistic expression that embraces nature as well as technology. And yet he was not a formally trained composer. The son of a violinist and a singer, he had decided to study at a French polytechnic. Even if he did later try to adapt his compositions to the conventions of classical music (they contain Andantes and Allegros, Scherzos and Intermezzos), Schaeffer had previously worked as a sound mixer and radio engineer, and it was on account of his technical and acoustic experiments during the Second World War that he had become a composer and the creator of a new style of music.

When Pierre Schaeffer described himself as a "scientist who plodded into the music",[7] it was only half-ironic – as a sound engineer without any formal musical training, he really was just that. At the same time, however, his book *A la recherche d'une musique concrète* is clearly the work of a French *homme de lettre* with a broad intellectual horizon.

Schaeffer's theoretical elaborations on the subject of *musique concrète* always result from a practical examination of his medium. He was neither a "pure" practitioner nor a theorist who was removed from practice. Basically, his musical experiments were a form of applied media theory that had resulted from his many years of working for the French State Broadcasting Corporation. He was already reflecting on the possibilities of conserving and broadcasting sounds in theoretical essays at the beginning of the 1940s, before creating his first compositions, coining the term *Arts relais*, or the broadcasting art, in the process. For Schaeffer, traditional art was about materializing an idea, while the new media, such as film and radio, had to get to an idea by starting from concrete materials. The "broadcasting art" that he described had to make use of the genuine qualities of radio, rather than trying to imitate other art forms, such as literature or theatre.

During his professional career, he had become acquainted with the developing modern media culture from ever-new perspectives, first as production manager at the *Strassburger Rundfunk,* then, in the 1930s, at the *Staatsrundfunk* in Paris. After the Germans had conquered Paris during the Second World War, Schaeffer worked on what today might be called an "alternative radio project" in an experimental studio in the provincial town of Beaune. In 1942, he founded the *Club d'Essai* there, a kind of research centre for radio art. Schaeffer used this studio in the spirit of the French Resistance. He recorded conversations and poems in which the surrealist poets Louis Aragon and Paul Eluard called for resistance against the German occupying forces. At the same time, he also prepared radio plays intended to be broadcast after the liberation of France. These included Saint-Exupéry's radio play *Nachtflug* [Night Flight], as well as Schaeffer's own work *La Coquille à Planètes* [The Planetary Shell], on which he spent almost a year, experimenting with genuine means of expression offered by the radio medium.

On 22 August 1944, 5 days before the arrival of the allied troops in Paris, Schaeffer's *Studio d'Essai* broadcast the first radio call for an uprising and reported on the fighting in the French capital. Schaeffer's studio also produced the most important audio documents from the Battle of Paris. Rudolf Frisius comments that "the radio of liberated Paris was down to Schaeffer".[8] For a short time in the same year, Schaeffer was even promoted to Director of French State Radio but was removed from office in October 1944.

Schaeffer's efforts in the *Résistance* contributed not only to the fact that in the decades to come, he received generous support for his musical experiments at French radio, but also to the fact that time and again, he held important administrative posts. He was studio manager at ORFT until 1974; later, he became supervisor of scientific projects and was often sent abroad to act as a representative of the station. Because his practical studio work was frequently interrupted by these international missions as well as other events, he often did not compose anything for years.

Schaeffer wrote down his initial thoughts about a "broadcasting art" during his time at Beaune in 1941, and these already hint at the development of a concrete music, with which he was to be preoccupied in the 1940s and 50s:

> Cinema and radio, the new aesthetic media, have, above all, developed new possibilities for concrete expression. This distinguishes these media from language. Cinema and radio are superior to language in terms of their potential for concrete expression and their concrete effects, on the other hand, they lack the potential for abstraction which language provides. Film and radio are the other way around from language – they move from the concrete to the abstract.[9]

Schaeffer here describes one of the central problems that confront music created from collected sounds. It is difficult to make music from these sounds without being constantly reminded of the original sound source. *Musique concrète* therefore has often been criticized for its "anecdotal character".[10] Schaeffer's very first concrete piece, *Étude aux chemin de fer* [Railway Study], composed in 1948, for example, seems more like a radio play than music. Schaeffer was well aware of this problem, as his theoretical texts and the subsequent development of his music show.

While Schaeffer's early pieces soon inspired the first imitators in some European countries as well as in the USA, his critics in France focused on the supposed inadequacy of Schaeffer's music. Claude Lévi-Strauss, for instance, wrote in *Das Rohe und das Gekochte* [The Raw and the Cooked] that:

> like abstract painting, its first concern is to disrupt the system of actual or potential meaning of which these phenomena are the elements. Before using the noises it has collected, *musique concrète* takes care to make them unrecognizable, so that the listener cannot yield to the natural tendency to relate them to sense images: the breaking of china, a train whistle, a fit of coughing or the snapping off of a tree branch. It thus wipes out a first level of articulation,

whose usefulness would in any case by very limited, since man is poor at perceiving and distinguishing noises, perhaps because of the overriding importance for him of a privileged category of noises: those of articulate speech. *Musique concrète* may be intoxicated with the illusion that it is saying something; in fact, it is floundering in non-significance.[11]

Schaeffer's former protégé Pierre Boulez, who turned to serialism after spending time in Schaeffer's studio, formulated this criticism even more radically. In an encyclopaedia article, he pronounces a quasi-death sentence on Schaeffer's work:

The term "concrete" reveals how much one was misled, and with what naivety one was looking at the problem; the word itself indicates that it is a matter of merely processing sonic material. There was no attempt to define or frame it. The question of the material was entirely ignored. Even though it is of the utmost importance for such an adventure, it was replaced by a kind of poetic crowding, which is on a level with surrealistic collages of images and words...Mediocre machines combined with a pleasant lassitude turned the studio of *musique concrète* into the sound equivalent of a bric-a-brac store. As far as the "works" are concerned, they only have their titles to show posterity: in the absence of creative intention, they are limited to montages that are neither very inventive nor varied, they always serve up the same effects, with locomotives and electricity providing the headlines. A *modus operandi* as disjointed as this leads nowhere...[12]

The polemic tone and numerous false claims that Boulez probably deliberately made bear witness to the merciless style of the disputes conducted in respect of post-war avant-garde music. In fact, in his theoretical texts, Schaeffer continuously dealt with the problems that arose from the fact that the sounds from which he created his music were in part easy to identify. The very first entry in *A la recherche d'une musique concrète* addresses the problem arising from the contrast between "abstract" music and "concrete" (word) material. "Sometimes when I write I am envious of more intense modes of expression", he writes.

"Writing is always making explicit at the expense of other things. Mystery is sacrificed, and consequently truth and so everything. At these moments I am overwhelmed by a longing for music that, as Roger Ducasse says, 'he likes because it does not mean anything'."[13]

While words stand for something, and sounds remind us of their origins, music is usually abstract, without meaning or reference. In the concrete music that Schaeffer would develop a few months later, he wanted to overcome this contradiction. In *musique concrète*, "the sound itself speaks" in a "sensually direct"[14] manner. Schaeffer coined the word *chosage* in contrast to *langage*, the French word for language – to let things (French: *les choses*) speak for themselves. They do not convey abstract ideas, only themselves.

Schaeffer developed a wide range of instruments in an effort to remove the "anecdotal" character of the sounds and to "refine" them into sounds without reference, so that a precise way of listening to their structure might replace any associations with their origins. Among the techniques designed to expose the "inner structures of sound" and to transform sounds into music were the fast, slow and reversed playback of recordings, as well as various montage techniques. But the most important design element of his early compositions was the uninterrupted repetition of sound fragments – loops.

How did Schaeffer get from his observations of a ski lift to these methods of sound manipulation? According to his notes, the idea that occurred to him during his skiing holiday, that of developing a music that arises from sounds and which expresses the modern contrast between nature and technology, had got a perpetual hold of him. As soon as he returned to Paris in March 1948, he began to put his plans into practice.

He writes that:

back in Paris, I have started to collect objects. I have a
"Symphony of noises" in mind...I go to the sound effects
department of the French radio service. I find clappers,
coconut shells, klaxons, bicycle horns. I imagine a scale of
bicycle horns. There are gongs and birdcalls. It is charming
that an administrative system should be concerned with
birdcalls and should regularize their acquisition on an official
form, duly recorded. I take away doorbells, a set of bells, an
alarm clock, two rattles, two childishly painted whirligigs.
The clerk causes some difficulties. Usually, he is asked for
a particular item. There are no sound effects without a text
in parallel, are there? But what about the person who wants
noise without text or context?[15]

Even in these early notes, Schaeffer formulates the problem of
musique concrète, which its critics, such as Boulez, would later
repeatedly bring to the fore – that the *chosage*, the language of
things, always implies a direct reference to things. "To be honest,
I don't think that any of these objects will be of use. They're too
obvious. After a few arguments, I do still borrow them, not without
first signing some receipts, of course. I take them with me with the
joy of a child who is allowed to plunder the attic..."[16]

Over the weeks that followed, Schaeffer experimented with his
finds from the radio archive, but didn't make much headway with
his idea of a "noise symphony". For 2 months, he struggled on with
shot grains and wind machines, tin cans and pans, and eventually
even with pipes from an organ that had been destroyed in the war.
His studio filled up with bits and pieces, but the music he produced
with these instruments did not satisfy him. Time and again, the
sound of things reminded of the things themselves, and therefore
could not be integrated into "pure" musical structures. Schaeffer
writes that he wants a "noise organ" that he can use to play his
sounds on a keyboard.[17]

Schaeffer only made headway with his search when he redirected his attention from the noises themselves to the recording device that was to record them. While experimenting, he noticed how much the sounds changed when he let go of a part of the sound. "I recorded the sound of a bell after it had been struck," he wrote in his diary on 19 April. "If you take away its transient response, the bell becomes an oboe sound. I prick up my ears."[18]

Schaeffer set about systematizing his observations. He recorded similarly "amputated sounds" onto vinyl records, arranged them on four turntables and began to "play" these sounds by switching the devices on and off. "If you listen carefully, this manipulation is cumbersome, unsuitable for any virtuosity," he writes in his diary, "but I own a musical instrument" – a simple precursor of the sampler used today, it might be added.

> A new instrument? I mistrust myself. I mistrust new
> instruments, be they waves, the *Ondes Martenot*, or what
> the Germans pompously call "electronic music"...My violin,
> my voice, I find these again in this whole mess of wood and
> tin and in my bicycle bells. I seek a direct connection to the
> sound matter, without any electrons getting in the way.[19]

Not without recording technology getting in the way, however. Schaeffer's experiments with the turntables prompted a change in his goals. Composing with objects that are not traditional musical instruments developed into working with the media reproduction of their sounds. "Playing" objects turned into playing with technology – the discovery of "amputated sounds" encouraged Schaeffer to manipulate the micro-structure of his sounds further. Instead of playing things as if they were instruments, he began to modify recorded sounds with the simple technological means he had at his disposal. He played the gramophone records he had recorded on faster and slower, and he listened to them backwards. And he enthusiastically noted down his observations about the "musical universe" which he had now entered.

In this painstaking work, Schaeffer proved himself to be an empiricist of sound. When he manipulated sounds, it was not to impose a compositional order on them, but rather, to emphasize their specific sonic character. Or, as he later called it, to listen to the "soul of things" through their sounds. He said in an interview, "I fought against [German] electronic music, which was another approach, a systemic approach, when I preferred an experimental approach actually working directly, empirically with sound."[20]

One characteristic that particularly distinguishes Schaeffer is his ability to step back from the seemingly obvious and to allow himself to be amazed. In his diary, he expresses surprise that no one had methodically used backward-running records in music production before him. "Everyone has played a recorded sound backwards before. But as far as I know, no one has ever extrapolated from this. After all, reverse playback doubles the number of available instrumental colours, at least *a priori*. No musician attends to this, yet this experience has been available for twenty years."[21] Schaeffer obviously didn't know the "record music" that Paul Hindemith and Ernst Toch had developed in Berlin in the 1920s, which uses just such effects.[22] Another composer who had worked with recorded music before Schaeffer was the Egyptian Halim El-Dabh.[23]

After Schaeffer had developed a series of methods with which he could manipulate original sounds and thereby "denature" them, he turned back to the search for suitable sounds. He came across a subject that had already fascinated experimental film-makers such as Dziga Vertov and Walter Ruttmann before the war – the railway. For the pre-war avant-garde, the railway had been an iconic object. Avant-garde films such as Vertov's *Mann mit der Kamera* [Man with the Camera], Walter Ruttmann's *Berlin – Die Symphonie der Großstadt* [Berlin – Symphony of the Metropolis] and other "city symphonies" of that time used the railway as the ideal subject for film due to its even, "rhythmic" mobility, and they represented it as a dynamic embodiment of modernity. The method Schaeffer used to assemble his *Étude aux Chemins De Fer* is very similar to the formal experiments of avant-garde film-makers of the 1920s.

Like these films, Schaeffer's composition provides a striking contrast to the technophobic trait that has shaped modern art and culture since Romanticism. His *Étude aux chemins de fer* does not celebrate the achievements of modern technology in the same way as exponents of the arts had done before the Second World War. Yet it does not articulate any criticism of it either; it simply integrates it into the compositional structure of the piece.

Schaeffer's decision to make technical repetition a basic element of his music stands in marked contrast to the general and far-reaching disapproval of modern technology, mass production and brain-numbing "industrialism", as formulated in the works of such diverse thinkers as Canetti, Spengler, Anders, Ellul, Huxley, Ortega y Gasset, Attali, Adorno and other members of the Frankfurt School. As can be seen from this list of names, this attitude ran through diverse political and ideological camps, from the extreme left to the extreme right, from bourgeois cultural pessimism to academic anarchism. At this point, it will suffice to present Theodor Adorno's position. It is especially his work that articulates critique of the phenomenon of repetition in all areas of social life; he views it as a result of the industrialization of the work process, a recurring topos. Adorno writes:

> the form of labour in industrial mass production is virtually that of the repetition of the non-changing. In terms of ideas, nothing new happens. But the behaviours that have developed in the sphere of production and the assembly line are spreading in an as yet unanalyzed way, potentially over all of society, even over sectors where labour is not carried out directly in accordance with those schemata.[24]

Adorno repeatedly attacked popular music, especially Jazz, as an example of industrial mass production in the field of culture, and

as a particularly blatant form of cultural capitulation in the face of
the repetitive machine:

> The cult of the machine which is represented by unabating
> Jazz beats involves a self-renunciation that cannot but take
> root in the form of a fluctuating uneasiness somewhere
> in the personality of the obedient. For the machine is an
> end in itself only under given social conditions – where
> men are appendages of the machines on which they work.
> The adaptation to machine music necessarily implies a
> renunciation of one's own human feelings and at the same
> time a fetishism of the machine such that its instrumental
> character becomes obscured thereby.[25]

Adorno's comments on the "idleness of Jazz" are well-known –
and well-known to be problematic. He uses his insights into the
musical form of Jazz primarily as ammunition to dismiss this and
any other form of popular music as regressive and dull. During his
excursions into the world of pop music, Adorno discovered among
other things the "rhythmically obedient type", which is seen above
all in the "so-called radio generation". This type is:

> most susceptible to a process of masochistic adjustment
> to authoritarian collectivism...This obedient type is the
> rhythmical type...Any musical experience of this type is
> based upon the underlying, unabating time unit of the music
> – its "beat". To play rhythmically means, to these people,
> to play in such a way that even if pseudo-individualizations
> – counter-accents and other "differentiations" – occur, the
> relation to the ground meter is preserved. To be musical
> means to them to be capable of following given rhythmical
> patterns without being disturbed by 'individualizing'
> aberrations, and to fit even the syncopations into the basic
> time units. This is the way in which their response to music
> immediately expresses their desire to obey. However, as the

standardized meter of dance music and of marching suggests the coordinated battalions of a mechanical collectivity, obedience to this rhythm by overcoming the responding individuals leads them to conceive of themselves as agglutinized with the untold millions of the meek who must be similarly overcome. Thus do the obedient inherit the earth.[26]

Adorno regards the rhythm of popular dance music as merely stereotypical and formulaic; for him, its rhythm imitates the mindless hammering of the structures of mechanical means of production.

The bodily functions that the rhythm recreates are themselves, in the mechanical rigidity of their repetitions, identical to those of the production processes that rob the individual of their bodily functions. The function of this music is ideological, not only in so far as it purports an irrationality that has no power over the discipline of their existence, but also in so far as this irrationality resembles the patterns of rationalized work. What they hope to escape from is not left out...It can be seen from the music that is consumed that there is no way out of the total immanence of society.[27]

The French theorist Jacques Attali takes Adorno's critique still further in his book *Bruits. Essai sur l'économie politique de la musique* [Noise. On the Political Economy of Music] published in 1977, where he refers to the recording media with which Schaeffer made his music.[28] According to Attali, recording media such as records and tapes turn music into one among many commodities, like saucepans or frozen fish. Sound objects such as records or CDs, which can be infinitely reproduced on a sound storage medium and sold as merchandise, make the experience of music infinitely repeatable and thereby devalue it.

For Attali, recorded music, which can be endlessly reproduced from a single original source, was the first precursor of today's world, where meaningful communication is replaced by a meaningless and joyless exchange of empty signs. "For death, more generally, is present in the very structure of the repetitive economy: the stockpiling of use-time in the commodity object is fundamentally a herald of death,"[29] he writes. He explicitly mentions Minimalist Music, which was internationally in fashion when the book was published, as an example of this development. He refers to Philip Glass' compositions as "background noise for a repetitive and perfectly mastered anonymity",[30] while pop music is "a pretext for noncommunication", its adherents finding "silence in repetition".[31] Adorno's and Attali's views are quoted in some detail because the hostility they express towards popular, rhythm-orientated music was a typical viewpoint of the post-war period. Especially in Germany, Jazz, Rock'n'Roll and other repetitive forms of popular music had many critics who struck a tone similar to Adorno's – often without necessarily being aware of him, which shows how deep such convictions were in post-war West Germany.

Those who were not scolded by their own parents for listening to "jungle music" were instructed by Günther Anders in *Die Antiquiertheit des Menschen* [The Outdatedness of Human Beings] that Jazz "inducts the listener and still more so the motoric co-performer into the *modus operandi* of the machine".[32] In the same year, the journalist Adolf Theobald became still more emphatic about the parallels between Jazz and the alienating (machine-controlled) working world. "The pedantically constant swing gives [Jazz] a regularity that makes one think of motoric music. This motoric characteristic makes Jazz the counterpart of a motoric, uniform way of working. It impresses many from offices and factories, where they are accustomed to an equally motoric, uniform working day." But it was not only in Germany that critics discovered parallels between Jazz and the machine. As early as 1937, American cultural critic Waldo Frank wrote that Jazz "is not an escape from the machine into the clear depths of the soul. It is itself machinistic! It is the music of a failed revolt. Its voice mimics our industrial wreckage."[34]

The disdain for such monotonously repetitive music (and the act of dancing to it) has persisted in some quarters of German society to the present day. It has also provided points of departure for the public debate on Techno — a type of music that is largely based on loops. In the 1990s, the debates that flared up annually in the press prior to the staging of the electronic dance music festival "Berlin Love Parade" still resonated with the antipathies of the 1950s towards rhythm-orientated "machine music" and its alleged dulling, regressive effect. Berlin journalist Gustav Seibt, for example, published an article in 1997 in *Berliner Zeitung*, in which he attributes to Love Parade "the levelling of hundreds of thousands" and a "celebration of the [merely] instinctual level", which "toys with the collective destructive impetus" and must soon end in "bloodlust"![35]

In post-war West Germany, the aversion to "machine-like" metrical music was rooted in the still-fresh memories of National Socialism with its instrumentalization of public parades, goose-stepping to march music, synchronized mass spectacles such as party congresses and sports events, and the celebration of rhythmic uniformity in the films of Leni Riefenstahl, as well as other mass media. Adorno's and Stockhausen's positions against rigid, straight rhythms are recognizably shaped by such memories of the recent past.[36]

In the 1990s, Karlheinz Stockhausen, who had produced most of his electronic compositions of the 1950s with loops, warned Techno producers emphatically against using rhythmic loops, this "musical drug". In an interview, he said that, "I wish those musicians would not allow themselves any repetitions and would go faster in developing their ideas or their findings, because I don't appreciate at all this permanent repetitive language. It is like someone who is stuttering all the time and can't get words out of his mouth. I think musicians should have very concise figures and not rely on this fashionable psychology. I don't like psychology whatsoever: using music like a drug is stupid."[37]

Pierre Schaeffer, of course, was far from composing "music as a drug". His notes show that the discovery of the loop as a means of refining noise into music was a coincidental product of his sound experiments and did not correspond to any artistic intention. However, once he had discovered this effect, he immediately recognized its potential. Unlike the countless gramophone owners who impatiently nudged the needle that had got stuck, Schaeffer began to listen. And unlike the previously mentioned artists and thinkers, who probably would have regarded jumping records as a prime example of modern media technology's tedious repetition, he began to view them as a compositional element. It is therefore of interest to understand how he came up with the idea of using vinyl record loops in his music.

At the beginning of May 1948, 3 months after his epiphany at the ski lift, Schaeffer began planning a composition for railways. He writes, "So here I am on my way to *Batignolles* station, escorted by a mobile sound unit and naively cherishing my wrongheaded bright idea."[38] He let the locomotives drive around, manoeuvre, produce noises. At the station in the Paris suburbs, locomotive drivers are required to "play" their locomotives like instruments, to drive them back and forth according to Schaeffer's directions. He directs the trains and prompts the drivers to make their locomotives "answer", as in a canon.

Back at the studio, he encountered the same problems he had experienced with other original noises – they suggest their origin; listeners see the locomotives in their mind's eye. The recordings he had made at the station didn't satisfy him. The sounds, which seemed to have had machine-like precision during those recordings, suddenly sound chaotic. "I imagined I had extracted a three-four, a six-eight from the moving coach. The train beats its own time, perfectly clear but perfectly irrational. The most monotonous of trains has constant variations of rhythm. It never plays in time. It changes into a series of isotopes."[39]

Due to the divergences, the recordings were not suitable for composing music with them. Schaeffer notes, "my composition hesitates between two options: dramatic or musical sequences. The dramatic sequence constrains the imagination. We witness events; departures, stops. We observe. The engine moves, the track is empty or not. The machine toils, pants, relaxes – anthropomorphism. All of this is the opposite of music."[40]

His search for methods that offered greater scope for musical organization led him to archive records that contained further railway noises. He decided to create a sound collage of various wagon noises. On 5 May, he noted in his diary, "I have composed a score. Eight bars getting under way. *Accelerando* by solo locomotive, then *tutti* of coaches. Rhythms. Some are very fine. I have isolated a certain number of leitmotifs that I must make into transitions and counterpoint. Then slow down and stop. A cadence of buffer clashes. *Da capo* and reprise, more energetically, of the preceding elements."[41]

But once he had assembled the selected sound fragments, he was once more disappointed with the result. He heard "nothing but a crude collection of rhythmic groups that refuse to conform to a beat". It may well have been this problem that made Pierre Schaeffer come up with the idea to use a technical trick to tame the sounds that did not want to submit to his ideas of order. Strangely enough, he later mentions in his diary how short sound fragments could be transformed into rotating sound surfaces that can be edited and combined at will once they are closed into loops.[42]

Strictly speaking, just like playing a record backwards or slowed down, the method of looping, which Schaeffer came up with in the spring of 1948, is known to everyone who has ever had a scratched record on their record player. Schaeffer systematized the error and made it into a fundamental technique, not only of *musique concrète*, but also of electronic music in general.

Since he needed loops to be as precise as possible for his compositions, it was not enough for Schaeffer to loop his noise records, for example by introducing a rough scratch. In collaboration with his sound engineer, Jacques Poullin, he developed a method that made it possible to create much more precise sound loops. Together, they manipulated the cutting machine which Schaeffer used to make recordings on gramophone discs.

At first glance, this cutting machine resembles a normal gramophone. A pliable vinyl disc is placed on the rotating turntable and a needle engraves the sound in a continuous groove. The resulting record can then be played on a normal gramophone. Cutting machines have two motors – one to rotate the turntable and the other to slowly move the needle towards the centre of the turntable. In this way, the sound is scratched into the vinyl in a spiral groove. Schaeffer's simple trick was to turn off the motor that was moving the needle towards the centre of the disc. This interrupted the spiral groove and closed the loop. It allowed Schaeffer to repeat a short fragment of sound over and over. The record no longer keeps the needle moving towards the centre and instead keeps returning to the same starting point, to form a locked sound fragment. Schaeffer had therefore isolated a moment of sound with which he could work. The short sound fragment had become a continuum, one might say that the sound became a condition. Schaeffer spoke of a "fragment of time torn out of the cosmos"; later he would rave about the "enormous effect" of such repetitions, "which radically oppose the logic of any known musical communication".[43] He was particularly fascinated by the idea that through repetition, sound fragments that were freed from their context acquired tonal autonomy. Later, he therefore spoke of a "sound object", which he compared to "words that had escaped the dictionary"[44] – quite obviously a reference to the poetry of the Lettrists, which was liberated from all semantic meaning, and which Schaeffer repeatedly refers to in his book. "It didn't matter that these sound objects resisted all syntax, that they didn't express anything. They were hot off the press and hit the ear without any conceptual ballast."[45]

How Schaeffer came up with this idea cannot be answered conclusively. Although he generally describes his own work in great detail, he neither mentions the time when he began to work with closed grooves, nor the method he used to extract a sound from his recordings. It is possible, however, that he used a practice that was already established in radio to produce background noises. Sound engineers who worked for radio or theatre in the 1950s and 1960s reported that tape loops (e.g. birds chirping or ocean sounds) were often used to provide continuous background noise for radio plays. It is just possible that this technique had already been used with records in French radio and that trained sound engineer Schaeffer was familiar with it. He himself writes that loops were a mere "trick", a "sound effect", before he elevated them to a musical method.[46] This remark seems to indicate that loops had indeed already been used in radio.

In respect of Schaeffer's early experiments, it is remarkable that he observes that the locomotive was simply not sufficiently "disciplined". It is only through media reproduction and repetition that the randomly pounding machine becomes a musical element. By looping its sound, Schaeffer came to control the machine on a symbolic level. While the futuristic composer Luigi Russolo had intoxicated himself in the 1910s with the idea of the uncontrolled noise of machines, Schaeffer brings this very noise back under his control – an act that can be read as a symbolic reversal of the subservient fascination with technology cultivated by some adherents of pre-war modernism. Instead of subjecting himself to the noise of the machines, he integrated this as a rhythmically pulsating element of his music.

Music that incorporates the rhythmic aspects of machines already existed, of course: compositions such as George Antheil's *Ballet Mécanique* (1924) or Arthur Honegger's *Pacific 231* (1923) used pounding machine rhythms during the pre-war period; in the case of *Pacific 231*, it was even about the railway, like Schaeffer's *Étude aux chemins de fer*. But unlike composers such as Russolo, Antheil or Honegger, Schaeffer was not interested in using musical resources to pay homage to technology. What is new about *Étude aux chemins de fer* is that the composition turns the rhythmically monotonous functioning of technology into an aesthetic element, instead of imitating it with traditional orchestral instruments. The notable feature of Schaeffer's method is that he "tames" the machine noise by organizing it into repetitions of mechanical precision.

The similarity between Schaeffer's methods and collage in the visual arts has been repeatedly pointed out. But even if Schaeffer's method can be said to be an acoustic counterpart of modernist collage, he actually pursues an opposite aesthetic goal. The technique of montage, for Gregory Ulmer the "most revolutionary formal innovation of artistic representation in our century",[47] served the purpose of articulating the modern experience of shock triggered by the new technologies and media. The most important sites of modernity – the battlefield, the factory, the modern metropolis – incessantly produced moments of shock. Modernist art reproduced such shocks – in the collages of the Dadaists and the montage techniques of the film avant-garde of the 1920s, for instance – by juxtaposing disparate elements.

In Walter Benjamin's critique of the idea of experience in the modern world, this kind of shock was a central element. But Benjamin also foresaw that this shock aesthetic was susceptible to running out of steam. In his essay *Über einige Motive bei Baudelaire* [On Some Motifs in Baudelaire] he writes that the more "readily consciousness registers these shocks, the less likely they are to have a traumatic effect."[48] When Schaeffer began his experiments with loops, this point seems already to have been reached.

After the Second World War – which had demonstrated the unleashing of technology in a terrible way – Schaeffer may have found it impossible, as well as aesthetically unnecessary, to articulate the horrors of modernism, let alone surpass them. In his early compositions, he is not interested in triggering aesthetic shock experiences through sound montages, like the Dadaists, for instance, aspired to. If it was the modernist collage method to isolate meaningful elements (e.g. from a painting, a photograph, etc.) and to contrast them with other elements, Schaeffer unites his sound elements into a harmonious whole by means of loop repetitions. If modernist collage emphasizes the element of contradictoriness and seeks to evoke shock through juxtaposition, Schaeffer dissects the noise of the modern world into tiny acoustic units and organizes them by means of an "organic" method, which everyone can intuitively understand – namely, by repetition. The isolation of individual sound elements allows their productive transformation. The loop transforms the noise of modernity into music.

Schaeffer's montage technology has also been compared with the collages of surrealists.[49] The surrealist artists gave their "found objects" new meaning by recontextualizing them. However, they generally avoided the direct, "shocking" confrontation of dissimilar materials, which the Dadaists foregrounded. Their combinations usually seemed "organically grown". In Max Ernst's montages of the 1920s, for instance, it is often only at second glance that it becomes apparent that his motifs are composed of divergent images.

Pierre Schaeffer's early pieces are composed in a similarly integrative way. In his *Étude aux chemins de fer* [Railway Etude], with the train rumbling rhythmically albeit unevenly, he almost paradigmatically subdues one of the machines that was one of the triggers of the shock experience of modernity: the railway. The railway gathers time and compresses the space it traverses. It makes "collages" out of the landscapes it traverses by bringing together places that are far apart. For the pre-war avant-garde, the railway was therefore an embodiment of speed and progress, and of the fragmentation of perception through technology. Wolfgang Schivelbusch writes in his *Geschichte der Eisenbahnreise* [History of the Railway Journey] that "akin to the notion of the railway as projectile, the train journey is experienced as being shot through the landscape, bewildering the senses".[50]

Ironically, it is a different modern technology with which Schaeffer arrests the ever-advancing energy of the railway and turns its movement into an idling state – electro-acoustic sound recording. Instead of passing by, the sound remains and is suited to sustained listening. The gramophone was actually built to reproduce linear time. But in Schaeffer's early compositions the passage of time is transformed into a moment that circles around itself. The rattling of the wagons suddenly no longer suggests the rushing past of a landscape, but stasis. The acoustic relic of a railway journey becomes a media fragment of its reality, which has detached itself from its cause and taken on a life of its own. Three seconds of railway noise are transformed into a musical unit of an exclusively technically-produced music.

Schaeffer was able to play this little reality shred and combine it with other, pulsating reality loops until a composition emerged from it. In his diary, writing about working on his railway composition, he observes that he has "succeeded in isolating a rhythm and in doubling it in a different timbre. Dark, light, dark, light. This rhythm can remain unchanged for a long time. In this way it creates a kind of character for itself, and the repetition makes one forget that it is a train."[51] It can be assumed that when he refers to "isolating", he means the first-ever implementation of record loops. Other forms of the sound montage were not possible with the technical means available to him at that time. "If I extract any sound element and repeat it without bothering about its *form* but varying its *matter*, I practically cancel out the form, it loses its meaning; only the variation of matter emerges, and with it the phenomenon of music."[52] The emptying of cultural signs, which Schaeffer describes here, is one of the most important aesthetic effects of all loops. Through repetition, the sound object is stripped of its original meaning, and a perspective of its purely acoustic properties, which normally recede behind its form, is made possible. At the same time, the loop technique creates an interesting tension between a sound within a certain sequence (which made composing with unprocessed railway noises so difficult) and its constant mechanical repetition. When Schaeffer writes about repeating a looped sound passage in different timbres, he does nothing other than what many House and Techno producers and DJs do today. House DJs, like DJ Pierre, have developed an entire stylistic instrument set by repeating sound fragments in "different timbres" by means of modulating with mixer filters.

Schaeffer was fascinated by the way repetition caused monotonous noise fragments to become acoustically autonomous, how variants suddenly seem to emerge from the never-varying. You can virtually see him sitting in front of the turntable and nodding to the beat of the looped rattling of wagons as he writes in his diary:

> as soon as a record is placed on the turntable, I am captivated, as if by some magical force that compels me to submit, however monotonous it may be. Maybe one gets seized when one is completely in the rhythm? Why not broadcast three minutes of "pure waggon" on the radio to let people know that it's enough to be able to hear that the whole art is to listen carefully?[53]

At the end of his description of the origin of the *Étude aux chemins de fer*, Schaeffer sums up that "music begins with two procedures: An element is *foregrounded* (so as to hear it as it is, its texture, its materiality, its timbre). Then it is repeated. If you repeat the same thing twice it becomes music."[54]

Of course, at that point, Schaeffer's insights were still far ahead of his concrete compositional work. Despite loops and other acoustic manipulations of sound elements, the *Étude aux chemins de fer* sounds more like a radio play than a piece of music. The dilemma that Schaeffer himself had clearly diagnosed can still be heard in the piece. In relation to the musical element, the "anecdotal" character of the "sound objects", as Schaeffer called his sound elements, are consistently pushed into the foreground and the technical manipulations cannot alter this. Although in several passages, the sound does take on a life of its own as abstract passages that no longer contain any reference to their original sources, the sound of a whistle brings the listener back to earth (or to the train station).

Schaeffer did not put his radical idea of presenting 3 minutes of unprocessed wagon noise into practice – the entire piece lasts barely 3 minutes. And yet, the passages where Schaeffer lets various looped "wagon rhythms" run on come closest to his idea of sound purged of tangible associations. Astonishingly, Schaeffer hardly relies on the rhythmic power of his newly invented loop. In the finished version, he has moved away from his original plan that different "wagon rhythms" would alternate over and over. Rather, he brought the "Eisenbahn-Ostinato" [Railway Ostinato] to a swift conclusion by editing it.

Nevertheless, loops are also the most important means of organizing his sound material in the etudes written in 1948. In the *Kreisel-Etüde* [Spinning Top Etude], Schaeffer uses the sound of a series of percussion instruments made of wood and metal, as well as that of two spinning tops. In the *Étude aux tourniquets*, he processes sound fragments from an orchestral tune-up. In *Etüde noire* and *Etüde violette*, he subjects some piano passages to the method of *sillon fermé*. (The piano parts were played by none other than Pierre Boulez, who would go on to criticize Schaeffer so harshly later on.) Schaeffer keeps returning to these early compositions and revises them several times, most recently almost a quarter of a century later, in 1971. He thus anticipated the contemporary pop music practice of updating music through ever-new remixes.

The most interesting composition from this period undoubtedly is the *Étude Pathétique*. I described the history of its spontaneous and inspired creation at the beginning of this chapter. In the *Étude aux chemins de fer*, it was a machine, the railway, that was brought back under the organizing control of human creativity with the aid of loops. In the *Pathétique*, Schaeffer organizes musical fragments from all over the world into a harmonious whole, again with the aid of loops – in addition to the rattling of a tin can, a slowed-down Balinese choir, an American Bluegrass harmonica and a few words spoken by French playwright and actor Sacha Guitry are brought together to form a harmonious whole. The *Étude Pathétique* is an early example of musical globalization, a world music mix *avant la lettre*.

Schaeffer writes that the aim of this composition was to integrate the human voice into a *musique concrète* composition, having previously focused on the sounds of things and machines:

The introduction of vocal elements has long excited me. I don't have an actor at my disposal, let alone a singer. Yet for weeks, I've done very well without them. There are always old, unused records lying around in a studio. The one that fell into my hands is engraved with the valuable voice of Sacha Guitry. "Sur tes levres, sur tes levres" [on your lips, on your lips], says Sasha Guitry. But the recording was interrupted by the cough of a script girl, which explains why the record went to waste. I grab this record, and on a second turntable put the strong, peaceful rhythm of a faithful boat, then, on two more turntables, anything that falls into my hands. An American record with accordion and harmonica music, a Balinese record. After that, a virtuoso concert for four volume controls and eight record players...The boat of the French fleet, the American accordion and the Balinese priests are amazingly willing to obey the god of record players. They form a clever ensemble, which is sparing in its effects, and which astonishes the listener who is invited to a first performance with a composition that is clever, harmonious and definitive in equal measure.[55]

One can tell from his *Pathétique* that Schaeffer has already gained some experience with music production on the turntable. His "mix" is still far from the tricks with which later Hip-hop DJs were to shine on the "Wheels of Steel".[56] But Schaeffer's "live mix" is fluid and bears witness to his familiarity with his "instruments". Additionally, by juxtaposing his sound materials, he emphasizes their diversity without playing them off "shockingly" against each other. Rather than highlighting their disparity, the different elements are joined as a loop that forms a rhythmically pulsating unity. The "non-musical" sounds in particular have lost their "anecdotal" character and fit organically into the musical construction. Music and noise complement each other; thanks to the loops they even form an almost synchronous rhythm. With the *Étude Pathétique*, which was created in a single take, *musique concrète* reached its first climax.

Interestingly, it was Schaeffer's pupil and later antagonist Karlheinz Stockhausen who, of all people, had been quick to recognize the ordering function of loops in Schaeffer's early etudes. In a WDR broadcast, he later commented on the composition:

> recorded noises from rolling tin cans, travelling trains, in addition to indefinable electrical sounds, evenly repeated speech fragments and some other sound events that are more or less easy to recognize are combined by means of a collage technique after they have been more or less deformed or transformed with electro-acoustic apparatuses. Things that seem to have nothing to do with each other in real life are brought into relation with each other by a simple musical means – a monotonous rhythm, for example.[57]

The *Pathétique* was to remain Schaeffer's last composition for a long time because he was busy attending international conferences for the ORTF. But he was able to make sure that his five sound studies were broadcast on the French State Parisian radio station on 5 October 1948. On 18 March of the following year, they had their premiere at a "live concert" – in actual fact, only the records were played – in front of an audience at the École *Normale de Musique in Paris*.

The "classics" of *musique concrète*, as Schaeffer confidently called his five early etudes, signal a "revision of modernity". The loops enabled Schaeffer to organize the noise of modernity into a harmonious whole. Through media repetition, Schaeffer tamed the acoustic turmoil of the twentieth century and reorganized it according to his own rules. This revision of modernity was not to be a permanent feature of his work; for Schaeffer, it seems merely to have resulted from the technically simple trick of the "closed groove". In the compositions he was to realize over the years to come, the technique of the loop was pushed into the background; repetition effects were no longer as prominent as they had been in his first recordings.

A period of cooperation between Schaeffer and the composer Pierre Henry followed. Over the next few years, Henry was to become one of the most important representatives of *musique concrète* alongside Schaeffer himself. Together, they produced the *Symphonie pour un homme seul* [Symphony for One Man Alone] in 1950, the opera *Orphée* (1951-53) as well as several shorter pieces. At the beginning of their musical partnership, tape machines did not yet exist on French radio and the *Symphonie pour un homme seul* was once again composed using Schaeffer's array of turntables.

Henry gave a vivid description of the prevailing production conditions for media music. At that time, the possibilities of sound manipulation were still quite undeveloped, yet also made possible some strange techniques. Each turntable was equipped with levers that enabled *glissandi* and transpositions. The modulation resulted from tapping the levers, akin to a "return to the instrument" since it required a targeted arm movement. Magnetic tape did not yet exist and jumping from one sound to the next, from one gramophone record to the next, was a precarious business. Henry outlines how accidental additions, produced by the needle on the record groove or by unexpected incidents during playback, could actually be enrichments that added an element of the unexpected and he describes himself as a "master at jumping grooves" since he jumped from one turntable to the next, making use of the eight turntables with which the studio was equipped.

The master of jumping grooves rarely used his newly acquired skills to build loops. The compositions which Schaeffer and Henry created together feature other methods of sound manipulation. In some passages of their music, loops do still appear (in "Erotica", in the *Symphonie pour un homme seul* of 1950, for instance). But the methods which Schaeffer and Henry now used to organize their sound sources generally were significantly more complex montage and manipulation techniques, rather than loops. According to Schaeffer, the lonely person of the composition's title is the *musique concrète* composer who has to spend days and nights working on his music in complete isolation and with only the simplest means at his disposal. If Schaeffer's early etudes indicate a "revision of modernity", however, then the *Symphonie pour un homme seul* comes across as a revision of this revision. Even the title is close to the existential rhetoric about "man" who is "thrown into the world" and "condemned to be free" (Satre), becoming modern in the company of European intellectuals. Instead of taming their brute yet appealing sound sources with loops, Schaeffer and Henry let it rain on the listener without the structuring element of repetition. Musically as well as thematically, *Symphonie pour un homme seul* is a return to central maxims of modernity. It's no longer about joining the noise of machines and media to make a harmonious whole. It's about estrangement and despair, which is given voluble expression. Satre's maxim "man is fear, man is abandonment, man is despair" has here found its acoustic pendant.

In their later compositions, Schaeffer and Henry didn't just work with magnetic tape, but also with two tape instruments, which Schaeffer had invented, and which sound engineer Jacques Poullin (who had already helped with the development of gramophone loops) built for him – the *phonogène* and the *morphophone*. Music critic Fred Prieberg, who had obviously seen both apparatuses in action, described them in this way: "the *phonogène,* which Pierre Schaeffer even had patented, is a magnetophone (tape machine) that is capable of running at 12 different speeds. Sensibly enough, the separate speeds reproduce the 12 intervals of the chromatic scale with mathematical precision, and since the motor also has random running times, transpositions across two octaves can be achieved."[58] To put it simply, with the aid of the *phonogène,* Schaeffer was able to play the tones of the scale at will, and in this way, could alter the frequency of any sound he chose – a forerunner of the digital sampler of today.

The sound manipulation possibilities which the morphophone made possible were even more diverse. This appliance, too, is based on a tape ribbon, which runs past ten sound levers. Depending on how these levers are set, not only bewildering echo effects, but also other types of sound manipulation can be achieved. Prieberg comments that, "it's even possible to alter the sound of a percussive element with the *morphophone.* A violin tone can be made to resemble a percussion instrument, a piano chord can sound like an organ, a dragging noise like a dry percussion sound that is hit with force."[59]

It was these kinds of sound processing that occupied Schaeffer and Henry over the years that followed. Loops had structured the early "incunabula" of *musique concrète*. Later, akin to Stockhausen, they were used as a means to create new sounds. While Schaeffer had used loops to transform noise into a harmonious musical unity in his five early etudes, the tape loops that featured in Schaeffer's and Henry's later compositions mainly served continually to create new noise.

And yet, as late as the 1960s, by which time his instrument set had long been refined, Schaeffer spoke of the "enormous effect" of loops and referred to them as *musique concrète*'s "point of departure".[60] In hindsight, it seems to have been the most effective and significant of his compositional techniques. He writes,

> without this surgery [of closed grooves], *musique concrète* would most probably have remained stuck in the "neither one thing nor the other" realm of electronic sound effects. But the closed groove, which is really just a procedure, prompted enormous effects – effects that contradicted the logic of every known musical "sound language" – so that a new point of departure can be referred to.[61]

Schaeffer didn't implement his discovery that "if you repeat the same thing twice, it becomes music"[62] as consequentially in his music as did the composers that were to come after him. As an old man, he even doubted his entire *oeuvre* with his typical mixture of irony and self-pity. "Unfortunately, it took me forty years to conclude that nothing is possible outside DoReMi...In other words, I wasted my life", he told an interviewer in 1987.[63] And yet it was precisely at this time that the idea of "jumping" gramophone records and of making music fragments repeat themselves endlessly was emerging as one of the most momentous developments in twentieth-century music. The producers of Hip-hop and the then emerging House and Techno music genres did just that with great success.

"WE SHALL RULE THE SOUNDS!" KARLHEINZ STOCKHAUSEN AND THE MUSIC OF THE SOUND LABORATORIES

Looking at photos of them, one might take them for natural scientists. The men wearing suits and ties, their hair combed back with pomade in the style of the 1950s, seem strangely ageless. They are bending over appliances that might have been found in a physics hall or a laboratory of that time. The walls are lined with cabinets with switches, controls, lighting diodes and display panels, which often reach up to the ceiling. Just occasionally, a tape player suggests that the place might be to do with music.

But the electronic music studios founded in Europe and the USA after the Second World War were places where serious work was done. After a number of composers had created the first electronic instruments and compositions for them before the war, these studios were systematically developing a new kind of electronically produced music. Often, the men standing before the apparatus – women are rarely to be seen in these pictures – have a concentrated facial expression, as if they were meditating on the machines in front of them. As if engaging in a deep dialogue with them. In the 1950s, one of them especially had mastered the art of posing in front of machines like an artist who was highly concentrated or deep in thought. He was to become one of the most important protagonists and propagandists of the men of the music machines – Karlheinz Stockhausen.

In the previous chapter, I presented the aesthetic differences that emerged between the French *musique concrète* and Stockhausen's German "electronic music" – its centre being the *Studio für elektronische Musik* [Studio for Electronic Music] at Cologne's *Westdeutscher Rundfunk* [West German Radio] (WDR). The competition between these two movements was fierce in post-war Europe and was fought out with great vigour. Yet beyond the very different musical expectations, the two schools had one important thing in common: both were to a large extent based on the use of loops.

Karlheinz Stockhausen had learned about this method in 1952 when he went to Paris to visit Pierre Schaeffer, although his application of it was to be completely different from that of Schaeffer, of course. While Schaeffer used loops to transform found sounds by means of repetition and to create music from the result, for Stockhausen, tape loops presented a way to manipulate pure sine tones from a generator and to turn these into compliant, malleable sound material for serial compositions.

"Abstract" composers like Stockhausen saw their composing as the most advanced point in the development of musical material since the beginning of the twentieth century, and their aim was to subject sounds to a completely controllable process of production. They referred back to the serial composition techniques developed at the beginning of the twentieth century by the Viennese School (Alban Berg, Arnold Schönberg, Anton Webern). Conversely, "concrete" composers such as Schaeffer and Henry opened their works to the sounds of the world. Pierre Schaeffer had rebelled against serial music from the start because he wanted his music to develop from the nature of sounds. The last thing he wanted was to impose a new musical structure on his chosen sounds – especially one as strict as that of serial music. "The countless puzzles that the auditory world presents seemed so complex to him that he considered it unthinkable to pre-construct sounds and sound structures."[1]

For the Cologne school of 'electronic music', on the other hand, it was a political issue to revive the serial methods of Schönberg, Webern and Berg. They wanted to re-establish a tradition that the National Socialists had wiped out in Germany and Austria. Stockhausen was just one of many German composers who wanted to tie in with this pre-war avant-garde school after the war in order to continue the kind of music that had been suppressed by the Nazis.

The rediscovery of Arnold Schönberg and the Viennese School in the post-war period was not least due to Theodor Adorno's *Philosophy of Modern Music*, first published in 1949. In his book, Adorno played off Schönberg against the far more popular Stravinsky and declared Schönberg's music to be an inevitable consequence of the historical development of music to become increasingly complex and logical. Schönberg and, above all, his pupil Anton Webern were to gain great importance in the development of European post-war music, especially in the German-speaking world. There, in the immediate post-war period, "serial music" developed from the "serial technique" of the Second Viennese School around Schönberg.

The principles according to which Schönberg and the composers who followed him created their serial music have been described as "the most complicated and abstract form of formal organization that has ever existed in music".[2] If I must nevertheless tax the reader with its basic principles in the discussion that follows, it is because these principles will keep playing a role throughout this book. For the average listener, serial compositions may sound chaotic and their structure incomprehensible. In fact, however, they are designed according to rigorous structural principles. Schönberg's 12-tone technique is based on the structural principle of the *series*. Each motif in his compositions consists of a series that contains each tone of the 12-step chromatic scale once. A composition is created by working through the series according to predetermined principles (basic shape, inversion [i.e. horizontally mirrored], crab [backward] and crab inversion). This method of composition was behind the emergence of a music based on mathematical principles, which limited the composer's creative freedom in favour of rational principles. Anton Webern extended the notion of total mastery over musical structure by determining not only the pitch of the notes, but also their duration according to the principles of series.

Post-war avant-garde composers developed these methods in still more radical ways. All the properties of music were to be determined by number or proportion series. In Webern's music, unlike Schönberg's, the duration of the notes was also determined by series. In other post-war serial music (such as that of Luigi Nono, Pierre Boulez or Luciano Berio), in addition to pitch and duration, other musical parameters, i.e. volume, timbre, tone density, articulation and mode, were also shaped according to the rules of the series.

This was the point when the use of electronic instruments became interesting to avant-garde composers. The demands of music that derived pitch and duration from quasi-mathematical operations had previously often overtaxed the skills of instrumentalists and singers. Further, the control of the timbre was impossible with conventional instruments, because their construction determines their timbre structure and allows only relatively small changes in this respect. (John Cage's "prepared piano" had been an attempt to extend the "built-in" sound characteristics of an instrument.)

Because the sound spectrum of conventional instruments has relatively narrow limits, their timbre was not amenable to precise serial control. The attempt to determine musical structures mathematically right down to the last detail met with a definite limitation here – until the possibilities of electronic sound manipulation opened up. Since every sound could be traced back to a mixture of simple sine waves, electronic manipulations of these sine waves had to be able to create any sound. The enthusiasm of German composers of the 1950s for electronic music came from the fact that they believed that electronics could be used to make sounds compliant in an ultimate way. Time and again, texts emerging from the Cologne School – especially those by Herbert Eimert – contain phrases referring to "commanding" the sound or wanting to "master" it, or conversely, that it was a matter of "overpowering it".[3]

It would be worth conducting a study in its own right to analyse this barracks-yard tone, which was widespread among German composers of the post-war period, and to examine the values associated with it in greater detail. In this context, the aversion to indeterminacy and "chaotic hustle and bustle", which is repeatedly expressed, and the desire for "pure" sounds as basic working material are striking. The rhetoric with which the composers of electronic music presented their ideas fitted West German post-war society, which wanted to get the Nazi past behind it as fast as possible. But in their desire to achieve a fresh new start, they apparently did not notice that the notion of a "pure" sound that was to be "mastered" or "commanded" could, in fact, evoke unpleasant memories of the recent German past.

The Cologne Studio for Electronic Music, where this tone prevailed, had first emerged from an initiative by the Nordwestdeutscher Rundfunk (NWDR) editor Herbert Eimert. Eimert, a composer and musicologist, was head of the night programme at NWDR. He was also a supporter of Schönberg and Webern, and was keen to apply their "serial" methods to electronic music. "The actual goal of the Cologne musicians," writes André Ruschkowski, "was to subject timbre to a serial continuum that encompassed all known and unknown, that is, all conceivable and possible sounds...Electronics were to make it possible to assemble timbre itself, to 'compose' it in a literal sense..."[4]

When the director of the NWDR gave him permission to establish a studio for electronic music, Eimert set about putting the idea of creating an electronic music that aimed to achieve an "iron system of sounding material" into practice. "Eimert argued that it was precisely the relentless severity of the 'serial' principle, which did not tolerate exceptions, that would succeed in taming the electronic material."[5] He shared this belief with a young composer who had returned to Cologne in 1953 after studying in Paris, and who was soon to become the hope of what became known as the WDR Studio for Electronic Music:[6] Karlheinz Stockhausen.

Stockhausen had studied with the French serialist Olivier Messiaen in 1952/53. While in Paris, he had become familiar with the work of Pierre Schaeffer, in whose radio studio he was temporarily permitted to work. He was therefore familiar with *musique concrète* as well as with musical serialism. In the then emerging electronic music, these two methods were soon to stand in irreconcilable opposition to each other. While Schaeffer was concerned with organizing recorded "concrete" sounds into music, Stockhausen and the Cologne School were looking for a completely abstract, non-referential music, in which they had complete control over every single sound element. Pierre Schaeffer, on the other hand, who repeatedly described himself as an anarchist, started from the sounds he had recorded. Looking towards models such as the Futurists and Varèse, he described his approach as "empirical" and tried to derive his music from the sound material. For him, "sound research" meant listening, immersion in sounds, and in noise.

The difference between these two approaches becomes particularly clear when comparing their respective approaches to their scores. For his first compositions, such as the *Étude aux chemins de fer,* Schaeffer noted down some short sketches for the structure of the piece. But he soon gave up writing down his ideas and instead developed his compositions entirely from the sounds he had recorded. His *Étude Pathétique* was mixed live, and subsequent compositions were made at the editing table with tape recorders.

Composers like Stockhausen, conversely, first worked out sophisticated scores according to the principles of serial music, and 'organized' their sound materials accordingly, sometimes taking months over this step. Time and again, the composers' "tools of the trade" are proudly displayed in photos of the Cologne Studio for Electronic Music and, in addition to tape snippets, rulers and stopwatches, such a score is always included. It is often written on arithmetic paper, or even graph paper, and reminds of flow charts or electronic circuit diagrams. The structure of the piece to be composed is recorded with numbers, graphs and symbols. The material that was to be processed in this way was often made of pure sine tones that had no tonal peculiarities, which could therefore be "subjected" effectively to the composer's will. And working with tape loops was an important means to achieving this end.

Pierre Schaeffer would probably have described his work in the 1950s as "sound research". In the case of electronic music from Germany, however, the term "sound control" would have been far more appropriate. The WDR studio worked on the creation of pure sounds created from sine tones, where every element could be shaped by the composer – the volume, the envelope curve, the frequencies, simply everything. "We will use electronic sound generation in the future. It will make everything easier, clearer, more reliable," Stockhausen wrote in December 1952 in a letter to his friend, the composer Karel Goeyvaerts, "and we shall rule the sounds – not the other way around."[7]

Even before his return to Cologne, Stockhausen was therefore already thinking along the "serial" lines which Herbert Eimert had established at the WDR. For him, too, the promise of gaining control over the musical material was the main reason for dealing with electronic music. Stockhausen wrote that through electronic sound production, "for the first time, the possibility to compose timbre in the real sense existed, i.e. to assemble the elements, and so bring the universal structural principles to bear in the sound proportions".[8]

Such ideas had already driven him when he composed the *Concrete Study* in Paris. In October 1952, through Schaeffer's mediation, Stockhausen was able to work in a little-used experimental studio at the Technical College of the French Post Office. The task of the studio, which was headed by physicist and information theorist Abraham Moles, was to conduct systematic sound research. As a starting point for his etude, Stockhausen opted for the sound of a prepared piano. He writes in a letter, "now I wanted to work the structure I wished to realize in an etude into the very micro-dimension of the single tone, so that the comprehensive principle of my idea would be present in even the smallest aspect".[9]

Since he had no access to sine generators at that time which could produce a "pure" sound, Stockhausen cut off the "head" of a piano note for his first etude – an idea that Pierre Schaeffer had already come up with at the end of the 1940s. He used a few centimetres of a tape recording with the relatively constant sound that followed in order to organize it – in accordance with the principles of serial music – into a predetermined structure. To do this, he glued the short pieces of tape containing the cut-off piano notes together to form loops. Then he transposed these tape loops with Pierre Schaeffer's phonogène – the previously described "magnetic tape instrument", with which it was possible to play a recorded sound up and down the scale. He made his manipulated piano sound at different pitches and assembled and combined them according to the predetermined principles.[10] Work on the piece was long and complicated. Forty years on, Stockhausen still remembered how time-consuming it was. He comments that:

since I was only able to access the studio plus technician for a few hours each week, I hammered a nail into my work table at my student digs, put a tape metal core around that nail, fastened a centimetre measure from left to right in front of me, put a series of assembled tapes with their metal cores, plus a core with an empty tape, side by side at the back of the table. Then I cut many pieces from a roll of white sticky tape and glued them side by side onto the table-top. Then, according to the instructions given in my score, I selected one of the tapes which contained a particular transposition of a sound, measured the notated length in centimetres and millimetres, cut the piece and stuck it to a longer piece of white blank tape, then wound the white tape and pieces of tape around the metal core on the nail. I used a pencil for this...Sometimes my wrapping equipment failed and then there was tape salad; I crawled around on the floor under the table looking for one end of the tape, laboriously untangled the mess of my good tape and carefully rewound it. When my studio time arrived, I synchronized two of my tapes with playback magnetophones, recorded the result onto another magnetophone, and, depending on the polyphony, superimposed that onto another zebra tape of brown tape pieces and snippets. When I listened to two synchronized layers, let alone three or four, I became paler and more helpless each time: I had imagined it all to be completely different! The following day, the sorcery continued – I changed my rows, chose different sequences, cut different lengths, glued different series, hoped for new sound miracles. I can't remember exactly how many weeks I spent cutting and gluing, incrementally achieving perfection in the art of winding while I did so."[11]

Pierre Schaeffer remembers Stockhausen's work on his first etude somewhat differently. In an interview with Stockhausen biographer Michael Kurtz, Schaeffer recalls that it was:

strange, when Messiaen came into the studio, he said, "I want almost no sounds at all", those were his words. When Stockhausen arrived, he said, "I'm going to work with a single tone"...[He took] a small sound fragment, ten centimetres of recorded tape, and pronounced, "I'm going to cut this sound into tiny pieces, millimetres in length, and create a permutation with it." I replied, "You unhappy soul, don't do that, you're just going to pile up lots of background noise, and that's not interesting at all!"...He didn't want to follow my advice, he really didn't want any advice at all, and since he could do what he wanted by himself, I sent him to Rue Barrault [the recording studio of the French post office school], where he could cut up his sound into millimetre pieces. So, he got going with his gluing and when eventually he came back perfectly satisfied, we said, "okay then, let's hear it", and we played the tape – it wasn't more than 10 centimetres long, with the permutations it was maybe 50 centimetres – and all you could hear was "chooooot". That was the upshot of Stockhausen's sound study, a kind of small "choooot". He himself was entirely satisfied – in contrast to me![12]

Stockhausen attributed Schaeffer's dissatisfaction with the result of his efforts, which had lasted for weeks, to the "impurity" of his sound materials. In a letter to Goeyvaerts, he writes, "but you're absolutely right about one thing. We can't do much with recorded sounds that are already 'finished' in front of the microphone. You really have to experience that for yourself, how a processed, transformed, dissected tone finally knocks the desired result from your hand! It's incredible how much chaos there is in a single note!!!"[13] Pierre Schaeffer had, of course, already had similar experiences when he tried to compose with the sounds of a steam locomotive for his *Étude aux chemins de fer*. However, Stockhausen could not accept the conclusions that Schaeffer had drawn for himself. "*Musique concrète*, and I felt this from the very beginning, is nothing but a surrender to the indeterminate, it's a really dilettantish gamble and unbridled improvisation."[14]

In Paris, Stockhausen had no further opportunities to work on his compositions. Kurtz mentions that, "Schaeffer declared his personal experiments finished and gave Stockhausen the task of systematizing certain sounds and noises. Stockhausen carried out this task without any enthusiasm."[15] It was only when Stockhausen returned to Cologne in the summer of 1953 and worked as a freelancer at the Studio for Electronic Music that he was able to draw conclusions from his experiences in Paris.

An almost Faustian gesture characterizes Stockhausen's early experiments – a search, as it were, for the innermost life of a sound, for that which holds it together on the inside. To him, the sine tones he produced with the aid of generators like those used in physics lessons were completely *pure sounds*, which he could mould according to his own will. Like Eimert, Stockhausen strove for complete control over all aspects of the sound. And with Stockhausen, it is even more apparent than with other serial composers that this idea of perfect control over sound is essentially about a form of human control over nature.

Time and again, passages appear in his texts that call to mind the idea of overcoming nature through human ingenuity.

> What does an architect do when he's tasked with building a cantilever bridge, a skyscraper, an aircraft hangar? Does he use clay, wood, bricks? New designs require pre-stressed concrete, glass, aluminium – aluminium, glass, pre-stressed concrete allow the realization of new designs. This is how the idea came to me to abandon pre-formed instrumental sounds and to compose the very sounds for a certain composition, to construct them artificially, according to the structural demands of this composition and no other.[16]

In order to be able to mould the sound entirely according to his ideas, Stockhausen edited it with a tape recorder. Only the output tones produced with the sine wave generator were actually electronic in this music. The entire composition emerged from the tape recorder that was used to process these sounds. Stockhausen writes:

> such sinus tones were the first elements with which we composed different spectrums according to the structural requirements of a certain composition. So, each sound is the

result of a compositional act. The composer determines the various properties (also called parameters). In practice, the work with sinus tones was done like this...a sinus oscillation is recorded on tape, then another, and another is added, and so on...[17]

Stockhausen used tape loops for this process of sound synthesis. It was to be another decade or so before the first transistor-based and voltage-controlled modular synthesizers were developed, with which such operations could be performed live. The modulations that became possible with the 1960s synthesizers of Robert Moog and Don Buchla were anticipated by Stockhausen with his systematic tape loop experiments, albeit in a very work-intensive way. Stockhausen had already begun to experiment with the frequency generator in the Paris PTT studio, where it was used for measuring purposes. He had by now learned enough about acoustics from his friend, the composer Karel Goeyvaerts, to understand that the entire sound spectrum could be produced from sine tones. This had led him to the idea of compiling the notes of a composition entirely from sine tones. As soon as Stockhausen had access to WDR's equipment, he set to work – not with the electronic instruments that the station had purchased by then, but with a set of instruments borrowed from metrology!

Later he recalled that:

when I started working in the Cologne studio in 1953, I immediately went to Mr Enkel [the head of WDR metrology] and asked him if he perhaps had a high frequency oscillator,[18] or a generator...He replied, "have you gone mad, we've got these expensive apparatuses, like Melochord and Trautonium!" – "Yes, but I want something else. *I want to know what each mix contains...!*" And for months I recorded individual notes, starting synchronously with two magnetophones and recording them onto a third magnetophone. The combinations weren't quite clean anymore and contained white noise, but still – it was a start.[19]

"Knowing exactly what's in it". "Clean combinations". It sounds like chemical experiments. Time and again the desire to take the sound apart is mentioned, like an element that can be broken down into its individual atoms – not only by Stockhausen, but also by other contemporary composers. At that time, the first atomic bomb had been detonated only a few years previously. It almost seems as if Stockhausen and other composers of that time wanted to reconstruct the splitting of the atomic nucleus in a musical clean room of electronic music.

The WDR used tape recorders to process the sine tones. By 1952, Robert Beyer and Eimert had already worked on tape-manipulated sine tones in their joint composition *Klangfiguren II* [Sound Figures II] where they had, among other things, pulled lengths of tape past the tape-head by hand in order to achieve unusual sounds, and – like Schaeffer and composers of American Music for Tape – they made sound fragments run faster or slower. More significantly, however, the sound engineers of WDR developed a process by which sound synthesis could be achieved through tape loops and therefore composed on the tape recorder. To achieve this, they exchanged the three tape-heads of a tape recorder, so that different frequencies could be "layered on top of each other". While a tape loop was running through the tape recorder, they were continually recording new sounds, which were combined in this way.[20]

Ironically, however, the magnetic tapes had their own way of resisting Stockhausen's urge for perfection. The white noise of the magnetic tape, which was constantly being re-recorded, increased in volume rapidly, and after eight to ten rounds the sounds became unusable. Nevertheless, the sound mixes that were produced in this way inspired Stockhausen. On 20 July 1953 he wrote to Goeyvaerts, who had encouraged him to carry out his experiments with the tape recorder.

I am assembling sounds from sinus tones for a new piece. This works very well, and I have already gained a lot of experience with it…I have, for example, superimposed ("composed") sounds or sine tones that remain completely stationary, but from which partial tones emerge one after the other at certain time intervals…without any direct intervention. It is incredibly beautiful to hear such sounds, they are completely balanced, "calm", static and "exposed" only by structural proportions. Raindrops in the sun…[21]

A month later, on 23 August 1953, he wrote in a letter to Goeyvaerts:

and finally, one-and-a-half minutes are ready! The piece lasts
9 minutes. I've taken to writing the score in the evening and
realizing it in the morning and afternoon. I am really happy –
this music is indescribably beautiful and pure!!! One wonders
how one could have thought and imagined differently for so
long!…The structure has placed the sounds in the world as
a "final process" – and as I was able to work in a completely
pure way for the first time, it feels like grace that this music
of beauty is so near. You can't imagine how happy I am.[22]

A few weeks later, Stockhausen's *Studie I* (1953) was finished, and the WDR Studio for Electronic Music had its first prototypical work. With historical distance, the sounds produced by Stockhausen appear less revolutionary. More than 40 years later, the musicologist André Ruschkowski judged that:

today, listening to Stockhausen's *Studie I*, it becomes clear
that, instead of a fusion of sinus tones into new, more
complex sounds, the separate components of the sinus
tones remain audible and easily identifiable. Rather than
a new sound quality, the impression of chords formed
from sinus tones was created. Moreover, thanks to their
easy identification, the separate sine tones have their own
acoustic quality, comparable to the sound of a simple

musical instrument, somewhere between a flute and pipe organ stops. That was probably what prompted Theodor W. Adorno to make the sarcastic remark that electronic music sounded as if Anton Webern compositions were being performed on a Wurlitzer organ.[23]

Stockhausen himself seems to have noticed that the "pure" sine tones he had created with the aid of the tape recorder were simply not acoustically interesting enough for longer compositions. He soon began to refine the technique of sound synthesis with the tape recorder. For his *Studie II* (1954), he layered even more sine tones on top of each other and sent them through a reverberation chamber. And for *Gesang der Jünglinge* [Song of the Youths] (1955/56), he ultimately combined syntheses of "clean" sine tones with the voice of a singer.

In *Gesang der Jünglinge,* Stockhausen also used a new method of sound generation, which was again based on tape loops. He mounted many short tape snippets on a tape loop and accelerated the tape so much that these short impulses merged into a single sound. The effect of playing this tape loop can be compared to the "buzzing" of a car tyre. When the car moves slowly, the unevenness of the tyre's profile creates a rhythm. The more the car accelerates, the faster this rhythm gets, until it finally turns into a buzzing whose pitch changes with the speed.[24] A knocking noise becomes a vibration. Stockhausen's sound compositions work in a similar way; they are rhythms that are accelerated to the point that they become vibrations. Probably no other composition method of the twentieth century embodies quite so well the desire of avant-garde music to transcend the limitations of physical reality with the aid of human reason and technology. In contrast to the layered sinus tones, the sounds that result do appear much more complex. In an interview, Stockhausen describes the work with the tape loops as follows:

I spent six weeks working on distinct sounds found within the young people's singing, which last six or seven seconds. There are sounds that consist of hundreds of cuts, tiny snippets. Sometimes I cut pieces of tape that were only two millimetres wide, and glued them onto white pause tape with acetone. Thousands of them! I was still working like this in *Kontakte*. I glued pieces of tape containing discrete impulses onto white tape with acetone, blew on each one until it was dry, then made a loop, let it run for four hours and recorded it onto large tapes that were subsequently accelerated enormously.[25]

In order to be able to work with such long loops, the sound engineers at WDR built special devices. Photos from the Studio for Electronic Music show, among other things, the so-called "loop table", a console with deflection rollers, on which metre-long tape loops could be wound and played. In a lecture he gave in the 1970s at the *Folkwang Museum* in Essen, Stockhausen described in detail how he "composed" the sounds from which his music was subsequently created.

> I formed almost all the sounds only from impulses – they sound like this: dock dock dock...I glued rhythms together from such sounds, then made loops from the rhythms, and let the rhythms on these loops run for many hours – a bit like in an alchemist's kitchen – and recorded the result. I went into the next room, prepared a new loop and the same thing again in a third room. So, there were loops playing everywhere, one could see them playing through the glass windows between the different studio rooms. Then I had the tapes accelerate with the aid of the magnetophone, so that they were transposed four or five octaves higher; the result was then transposed another four octaves up – it was then eight octaves higher altogether – until I finally reached a point where the rhythms could be heard as pitches and timbres. A terribly primitive process! It took me a whole day to produce a sound that lasted eight seconds – to assemble

and "compose" this sound colour, to define it through the micro-structure of the accents and then generate a whole family of sounds.[26]

And what was the sound of these tape-loop manipulations like? Holger Czukay, temporarily a student of Stockhausen and later bassist in the rock group Can, describes his first impression like this: "it sounded like a toilet flushing in space...I couldn't stop laughing".[27] To this day, the sounds which Stockhausen came up with using his techniques are baffling, their tonal originality hardly being equalled by modern electronic music. Stockhausen took the fact that they made 1950s audiences laugh calmly.

"When this piece is performed, the audience usually laughs at three particular points," he observed during György Ligeti's Artikulation, which was written in 1958 in the Cologne studio. "While the piece was being developed in the studio, the composer and his team laughed, too."[28]

The pieces, which were so novel that they inevitably provoked laughter, had been produced to a large extent with the aid of tape loops. Today, they are regarded as being among the canonical works of early electronic music. By the 1960s, however, questions of production methods were receding into the background. After *Hymnen* (1966/67), Stockhausen began to work with synthesizers instead of tape loops, and later he also used computers.

For rock musicians like Holger Czukay, bass player of the band Can, Stockhausen's early compositions from the 1950s and 1960s, which were created with tape loops, were an important inspiration. And Stockhausen was also of great importance to other German rock groups that began experimenting with electronic music in Germany in the 1970s. Krautrock groups like Tangerine Dream, Kraftwerk, Cluster, Neu and Faust were all influenced by him in one way or another.

Further, it was not only in Germany, but all over the world that rock musicians began to be interested in Stockhausen's electronic music and his production methods. For many of them, it was the first time they had heard musical works created with tape loops. The Beatles were among the first to be inspired by Stockhausen's methods – which they misunderstood, however, with creative results. And they were not the only ones to be inspired by him. Frank Zappa and the Mothers of Invention, Soft Machine and the Grateful Dead also learned from Stockhausen, who himself never sought contact with the rock scene, even though the admiration of The Beatles obviously flattered him. After John Lennon's death he claimed that they had been in touch a few times. But when, in 1997, the publication *Zeit* presented him with a selection of German Krautrock records and requested that he evaluate them, he responded haughtily and dismissed them for their "banal melodies", their "conventional structures" and "sonic sickly-sweet harmonies".[29] Further, when BBC Radio 3 played the productions of some contemporary Techno musicians to him, he recommended his own compositions to them for further study.[30]

He reacted particularly indignantly to the use of repetitive rhythms in the Techno pieces. He condescendingly remarked that the Techno avant-gardist Aphex Twin, "would find listening to my work *Gesang der Jünglinge* instructive...He would then immediately quit these post-African repetitions and strive for changing tempi and rhythms instead." Invited by the station to reply, the recipients of this critique were not slow to respond in kind. David Pemberton, for instance, whom Stockhausen had criticized for using loops ("that old hat") remarked, "he keeps talking about our music being so repetitive, but his music is the exact opposite – it's so non-repetitive that it never gets anywhere". To Pemberton, Stockhausen's music was, "not necessarily bad, but there is no development in it...I think he should develop his music a bit more. Try repeating a few ideas, working on them, expanding them..."

The composer Scanner recalls Brian Eno's paradoxical insight that repetition is a form of change – "this is a concept you either agree or disagree with. I like repetition; I like Richie Hawtin's work for that very reason. It's a religious experience...it's an incredible feeling how it grabs you, especially on the dance floor."[31]

It is precisely the rhythmic qualities of loops (which were to fascinate producers of electronic dance music) which Stockhausen ignores in most of his canonical electronic compositions of the 1950s and 1960s, using them only in homeopathic doses, if at all (there is a short sequence at the end of *Hymnen* [1966/67] and some experiments with tape delay in the compositions *Solo* [1965/66] and *Spirale* [1966]). Only when sounds were transformed into pitches did loops become musical material for Stockhausen. He used tape loops to subject the world of sound to a rigid, man-made order, and to tame the "chaotic hustle and bustle" of a single note. In an attempt to exclude human subjectivity as much as possible from the compositional process, and to replace it with objective "laws of form", he developed a music that, like no other, embodies a rationalism that aims for total control over nature.

Loops served Stockhausen to shape sound like a sculptor shapes their material. The inherent laws of natural sounds, which fascinated Schaeffer so much and which he emphasized with his loops, were something that Stockhausen wanted to eradicate, and, using exactly the same technique, he aimed to bring the sounds completely under his control. While Schaeffer was using tape loops to bring "concrete" sounds from the environment to life, Stockhausen used loops as a technique to produce completely abstract sounds. The fact that they can be used for such different purposes speaks for the flexibility of loops as an aesthetic means.

Fear of regression and loss of self resonates in Stockhausen's rejection of any rhythmic use of loops. In the previously mentioned radio interview, commenting on Scanner's Techno music, he remarks that, "I know he wants to achieve a special effect in discotheques or wherever the audience wants to be lulled into dreaming along with these repetitions, but he should be very careful there, because the audience will immediately give him up for something else when a new musical drug appears on the market."[32] Music as a drug, music for dreaming – with such formulations, Stockhausen stands in a modernist tradition that sees repetition as a way to arrive at states that are either infantile or degenerate, which precede human consciousness proper, or the development of subjectivity. The fear of lapsing into an irrational state lies behind the refusal to make use of the repetitive possibilities that loops have to offer. Loops as regressive, lulling, mindless, a path to ego extinction – these are arguments that seem to come directly from the repertoire of such thinkers as Adorno (whom Stockhausen read and met several times). Both Stockhausen and Adorno had experienced how the National Socialists used marching music for propaganda purposes, and for Stockhausen especially, the military marches he had heard on the radio as a child triggered a lasting and well-documented aversion to repetitive rhythms. He told Jonathan Cott of Rolling Stone in an interview, "you know, marching music is recurrent, and it looks like most marching music is about collective synchronization, and that has a very dangerous aspect. For example, when I was a boy, there was nothing on the radio from morning to night than this typical marching music with wind instruments, and it really conditioned people."[33]

Stockhausen and other tape experimenters in avant-garde music of the 1950s regarded loops as an invocation of Thanatos, the ancient embodiment of Freud's death instinct. Not only Stockhausen, but the entire generation of composers who created electronic music in the period after the Second World War, ignored the obvious quality of tape loops. In many respects, the approaches of French *musique concrète*, German electronic music and American Music for Tape were very different. But what they had in common was that they all worked with tape loops. Listening to their music, however, one would never guess it.

It was not until the mid-1960s that composers like Terry Riley and Steve Reich began to use that most characteristic quality of tape loops in their compositions – the incessant mechanical repetitions and the rhythms that can be produced with the aid of them. Minimalist composers found the serial music of composers like Stockhausen increasingly paralyzing and sterile. In the mechanical banging and beating of tape loops, on the other hand, they perceived Eros, rather than Thanatos, which seemed productive and alive to them.

Other people, who had never heard of Schaeffer or Stockhausen, also noticed that tapes can be looped to create new sounds. People with no musical education to speak of, and without knowledge of the contemporary avant-garde music of the time. One of them made his first record in August 1953 in Memphis, USA – around the same time that Karlheinz Stockhausen used tape loops to overlay sine tones for his *Studie I* in Cologne. For this young man, like for Stockhausen, tape loops were to play a decisive role in his musical development. Unlike Stockhausen, however, he was not afraid of exposing himself and his music to media repetition. When his producer came up with the idea of editing his voice with tape loops, one of the most successful careers in the history of rock music was launched. The singer's name was Elvis Presley.

CHAPTER 5

THE PROSTHETIC GOD: ELVIS PRESLEY AND THE *BEL CANTO* OUT OF THE MACHINE

I think the echo on Elvis' Heartbreak Hotel is better than the song itself, by far. Nobody could tell me what that was, in my family. They didn't know what to make of that sound. It turns the studio into a cave.

Brian Eno

5.1. "I just wanted to see what it sounds like"

In the history of rock music, there is a scene that gets repeated over and over, as if it were itself a loop – a somewhat insecure young man with a cheap guitar under his arm enters Sun Records music studio in Memphis on a hot Saturday in August 1953. He approaches the secretary, who is typing in an outer office. When Marion Keisker asks how she can help him his mumbled reply is almost incomprehensible. "But, of course, she knew what he was there for, what else could he be there for with his guitar and that desperate look of *need* in his eyes?" Peter Guralnick writes in his biography of Elvis.[1]

The young man with that look of need in his eyes was there to make his first record. His name was Elvis Aaron Presley. Contrary to legend, the record was not meant as a birthday present for his mother – Gladys Presley's birthday had been back in April, 4 months before her son showed up at Sun Records for the first time. Elvis just wanted to know what a recording medium would do to his voice – "I just wanted to hear what I sounded like," he would later recall in an interview.[2]

This anecdote is an appropriate beginning for the unique career of a singer who, like no other before him, was to become a product of the media of his time. Much has been written about the fact that radio and the then new medium of television had made Elvis into a star. The record company RCA, which signed Elvis in 1955, owned the TV station NBC, and this regularly broadcast Elvis' performances. Footage showing Elvis performing on *The Ed Sullivan Show* in front of hysterically screaming fans has become an incunabulum of music history. As an artist, Elvis was a creation of the media. But not only his popularity was the product of a well-oiled media machine. What we are hearing on Elvis records, that voice with the unique flexion, is also the result of a media procedure.

Elvis worked in producer Sam Phillips' "Memphis Recording Service Studios" using technology that was state-of-the-art then, but which seems incredibly primitive today. Sam Phillips and Elvis' guitar player, Scotty Moore, compensated for the simple equipment with their ingenuity and technical experiments. While similar strategies were being tried in other recording studios in the USA, none had such resounding success and such far-reaching consequences as did Elvis' "Sun Sessions".

These media innovations produced what is recognized as the sound of Rock'n'Roll today. At the time of the Sun Sessions, Elvis was an inexperienced singer who had never performed live and who had no background in studio recordings. Yet he developed the singing style that would turn him into an international star from his exposure to media technologies. While it would be a step too far to say that the new media technology was solely responsible for Elvis' success, it is equally impossible to imagine that he would have found his unique sound without it. And this technology was a predecessor of the tape loop.

The tape effect is responsible for the gurgling slapback echo on Elvis' recordings. It brings one thought to mind when you hear it, even today – Rock'n'Roll! This slapback echo, which Sam Phillips produced with two tape recorders and which is the focus of this chapter, was a business secret kept within the confines of the studio's control room. Even Elvis himself did not know how Phillips had managed to clone his voice. When he changed from Sun Records to the much larger record company RCA, studio technicians and producers tried in vain to copy the effect.

After he sold his contract with Elvis to RCA for the then-sensational amount of $35,000, Phillips continued to process the voices of other artists on his label with the tape echo – Carl Perkins, Johnny Cash and Jerry Lee Lewis, for instance. Producers of aspiring Elvis wannabes, like Eddie Cochran and Gene Vincent, did manage to copy the trick and turned the wobbly echo into *the* trademark of Rock'n'Roll.

If anyone wants to reconstruct the sound of original Rock'n'Roll today, it is not enough to reproduce the simple chord sequences and the slapback bass. Really authentic retro Rock'n'Roll works only with the effect that Sam Phillips used to enhance Elvis' first recordings. Therefore, the Sun Sessions are of great importance – and not only for the development of Rock'n'Roll. They also mark the beginning of a music that can only be produced in the studio, the live performance of which is secondary to its recording.

But what had made Elvis approach Sam Phillips in the first place? In the 1950s, long before tape players and dictating machines had found their way into the mass market, if you wanted to hear your own voice recorded you had to pay for it. In August 1954, Elvis could have gone to the WT Grants department store on Main Street, where recording a song and having it cut on disk cost 25 cents. But he preferred to get in touch with a producer he had read about in the newspaper, and whose recordings of black Blues singers had become regionally successful. "We record anything – anywhere – anytime. A complete service to fill every recording need," Sam Phillips' business card read. It was 3 dollars 98 cents to record two songs that could be taken home on acetate record (just like the one that Pierre Schaeffer had used).

Today, Sam Phillips' Sun Records may have a place of honour in the history of pop music and the Rock'n'Roll Hall of Fame as "the place where Rock'n'Roll was invented". But in 1954, Sun Records was a minor player. There were around 800 similar studios in the USA in the 1950s[3] – the "independents", small labels that recorded the majority of black artists, and which were the forerunners of the Rock'n'Roll and soul music of the future. These small labels published music that the larger labels did not touch. This included Sam Phillips' sound experiments – professional sound engineers of the big record companies most likely would have regarded them as technical shortcomings.

The majority of the small companies, Sun Records included, were founded after the Second World War. They were called "independent labels" or "indies" for short because they were independent from the four main record companies, RCA Victor, Decca, Columbia and Capitol, which controlled the American music market. The major labels released mainly soft pop music, for which there was a reliable, national market. This presented an opportunity for the smaller labels, which often specialized in local artists and regional musical styles, such as western swing, honky-tonk, square dance or bluegrass. Apart from those styles, it was African-American music that ensured the survival of many of those small labels. They published musicians who played doo wop, jump or club Blues. The better-known ones include Chess, which specialized in Chicago Blues, and Atlantic, which published Rhythm & Blues.

Not all the founders of these labels were music lovers; they often ran their labels alongside another business. The Chess Brothers, for example, owned a number of nightclubs, and the artists on their label were predominantly performers at those venues. Sam Phillips himself worked at the local radio station WREC until the double workload of being a radio moderator by day and studio owner by night got too much and he quit his day job to dedicate himself to Sun Records. (Incidentally, his responsibilities at the radio station had included the production of sound effects – a task that would have music-historical consequences once he came to work as a producer.)

Many indie label founders were shrewd businessmen who were less interested in innovative music than in quick profits. "Influencing music did not top the agenda of these visionaries and entrepreneurs; first and foremost, they wanted to earn a living," Rick Kennedy and Randy McNutt note in *Little Labels – Big Sound.* "Records happened to be less expensive to produce and distribute than other products..."[4] And many did very nicely out of it – "one invested a little and directly reached the audience for which these records were made. The distribution initially was inadequate, but it was sufficient for record impresarios to sell one or two thousand records in their hometown to make a satisfying profit."[5] Sam Phillips was able to afford his sound experimentations mainly because he kept his overheads low. When he unexpectedly became hugely successful with Elvis and Carl Perkins in the mid-1950s, he "was approaching the volume of a major label, with the overheads of the smallest independent".[6]

Since they often produced only for a local market, the independent labels were able to move fast and respond quickly to new trends. Like many of the other small labels, Sam Phillips initially issued exclusively African-American music on Sun Records. In interviews, he kept pointing out that his fascination with black music went back to his youth. As a child he had known African-Americans who worked on his father's farm: "I listened to that beautiful *a cappella* singing – the windows of the black Methodist church just half a block down from Highland Baptist would all be open, and I was just fascinated by the rhythms."[7]

His father's black agricultural workers were also the first to tell Sam Phillips about Beale Street in Memphis. Beale Street was a nightclub district in Memphis where Blues and Jazz was played. "To me, Beale Street was the most famous place in the South," Phillips later reminisced about his encounters with that legendary road.

> We arrived in the city at five or six o'clock in the morning and it was pouring down with rain, but we just drove up and down, and it was much more than I had even envisioned. I don't know if I can explain it to this day – my eyes had to be very big, because I saw everything, from winos to people dressed up fit to kill, young, old, city slickers and people straight out of the cotton fields, somehow or another you could tell: *every damn one of them was glad to be there*. Beale Street represented for me something that I hoped to see one day for all people, something that they could say, I'm part of this somehow.[8]

Phillips did not say it explicitly, but those able to read between the lines would have known what he meant. What he saw on Beale Street was what American president Lyndon B. Johnson called the "the great society" at the end of the 1960s – a society without racism and without segregation. Beale Street was in a black neighbourhood and the patrons of the music bars there were predominantly African-American. But white people went to Beale Street too, to listen to the music and be entertained. According to some of his biographers, Elvis first heard the song *That's All Right, Mama*, his first local hit, at a concert given by black Blues guitarist Arthur Crudup in a bar on Beale Street. In the American South, where black people were not allowed to sit on most park benches and could only use specially designated public toilets, Memphis was a city of relative tolerance, and Beale Street symbolized this tolerance.

Sam Phillips has often been quoted to have said, "if I could find a white man with the Negro sound and the Negro feel, I could make a billion dollars". This sentence seems to be an invention of Albert Goldman's controversial Elvis biography, however – Phillips himself repeatedly denied that he ever said anything of the kind. It was Elvis himself who more or less supported this notion in an interview with the *Charlotte Observer* in 1956. It was one of the few candid interviews that he ever gave, before his manager Colonel Parker whisked him away from nosy questions. Elvis told a reporter of the local newspaper that:

> the coloured folks been singing and playing it just like I'm doing now, man, for more years than I know. They played it like that in the shanties and in their juke joints and nobody paid it no mind until I goosed it up, I got it from them. Down in Tupelo, Mississippi, I used to hear Arthur Crudup bang his box the way I do now, and I said that if I ever got to the place where I could feel like old Arthur felt, I'd be a music man like nobody ever saw.[9]

Elvis expresses a respect for African-American culture that seems to exceed even that of Sam Phillips. He indirectly mentions the segregation in the south of the USA ("*their* juke joints"). But unlike Phillips, who does stress the originality of an African-American music and an authenticity unspoilt by Western influences, Elvis doesn't acknowledge any hierarchy between black and white music. Troubled race relations in the American South also played a significant part in the recording of Elvis' first single, and in some strange way, the tape loop effect made its own contribution to the historic cross-over that *That's All Right, Mama* turned out to be.

5.2. "Try to find out what you are playing, and then we'll record it": the Sun Sessions

It must have seemed unlikely in 1953 that Elvis would become the first superstar in rock music history and it was even more unlikely that he would rise to fame with a version of an African-American folk song. Elvis had originally wanted to be a crooner. At his first session in Phillips' studio, he recorded the tearjerkers *My Happiness* and *That's When Your Heartaches Begin*. Sam Phillips said politely that he was an "interesting" singer and that "we might give you a call sometime". He had Marion Keisker make a note of the boy's name, which she misspelled, and he annotated this "good ballad singer. Hold..."[10] She typed the two song titles on the label, gave Elvis his acetate disk, and that was that for the first recording session. Elvis, who was earning his living as a truck driver and at an assembly line at the time, stopped by Sun Studio every so often to see if anyone needed a singer. But Marion Keisker never knew anyone who did, and it was almost a year until Sam Phillips did eventually decide to give him a call.

The recordings that Elvis finally made in Phillips' studio on 5 July 1954 have become so legendary that they take up a unique place in the history of Rock'n'Roll, which has no shortage of legendary successes. The Sun Sessions were the first professional recordings of Elvis Presley, who was then 19 years old. For many decades, they were only available as illegal bootlegs, so that the myth could flourish freely. It was only after Elvis' death that *The Complete Sun Sessions* were released as a two-LP set, which enabled critical evaluations by fans, writers and musicologists. By now, the elite of American music journalism has examined the circumstances of these sessions with the thoroughness of classical philologists. Writers like Albert Goldman, Dave Marsh, Greil Marcus and Peter Guralnick have published detailed analyses of the different takes and outtakes. The circumstances in which the first Elvis single was recorded have been studied as meticulously as the Dead Sea Scrolls.

In the United States, the Sun Sessions are not just considered a landmark in the history of Rock'n'Roll, but a unique piece of Americana. The songs that Elvis recorded during these sessions were not like *Hound Dog*, *Heartbreak Hotel* or *Blue Suede Shoes*, which were to catapult him into the limelight 2 years later, but they did mark the beginning of his ascent to international stardom. Within a few months, the resulting record had sold 20,000 copies in and around Memphis.

Yet initially, the first sessions had not seemed promising. Together with guitar player Scotty Moore and bass player Bill Black, Elvis arrived at Sam Phillips' studio on the evening of 6 July 1954. When the recording session started, the musicians weren't even sure what song to record. Elvis, with his preference for slow pieces, suggested the ballad *I Love You Because*, and the trio spent most of the evening working on that song. These recordings have been preserved, and they are not very good. The tempo is sluggish; Elvis staggers through the song with an expressionless, insecure voice. Listening, one is afraid that the group might just give up at any moment. After several fruitless attempts, the musicians took a break.

Before that session, Sam Phillips had suggested that Elvis might try a song by Arthur "Big Boy" Crudup. During the break, Elvis did start to play the song, probably to brighten the mood. "Elvis just started fooling around," Scotty Moore remembers. "I played along as soon as I found out what key it was in. Then the door to the control room opened. Sam was doing something in there and he came out and asked, 'what are you playing?' Elvis answered, 'I don't know, we're just fooling around.' Sam replied 'well, that sounds good. Try to find out what you're playing, and then we'll record it.' So we briefly talked it over and decided to play it. We played it again, and Sam listened. After we had played it three or four times, we just recorded it – and that was that! Basically, it was a *rhythm record*. It wasn't a big deal. Sam didn't tell him what to do. Elvis fooled around, just did what came to his mind, what he liked."[11]

Moore got one detail wrong – they recorded *That's All Right, Mama* not once, but twice. On *The Complete Sun Sessions*, there is an outtake which was obviously recorded before the take that was later released. On that first take, the band needs three attempts to get through the song. Scotty Moore's guitar riffs are more improvised and somewhat aimless; during his solo he makes a mistake. But the biggest difference between the first and published takes is Elvis' singing. In the first, he still sounds a bit insecure and in the chorus he gets lost. By contrast, in the second take, his voice sounds more self-assured and consistent; his phrasing is more focused. He knows the song better now, understands its structure and has found his own interpretation. But there is something else. His singing sounds – how to describe it? Clearer? Brighter? More rhythmic? It is all those things, but above all, it is more professional – the record sounds accomplished and not like three amateurs practising a new song.

How was this transformation accomplished? Elvis did not suddenly become a better singer between the first and second recordings. The crucial difference lies in a sound effect that Sam Phillips added to the final recording. This effect was Sam Phillips' secret ingredient, which would turn the song into a Sun single. It characterized the Sun sound, just like the fusion of African-American Rhythm & Blues and white hillbilly music that Elvis introduced to this session did. It was an echo effect, which was accomplished with two Ampex tape recorders.

Even though all Elvis biographies mention this recording technique, they do not explain how exactly Phillips had accomplished it. In order to answer this question, I contacted the only participant of the Sun Sessions who is still alive – Elvis' guitar player, Scotty Moore.[12] He explains Phillips' secret ingredient like this: "Once he was content with a recording, he would play the final take with the first tape recorder, before the tape went through the second tape recorder, where it was replayed with a slight delay, creating an echo that is just 100 milliseconds long." Phillips recorded these two minimally deferred signals. This is how the sizzling "slapback" sound came about.

Since there was no multi-track recording at that time to separate the different recording tracks, all instruments and the vocals were recorded to the same tape and, therefore, the whole sound was subjected to this "tape delay" effect. It is confusing how differently the tape echo affects the different instruments. Elvis' voice acquires a strange eerie quality. The guitar sounds fuller and somewhat blurred. Bill Black on the double bass uses a raw Pizzicato technique, the so-called "slapping", where he pulls the strings so strongly that they hit the neck of the instrument and thereby produce an additional striking sound. Due to the echo effect, the bass suddenly sounds like a tuned percussion instrument. It makes it easy to forget that this early Rock'n'Roll song was recorded without drums.

Peter Guralnick notes that the slapback effect added to the "presence [and] to the excitement of the take".[13] It most certainly heightened the tension of the music, but has it really increased its presence? The sound is mushy, less material than in the first take, as if it were out of this world and in this sense, less present. Albert Goldman articulates the fascination of *That's All Right, Mama* when he writes:

> Sam Phillips enhanced [Presley's] high ecstatic voice with a subtle aura of quavering echo. It was a stroke of genius – perhaps the most brilliant inspiration of this famous producer's career. Indeed, when you weigh the forces that contributed to Elvis Presley's breakthrough, Phillips' claim to importance appears completely justified. Not only did he give Elvis the right steer in directing him away from lugubrious ballads to the currently fashionable R&B material, but he attached to his new star's raw and untrained voice the electronic prosthesis that masked his vocal faults, while it transformed – or should we say transfigured? – his vocal quality into the now legendary Presley sound.[14]

Should we simply say that what we know today as Elvis is the product of recording and media technology? The star, who owed his rise to radio, television and cinema, is – to use Freud's magnificent term – "a prosthetic god", and he has a media operation to thank for his voice – the tape delay.

When the importance of Elvis' first single is emphasized, it is usually pointed out that Elvis imposed his own style on an African-American Blues song. The question of whether *That's All Right, Mama* is a black or a white song accompanied Elvis' first record from the outset – the song entered into the Rhythm & Blues charts in Memphis together with black Blues singers such as Muddy

Waters and Johnny Ace; the magazine *Cash Box* discussed it as a Blues record.

The success of the record was:

> an event, to some a scary one, but if *That's All Right* brought home the racial fears of a lot of people, it touched the secret dreams of others; if it was a threat, it was also another ride on the raft. "It was like a giant wedding ceremony", said Marion Keisker, Sam Phillips' working partner and the one who had first heard in Elvis' voice everything that Phillips was after. "It was like two feuding clans who had been brought together by marriage."[15]

But the combination of black and white folklore, which Elvis introduced in *That's All Right, Mama*, was only one historical aspect of the recording. The other was technological – the recording technique, the echo effect that put an acoustic polish on the fusion of Country music and Rhythm & Blues.

After the song was recorded, the musicians were apparently somewhat intimidated by what they had created. When Sam Phillips played the finished recording to them, Bill Black remembers that:

> we couldn't believe it was us. It just sounded sort of raw and ragged...We thought it was exciting, but what was it? It was just so completely different. But it just really flipped Sam – he felt it really had something. We just sort of shook our heads, and said, "Well, that's fine, but good God, they'll run us out of town!"[16]

5.3. Media Music

Phillips was among the first producers who permitted sound effects and studio technology to be pushed into the foreground in such a way. On his recordings, the slapback echo does not contribute to any "subtle refinement", as had been the case with studio recordings of pop music. Instead, the technical effect became an entity in itself during the recording process. It was as if the machines had developed a will of their own, they dominate the sound of the early Elvis songs, and subsequently of many other Rock'n'Roll and Rockabilly records.

A comparison of Sam Phillips' method with that of another important innovator of American pop music, Les Paul, serves to elucidate its special character. Ten years before Sam Phillips, guitarist Les Paul had experimented with an echo effect he had produced using a recording medium that was common at the time – magnetized wire, the forerunner of magnetic tape.[17] Les Paul, however, attached great importance to the idea that listeners should not notice his manipulations. "All I want to do is to reproduce sound as it really is, and with depth perception, so you can *see* the performer," he observed.[18] What would Elvis look like if he were made perfectly "visible" on *That's All Right, Mama*? A double figure before a blurry background? A monster with two mouths?

Sam Phillips' productions achieved just the opposite of Les Paul's ideal of a "pure, unadulterated" sound. Phillips did not buy into the illusion that one could capture a sound as it really was with recording technology. Instead, he suggested that sound is a malleable raw material which can be shaped and modified. This makes Sam Phillips a modernist of pop music – what his work has in common with the modernists of the twentieth century is its self-referentiality. He does not focus on the song as such, but rather, on the sound material, which becomes the actual focus of his work. His productions are the beginning of a development where the recorded sound is not a referent of an acoustic quality "before the recording", but rather, a flexible material which can be modified according to the requirements of the composition. Without much ado and without any publication of manifestos, the conflict between "abstract" and "concrete" art that I have outlined in the chapter on Pierre Schaeffer is here evident once more.

The painter Auguste Herbin's definition of concrete art comes to mind: "When the painter separates himself completely from the object, in his act and in his thoughts, he creates a work in which the forms, the colours, the relations are pure conception."[19] One might say that, similarly to this concept, pop music started to work increasingly with sounds that were divorced from the actual sounding object from the 1950s onwards. A song that no human voice can sing, a guitar sound that exceeds the sound capabilities of a guitar, a bass that turns into a percussion instrument – Sam Phillips allowed sound to take on an independent electronic existence which not only departed from the original source, but even escaped his control to some extent. That's the difference between him and Les Paul's illusory perfectionism. Sam Phillips used the sounds he created with the aid of the tape delay to enhance the strange combination of Country music and Rhythm & Blues that was pouring from Elvis' subconscious. In his monograph on Sun Records, entitled *Good Rockin' Tonight*, Colin Escott calls him "possibly the first producer in the later sense of the word".[20]

Before this, a music producer – the title was borrowed from the film business – was a manager who made money available for recordings, enlisted musicians, selected songs for the artist and did other organizational tasks. Due to improvements in recording technology, which were a consequence of intensified research during the Second World War and which made their way into recording studios during the 1950s, the producer's remit changed. He effectively became a designer of recordings, and these began to bear his trademarks. Today, the contribution that important producers make to the music of their clients is often regarded as almost as important as that of the artists themselves. Icons like George Martin (for The Beatles), Norman Whitfield (The Temptations, Marvin Gaye, Edwin Starr), Brian Eno (Devo, Talking Heads, U2), Trevor Horn (Frankie goes to Hollywood, ABC), Dr Dre (NWA, Eminem) and Diplo (Major Lazer, MIA, The Weeknd) come to mind here.

Elvis was not the first artist who was treated to a technological special treatment that enhanced his artistic potential, but he was the first Sun artist whose music was subjected to the tape slapback effect. This effect can be heard even more clearly on the B-side of Elvis' first single than on *That's All Right, Mama*.[21] This song was originally performed by white Country singer Bill Monroe. If Elvis interpreted the black Blues song *That's All Right, Mama* as if it were a white Country song, he used the opposite approach with *Blue Moon of Kentucky*. "Presley changed the meter and the tempo, bringing Arthur Crudup's sparse, free-wheeling approach to the Country song."[22] At the end of one of the takes of *Blue Moon of Kentucky*, which was later published on the album *The Complete Sun Sessions*, Sam Phillips can be heard calling out at the end of the track, "hell, that's fine. That's different. That's a pop song now, little Vi! That's good."

Thanks to the tape echo, Elvis seems to duet with himself in the final version, which was released as a single. His untrained voice turns into a smooth tenor that sounds silky and ghostly at the same time. A comparison of the first take of *Blue Moon of Kentucky* and the later version with the tape echo effect again reveals a strange media metamorphosis – an insecure young man and inexperienced singer turns into the Elvis we know today. On close listening, one starts to ask oneself where these sounds actually come from, since they cannot emerge from a human throat, and these legendary recordings begin to sound mysterious, almost a bit uncanny.

What influence did the echo have on Elvis' singing style? In this respect, it is important to point out that the singer never heard the tape echo while he sang; Sam Phillips added it in post-production. Nevertheless, it seems like Elvis also adapted his singing style to the effect. He blurts out the syllables with a vengeance, or stutters, seemingly aiming to intensify the echo. At the beginning of *Blue Moon of Kentucky*, he repeats the words "blue moon" with relish, while the echo adds a canon effect to his vocals. In *Baby, Let's Play House*, another Sun single, Elvis stammers a "B-B-B-b-baby" staccato at the beginning of the song, accentuating the echo effect. This "hiccup"-style has been imitated by all his successors, from Eddie Cochran to Gene Vincent and Buddy Holly.

In *The Raw and the Cooked*, Claude Lévi-Strauss writes:

> even at the babbling stage [of a baby] the phoneme group / pa/ can be heard. But the difference between /pa/ and / papa/ does not residue simply in reduplication: /pa/ is a noise, / papa/ is a word. The reduplication indicates intent on the part of the speaker; it endows the second syllable with a function different from that which would have been performed by the first separately, or in the form of a potentially limitless series of identical sounds /papapapapa/ produced by mere babbling. Therefore, the second /pa/ is not a repetition of the first, nor has it the same signification. It is a sign that, like itself, the first /pa/ too was a sign, and that as a pair they fall into the category of signifiers, not of things signified.[23]

The operation that Sam Phillips performs on Elvis' voice reverses the process that Lévi-Strauss describes. Baby – a word, which in itself stems from the babbling of infants – is a term that signifies something. The Ba-ba-ba-ba-ba, which the tape recorder reduces the word to, is a placeholder for the chaos that hides behind each syllable. The echo turns meaning into pure sound as it repeats the meaningless syllables, which have been torn out of their context. The words "blue moon" become liberally cascading syllables and the word "baby" turns into a kind of technologically enhanced baby babbling. Or, in Lévi-Strauss' terms, with the support of two Ampex tape machines, a sign turns into "wild sounds" that do not refer to anything any longer.

In the years that were to come, pop music turned the draining of meaning via technological manipulation into one of its most important subjects. Words were emptied of their implications with the aid of repetition, or loops; voices were speeded up or distorted and sequenced with effects like the tape echo until the technological treatments themselves became the focus, and eventually, more important than what was being said or meant in these songs. When Elvis' voice took on a technical life of its own, it anticipated those practices.

But Sam Phillips is not a sorcerer's apprentice who is overpowered by his equipment – and this is precisely because he lets it do what it wants. He leaves his media equipment to play and produce semiotic nonsense and turns this into a boon, into the essential strength of his productions. In the process, he created a celebrity who remains one of the main icons of pop culture to the present day – Elvis Presley, whose greatest artistic achievement was, perhaps, to be a willing subject of technical innovation.

Did the teenagers who went crazy over Elvis' first single ever wonder where this mysterious echo came from? One can only speculate about how conscious his listeners were of this effect in the 1950s. But they perceived it at some level, and they wanted it. Elvis' guitar player, Scotty Moore, was concerned with how to reproduce the echo sound on stage, which was not easy to do with the simple equipment they had at their disposal.[24] Eventually, he discovered a new type of amplifier, which had been developed by engineer and amateur musician Ray Butts.[25]

In the mid-1950s, Butts built the first guitar amplifier that could produce an echo effect on stage. Only a few of these amplifiers still exist today. When the back of the box, which is about the size of a large television set, is opened, what meets the eye is precisely what this book is about – a loop! A short tape loop twists around some pulleys at the bottom of the box. It can be argued that the Echosonic was the first commercially available piece of equipment that enabled the production of tape loops. Butts radically simplified Sam Phillips' construction with the two tapes, and instead, one finds a tape loop that passes a record head, and which records the guitar sound. Only a few centimetres away there is a playing head, which replays the signal. It is a simple construction, which the many tape delay echo units that were to follow in the 1960s and 1970s improved upon, taking the Echosonic as their model.

Scotty Moore noticed the amplifier when he heard it in a song by well-known Country guitarist Chet Atkins,[26] and Carl Perkins, Roy Orbison and Luther Perkins, the guitarist of Johnny Cash, would later use the Echosonic amplifier, too. Thus, the majority of the protagonists of the new Rockabilly sound – all under contract at Sun Records and, therefore, all treated to Sam Phillips' slapback echo – used a tape loop on stage in order to reproduce imaginary sound landscapes similar to those that could be created in the studio. Life started to imitate (media) art. Scotty Moore used the new amplifier in the studio as well as in live concerts. The Echosonic tape loop was also utilized in Elvis' final Sun session. Its short, firm sound can be heard on *Blue Moon* and on *Baby, Let's Play House*.[27]

The tape echo from Sun Studio is the beginning of a development where music changed from what musicians performed to what they recorded. What came to matter was not what was written on a sheet of music, but what came out of the loudspeakers. In the pop music that was to come after the Sun Sessions, the difference between the musical work and its recording disappeared, and in that sense, Elvis' early singles are the forerunner of music genres such as Techno, which are produced exclusively with media technology and can only be performed live with difficulty.

The American philosophy professor Theodore Gracyk defines Rock music as a type of music that "paradigmatically exists as *recorded* music".[28] His characterization applies to the Sun Sessions, as American Rock journalist Dave Marsh argues:

Elvis, Scotty, Bill and Sam built their music in the recording studio, the first time anyone had ever created major musical innovations except by working it out in front of a live audience or by laboriously composing in on paper first. Magnetic recording tape had only recently made it possible to do a take of a song, listen to a playback, analyze it, then try another rendition and repeat the process...This approach was liberating in two ways – it freed them from the inhibiting effects of audience disapproval while their music developed, and it liberated them from a dependence on tyrannical songwriters, since their new style would obliterate any previous version...none of the members was a skilled songwriter.[29]

A year-and-a-half after the Sun Sessions, Sam Phillips sold his contract with Elvis to RCA in order to pay off its debts and Elvis' international career really took off. Many Elvis fans feel that he never reached the freshness and the candour of his Sun Sessions again. But as an artist on the RCA label, he instantly became an international star. His first hit for the new company was *Heartbreak Hotel*. The producers wanted not only Elvis, they also wanted the echo on the record. Yet nobody, not even Elvis himself, knew how Sam Phillips had produced this effect.

In order to imitate the slap-back echo, sound engineer Bob Ferris turned a corridor of the RCA building into an echo chamber out of glass and tiles. Elvis' voice was pumped into the soundproof corridor with a loudspeaker. At the other end of the corridor, a microphone recorded his voice, encompassing the natural echo of the room in the process. When Steve Scholes, head of the A&R department at RCA, heard *Heartbreak Hotel*, he called Ferris' idea a "terrible mistake". He felt that the sound of the song did not fit into the radio programmes of the time. But perhaps that was precisely the magic ingredient – some weeks later the title entered the charts and went on to become Elvis' first international hit.

What is the significance of the slapback echo, which caused a sensation as a novelty in the 1950s and has a fascination that has not faded to this day? Does this echo have a meaning beyond being a unique sound effect? The music that Sam Phillips, Elvis Presley and his band recorded was produced in a specific social context and can hardly be isolated from this. Unlike Pierre Schaeffer, who conducted his experiments in the solitude of a French broadcasting studio, the development of Rockabilly and Rock'n'Roll was embedded in the social conditions of the American South.

Rockabilly originally was little more than a dance and party fad in the South of the USA and was a national success for only a short period of time. But by combining elements from white and African-American musical styles, it deals with an issue that also plays a perennial role in loop-based music – the fusion of "black" and "white", of European and non-European music.

Another issue, which was to recur throughout the history of loops, is already audible in the Rock'n'Roll that emerged from Sun Studio. Most Rockabilly songs were pure dance music. In his book on Sun Records, music journalist John Floyd calls Rockabilly the "probably most limited style in music history, which consists mostly of endless cheers to 'rock rock rock' and 'go, man, go'".[30] Rockabilly was also a short-lived phenomenon. Three years after Elvis' first recordings it was already past its peak. If Elvis had remained faithful to this style, his fate would likely have been similar to that of the other Sun star, Carl Perkins, who never had another hit after *Blue Suede Shoes*.

But despite its limitations, Rockabilly from Sun Studio, in its best moments, expresses insatiable desire and total passion, transgression and the end of all moderation.

Rockabilly and Rock'n'Roll were the first musical styles of a genuine youth culture that started to develop after the Second World War. They speak of its hedonism and the "right to party", yet are still far from celebrating community, solidarity and unity, as the psychedelic rock of the 1960s, disco in the 1970s and rave in the late 1980s and early 1990s were to do. Rockabilly, a music that – just like these later musical styles-developed to accompany dance marathons, was nevertheless still far from the fraternization on the dance floor which the coming dance movements would celebrate. Its ecstasy is undifferentiated, if not downright violent.

But in his book *Mystery Train*, Greil Marcus points out how Rockabilly, despite its crudeness, paved the way for more emancipatory and more liberal ideals than those of Country music, from which it had developed:

Country music (like the Blues, which was more damned and more honestly hedonistic than Country had ever been) was music for the whole community, cutting across lines of age, if not class. This could have meant an openly expressed sense of diversity for each child, man, and woman, as it did with the Blues. But Country spoke to a community which was fearful of anything of the sort, withdrawing into itself, using music like a bond that links all together for better or worse, with a sense that what was being shared was less important than the fact of sharing...All that hedonism was dragged down in Country music; a deep sense of fear and resignation confined it...[31]

Marcus argues that Country music, which was often about the depressing and miserable lives of the Southerners, at the same time made their lives bearable. By reflecting these circumstances, it also validated them.

By contrast, Rockabilly placed hedonism and individual pleasure in the foreground and opted to rock, rock, rock away fear and resignation. Lux Interior from the band The Cramps, which was instrumental in the revival of Rockabilly in the early 1980s, put it this way:

The people who originally played Rockabilly were genuine rebels who made underground music – the wildest stuff never became famous. Today's modern "rockabilly" bands try to copy the mannerisms from this time, but if one tries to copy the hiccup singing, one is on the wrong boat. These lunatic emotional outbreaks came from inside; they were perfectly unrestricted expressions of passion. And if this music should make you do anything, then to lead a perfectly unrestricted life.[32]

This rebellious energy of Rock'n'Roll was the foundation of an independent youth culture, which began its triumphant advance around the world in the 1950s. Without Rock'n'Roll and Rockabilly, the more democratic and egalitarian youth and dance movements would not have been possible. Of course, this revolt was not the result of an echo effect or tape loop. On the other hand, it is more than mere coincidence that in the early days of this revolution, some of the most important records featured the tape echo. Tape echoes did more than ensure a smooth fusion of Country and Rhythm & Blues. They did more than enhance the singing of Elvis to a *bel canto* or extend that ecstatic shriek of Jerry Lewis to an echo that could not have come from the world this side of the machines.

They added a technical dimension to music making in which recording technology increasingly took centre stage, subjecting the music to its logic in the process. Additionally, they were the beginning of a development in pop music that would dissolve the boundaries between "black" and "white" on both sides of the spectrum, until (with House, Techno, Drum & Bass, Trap) they finally seem to disappear completely. In this music, the erosion of boundaries between those who listen to it, the "brothers and sisters on the dance floor", is described over and over again. Often this music paints pictures of ecstatic bliss, or of the sleep of reason. It does this with words, but more importantly, it does it with sounds, which – just like Sam Phillips' tape echo had been – are of technological origin.

In the 1960s – when Elvis had become a caricature of his younger self – other artists would grant even greater artistic licence to a technology that had advanced only slightly since Sam Phillips' tape delay. In some of the following chapters, I will discuss Terry Riley and others in greater detail. Interestingly, they used elements of African-American music in their tape compositions, be it Junior Walker's *Shotgun*, which Terry Riley looped into his *Sweet Bird of Paradise*, or the voice of the black preacher that is the foundation of Steve Reich's tape composition *It's Gonna Rain*.

What these artists have in common with Sam Phillips is the fact that they worked either on the margins of, or outside established practices of music production. Sam Phillips belonged to a musical cottage industry, not unlike the Techno and Hip-Hop producers of today, who make their music on computers at home, and not in the studio of a record label any longer. They take advantage of the possibilities which the new media technologies make available to them, rather than primarily using them to compensate for their vocal shortcomings. To them, these machines are the means to a new musical aesthetic. Many musicians do regard the partial automation of musical production, loops and the devices that produce them as interfering with their artistic autonomy. Yet those who took advantage of these possibilities gained new autonomy in their music production. Sam Phillips' tape echo was the beginning of this development.

A COCKPIT OF DREAMS: RAYMOND SCOTT, MUSIC ENGINEER

"I had two single mellotrons and a double mellotron built specially for me," said Rick Wakeman, keyboard player of the band Yes, in an interview.

> And I was frustrated by the mellotrons because of the problems with tuning and because of the tape recorders... Exasperated, I took them into a field, poured petrol over them and set them on fire. It all burned, the wood, the metal...I enjoyed that because [the mellotrons] had ruined so many recording sessions; they were forever breaking. But later, I did regret it.[1]

The mellotron that made Rick Wakeman take such extreme measures is one of the most obscure instruments in music history.[2] It is based on loops created with audio tapes featuring original recordings of instruments, such as a flute, an organ, a violin or even a mandolin. For each note of the scale that could be played on the instrument, a separate tape loop was concealed inside the mellotron's frame. When a key was pressed, a sound head was lowered onto the tape to play it back – theoretically, anyway.

In practice, the tapes frequently got tangled while being played and had to be threaded back onto their spools, which could take hours. If the sound was to be altered, the tape loops had to be exchanged for those of another instrument. In addition, the mellotron was difficult to tune, and, once tuned, did not hold the key well even then. The magnetic tapes also gradually wore out so that eventually the sounds that were produced were hardly distinguishable.

These technical problems present an ironic contradiction to the mythology that developed around rock keyboard virtuosos like Rick Wakeman in the 1970s. They seemed like wizards as they hid behind the machinery of synthesizers and other keyboards, appearing like rulers of technology. In the studio, but more especially during live performances, the mellotron regularly humiliated the player when it gave up the ghost. No wonder Rick Wakeman got so exasperated that he just wanted to destroy it. Technically, the mellotron resembled Pierre Schaeffer's *phonogène*, another keyboard instrument that played back tape loops. But Schaeffer's instrument openly displayed its tape loops. In the mellotron, they were hidden in a deceptively minimalist frame which resembled a cocktail bar. So the design of the mellotron gave players the illusion of having complete control over the sound – a problematic illusion, as they quickly found out.

Rick Wakeman was not the only one who had difficulties with this instrument. Its strangely muffled sounds may have lent a unique sound to hits like *Strawberry Fields Forever* (1967) by The Beatles, or *A Space Oddity* (1969) by David Bowie. But its technical limitations meant that it never became very popular. Most musicians developed a similar love-hate relationship to it as Rick Wakeman – although not many went so far as to set it on fire.[3]

Wakeman's dramatic gesture not only marks the end of a very particular relationship between musician and instrument. It also signals the end of a brief period of instrument-making where attempts were made to build instruments from electromechanical parts. This period began after the Second World War. Its end – or culmination – came with the introduction of digital instruments, such as samplers and sequencers, which delivered what electromechanical instruments could only attempt to do.

A sampler enables digitally stored sounds to be played on a keyboard, and further enables them to be modified beyond recognition. With a sequencer, it is possible to save and repeat sound sequences; in other words, to structure sounds. Both these instruments are indispensable in today's studio environment.

Most of the analogue predecessors of today's digital sequencers and samplers were based on tape loops.[4] It is not my intention in this chapter to provide a comprehensive overview of the long and at times confusing, as well as fascinating, history of these "tape instruments". Rather, the focus will be on the work of one instrument maker who played a particularly prominent role in the development of instruments based on tape loops: Raymond Scott. Scott is an extraordinary figure in the history of electronic music, and it's a history that's not exactly lacking in eccentric and dazzling figures. He was born in 1908 in Brooklyn and named Harry Warnow. From the 1930s onwards, he and his swing band earned so much money with his songs, soundtracks for animated films and commercials that in 1957 he was able to retire at the age of 49. From then on, he lived on royalties and spent his time developing electronic instruments until his stroke in 1984.

Although in many respects, these instruments were groundbreaking, they are barely known today.[5] But even though both the historiography of Jazz and electronic music has hardly taken note of Scott, almost everyone has heard his music. Founder of the Raymond Scott Quintet, he wrote eccentric swing music that was used to accompany the Warner Brothers *Looney Toons* cartoons (with characters like Porky Pig, Bugs Bunny and Road Runner, among others) in the 1930s and 1940s.[6] His music was later played by such diverse bands and performers as Louis

Armstrong, Benny Goodman, the Kronos Quartet, Rush, They Might Be Giants and Devo.

Even if he is little known today, Scott was an important figure in the development of electronic pop music. He was not only one of the first to build instruments based on tape loops; more importantly, he is considered the inventor of the sequencer, and it is above all the sequencer which caused loops to become an important foundation of modern pop music.

What is more, the sequencer was not Scott's only innovation in the field of repetitive music. With his *Circle Machine*, he created the first electronic instrument that turned repetitive tone sequences into the foundation of complex compositions consisting of permutations of these sequences. This in turn gave rise to an instrument capable of generating its own musical pieces based on repetitive sequences: the Electronium. Scott was one of the first composers who – long before Brian Eno and other promoters of generative music – actively worked on instruments that could "compose" music autonomously.

At the same time, his inventions are an expression of a technocratic optimism about the future, which characterized the post-war period in the USA. The sequencer, Circle Machine and Electronium were Scott's contribution to a utopian future in which a leisure class would delegate all kinds of work to machines – including that of composing music. In photos for advertising brochures and newspaper articles, Scott liked to present himself as a casually dressed householder who sits, arms crossed, in front of his music-making paraphernalia, or who calls up pieces "at the touch of a button". These images suggest that it was not only physical, but creative work which had been handed over to technology.

In many respects, Scott fits the cliché of the "mad inventor". He was an eccentric and his foibles provide his biographers, who have brought him back from obscurity in recent years, with welcome material to embellish the history of his technical innovations: Raymond Scott worked on his magnum opus, the Electronium, with such zeal that it broke up his second marriage. He continuously made improvements to the instrument and the Electronium remained a work in progress until his death. He generally had little luck when marketing his inventions, however – among them are an electronic children's rattle, an alarm clock that wakes the sleeper to the sound of their own voice, and women's jewellery made of LED components.

The self-playing Electronium also seems to encompass his personal idiosyncrasies. Scott was the prototype of the isolated studio tinkerer who preferred to produce his music in isolation. And if some of his contemporary colleagues are to be believed, he was a veritable misanthrope. "All he ever had was machines – only we had names," grumbles singer Anita O'Day, who had worked with him. And anyway – he had "downgraded musicians to a kind of wind-up toy".[7] Scott, consequently, sent his fellow musicians home, and built machines that would make music for him instead.

The Electronium was not just intended to spare Scott from working with human musicians. It was also to make an old human fantasy come true – the fantasy of machine-created art which does not require human intervention. "He wanted music composition not to be onerous," his former employee Herb Deutsch recalls. "He said, 'you know, I just want to sit here and run this machine and whenever it does something good, I want to record it'…And he really wasn't lazy – on the contrary. He worked incredibly hard at not having to work as a composer."[8] For over 30 years, he surrounded himself with circuits in preference to rebellious musicians, so that he would be able to eliminate the human element from music production. "He was more comfortable around machines," Jeff Winner and Irwin Chusid, his re-discoverers, comment. Scott "spoke their language – or taught them to speak his language".[9]

The various sequencers and sound generators which Scott developed were components of one gigantic electronic instrument that occupied several rooms in the basement of his home on Long Island. Work on this instrument – and its predecessors, which bore names like Karloff or Orchestra Machine – is said to have cost this large man with the crew haircut over a million dollars; almost all the royalties he received for his Jazz compositions were invested in his electronic instruments.

He never recouped these costs. He did use the instruments to record music for commercials and industrial films and also developed audio logos for a number of US companies. These audio logos – short sound sequences intended to characterize a brand much as visual trademarks do – were one of Scott's ideas that proved to be remarkably future-orientated. Yet when he died in 1994, not only was he largely forgotten, he was also completely impoverished.

Scott belonged to a generation of "music engineers"[10] who, in the 1950s, 60s and 70s, continued the development of electronic musical instruments that had been started during the postwar period by composers like Pierre Schaeffer and Karlheinz Stockhausen. Among these engineers were Hugh Le Caine, Bob Moog, Don Buchla, Peter Zinovieff and the brothers Leslie, Norman and Frank Bradley.

Schaeffer and Stockhausen had begun their work with the technology that was available to them at their respective workplaces, which in both cases were publicly financed broadcasting companies. Schaeffer used record players and tape recorders; Stockhausen, sinus generators and tape recorders. Their most notable achievement was probably to spot the musical potential of these apparatuses, and to re-purpose recording devices and measuring instruments originally intended to serve other purposes. When bespoke apparatuses were made for them subsequently, they were created with specific needs in mind and without any thought of series production. Sam Phillips, likewise, had used the tape echo effect with which he edited Elvis' Sun Sessions solely for his own productions.

The music engineers, by contrast, did not build instruments primarily for their own use but as prototypes for marketable products. It's true that Scott composed pieces for his instruments. But his work was always motivated by the idea of creating instruments for others to use. He never did achieve this ambition. Yet even if his instruments were scarcely made use of by other musicians, their development marks an important point on the way to the digital instruments and computer programs with which most contemporary music is produced today. And many of Scott's inventions were based on the loop principle.

As early as 1949, he created the *Orchestra Machine*, which used tape loops to simulate the various instruments of an orchestra – a little-known precursor to the mellotron. Even his *Talking Alarm Clock* (1946) functioned with a magnetized wire loop on which the user could record their own voice. Before Scott developed the *Circle Machine*, an electronic instrument that automatically generates its own music through varying repetitions, at the end of the 1950s, he built the first electro-mechanical sequencer in 1953. Around that time, he submitted a patent for a musical instrument which "automatically finds a certain place on a tape and repeats it as often as desired".[11] As discussed in the chapter on Karlheinz Stockhausen, until well into the 1960s, most of the so-called "electronic music" was actually music produced using tape recorders, often with the aid of tape loops. It was not until the end of the 1960s that a number of technical developments made it possible to build instruments that could make actual electronic music – the first synthesizer models.

The development of the synthesizer was, to a large extent, driven by the frustration of composers and musicians who found working with tape too complicated. For Peter Zinovieff, founder of British synthesizer company EMS, it was the difficulties with tape recorders in the production of electronic music that were the most important reason to dedicate himself to the construction of synthesizers. "I'd had just about enough of snippets of tape."[12] American synthesizer pioneer Donald Buchla, likewise, built his first electronic sequencer because he found working with magnetic tape too laborious. "If you wanted a sequence of 16 notes, you no longer had to cut 16 pieces of tape together. All you had to do was to take my sequencer and set the length and pitch for each interval."[13] In developing this sequencer, he took account of the wishes of two composers, Ramon Sender and Morton Subotnick of San Francisco Tape Music Center, who were also tired of cutting tapes and wanted a machine capable of sequencing sounds.

Since Scott was financially independent, he was, to a large extent, able to be the "author" of his instruments and used them to advance the utopian fantasy of automated creativity. His second wife, Mitzi Curtis, recalls domestic scenes that seemed to come straight out of *Star Trek*:

> We'd be having lunch, the Electronium was in the next room playing something very nice. I'd say, "Oh, isn't that a pretty melody?" As if it had heard me and was saying to itself, "okay then, if you like it so much, I'll play it again", it repeated the same melody...It was a self-playing machine. It simultaneously composed and played. It was so *out of this world*."[14]

And it still is – to this day, the compositions which Raymond Scott created with his self-built electronic instruments sound futuristic.

With his electronic music for commercials and industrial films, he served the American zeitgeist of the 1950s and 1960s, which was confident and technology-friendly. It was a time characterized by a naive belief in technology and the future, especially in the USA. Even though by dropping atomic bombs on Hiroshima and Nagasaki in 1945, the USA had demonstrated the destructive potential of technology, which was then rapidly developing, the post-war period was characterized by an obsession with technical progress and the period has been described as the space age, or nuclear age. This *zeitgeist* found popular-cultural expression in the animated series *The Jetsons*, in Disney World's Tomorrowland and in the space pop compositions of Harry Revel and Attilio Mineo, among others.[15]

It was this music, classed as Easy Listening, that first introduced many music listeners who had no interest in avant-garde music à la Stockhausen or Schaeffer to electronic instruments such as the Theremin, as well as to tape loops. One of the most successful musicians working in this field had even been a student of Pierre Schaeffer. Through the agency of Edith Piaf, Jean-Jacques Perrey worked in Schaeffer's radio studio in the mid-1950s, where he became familiar with tape loops. After emigrating to the USA, he became successful with his playfully bizarre pop songs. His version of Rimski-Korsakov's *Flight of the Bumble Bee*, for instance, consisted of glued-together recordings from a beehive, which were rhythmically underpinned by tape loops. Although this composition clearly is in the tradition of *musique concrète*, the result was a catchy pop hit, and in a way, Perrey anticipated the use of found sounds and tape loops in 1970s, 80s and 90s pop music.[16]

Like Raymond Scott, Perrey composed soundtracks for some of the attractions in Disney World's Tomorrowland, while Raymond Scott also produced music for General Motors' futuristic pavilion at the 1964 New York World Fair. The world exhibition, which took place in Queens, was in many ways the pinnacle of naive American euphoria about the future and postwar technology.[17] It was used by the American government as well as by companies and the advertising industry to propagate their versions of the world of tomorrow. The General Motors pavilion served as an embodiment of their strategy. The so-called Futurama was the largest building at the World Fair and intended to introduce the public to Saint-Simonesque utopias of a second modernism.[18] Attractions included a 'City of Tomorrow', where huge skyscrapers were linked by moving pavements, and high-speed commuter trains transported passengers to airports in the city centre. Additionally, visitors could witness a journey to the moon, watch holidaymakers in deep-sea resorts and watch trees in the jungle being felled with laser beams. How much Scott contributed to this spectacle is not clear. It is known that he accompanied a radio commercial for the General Motors pavilion with electronic sounds. However, materials in his estate suggest that he also composed the music which visitors heard in the Futurama building.

Like numerous other exhibits at the world exhibition, the Futurama celebrated a future in which all human needs are provided by technology. Physical work was to be made redundant, or at least significantly easier, by machines. The technocratic programme of the New York World Fair was entirely in keeping with Raymond Scott's declared goal of transferring the work of composing to electronic instruments. Interestingly, Scott describes his invention in analogy to literature, probably without being aware of similar experiments in other artistic disciplines, like those conducted by the Stuttgart School.[19] "It's like inventing the typewriter, but this typewriter also develops the plot and reads out the result in its own voice. You stipulate form and structure, but the machine works out the details. If you like what it has produced but want a different pitch or tempo, you just press the appropriate buttons..."[20]

How did Scott come up with these ideas? One can only speculate about whether he knew about the computer-generated *ILLIAC-Suite* (1955) by Lejaren Hiller and Leonard Isaacson, because he steered clear of the "official", academic electronic music scene. Yet he does seem to have been well informed about developments in this field. His company "Manhattan Research" advertised that it produced "electronic music and *musique concrète*", which also shows that Scott was familiar with pertinent keywords.

He cultivated occasional contacts with academic composers, such as Vladimir Ussachevsky, but otherwise stayed away from the serious music milieu where electronic music was being played in the USA at the time. His former colleague Herb Deutsch says that, "it should be acknowledged that Raymond knew what was happening in academic music. But his own world was completely different, and he was more comfortable there. I think he didn't appreciate some of those academic types. They don't seem to have given him his due, and he was very sensitive about that."[21]

So only a few insiders were aware of the instruments Scott built in his basement on Long Island. During the last years of his life, Scott obviously regretted having kept them a secret. In an unaddressed letter found within his estate, he writes:

I have a story that might interest you. It is not well-known nowadays who developed the circuit for sequencing successive musical pitches – which today is called a "sequencer". I, on the other hand, know well who the inventor was – since it was I myself who first developed and built an electronic sequencer in 1960. The concept for my musical pitch sequencer was inspired by the introduction of the Wurlitzer drum machine in 1959, which was called Sideman.[22]

The Sideman was the first electronic rhythm machine.[23] The Wurlitzer company developed the instrument in 1959 to go with their home organs, so that organists could have a rhythmic accompaniment. It could play 12 different, electronically-generated rhythm patterns at different tempi. The sound source was a series of electron tubes (like those in the retro radios of the 1950s), which were activated by contacts on a rotating disc.

In his letter, Scott describes:

[Sideman's] rotating, mechanical, disc-shaped switching mechanism that triggered electronically generated drum sounds. I immediately thought, why not build an instrument that plays a series of musical pitches automatically? I used thyratron tubes and relays and built my first sequencer in the spring of 1960...I can still understand this need I had for secrecy in the past. My income depended on electronic music – and I thought I had this great advantage, because it was my very own sequencer ... But now, after all these years, I regret the secrecy and I want people to know what I achieved.[24]

The sequencer was only one element of Scott's Electronium. "The entire system is based on the concept of artistic collaboration between man and machine," Scott wrote in a patent application for the Electronium. "The new structures created by the machine are unpredictable in their details." The manual for an early version of the device states that:

the composer "asks" the Electronium to "suggest" an idea, a theme or a motif. To transpose it into another key, the composer only has to press the appropriate button. There's everything the composer needs; faster, slower, different rhythm, interval, rest, an additional theme, variation, extension, prolongation, transposition, counterpoint, a change of phrasing, an ornament, ad infinitum. It is capable of producing a seemingly inexhaustible palette of musical sounds and timbres, rhythms and harmonies. Whatever the composer wants, the Electronium processes it and follows his instructions. The Electronium adds something to the thoughts of the composer.[25]

The world's first sequencer was an early element of Scott's Promethean project of building an instrument that plays itself. Later, he built more advanced versions of the sequencer, which bore names like Circle Machine, Pitch Sequencer and Bassline Generator. Anyone who sees pictures of these devices today probably won't realize that these metal cabinets covered with buttons, switches, display panels and sockets encompass a musical instrument. The entire apparatus, jokingly referred to as the "Wall of Sound", resembles the control panel of a nuclear power plant, or a mainframe computer from the 1960s. Scott himself was well aware of the similarity of his apparatus to the control electronics of his time. In 1971, he said in a newspaper interview, "I want [the Electronium] to engender a feeling of driving a control machine, a cockpit of dreams."[26]

Due to Scott's secrecy, it is difficult to understand today how his cockpit of dreams actually worked. The initial sequencer he had constructed in 1953 (7 years before the sequencer he mentions in the letter cited above) apparently was still a semi-mechanical instrument constructed of switching relays, which had little in common with the later models. Bob Moog, who saw the instrument, later remembered:

He had one rack next to another, and they were full of these relays, like those used by telephone companies. You dialled and the relay went through all sorts of positions. He'd wired the things together so that he could switch the sounds on and off... The whole room was just going clack- clack- clack- clack, clack- clack- clack- clack, and sounds were buzzing about the room. Not everyone could afford something like that, that's for sure. It took a hell of a lot of money and a hell of a lot of imagination. And madness, as well.[27]

Herb Deutsch, who had also seen the instrument in action, describes it like this: "It was about two meters high and ten meters long; the sequencer consisted of hundreds of relays, solenoid coils, sound circuits and 16 different oscillators. If you went behind the wall while music was being produced, all you could hear was a cacophony of clicking relays going back and forth."[28]

The Circle Machine, which developed from the electronic sequencer, was controlled by light pulses. In the few surviving pictures that show Scott with his "Wall of Sound", this device is difficult to detect. The Circle Machine is mostly a blur in the background, a round object with a bracket. The American musicologist Thomas Rhea, who worked for Scott in the early 1970s and had seen the Circle Machine in action, assumed it to be an analogue waveform generator. He remembers a, "crazy appliance that whirled about like a dervish. It had a ring of incandescent lamps, each with its own heating resistor and a photo-electric cell on a spindle that rotated above the lights."[29]

This sequencer seems to have been used on three records, which Scott released under the title *Soothing Sounds for Baby* in 1962 and 1963, and which belong to the most obscure works of electronic pop music. The exact genesis of these records cannot be reconstructed. The cover of the original releases merely shows that the three EPs had been produced in collaboration with the Gesell Institute of Child Development. The Gesell Institute practised methods developed by the American child psychologist Arnold Gesell. Apparently, these records, which were offered for three different age groups, were intended to be a kind of "acoustic toy". An insert in the original editions of the records indicates that the music was intended to have a comforting effect on babies because they mimicked the "rhythmic jingling of a music box" or resembled "the ticking of a clock held close to the ear".[30]

For today's listener, however, the monotonously repetitive pieces are reminiscent of Minimal Techno. In the longest and most radical piece, *Toy Typewriter*, the electronic reproduction of typewriter key clatter raps on for over 17 minutes. Most of the other pieces, which bear titles like *Tic Toc*, *The Playful Drummer* and *The Happy Whistler*, contain at least some beginnings of melodies, in spite of their uniformity, but do repeat these over and over. *Toy Typewriter*, by contrast, is pure electronic percussion.

Whether Scott used the Circle Machine or another of his sequencers on *Soothing Sounds for Baby* is not entirely clear. No definitive documentation was found in Scott's estate, even though a diligent group of electronic music archivists is attempting to process his estate in an exemplary manner. How the project first came about is as unclear as the instrumentation of the pieces. Nevertheless, the hammering uniformity of the music suggests that Scott did use either the Circle Machine or another type of sequencer in the production of *Soothing Sounds for Baby*. What is known is that the Circle Machine was used in some commercials where, among other things, it produced the sound of a dying car battery as well as rhythmic patterns to accompany the music.

Time and again, Scott toyed with the idea of selling his Electronium, especially since at the end of the 1960s, the royalties for his Jazz compositions were no longer flowing in so freely. Financial salvation came in 1970 through an unexpected kindred spirit: Berry Gordy, founder of the legendary soul label Motown (Diana Ross & the Supremes, Marvin Gaye, Temptations), bought a half-finished Electronium from Scott in 1970. Like Scott, Gordy was fascinated by the idea of being able to compose music quasi-automatically, and to have pop songs composed by a machine instead of well-paid songwriters. In an interview in 1997, former Motown manager Guy Costa recalled:

Berry believed that the Electronium's ability to transform
the musical process into numbers was important...Berry
had always been a formula man; he'd find a rhythm or a

sequence of harmonies and developed something from it. The Electronium offered the opportunity to play a chord, to store rhythms, and then to rearrange them. All these new possibilities appealed to him.[31]

Although Gordy also invested substantial sums to develop the Electronium, Motown never seems to have derived any commercial benefit from it. At any rate, the sound of the Electronium does not appear on Motown records. Therefore, one can only speculate about what such gifted Motown producers as Norman Whitfield might have done with it.

Although Barry Gordy made Raymond Scott head of the research department of his record company in Los Angeles in 1972, the Electronium was never developed to the point that would have made it possible for the instrument to be used by other musicians. Part of the reason was that Scott had also found a kindred spirit in Gordy in terms of continuously wanting to effect changes and improvements to the Electronium. In 1977, aged 69, Scott retired. He died in 1994, aged 85. The remnants of his still unfinished Electronium were bought up by Mark Mothersbaugh, founder of the American new wave group Devo.

Scott's sequencer and Circle Machine would have been capable of producing repetitive music such as composers of Minimal Music and producers of Techno were to do years later —in fact, some of the pieces on *Soothing Sounds for Baby* come surprisingly close. But most of his compositions do not make use of loops. The idea of simply letting the machines run, relinquishing control and turning the listener into a co-producer of the musical experience was not yet conceivable for Scott. He was still committed to the spirit of modernity, which can only ever imagine *being* in terms of a linear, teleological process – as time's arrow, to use Stephen Jay Gould's phrase. In keeping with this spirit, when Scott wasn't using loops as sound effects, he organized his compositions according to parameters of development, progress and musical dissolution. Excepting pieces on *Soothing Sounds for Baby*, he did not create any compositions that could be said to represent Gould's circular time. It was the next generation of composers, who were subject to a "postmodern" sensibility, who allowed their music machines to unfold their own monotonously repetitive processes and to confront the listener with the unrefined results of these processes.

Although these developments were not widely known in his own time, they were conceptually superior to better-known instruments, such as the mellotron, and possessed a flexibility that anticipated many of the features of today's digital samplers and sequencers.

Over the past 50 years, an entire industry and entire branches of instrument-building have developed around the production of repeated sounds. Today, every synthesizer includes a sequencer that allows sound sequences to be repeated *ad ultimo*. With digital samplers, it is possible to join any digitally stored sound into an endless chain. Both types of instruments are available in numerous designs and models, and it has become impossible to imagine music production without them.

The number of software programs that produce uninterrupted repetitions of images and sounds is also immense. It's not just programs for professional music production and digital video editing that contain a loop function. Audio and video programs such as VLCr, which most private individuals have on their computers, have this function, too.[32] The same goes for the majority of CD and DVD players. Even if most users of these machines and programs never avail themselves of this facility, the instruments for the production of loop-based art are available to almost everyone.

Simpler loop-producing instruments were initially more effective than Scott's Electronium when it came to the dissemination of loop techniques. In 1968, Robert Moog began offering a sequencer for his influential synthesizers. This sequencer, which quickly became popular, especially among pop musicians, was much simpler than what Scott had built, and perhaps this was the reason for its popularity.

Moog's sequencer (and soon, other synthesizer sequencers as well) generated entire musical genres over the decades to come – the electronic *kraut rock* of Tangerine Dream and Klaus Schulze; Giorgio Moroder's electronic disco of the 1970s; the electronic body music of the 1980s; Techno of the 1990s. Raymond Scott provided an initial draft for such loop-based music with the proto-minimal Techno of *Soothing Sounds for Baby.*

And Scott's influence on the development of the Moog sequencer, and therefore on the music styles mentioned above, is a very direct one: Bob Moog had worked for him as a young man, had seen the early sequencer in action and had been impressed by it, commenting, "I had never seen anything like it!" Even though his own sequencer was simpler (and other synthesizer makers also developed sequencers in the late 1960s), Scott's original sequencer seems to have been an important influence. Moog himself never tired of highlighting Scott's pioneering role. "He was the first. He foresaw the use of sequencers and electronic oscillators for sound production. Those were the turning points"[33] in the development of electronic instruments, he wrote in a tribute to Scott in the late 1990s.

Of course, with the exception of *Soothing Sounds for Baby* (where loops are intended to calm children), Scott never foregrounded the rhythmic characteristics of his instruments, like Techno *et al* were to do. He was still attached to traditional ideas about his role as a composer, and about musical structure. Yes, his instruments were to compose for him. But they were envisaged to produce melodies, rather than rhythms or repetitive beats.

It was only when the *will to repeat* began to spread through music and the visual arts in the early 1960s that such compositional methods became conceivable. This will to repeat made it possible for a new generation of composers to let their music machines function and repeat on their own. In the second part of this book, the discussion will focus on how the repetitive loop was transformed from a technical trick for the production of unusual sounds into a genuine aesthetic means of expression.

"PRECISE, UNPRETENTIOUS AND SIMPLE SEQUENCES": PETER ROEHR'S FILM MONTAGES AND THE "WILL TO REPEAT" IN 1960S CULTURE

I feel identified with what I do. In the 'montages', I realize everything that's important to me, without reservation. I think I am free.

Peter Roehr, 1964

It's a weekend in the spring of 1966. Together with a photographer and his wife, artist Peter Roehr sneaks into the studio building of *Hessischer Rundfunk* [Hessian radio]. Frankfurt radio station had produced a series of his sound montages. They consist of short sound sequences that are repeated several times unaltered. Water level reports, excerpts from commercials, the news or a few bars of background muzak are played some ten or twenty times. *Hessischer Rundfunk* did not broadcast these sound montages, however. An editor wrote to Roehr that one must "consider the general listener, who has little appreciation for this".[1]

There is a photo featuring Roehr as a West German dandy in suit and tie, sitting grinning on a chair while a woman works at the editing table. She is placed in front of him, so it's not possible to be sure, but it looks as if Roehr is folding his hands demonstratively in his lap. In another picture, he looks absent-mindedly at the floor while a piece of tape slips through his fingers. It seems as if he wanted to show that he is not taking part in the production process and is merely observing how his instructions are being carried out by others.

These pictures weren't taken at the time the sound montages were produced. Roehr had them made retrospectively. Even the tape on the editing table was probably just one that was lying about the studio. The woman in the picture is not a professional editor employed by *Hessischer Rundfunk,* but rather, the photographer's wife. So Peter Roehr went to a lot of trouble to document that he wasn't involved in the manual labour of producing his sound montages.[2]

The multiple repetitions of the sound fragments of Roehr's sound montages are part of an overall work dedicated to one basic principle with impressive consistency – the repetition of found material. "I place things of the same kind together," Roehr wrote in 1965. "These can be objects, photographs, stand-alone forms like letters, texts, tones and sounds, film material, etc. and I call the results 'montages'. I do not use organic objects, just constructed ones, and preferably industrially produced objects...I arrange the objects without interruption, as this would impede their relationship to each other, and attract some of the attention."[3] Roehr sorts cardboard letters, photos, stamps, stickers, pocket mirrors into grids with meticulous orderliness.

He is not the only serial artist of that time. In the art of the 1960s, things start being arranged in rows, grids, structures. It is a period where artistic methods of technical reproduction and repetition often coincide for aesthetic purposes. This influenced the pop art of Andy Warhol, the Minimal Art of Carl Andre and Donald Judd, and the Conceptual Art of Sol LeWitt and Hanne Darboven, which emerged almost simultaneously. Repetitions, sequences and systems, organized according to simple rules, became the most important structural element of art forms that had lost the taste for staging shocking contrasts or for presenting constant innovation and progress, which had characterized the art of classical modernism.

Authors like William Burroughs and Byron Gysin continued such modernist approaches in the 1960s in their literature and in tape cuttings, where text or tape snippets were randomly assembled, often with dismal results. At the same time, however, numerous artists chose elementary and easily comprehensible structuring methods for their material. One of these was the loop. These artists sought refuge in the arrangement of elements that accorded with simple, comprehensible formulas, such as arranging their material "one after another" (Donald Judd) or by incorporating it in "systems set up in advance" (Peter Roehr).[4] If any difference emerges from this, then it arises paradoxically, from an arrangement of elements that emphasize sameness. "I alter material by organizing it without changing it," Roehr wrote laconically in November 1964. "Every work is an organized territory of equal elements. It's neither successive nor summary, there is no conclusion and no sum total."[5] Half a decade before Roland Barthes was to proclaim the "death of the author", Roehr had renounced the will to artistic self-expression in his art.

Although Roehr's artistic method was part of a development that was gaining momentum in the international art scene of that time, to this day, his work does not receive the recognition it deserves, despite the fact that his immersion in repetition precedes that of American Minimal Art. In recent years, his works have been shown in exhibitions on Minimal Art and 1960s art, especially in the USA.[6] Nevertheless, in his own country, Germany, his importance as a pioneer of repetitive art is still not as well-known as it should be on account of his radical aesthetics – even though, with the exhibition Serial Formations[7] in 1967, he staged one of the earliest events of such aesthetic positions. The exhibition included works by contemporary artists like Carl Andre, Donald Judd, Dan Flavin, Sol LeWitt and Agnes Martin, shown for the first time in West Germany. Roehr himself, however, has not yet been included in the international canon to which these artists belong.[8]

The fact that Roehr and his work are not well-known is probably also due to his early death – he died of cancer in August 1968, at the age of 23. But the fact that his work seems like a foreign body in the post-war art scene of West Germany, which was characterized by abstract expressionism and informal art, is undoubtedly a contributing factor. His emphatically "unimaginative" works must have seemed like a provocation within a context that in many respects still paid homage to the genius cult of Modernism, even if they were not intended as such. At a time when artists were expected to present themselves as other than the ordered rationality of the "administered world" (Adorno), it was hardly fathomable why an artist would want to repeat the same thing, akin to an assembly line worker. It didn't help that Roehr himself made comments like, "I haven't come up with anything!"[9]

When his work is placed in an international context, however, it becomes evident that around 1964, Roehr unswervingly radicalized the will to repeat, which was also felt by many other artists of that time. In the first half of the 1960s, an entire generation of artists replaced individual self-expression with objectivity, schematic clarity, depersonalization and rigid systems of order, like that of repetition. As with the American minimalists, Roehr's work is about shifting the construction of meaning from the artwork itself to the outside, to turn it into a "function of organizing interfaces".[10] In contrast to Judd and Andre, however, Roehr used prosaic everyday objects, such as drawing pins, marbles, coins, corks and advertising photographs for this purpose. He used them to emphasize their prefabricated, impersonal character. Only rarely did he go so far as to admit that by sequencing them, he wanted to reveal "the poetry that is in them, eclipsed by environment, origin and purpose".[11]

Roehr's most famous works are his serial montages of everyday objects like labels, matchboxes, coasters and airmail stickers. Later, he arranged advertising pictures using the same method. Time and again, he emphasizes the absolute uniformity of his method. Roehr even found the silk screens of Andy Warhol too varied because they differ in terms of colour application details. He combatively comments, "I've always liked Warhol's pictures, even if I didn't find them as consequential or as good as my own."[12]

Roehr was happy to emphasize that his works were "not composition[s]" as such – "the picture itself is infinite, it could spread out in all directions and keep continuing."[13] Like the works of Judd and Andre, Roehr's material collages show a world without a centre. In this world, things acquire meaning, not through their individual properties, but through the structures in which these properties appear. The artist creates an arrangement that is as neutral as possible and leaves it up to the viewer to find their own meaning in it. This kind of art is no longer about externalizing artistic subjectivity, but about giving the viewer the opportunity to give free rein to their own subjectivity in the work of art.

In the context of this book, Roehr's audio-visual works using film and tape are more important than his material collages. Peter Roehr was the first artist who had the courage to string together image and sound sequences completely unchanged. He does not vary, or modulate or modify. That's why he plays a very particular role in my history of the loop. The first part of this book is about composers who used specific characteristics of the recording medium of tape – reproduction and repetition – for their music. They used tape loops to create sound effects (like Raymond Scott) or to gain control over the sound (like Karlheinz Stockhausen). Tape loops were also used to modify existing sounds (as Sam Phillips did), or to denature and separate sounds from their original source (as Pierre Schaeffer did). But none of these experimenters came up with the most obvious idea: simply to make loops repeat and to let their repetitive properties create metric structures. It was not until the 1960s that the cyclic, periodic nature of loops was discovered and used as an aesthetic means in its own right.

The second part of this book is about artists who focused on the endless, machine-like repetitions that recording media are capable of producing. For reasons to be discussed, it seems that working artistically with this constitutive characteristic of recording media only became possible in the mid-1960s. Composers like Terry Riley and Steve Reich began to use repeated tape fragments to organize their music at this time. The following two chapters will show how these composers developed a musical language from an examination of the propagative characteristics of tape – the musical style that has gone down in music history as pulse music, repetitive music, ac' art, or, in other words, Minimal Music. But although (or perhaps because) Riley and Reich focused on the repetitive potentials of tape recordings, they tried to obtain a maximum of variation from the repetitions. Neither of them goes as far as Roehr, who really only strings together identical sound elements and nothing else, leaving the production of difference, "variety", or even transcendence entirely to the listener.

The will to repeat is palpable, not just in visual arts and music, but in the experimental film and media arts of the mid-1960s. During this period, film-makers and visual artists discovered the loop as an aesthetic tool in a big way. This had a variety of reasons. Some merely made a virtue out of necessity and looped their films for exhibitions, so that they didn't have to be re-inserted into a projector over and over. Artists like Marcel Broodthaers, Michael Snow, Valie Export and Dieter Roth are examples.

In experimental and structuralist films of the time, many film-makers and artists worked with loops as an aesthetic tool. Among them are Bruce Connor (*A Movie*), Lutz Mommartz (*Railway*), Dick Higgins (*Invocations of Canyons*) and Nam June Paik (*Zen for Film*), the latter producing the arguably most interesting film loop besides Roehr's work. *Zen for Film* (1964/1965) is merely a piece of transparent film strip. When it is projected, a white rectangle appears on the screen. Michael Glasmeier comments that:

> what [the film] shows is the optical answer to Cage's 4'33, namely, there is nothing at first. However, gradually, dust and dirt accumulate, to create a kind of rhythmic visibility. This piece of film not only refers to the Zen Buddhist movement in a static way, but also proves beyond doubt that even a perfectly rounded loop without any perceptible perforation at its beginning or end is subject to minimal changes. The possibility of a radical falling out of time leaves traces in time.[14]

At the same time, *Zen for Film* is a piece of self-reflexive filmmaking – it's a film that shows nothing but itself and its specific media properties. Its lack of images has also been interpreted as a protest against the flood of images of modern mass media, encouraging the viewer to counter this bombardment with his own images. What escapes such judgements, however, is that the film uses the technical properties of film-as-mass-medium to arrive at its own technological images, which the projector literally inscribes into the film strip. Around this time, experimental film-makers such as Malcolm McGrice, Paul Sharits, Robert Breer, Peter Weibel, Peter Kubelka, Kurt Kren, Werner Nekes, George Landow and James Collins were also beginning to focus on media repetition and film loops. In contrast to the films of Peter Roehr, however, their films hardly ever consist solely of unmodified loops. These films use loops as one of several methods to explore film as a technical medium. For the film-makers mentioned above, the use of loops became such a versatile stylistic device that it would require a separate chapter and a more comprehensive book to do them justice. Explorations of the aesthetic possibilities of film loops, whether as an element of an installation or as part of the film itself, are so pronounced during this period that P. Adams Sitney refers to them as one of four defining elements of structural film in his canonical book *Visionary Film*.[15]

The 1960s were a time when serial structures – including loops – began to become established in such diverse artistic scenes as fluxus, Minimal Art, conceptual art, expanded cinema, structural film and video art. Artists simply let the media machines run and repeat. But no one is more consistent in this than Peter Roehr, who does nothing more than string together short sequences of images without modification, even in his film montages. It wasn't until the end of the 1970s, almost a decade-and-a-half later, that video artists like Klaus vom Bruch or Dara Birnbaum dared to assemble films from unvaried repetitions of short image sequences, and even these video loops don't have the unwavering austerity of Peter Roehr's film montages. The scratch video artists of the 1980s in their turn made use of such repetition. But it wasn't until the 1990s that artists like Daniel Pflumm, Paul Pfeiffer and Klaus vom Bruch, in his later work, used truly unmodified repetitions of film or video sequences.

Even if Roehr's film and sound montages were not recognized by the German and international cultural scene at the time they were created, looking back, they appear to have been a watershed. With his montages, Roehr anticipated some of the dominant artistic themes of the years to come – the absence of the "artist's touch" in the creative process. The belief in a form of art that replaces notions of artistic genius and inspiration with sheer regularity. The method of arranging (audio-)visual elements according to predetermined structures that are free from hierarchy or other "superordinate" principles of composition. And above all, the belief that such sheer arrangements allow for a different or an unbiased view of the repeated phenomena, a notion that will be returned to in later chapters, when considering the minimalists and the tape experiments of writer Ken Kesey.

Roehr notes in 1965 that, "I believe that each thing contains detectable properties that we rarely perceive. If we perceive a thing several times in a row, adjacent (in space) or sequentially (in time) – without there being a gap in between...then we notice these qualities."[16] The same, over and over, to enable perception of an object beyond context – early on, Peter Roehr takes this project to the nth degree.

In the notes that accompany his work, Roehr points out the influence of mechanized serial production: "the machine and new production systems that are associated with it have transformed our entire way of life. This affects not only the social and economic situation, but also the aesthetic one".[17] And yet, while technology and media did have an effect on Roehr's work, they were apparently not the most important influence. In a short autobiographical text, Roehr describes the beginning of his fascination with repetition:

> shortly before I started making montages – I was 18 at the time – I had read a book on Zen Buddhism. Perhaps it was no coincidence that the first ideas for the montages came about during this period. I remember clearly that I attached great importance to the idea of sequencing, to precise, unpretentious and simple sequencing, straight away. Back then (in 1962), I guess I felt like I had discovered the circle or the square and wondered why others hadn't found it before me...When I went to Italy in mid-September 1963, I saw a large construction fence that was covered with several rows of evenly spaced identical posters. I remember being amazed by this.[18]

For Roehr, an important impulse to start using monotony, series and sequences came from a fascination with Far Eastern religion, rather than from a preoccupation with the replicative techniques of his time.[19] He notes, "I think I felt very strongly what it [Zen Buddhism] meant, and was determined to go into the desert to meditate as soon as my circumstances allowed...It was not intoxication, but rather, a lightness and serenity in the face of many problems."[20] Interestingly, others have observed Roehr's work to have a similar effect. Art critic Norbert Messler notes, "when we look at such a montage, we ourselves enter into a state of pronounced detachment".[21]

The picture collages soon turn the observer's attention from their motifs to the pattern formation, and to a kind of abstract, optical dynamism that is lacking in the discrete components. In these works, it is repetition that forms the structure. Roehr himself was well aware of this effect of his work. "If the number of objects in a sequence exceeds a certain flexible limit, they dissolve and become basic units of a structure that is specific to them. But if another, given flexible number is not reached, then they remain just a collection of objects."[22]

In his image and sound montages, Roehr struggled with the question of exactly how many repetitions were optimal to make the subject matter more than a mere collection of audiovisual elements. It can be argued that he did not find that optimal number in his sound montages. Just as Pierre Schaeffer had found out before him, Roehr's sound montages push the recorded objects' "anecdotal" character obtrusively to the fore.

The sound montages tend to evoke the stuffiness of the late 50s and early 60s with their tube radio sound. When an agitated man lectures in an authoritative voice, "I'll tell you how the air gets into children's chocolate", when a distraught housewife recites rhymes about a stain on her wallpaper, or when an indistinct "inner voice" muses, "a cup of Fox coffee would do me good now", it often seems as if Roehr had intended to parody the dullness of advertising through the endless repetitions of these sound fragments. Of course, that was the last thing Roehr wanted. Rather, as he said in an interview, he was looking for sequences that "reveal themselves". What I mean by this is visibly exposed aesthetic qualities that reveal an unexpected structure.[23]

Roehr's film montages, which he showed for the first time in the autumn of 1965, do this more successfully than his sound collages. For the former, he used excerpts from American TV commercials. His friend and gallery owner Paul Maenz was working for an advertising agency in New York at the time and sent film reels, which had been returned to the agency after being broadcast on television, to Roehr. Since these films were sometimes broadcast by dozens of American local stations, Maenz often had 20 or 30 reels with the same film commercial, which he put at Roehr's disposal.

Roehr selected short passages from the film, often just a few seconds long, and then had an editor join identical copies of these passages together. As with the sound montages, he emphasized that he did not undertake the manual work himself. He didn't even need to be present once the film clips had been marked with lengths of string. In his notes he observes, "[due to scheduling issues], some of my films were produced and shown by [editor] Roland Kress without me having seen them previously. They were such that we didn't have to make any retrospective changes."[24]

Boxers box, wrestlers wrestle, an illuminated advertisement on a gas station scurries by, a tracking shot shows New York skyscrapers from below, rising up like monoliths in plunging perspectives. Time and again, over and over, without will, obediently, automatically, as though led by some higher power. Even more than with the picture collages, the material seems to take on a life of its own, detached from its "content". The constant repetitions don't just facilitate a more conscious awareness of certain details and an analysis of movement structures within these short film clips. No, when something is repeated, it changes.

Roehr notes about his "films without story" that "the amount of repetition is such that the montage ends when individual movement begins to fade into a movement structure".[25] As with the montages, differentiation, which Roehr seems to eliminate through the non-hierarchical treatment of the material, returns by way of subjective perception. The intransigence of the rule is negated by the dynamics of the viewing process.

Peter Roehr's montages therefore confirm David Hume's insight about repetition and difference, which Gilles Deleuze often quotes: "Repetition doesn't change the repeating object, but it does change something in the mind that contemplates it." It was the rediscovery of this maxim that allowed Deleuze to stop viewing repetition as an effect of Freud's death drive, and to turn it into a way of producing difference. In accordance with the much-cited formulation in *Anti-Oedipus*, for Deleuze, the subconscious is not theatre (as it is for Freud), but factory and machine.[26] Their repetitions can also be experienced as a means of the pleasure principle, in other words, as Freud's Eros. Roehr's films are an artistic expression of the insight that constant repetitions can change "the mind that observes them". The more the identity of an image or a film scene are emphasized through repetition, the clearer the differences become to the viewing consciousness. Roehr observes that "in my films, the story can be summed up in a simple statement – something like 'a woman is drying her hair', or 'two cars are driving through a tunnel'. By repeating the situation, the initially perceived action begins to dissolve and expand."[27] It is precisely this desire for the dissolution and expansion of perception, which Roehr's films and collages work towards, that characterizes the visual arts of the 60s, pop culture, minimalist art and the psychedelic culture of the late 60s.

On the one hand, there are the dry, modest and methodical arrangements of Peter Roehr or the American minimalists, on the other, the colourful, unrestrained and drug-infused beatnik and hippie folklore of the "swinging sixties" – at first glance, these movements seem to have nothing in common except the fact that they came about in the same time period. But in fact, they pursue the same project of creating a perception of objects that are removed from external contexts, of making it possible to perceive the essential. In the case of American minimalism, there are Judd's geometrically arranged cubes, Andre's square base plates, Robert Morris' mirror cubes and Larry Bell's glass cubes. In Roehr's work, everyday jumble is intended to open the "gates of perception" through its strict and regular ordering. In psychedelia, it was drugs like marijuana and LSD.

Diedrich Diederichsen notes that what minimalism and psychedelia have in common "can only be understood when one accepts that the psychedelic drug culture was not purely a culture of intoxication, and that it had a heuristic component that is understood by many authors as a practical, often mystical, and sometimes also a political means of cognition which frees objects from various illusory components...and makes one see more clearly."[28] I am aware that by following such a line of argument, I enter a problematic area. I run the risk of being drawn into a kind of culture-war, which is still being fought about the 1960s, and make it worse by focusing on the central role that drugs played in the cultural production of this decade.

Nevertheless, it is impossible to overlook the fact that the use of LSD, cannabis, mescaline and amphetamines played an important role in much of the artistic production of the time, as I will show. For one thing, drugs were used to trigger certain artistic experiments, and for another, artists wanted to record and make comprehensible the experiences which drugs triggered – if they did not advocate them immediately.

Terry Riley, The Beatles, La Monte Young, Andy Warhol and a few others who will be discussed were all acknowledged drug users in the 1960s. While it is less taboo in pop music to use drugs, artists operating in so-called "high culture" are reluctant to present their works as having been influenced by intoxicants. In self-testimonies about the 1960s, however, their drug use is mentioned quite explicitly in some cases, and titles like Terry Riley's *Mescaline Mix* leave little doubt as to their inspiration.

Minimalist composer Steve Reich has repeatedly emphasized that he does not regard questions about the influence of drugs on his music as a "profitable topic of conversation",[29] and in critical literature on Minimal Art, drugs are generally not discussed, even though their use by some artists is anecdotally documented. But in an interview about his music from the 1960s, composer Terry Riley, one of the founders of musical minimalism, does admit with gratifying honesty that:

I think you really have to look at the sixties, and what was going on then. I was never concerned with minimalism, but

I was very concerned with psychedelia and the psychedelic movement of the sixties as an opening toward consciousness. For my generation that was a first look towards the East, that is, peyote, mescaline and the psychedelic drugs that opened people's perceptions to a higher form of experience.

When asked if *In C* was a "drug piece", however, Riley replied:

> well, no, not specifically. But the drug experience leads towards some kind of satori, some kind of enlightening, and that was what I was after. And for a lot of people, the drug experience was the only way that they had of getting into that world. No, I don't think drugs are the answer and I don't advocate that. What I'm saying is that during the sixties that was the way a lot of us entered into as a search for higher consciousness.[30]

For our purposes, it is particularly interesting to note that the artistic production of the 1960s, which was created under the influence of drugs, often worked with repetition, and that this was achieved by means of industrial production, such as screen printing or the use of technological media, like tape recordings. German music critic Ulrich Dibelius tries to explain the points of contact between repetitive technology, Minimal Music and psychedelia:

> the psychedelic in the equation is based, so to speak, on an auto-intoxication of the civilized human being. For it was he who forced the overflowing abundance of fantasy and the wealth of natural forms into the limited regularity of specific ways of perceiving, into an exploitative mode of being and into technical-industrial production. The sterile identity of his serial products was the consequence, the absolutism of his norm became the self-imposed principle of his life. And this to such an overwhelming extent and with such general validity that human consciousness had almost no

choice but to increasingly regard this trimmed-down second nature as the true and first. One becomes accustomed to the uniformity of house facades, customary opposites, habitual behaviours, social and political processes, when there is nothing else or this is the main thing observed on a daily basis ...The only artistic reaction that probably remains is the attempt to understand the insidiously narcotic effects of such endless lines of uniformity ...or, to put it in general terms, to accept perspectives that get lost in nothingness as a new, peculiar kind of aesthetic value. Who knows if this gentle, befuddling poison, imbibed as decoctions from a mechanized, industrialized, computerized world, isn't suited to being used as a modern artistic means geared to coping with existence by means of corresponding puzzles of the imagination.[31]

Dibelius here argues similarly to Adorno to protect Minimal Music from cultural-critical damnation, as initiated by him. In doing so, he overlooks the fact that the "overflowing abundance of fantasy and the wealth of natural forms" are themselves the result of repetitive processes (such as cell division and DNA reproduction). Further, he mistakenly declares Minimalist repetitive processes to be a kind of parody of the mechanisms of contemporary technical culture. His argumentation is reminiscent of Henri Bergson and his essay on laughter, according to which grotesque comedy comes into being when organic life (or art and music) are repeated like a machine. Yet for Roehr and other Minimal Artists of the 1960s, it was about an autonomy of experience. This is the desire that artistic and musical minimalism and psychedelia have in common.

American minimalists have often been accused of putting an artistic mantle around modern mass production. Jutta Held, for example, argues that the resemblance of minimalist sculptures to terraced houses, freezers or washing machines from the 1950s and 60s is not coincidental, and that they also reproduce the structures and ideology of capitalist mass society.[32] Roehr and his arrangements of advertising photos, mark pieces and beer mats would probably have been similarly criticized had his work received critical acclaim during his lifetime. But they are neither that, nor a parody of modern industrial society's mechanisms in Dibelius' sense.

The repetitions of Minimal Art and Minimal Music, similarly, are not repetitions in the tradition of European modernism, nor the agonizing repetitions of Beckett and his "I can't go on. I'll go on". Nor yet are they parodic assembly line repetitions, like Chaplin's *Modern Times*, in which horror of the monotonous world of machines is comically expressed. Rather, they remind of the concise and strictly descriptive repetitions of Gertrude Stein. Especially in the USA, the method of repetition seems to have been a way of distancing oneself from the suffering of a monotonous world, as well as from the existentialism of European art.[33]

When the artists of the 1960s, who will be the subject of subsequent chapters, used repetition techniques like the loop, they neither adopted them unquestioningly, nor did they implement them in order to criticize them. They used them to produce objects that would transfer the "meaning" of a work of art to the realm of perception, and repetition was an important element of this strategy.

Two schools of thought played a more important role in this development in the USA than high-profile "sixties philosophers", such as Herbert Marcuse, Marshall McLuhan and Buckmister Fuller – the phenomenology of French philosopher Maurice Merleau-Ponty and the Gestalt therapy of German psychotherapist Friedrich Perls.

Phenomenology had become known in the USA through the books of Maurice Merleau-Ponty, whose writings first appeared in English translation in the 1960s. Anja Osswald even refers to phenomenology as the "go-to philosophy of Minimalism".[34] The reception of Friedrich Perls' Gestalt psychology can be gleaned from the work of a number of post-minimalist artists, such as Bruce Nauman and Dan Graham. But it is Perls' work that was particularly important to the American psychedelic movement. Perls' approach to promoting awareness, the consciousness of being in the here and now achieved through therapeutic methods, influenced the tape experiments of Ken Kesey, who will be the subject of a later chapter.

In her book *Chronophobia*, American art historian Pamela M. Lee provides an interesting account of the obsession with time, its slowing down and eventual arrest in the culture of the 1960s.[35] Her approach can help to understand the propensity of minimalist art and music, as well as of psychedelic culture, to obsess about time. For Lee, the visual arts of the 1960s are characterized by "chronophobia" – that is, a pathological fear of time and its passing. While I don't agree with the view that fear of the passage of time is encapsulated in the art of this period, it undoubtedly does play an important role in 1960s art. It explains not only the emergence of certain new art forms, such as Happening and Performance Art, kinetic art, process art and systems art, but also the increasing use of audio-visual and time-based media, like film, video and tape.

In her focus on the visual arts, Lee overlooks the fact that in music of the 1960s, the passing of time also became a focus for contemporary composers. In contrast to painting and sculpture, music has, of course, always been a more "time-specific" art form; the well-known dictum from Lessing's *Laocoon* ("It remains true that the passing of time is the territory of the poet, just as space is the territory of the painter"[36]) applies especially to music. But in Minimal Music of the 1960s, the passing of time is emphatically foregrounded; indeed, it becomes the object.

Where does this sudden fascination with time come from? Pamela Lee sees one reason in the enormous technological progress of this epoch. In Europe and North America, the transition from an industrial to a post-industrial information society began in the 1960s. New communication technologies, which enabled the accelerated transmission and processing of data, form the backdrop against which artists increasingly dealt with time as an object.

One reason why tape loops became so popular in the 1960s is undoubtedly the fact that the scientific breakthroughs that had resulted from accelerated research during the Second World

War had by then emerged as products for the mass market – tape recorders, and, later, video recorders, for example. In the 1960s, tape recorders had gone from being expensive high-tech equipment to products for the mass market and the same happened in the 1970s and 1980s with video recorders. These items were no longer found only in the studios of radio stations and production companies but were offered in department stores and electronics stores. Paul McCartney explicitly pointed out that one reason for the creation of the composition *Tomorrow Never Knows* was that The Beatles had bought their own portable tape recorders and were able to experiment with tape loops at home.

The fascination with media was generally a more important element of 1960s pop culture than it may seem today. Experimenting with media was a central element for American hippies in particular. In an interview in the early 1990s, Timothy Leary, one of the voices of America's 1960s counterculture, underlines the connection between the new media and alternative culture: "Once there was modern technology that could produce psychedelic drugs for a mass market and electronic amplification for the recording and playback of sound, these things were historically pretty much inevitable, I think."[37]

Leary seems to allude mainly to the psychedelic rock music of the 1960s. In fact, electronically amplified music – such as that of Jimi Hendrix or the Grateful Dead, Tangerine Dream and Amon Düül – dominates our image of this decade today, as do major music festivals, like Monterey and Woodstock. And even after the hippie movement temporarily withdrew from the big cities and founded rural communities, it was not as technophobic as it may appear today.

The use of media in the 1960s focused on appropriation and on self-empowerment, and the potential of the new medium of video for political activism was quickly recognized by the American counterculture of that time. Collectives like Videofreex or Raindance sought to use video as a catalyst for social change and to make it the central tool of an alternative media culture. Computers and synthesizers, likewise, were quickly discovered and tried out by the hippie generation. The synthesizer was to play an important role in European progressive rock of the late 1960s and early 70s, while subcultural groups like the "Homebrew Computer Club" saw the PC as a tool to be developed for creativity and to enhance individual talent, having until then only been available to a small elite of scientists and industrial staff.

What is more, the fascination with new media was not limited to pop culture. In 'high-brow' art, artists of renown also began to experiment with technology and media. The technological installations and performances produced by Robert Rauschenberg, John Cage, Nam June Paik and Merce Cunningham with the aid of engineer Billy Klüver and the organization "Experiments in Arts and Technology" (EAT) led to a real boom in collaborations between technicians and artists during the second half of the 1960s, especially in the USA.[38] It can certainly be argued that these media experiments were in many ways more characteristic of the art of that time than the panel paintings of Warhol, John or Richter, which shape the perception of that time today.[39]

But the 1960s, when such often naively technophile works were created, were also a time when the euphoria of progress that is expressed in them was critiqued. The writings of Herbert Marcuse, Jacques Ellul, Günther Anders, Theodore Roszak, Theodor W. Adorno and Max Horkheimer – to mention just a few of the much-read thinkers of that era – paint a deeply ambivalent picture of progress, and of the future. Their pessimism about – depending on the terminology used – "late capitalism", the "managed world", "advanced industrial society" or "technocratic society" shaped the student revolts in the USA and Western Europe in the late 1960s.

At the same time, the rise of postmodernism makes this an epoch when an intellectual line of thought emerges which no longer regards history as linear or progressive. With it, the topos of the "end of history" arises, or rather, of a history without end. If postmodernism is understood along the lines of Frederic Jameson as an "ultimate and extreme contamination of our social, historical and existential present, which takes the past as its 'referent'",[40] then it coincides with American literary scholar Nic Bromell's description of the 1960s as the beginning of a kind of eternal present – "whatever else the 60s were...they were also a concentration of cultural energies upon the consequences of growing up in an age when the fatigue of metaphors has become obvious, when the idea of change has collapsed into the idea of continuity, and when narratives about the past, present and future must find a way to think of these as something other than a sequence".[41]

Today we are accustomed to viewing the 1960s as an epoch of supposed or actual revolutions – "cultural revolution", "student revolution", "sexual revolution", "women's revolution". Revolution means the sudden overthrow of a historical situation, a sudden change. What Bromell outlines contradicts the picture that the protagonists of the 1960s painted of this decade as an epoch of progressive change. Artistic practices like Pop Art, Minimal Art and Minimal Music deal with the fact that the concept of revolution, and with it, the notion of time as something that progresses teleologically with an inner consistency towards a specific goal, had become tired. Even if hippies and radical students may have seen themselves as agents of inevitable, revolutionary upheaval, from a historical perspective, the changes that the 1960s brought about seem far less revolutionary and sudden than they may have seemed to be at the time. Today, the inflationary use of the word "revolution" seems more like a final rebellion of modernist rhetoric than an apt description of the innovations that the 1960s brought. It is one of the contradictions of this epoch that, on the one hand, left-wing students and cultural revolutionaries preached ground-breaking progress, while on the other, time is slowed down and stopped in art and music.

Minimal Art was the first art movement in which time and temporality became the dominant theme. It expresses the idea of stopping time, of ending history. Minimalism subjects music, sculpture and painting to the primacy of temporality by arranging pictures, materials and sounds into sequences and series. American art critic Michel Fried astutely pinpoints the temporal quality of repetitive art and its consequences – if only to turn it into an argument against the art movement. In his much-cited essay *Art and Objecthood*[42], he argues – in line with Clement Greenberg, who had formulated a similar critique of minimalism – that the emphasis on temporality gives these works a kind of "stage presence". Minimalist art was to be circumnavigated and viewed from different perspectives. Fried therefore recapitulates Lessing's previously quoted dictum (which, however, he does not explicitly mention) that works of art which are to be experienced in time are more closely related to literature than to art.[43]

American art historian Hal Forster points out that the series and sequences of Minimal Art, which Fried dismisses as time-bound and therefore contrary to the intrinsic nature of visual art, require different forms of perception. Because minimalist works of art, due to their repetitive and spatially expansive forms, "are constantly redefined by our temporal perception, they are thrown back on themselves and works become complex as a result of this...Through this change, the viewer, who is denied the safe space of formal art, is thrown back into the here and now."[44]

Just as the mysterious monolith in Stanley Kubrick's *2001* triggers an evolutionary leap because its enigmatic, unexplained existence compels reflection, so the cubes and rectangles of Minimal Art demand to be experienced and to have meaning ascribed to them by the viewer. The point of contact between minimalism and phenomenology is the fact that Minimal Art, by presenting meaningless sequences of blocks and other "primary" structures, induces viewers to make themselves the subject of their experience of the world, instead of presenting them with an interpretation of the world.

Phenomenology, as developed by Edmund Husserl at the beginning of the twentieth century, wants to adhere to what is immediate to consciousness when observing critically, to "the things themselves", as Husserl's well-known formula puts it. From a phenomenological perspective, to recognize the true nature of an object, one must put any foregoing theory to one side. Only when all assumptions and all (pre-)judgements are suspended does the world appear in its actual structures. In Merleau-Ponty's development of this approach, meaning results directly from the act of perception. This idea is in line with minimalism and the art of Peter Roehr. For Merleau-Ponty, subject and object are not opposites, rather, they exist in a dynamic relationship of tension. The object exists only through the perceiving subject, which in turn is constituted by the perception of things. Merleau-Ponty therefore contradicts a basic maxim of Western rationalism – Descartes' "I think, therefore I am." In phenomenology, there is no autonomous intellect. The subject emerges through the confrontation with the world of objects. Minimalist art is therefore always also a critique of Western rationalism, which regards the cognitive mind as independent from the phenomena it experiences. In many respects, the minimalists' perceptual experiments (and the drug and media experiments of the hippies) seem like a handson version of Merleau-Ponty's "corporeal thinking". Their activities can be understood as experimental investigations of the "physical" conditions of perception. Minimal Art achieved this through simple geometric primary structures and their placement and repetition in space, which refer the perceivers back to themselves and their perceptions. Through tape echoes, drugs like LSD and dance marathons with loud music and repetitive light effects, the psychedelic movement also impacted on perception, which was at the heart of Merleau-Ponty's phenomenology. If the body is our connection to the world, then one could override its activities by influencing the body with all available means to enable moments of heightened perception.

The desire to break with the conventions of perception in order to arrive at a "truer experience" is therefore shared by Minimal Art and psychedelia. The contrast between the two movements lies in the methods they use to try to achieve moments of pure being. Diedrich Diederichsen notes, "the key difference between the epistemological ideas of Husserl's phenomenology...and the drug practice of beatniks, hippies and other counter-cultural movements is that the one consists of the controlled, theoretical components of a philosophical system, and the other of events that are usually overwhelming, and which occur by chance. What they have in common, however, is that they construct an experimental arrangement which claims to be able to determine, or to have experienced the essence of an object beyond its everyday function..."[45]

Stoic, pedantic repetition of the ever-same in Minimal Art on the one hand, drug intoxication and dance excesses on the other – the one is as Apollonian in approach as the other is Dionysian. Both, however, aim to enable experiences beyond normalized everyday perception. The two developed in parallel, and their points of contact are cursory. Yet there are also too many of these to be mere historical coincidence or the product of a vague "zeitgeist" of the 1960s.

Over the following 2 decades, pop music was to develop styles that were characterized by the use of media loops – Krautrock and electronic varieties of Disco, dub and Hip-hop in the 1970s; electronic body music, Electro and Industrial in the 1980s; rave, house and Techno in the 1990s. Not forgetting dubstep and the numerous varieties of electronic dance music of the present. Many of the musicians and producers who developed these genres were not aware of the minimalism of the 1960s and certainly didn't know about Peter Roehr and his media experiments, which subjected sound and moving images to the order of strict sequences.

Others, however, do consider themselves to be influenced by artistic minimalism. Richie Hawtin, one of the leading Techno producers and DJs of the present day, says in an interview:

a lot of what I do is influenced by other art styles, for instance, by the minimalists of the 1950s and 60s...Minimalist artworks are often composed of a collection of smaller elements – if you allow yourself to enter into them, the sum of these individual parts is much greater: you notice what they have left out. I use these visual ideas and apply them to sound.[46]

The play with repetition and minimal difference and the phenomenological effects of Minimal Art have become defining elements of Techno aesthetics.

In the final year of his life, Peter Roehr tried to bridge the gap between his art and 1960s pop culture. Early in 1968, together with Paul Maenz, he opened the first Headshop in Frankfurt. "Pudding Explosion" sold hippie posters, pins and underground magazines. Maenz later wrote that the shop on Frankfurt's *Holzgraben* was "a combination of improvised corrugated cardboard architecture, flickering light bulbs and loud rock music that was as colourful as it was rugged, as was legitimately possible only in those days. For nearly two years, there was something like a small, radical underground that did not fit into any existing scheme."[47]

The flickering light bulbs and the loud rock music may only have been "legitimate" in the late 1960s. What it did not represent, however, was an attempt to create a situation which does not fit into any "existing scheme" on account of making authentic experience possible. Rather, it was intended as a unifying project of all the most radical art forms of the 1960s. In contrast to the pre-war avant-garde, the art of this era no longer wanted to open the viewer to new experiences through a clash of incongruent opposites. Rather, it made use of repetition and stasis, of reproduction and inactivity. Or, as Roehr himself called it, of the "precise, unpretentious and simple" sequence.

Unfortunately, he did not live to see the mass-cultural triumph of this method. However, his paintings and film montages show that he was one of the first artists to understand the aesthetic power of media repetition. In the second part of the book, some of the characters who made this method into a (pop-) cultural phenomenon and aesthetic tool will be examined.

"ZENNISH? THAT'S A GOOD WORD!" LA MONTE YOUNG, ANDY WARHOL AND THE SUSPENSION OF TIME

Andy Warhol looks a scream, hang him on my wall
Andy Warhol, silver screen, can't tell them apart at all.

David Bowie

The 'Lecture on Nothing' was written with the same rhythmic structure that I used in my musical compositions at that time... One of the structural means was the repetition, fourteen times, of a single page in which the chorus occurred: Jeanne Reynal, as I remember, stood up at some point in the middle of it, screaming and saying as I continued speaking, "John, I love you very much, but I can't take this for another minute. Then she went out.1

John Cage

In the autumn of 1964, a remarkable collaboration took place in New York between two artists who at first glance seem to have little in common: artist Andy Warhol and composer La Monte Young. At the New York Film Festival, they mounted a joint installation – an awkward arrangement, because Warhol had not been invited to the festival's actual film programme and had to make do with a place in the foyer.[2] Yet Warhol managed to turn the situation to his advantage. He made use of four Fairchild 400 projectors, which had newly arrived on the market and which could project 8-millimetre film cassettes onto a display no larger than a television screen. He showed short excerpts from his films *Eat, Sleep, Kiss* and *Haircut* on these four rear projectors as a loop.[3]

Warhol's films from this period don't have a plot in the conventional sense. They merely show what their titles declare – a haircut, a couple kissing, a man sleeping, and artist Robert Indiana eating a mushroom. The original versions last between half an hour and several hours, while the cinematographic endurance test *Empire*, which shows nothing but the Empire State Building at night, goes on for 8 hours. On the Fairchild projectors monitor, the films could be viewed as panels.

By reducing their length to 3 minutes, the last bit of action that these largely improvised films might once have had has been removed. A press release of the festival states that "according to the artist's own definition, Warhol's film quartet is 'never-ending'".[4] The fact that Warhol showed the films as endless loops was, however, due to the exhibition situation and the technology; the Fairchild 400 worked with closed cartridges containing loops of film.

These cinematic exercises in interminability were accompanied by La Monte Young's minimalist piece *Composition 1960 # 9*, which perfectly complemented the suspended animation of Warhol's kissers and sleepers. The famous "score" of this composition merely consists of a straight line on a piece of paper. La Monte Young and his wife Marian Zazeela interpreted it by continuously stroking a brass mortar with a violin bow for the collaboration with Warhol, which produced a seemingly "infinite" tone. The piece was played on four tape machines simultaneously and at a deafening volume. This installation, shown in the lobby of a concert hall, thundered throughout the Lincoln Center. After a short time, the festival management ordered La Monte Young to turn down the volume. Young withdrew entirely from the event.

La Monte Young and Andy Warhol were a strange pair. On the one hand, there was the artist-entrepreneur and pop-art icon Warhol, who pursued art as mass production, and for whom virtually any means were justified to popularize his work. On the other hand, there was the difficult and solitary La Monte Young, who today is considered the founder of musical Minimalism, but whose work is primarily known as a kind of legend – beyond rare live performances and museum installations, almost none of his music is heard today while published recordings of his music, at times consisting of only two or three sustained notes, likewise are very scarce. This may be partly due to the fact that their physical impact cannot really be reproduced on media such as LPs or CDs, but may also be due to the fact that Young himself was reluctant to let others take control of his music.

As much as popularity was a central aspect of Warhol's artistic project, La Monte Young appeared as the recluse of contemporary avant-garde music. His decision to withdraw from the collaboration with Warhol is typical of his career – the composer preferred to forego an opportunity to perform his work to a wider public to being obliged to make artistic compromises. His reputation is therefore above all based on his being the founder of musical Minimalism, and, of course, on the influence he exerted on rock groups like Velvet Underground, Suicide, Sonic Youth or Sunn O))).

The principle of repetition is central to Andy Warhol's work. That's why it was logical for him to develop an interest in loops in his cinematic work, like those he showed at the New York Film Festival. But in fact, apart from the installation at the Lincoln Center, he only used loops on one other occasion – *Sleep* (1963), one of his most famous or infamous films.

Why didn't Warhol make more use of the repetition methods he used in his paintings in his work with video and film, when the technical capabilities of film readily suggested such possibilities? Most of his experimental films from the 1960s are simply recordings of reality in real time, which appears as unfiltered and unprocessed as possible. In the 1960s, film montage played virtually no role in Warhol's film-making style. Nevertheless, I will discuss Warhol's few experiments with film loops in detail, because they enable interesting new interpretations of some aspects of his work. At the same time, I will discuss the often overlooked influence that minimal music, like that of La Monte Young, had on Warhol's work.

Both Warhol and Young developed an aesthetic of monotony. Their interest in stasis and idling prompted their experiments with repetition and loops for a short while, but neither of them pursued this technique further. Warhol worked with loops for the installation at the Lincoln Center and also in *Sleep*, but thereafter, only used repetitive structures in his paintings. Similarly, there are only two short compositions by La Monte Young that consist of repetitive patterns. He did not continue to use this compositional technique and left its further development to others. This music, based on repeating patterns, is what is commonly regarded as Minimal Music today.

Considering Warhol's documented interest in Minimal Music, he no longer appears solely as the ironic critic of media society/late capitalism/commodity fetishism, as he is often portrayed to be. Suddenly, his work seems to be about different views of the world. Seen from this perspective, an interest in perceptions that differ from the conventionalized experiences of everyday life is suggested, and in this respect, Warhol's project resembles that of La Monte Young and his ensemble Theatre of Eternal Music. Unlike Young, however, Andy Warhol was not concerned with a kind of ecstatic immersion; on the contrary, he aimed to keep phenomena at a distance and to enable an abstracted, distanced view of them.

The fact that the collaboration between Andy Warhol and La Monte Young was possible at all seems to be an important key to understanding the work of both. While the work of Andy Warhol is well-known today, the work and person of La Monte Young have remained shrouded in mystery. Before examining his collaboration with Warhol further, the section that follows will therefore offer a short biography of the composer, whom Brian Eno has described as "the daddy of us all".

My own first experience with La Monte Young's music was in 2004 during a visit to his *Dream House* in New York. This occupies a floor of a residential building on Church Street in Soho and is open to the public from Thursday to Sunday, two o'clock in the afternoon until midnight. The building also houses the private apartment of La Monte Young and his wife, the light artist Marian Zazeela, with whom he has worked since 1962.[5]

The *Dream House* presents a kind of uninterrupted concert. La Monte Young says about its creation that:

> I developed the idea of a place where music could be made non-stop. I had just composed *Four Dreams of China*, [which...] combines the long notes from the *Trio for Strings* with group improvisation. And I thought that if you had a piece that can potentially go on and on, it would also be nice to have a *place* where the music can go on and on.[6]

This idea initially resulted in discrete installations, and eventually in a permanent version that took up an entire house on Harrison Street in New York. However, this version of the *Dream House* was closed in 1985 when the Dia Art Foundation, which had been supporting the project, ran into financial difficulties. Young and Zazeela have had a smaller version of the *Dream House* underneath their own apartment, a "Dream Apartment", so to speak, since 1992.

As soon as you climb the stairs to this *Dream House* on the second floor of the typical New York tenement building, you hear a buzzing sound that gets louder and louder and which makes you think of an engine room or a generator. After one of Young's elevators have let you in (please take off your shoes!), you find yourself standing in a large loft, where two rooms are connected by a narrow corridor. These rooms are almost empty. There are some cushions lying on the floor; in one corner there is a portrait of Indian raga singer Pandit Pran Nath, with whom Young studied in the 1970s, and with whom he recorded a series of records featuring traditional ragas. Incense burns in front of the picture; the smell permeates the whole room. Magenta-coloured foils are stuck to the windowpanes, which bathe the rooms in a reddish light, darkened further to an iridescent violet by the blue and purple lights inside. In each corner of the larger room there is a large black amplifier that fills everything with a continuous, humming vibration that is reminiscent of the roar of a wind tunnel.

This sound represents the actual interior of the *Dream House*. There are 32 different sinusoidal frequencies, played simultaneously and without interruption by a synthesizer.[7] While the sound objectively remains the same, the impression gained by the listener can change dramatically with the slightest movement. The frequencies are selected according to complicated mathematical principles, in such a way that both the overall sound and the overtones that result from the concurrence of the different tones are heard differently, practically everywhere in the room.

The music appears constant and steady only as long as you stand completely still. Like a jackhammer, a deep roar is throbbing in the sound spectrum at the very bottom of the scale, overlapping and forming complex rhythms. The sound is densest in the middle of the room, while high, shrill, whistling frequencies dominate around the walls. This sonic mass is the principal impression in the room. Sound rarely has such a physical, object-like presence as it does in the *Dream House*. While Marian Zazeela's light installation makes the physical space seem ethereal and intangible, the sound appears like a concrete, massive thing that can be experienced by the listener in a quasi-tactile way. Gently moving the head back and forth makes the different frequencies modulate each other, and thus hypnotic melodies are created in the listener's head by simply nodding.

The title *Dream House* is actually misleading because it suggests that the composition/installation transports the listener into dream worlds. But in fact, this experience of sound does not make him absent-minded or sleepy. Rather, the visitor to the *Dream House* soon finds him/herself in a state of heightened, intensified perception, because attention increases with the attempt to listen to the smallest variation in the initially seemingly completely monotonous, electronic sound monument.

Similar to Terry Riley's Time Lag Generator, which will be the subject of the following chapter, here, too, it is the audience who complete the work in a very physical sense. The sound that surrounds the visitor only becomes music in the ear and body of the listener. What is heard is a completely unique experience, which varies from one perceiving subject to another.

No matter how close two people are standing or sitting next to each other in the *Dream House*, they do not hear the same thing.

Like Riley's Time Lag Generator or Ken Kesey's tape echoes, like the sculptures of Minimal Art and, in some ways, like Andy Warhol's Pop Art series, the *Dream House* throws audiences back on their own perception. Young's music almost seems like a demonstration of the central ideas of Maurice Merleau-Ponty's phenomenology.

The spatially contingent composition illustrates the idea of a subject that only ever constitutes itself in the act of perception.[8] The *Dream House* is an attack on Cartesian body-mind-soul dualism, since it demonstrates that Descartes' separation of body and mind cannot be maintained. In the *Dream House*, the body is not simply a transmitter of sensory impressions. It also listens; it is an integral part of the acoustic experience.

Drones, long notes that may be sustained for hours, have been at the centre of La Monte Young's work since the early 1960s (he was born in 1935). In biographical accounts, much is made of the fact that he lived in a wooden hut in Oregon as a child and is said to have listened to the sounds of nature undisturbed there. The whistling of the wind in the roof truss, the chirping of crickets and eventually, the humming of power lines are said to have been formative influences.[9]

His time in the Los Angeles jazz scene in the 1950s, where he played saxophone with Eric Dolphy, Ornette Coleman and Don Cherry among others, seems to have been at least as important, however. The first signs of a Minimalist aesthetic become apparent in the three compositions *For Brass* (1957), *For Guitar* (1958) and *Trio for Strings* (1958), which he wrote as a music student. They consist of long, static tones without any rhythmic invigoration or traditional melody.

Young therefore made a compositional technique out of a practice that exists in many types of folk music. Traditional instruments like the hurdy-gurdy, the bagpipes, the Australian didgeridoo and the Indian tambura enable the playing of a single, long-lasting tone or the accompaniment of a melody with a static key note. In Western church music, such long- lasting notes also exist in Organum, which was developed in the twelfth century.[10] After that, however, they rarely appear in European art music. Barring exceptions like the pastorales in George Frideric Handel's *Messiah* (1741) and *Pastorales* by Ludwig van Beethoven (1808), it is striking that they usually serve to represent rural idylls – another kind of dream music.[11]

After initially performing as a member and organizer of the Fluxis Group in New York from 1960 onwards, Young turned his attention entirely back to music.[12] In group improvisations with the group Theatre of Eternal Music, he turned drones into his own musical style. That said, there are contradictory accounts of the contribution the various members of the ensemble made to the development of this style, and the conflict over the copyright of their music continues to this day. Fellow musician Tony Conrad claims to have contributed the mathematical principles by which the pitches of the individual long-lasting tones were determined, as well as the electronic amplification of the instruments. John Cale, subsequently viola player for Velvet Underground, writes about his time in La Monte Young's ensemble in his autobiography *What's Welsh for Zen*:

> the members of Dream Syndicate were fascinated by sound, both scientifically and mystically, and spent hours of rehearsals learning how to perform long-lasting, meditative drones and chants. Their rigorous style kept me disciplined...I also learned to amplify my viola electrically, which was to lead to the strong drone effect that is so pronounced on the first two Velvet Underground albums. That came about because Tony [Conrad] brought an electronic pickup with him one day that could be plugged into the guitar...Tony plugged it into his violin and I plugged it into my viola, and we had a mixer, and it made a din that sounded like an airplane jet.[13]

At that time, La Monte Young was still improvising on the saxophone, until it was agreed that it would be more interesting musically if all the musicians would play individual notes for a long time. The intervals that the members of Theatre of Eternal Music finally agreed on were thirds and sevenths. "That was the system we eventually came up with," writes Cale. "It took one-and-a-half years. But to this day, [La Monte Young] refuses to acknowledge our contribution."[14]

From 1966, Young's wife, Marian Zazeela, had been bathing the concerts of the group, of which she was also a member, in coloured light. Their performances, often lasting all night long, were the forerunner of the multimedia installations, as well as environments that Young and Zazeela showed at various exhibitions. However, their concerts and installations are not intended to question the conventions of the traditional concert. Above all, they are an attempt to increase the perception of the music. The extended duration alone represents a special physical experience. And the perception of tiny nuances, which is at the heart of Young's music, makes the experience of listening intensely physical.

In an article, John Perreault, a former art critic for *Village Voice*, describes a performance by La Monte Young on 22 February 1968 as an intense physical challenge. He says, "at first it seemed too dangerous even to enter the auditorium, because the sound was already painfully loud through the closed doors. When you did enter, it was almost as if a torrent of hot wind was blowing in your face, or as if you were entering a room full of brine, only to discover that you could still breathe surprisingly well…It was like hearing a little piece of eternity…"[15]

The embedding of music in performance situations which involved other senses besides hearing seems to have been in the air at the time. There is little doubt that Zazeela and Young had begun to transform concerts into situations that could be experienced with all the senses before Andy Warhol let his multimedia spectacle *The Exploding Plastic Inevitable*, with the drone-inspired music of Velvet Underground in 1964, off the leash, and before John Lennon and Young's former Fluxus ally Yoko Ono's Plastic Ono Band frightened the audience with similar attacks of long-lasting, barely modulated noise. The desire to turn a concert into a potentially life-changing experience for all the senses also connects the Theatre of Eternal Music with the raves and dance parties that were to come after them: the Acid Tests of the Merry Pranksters in the 1960s, which will be discussed in one of the following chapters, and also the raves, Maydays and other contemporary Techno parties.

The ensemble name Theatre of Eternal Music describes Young's method of composition to this day; almost all of his works tend to have no end. (Even his comparatively conventional piano composition *The Well-Tuned Piano* grew longer and longer from one of its rare performances to the next). In this sense, he can be considered the founder of Minimalism, even though he wrote hardly any compositions that correspond to the contemporary idea of Minimalism as a music with constantly repeating structures.

While La Monte Young's work is primarily characterized by drones and long, hardly varied notes, two of his compositions from the early 1960s do anticipate the repetitive Minimal Music which Terry Riley, Steve Reich and Philip Glass were to pioneer. The first is *[X] for Henry Flynt* (and later, *Arabic Numerals (Any Integer) for Henry Flynt* as well), in 1960. Henry Flynt was an artist friend of Young's who was known for his radical approach to art, and who is regarded as the creator of the term "conceptual art". The composition consists of the instruction to repeat a loud, heavy tone every 1 to 2 seconds, as often and as regularly as possible; the "X" in the title stands for the number of repetitions that the performer plans to make. Frequently, this sound simply consists of clusters played on a piano, with the performer pressing down as many keys as possible, using the arms. Other versions have been performed with a spoon on a frying pan or with a drum beater on a gong placed on the floor. A radical version of this composition is *1698*, where the title indicates how many times Young struck a dissonant chord on the piano – 1698 times, to be precise, with the performance lasting just under an hour.

In this piece, basic ideas of minimalist playing with repetitions and loops are already present. It anticipates the seemingly endless stringing together of a repetitive structure on the one hand, while on the other, the inevitable deviations of interpretation of the ever-same sound introduce minimal variation. Composer Cornelius Cardew, who performed the piece, notes that, "the listener can hear and appreciate errors in the interpretation. If the piece were performed by a machine, this interest would disappear and with it the whole composition."[16]

Not long after, Terry Riley was to demonstrate that machines could also do the job of producing "errors" with his first tape compositions, which can turn listening to repetitive structures into interesting acoustic experiences. Large parts of electronic dance music still consist of slightly modified variations of a more or less constant same. They are designed to trigger precisely the perceptual processes and experiences that *[X] for Henry Flynt* was aiming at. Through repetition, it is possible to notice tonal details and minimal differences that would otherwise remain hidden. In the process of following different elements as they move into the foreground and recede into the background, perception shifts incessantly, making the sound seem to transform itself.

Brian Eno, who performed the piece *[X] for Henry Flynt*,[17] describes the physical effects which playing has on the performer.

It sounds horrible I know, but if you last ten minutes it gets very interesting. My first performance of it lasted an hour and the second one an hour and a half. It's one of those hallucinatory pieces where your brain starts to habituate so that you cease to hear all the common notes, you just hear the differences from crash to crash, and these become so beautiful. They're just entrancing…just missing one note out of the fifty or so you're covering is a very noticeable difference, you really can hear that. You start to hear these omissions as melodies…Since I had the sustain pedal down as well it was just a continuous ring and eventually the whole piano was just really resonating and the richness of the sound was just amazing. After a little while you start to hear every type of sound, it's the closest thing in music to a drug experience I've heard. You hear trumpets and bells and people talking clear words…It's like the opposite of sensory deprivation, but it's the same effect. You start to hallucinate, because you telescope in on finer and finer details, like for instance the acoustics of the room become very, very obvious to you. You notice that one note always echoes off that wall…And you can hear interplays like that in space as well, which of course are facts that in a normal performance you wouldn't be aware of, since things are going by so quickly and they don't repeat.[18]

[X] for Henry Flynt therefore represents a quintessential source of the Minimalist Music style, one of strictly repeated elements.

Another composition by La Monte Young from the same period is much less well-known. It anticipates the repetitions and permutations of musical cells as they are known from the later compositions of Steve Reich and Philip Glass – *Death Chant* (1961), a piece Young wrote for friends whose child had died. This composition for male voice is to be accompanied by glockenspiel or carillon and consists of short cells, similar to Glass' later compositions. Initially there are only two notes, to which further notes are added as the piece progresses. The instructions provided with the composition read, "to be repeated for a very long time, or *ad infinitum*". This is the template for what is usually understood by Minimal Music today: Short, minimally varied motifs that are repeated very often. Or *ad infinitum*.

But Young did not pursue this method of repetitive patterns. His friend Terry Riley's experiments with tape loops also had no influence on his work. From the late 1960s, he did begin to work with sine wave generators, and later on with synthesizers, using technically generated repetitions – if not in the form of loops, then at least in the form of pure vibrations. These experiments ultimately led to the *Dream House* sound installation.

Today, Minimal Music is understood as music with modular repetitions, or repetitive patterns. La Monte Young's drones are far less well-known. But at the beginning of the 1960s, they shaped the intellectual space in which the music that is now known as Minimal Music would develop. Young formulated his programme succinctly as "no theme, no development, no variations, no contrasts, just an interest in time and relationships between pitches".[19] His interest in time and how to halt it was shared by Andy Warhol, whose loop installation at the Lincoln Center he came to accompany.

The New York art scene of the early 1960s was smaller and more easily surveyed than might appear in retrospect. Artists, later to be sorted into different categories, cooperated with each other across genre boundaries. "Everyone in the Downtown Lower East Side scene was connected through their work and their lovers," John Cale recalls in his autobiography a quarter of a century later. "It was a great web of networks grouped around such figures as La Monte, Andy Warhol, Allen Ginsberg, Robert Rauschenberg and Ed Sanders."[20]

An example of this joyous muddle is a band which artist Claes Oldenburg was in the process of forming at the beginning of 1963, and where Andy Warhol and La Monte Young apparently first met. The band's line-up seems extraordinary today. It consisted almost exclusively of artists who would later become international stars of the art market. Besides Young (saxophone) and Warhol (choral singing), it included Larry Poons (guitar), Walter de Maria (drums) and Patti Oldenburg (vocals); Jasper Johns was to write lyrics for the group.

But it did not go beyond a few rehearsals. It established the initial connection between Warhol and La Monte Young, which was to be refreshed again and again, finally to result in their joint installation at the Lincoln Center. When the work of Young and Warhol is viewed from this perspective, a number of astonishing parallels emerge between the two artists, which do not fit into any simplistic contrast of Warhol, the successful pop artist with high-fashion ambitions on the one hand, and Young, the original and stubborn composer-hermit from the Lower East Side on the other. And it is not only the structural similarities between Young's and Warhol's work that are more striking than might at first appear. The list of joint collaborators is also longer than one would expect.

I have previously mentioned the fact that viola player and composer John Cale was a member of the Theatre of Eternal Music before co-founding the influential band Velvet Underground. "Andy Warhol's Velvet Underground", as the band was called on its first record, featured the famous banana cover designed by Warhol and quickly became his Atelier Factory's house band, as well as the focus of his multimedia spectacle *The Exploding Plastic Inevitable*. In the process, Cale popularized drones, which he had developed with the Theatre of Eternal Music with La Monte Young, Tony Conrad and others, in long solos consisting only of a long, sustained tone on his viola. What is less well- known is that Billy Name had also first made music with La Monte Young before he became the outfitter and in-house photographer for Warhol's Atelier Factory, in whose darkroom he even lived for a while. Warhol had met Billy Linich (his real name) in 1964 at a "haircutting party" in his apartment, when Linich cut his friends' hair. The walls of Linich's apartment were painted silver.

The meeting between Warhol and Name is important for three reasons: firstly, after their brief affair, the two artists began a long-standing collaboration. Secondly, it was the inspiration for Warhol's film *Haircut*, the 3-minute version of which was shown at the film festival in Lincoln Center. But most importantly, Warhol was in the process of moving into the new studio, which would later become known in art history as the Factory. And this 1500 square metre loft was painted completely silver by Billy Name in January 1964. The silver spray paint, which would also play an important role in Warhol's work in the years to come, will be discussed further later. For me, it represents the complementary, visual counterpart to Young's long-held sounds. Aphoristically, one could say that Warhol didn't need loops because he had the silver paint in his aesthetic repertoire, just as La Monte Young didn't need loops because he used drones.

Warhol was closely acquainted with the music of La Monte Young. He was at a concert in New York's Judson Hall in October 1962, where the two 1-hour pieces *Composition 1960 #7* and *Trio for Strings* were performed. The director, Jonas Mekas, who was there with Warhol, is convinced that it was this concert that inspired Warhol to make the film *Sleep*. In his autobiography, John Cale also mentions a Theatre of Eternal Music concert at the home of Henry Geldzahler, then curator of modern art at the New York Metropolitan Museum. "He took the mattress off his loft bed and the four of us sat on it and played this outrageous music. Jackie Kennedy was there, and Andy Warhol too."[21] When in June 1963, Andy Warhol's photo booth pictures of newcomers to the New York art scene were published in *Harper's Bazaar* under the headline "New Faces, New Forces, New Names in the Arts", La Monte Young was also there. The caption quotes John Cage saying that Young "can, either by repeating a single sound or by playing a single sound for 20 minutes, make that which I had thought the same actually appear as full of diversity. I find his work remarkable."[22]

So Warhol was familiar with Young's work, and it was not his only encounter with Minimalist Music. In September 1963, he was present at one of the most important events in twentieth-century avant-garde music – the premiere of Eric Satie's *Vexations*, which John Cage organized at New York's Pocket Theatre. The infamous piece, whose 180 notes were to be repeated 840 times, was performed by Cage and a whole team of performers, including John Cale, who took turns. "The entrance fee was $5," Cale writes in his autobiography, "but the audience got a five-cent discount for every 20 minutes they stayed, and those who held out to the bitter end even got 20 cents back."[23] Even though the event took place in a small and relatively unknown location, the *New York Times* covered the event, with newspaper reporters attending in shifts, like the pianists.

One of the attendees was Andy Warhol, who later referred back to this concert time and again. Journalist George Plimpton, who belonged to Warhol's circle in the 1960s, describes an encounter that took place shortly afterwards.

In the early 1960s, I happened to meet Andy Warhol
and told him that I had read an article about a piano
composition by Erik Satie that lasted only a minute and a
half...but was to be played for 18 hours on the composer's
instructions. I mentioned this to Andy because I thought
it might interest him somehow – after all, he'd made eight-
hour films of people sleeping and that 24-hour film with
the camera pointing at the Empire State Building. It never
occurred to me that he already knew about this concert,
or – bearing in mind his somewhat limited intellectual
parameters – that he had heard of Satie before. His reaction
baffled me. He said, "ohhh, ohhhh, ohhhh!" I had never
seen him so excited. Between the ohhhhs, he told me that he
had actually gone to the concert and had stayed to the end.[24]

According to some reports, Warhol discussed the role of repetition with Cage after the concert, but in an interview in the early 1980s, Cage could not recall this.

> I hadn't realized that Andy was there. But even if he wasn't, it doesn't surprise me that his work followed the same lines. Of course, artists are encouraged by other things that happen, but mostly by what is either in the air or already inside them. Andy has fought by repetition to show us that there is no repetition really, that everything we look at is worthy of our attention. That's been the major direction of the twentieth century, it seems to me.[25]

In another interview, Cage describes the effect that the performance of the piece had on him:

> I slept for an unusually long time, and when I woke up, I felt different than before. My surroundings suddenly seemed unfamiliar, too, although I had lived there for a while. In other words, I had changed and the world had changed...I wasn't the only one to have had this experience, other people who had been there wrote to me or called me to say that they had had the same experience.[26]

Cage describes the performance of *Vexations* as almost a mystical experience. *The world looked different.* Unfortunately, there is no direct testimony from Warhol himself as to what effect his visit to the concert had on him, and whether he was affected by similar changes in perception. But he seemed to be concerned with a comparable effect when he used repetition in his art.

Art historian Rainer Crone describes his serial techniques as a way of applying Brecht's alienation effect to painting. Crone, writing in the 1970s, says that unlike with Cage, the repetition of motifs was not a method of approaching the essence of being, but a form of social criticism. The repetitions and silk screens of motifs from advertising and mass media, always slightly varied due to irregular applications of paint, reproduced "the state of a social system where manipulation for consumption is understood to be the most exalted (current) commodity of the nation, and where ideology has led to the destruction of the personality, the individual."[27]

This view, which still has its followers, sees Warhol's pictures as a disapproval of their subjects. Barbara Rose, who compares Warhol's portraits with those of Goya's Spanish aristocracy, argues in a similar vein. "Warhol's grotesque portraits of his patrons, in which every feature of their empty narcissism is magnified, his grotesquely adorned Marilyn Monroe and tearful Jackie Kennedy will always remain as a scathing indictment of American society in the 1960s, just as Goya's portraits mercilessly scourge the Spanish court."[28]

The fact that Warhol and his serial images can be read both as an invitation to pay attention to things (John Cage) and as a merciless criticism of American society (Rainer Crone, Barbara Rose) speaks for their ambiguity. Or perhaps "indifference" would be a more appropriate term. Warhol's own comments on the choice of his motifs are so ambivalent that they can be understood both as mockery and as naive admiration for his subjects. But if one considers them in the context of Minimalist Music and its programme to show its elements as themselves, without development, final logic or theme, then a third reading seems more plausible. They are neither a critique nor a celebration of their subjects, but a method of adopting an impenetrable, cool attitude towards them, without inner involvement or affinity.

Returning to Satie and his *Vexations*, the peculiarities of the piece may help to understand Warhol's work better. Satie had never actually asked to repeat the composition 840 times. The handwritten instructions on the original manuscript merely state, "if this motif were to be played 840 times in a row, it would be advisable to make advance preparations by assuming a stance of genuine immobility and greatest possible silence". *Genuine immobility* – the programme of Minimalism, and even La Monte Young's electronically amplified, deafening drones, could be described in this way. What this and other variations of Minimalism share with Andy Warhol's paintings is the impulse to bring time to a standstill, to enable attention, which otherwise rushes past unchecked, to be in the here and now. The aesthetic result can be increased perception of reality on the one hand, and its neutralization on the other.

Satie himself emphasized the unobtrusive effect of his repetitive compositions, like *Musique d'ameublement* (Furniture Music). These compositions were intended to resemble the effect of furniture, that is, not to push themselves into the foreground, and they have therefore been described as precursors to contemporary ambient music. Satie's compositions neutralize themselves, so to speak:

> one must try to realize a *Musique d'ameublement*, that is, a type of music that becomes part of the sounds of the environment, which it encompasses. I imagine it being melodious, it should soften the noise of the knives and forks without drowning it out, without imposing itself... At the same time, it should neutralize the street noises that obtrusively enter in.[29]

Satie's fascination with cool neutrality is well documented and ranges from aspects of his work to his own private tics, from the desire to create work that is as "white and pure as antiquity"[30] to the attempt to live exclusively on white food. Warhol expressed similar sentiments in his book *Popism* when he says that "empty, hollow Hollywood was all I ever wanted to live my life by. Plastic. White-on-white".[31] It is characteristic of Warhol's world view that he links Hollywood, *the* metaphor of a mass media phenomenon in the twentieth century, with the void he longs for – for Warhol, it was probably just as important a reference point as antiquity was for Satie.[32] What is the relationship between Young's musical *tabula rasa* and the cool emptiness that characterizes Warhol's pictures from the 1960s? A depiction by Tony Conrad provides a key to the similarities between the two artists. As previously mentioned, the composer, film maker and artist belonged to the Theatre of

Eternal Music in the early 1960s. Former school friends Conrad and Young later fought a decade-long feud over the release of their joint recordings from that time, which went so far that Tony Conrad held one- man demonstrations outside Young's apartment in New York. Yet the description he gives of La Monte Young's musical development seems fair and unaffected by these disputes – they are, barring one crucial detail, identical with other accounts, such as that of John Cale. This crucial detail is the importance which Conrad attaches to Jazz as a major influence on La Monte Young's music. It is true that other publications mention that Young performed in Jazz bands and that some of the techniques he developed originated in the canon of cool Jazz forms of the 1960s. What distinguishes Conrad's presentation from others is that he writes from a musician's perspective and places La Monte Young's Jazz experience in the foreground.

Young "played with Ornette [Coleman], with Don Cherry... and with others as a young saxophonist," writes Conrad in the accompanying book to the CD Early Minimalism. "The black musicians had tried to get him to swing; he didn't want to (or couldn't) and therefore he played cool (like other white jazz musicians of 1950s California). It was typical for him to play even cooler than the others, and to incorporate long, drunken notes into his classical pieces. His early String Trio is a kind of hyper-cool, California modern classical piece. At the time, he prided himself on being slow and cool, and that was a common denominator of our musical taste. We were slow, cool, and (although we both would never admit it to ourselves), nerdy."[33]

Where does this idea of cool Jazz, which has become an important concept not only in African-American culture, come from? The idea behind the term seems to have its origins in the language of the African Yoruba and describes the property of the gods to stand above things.[34] For the Yoruba, *fun fun* – a term that reappears as *cool* in the idiom of the black African-Americans – means a cool, distanced restraint, as well as the ability to face adversity and problems with grace and dignity.

In his book *Blues People,* LeRoi Jones (who later became Amiri Baraka) writes about the meaning of the word "cool" in African-American culture.

> To be cool at the simplest level means to remain calm, even unimpressed by the horrors which confront you in the world every day. As an expression used by blacks, the horrors etc. were the spirit of white America in its mind-numbing predictability. In a certain sense, this quiet or stoic suppression of suffering is as old as the arrival of blacks in slave society, or the slaves' pragmatic acceptance of the gods of their masters. It is perhaps the flexibility of black people that has allowed them to survive; their ability to be cool – that is, calm, unimpressed, distant…In a world that is fundamentally irrational, the most legitimate way to relate to it may be by not to participate…[35]

Jones' account of the "cool" attitude is not very different from the way Warhol liked to present himself in public – as a distanced observer who does not join in. A voyeur. A stargazer who passively follows events around him, instead of actively participating in them. Unconcerned. Without sympathy and without pity. Warhol has also often been described as "calm, unimpressed and distanced". Warhol was not an African- American, but the son of bitterly poor immigrants from Eastern Europe, and he had long felt like an underdog and outsider, especially in the New York art scene, which was dominated by white Anglo-Saxon protestants (WASPs). So his display of coolness may also have been a way of compensating for what he felt to be a social deficit.

For Tony Conrad, it's clear that the cool attitude came to the Factory along with the method for extending time, which had started with the Theatre of Eternal Music. Billy Name, who had been rehearsing with the group for a while, "moved into the Factory and brought with him the legend of cool, long-lasting aesthetics (this fell on fertile ground there and soon appeared in Andy's first films)".[36]

This is perhaps an overly simplified description. But Conrad's reference is of interest especially since it highlights a parallel between the work of Young and Warhol that is often overlooked. What the art of Andy Warhol, the music of La Monte Young and the Theatre of Eternal Music have in common is their work on an aesthetic of stasis and coolness. While Warhol's Pop Art, and more especially his cinematic work, may not have been born out of the spirit of Young's Minimalist Music as directly as Conrad suggests, there are obvious similarities between Warhol's and Minimalist art, whether musical or visual, which the categorizations of art history tend not to recognize. Minimal Art and Pop Art are often portrayed as two opposite currents of the 1960s – on the one hand, there is hedonistic Pop Art, which celebrates the superficialities of capitalism, on the other, profound Minimal Art, in retreat from the world. It is an antinomy that has been constructed retrospectively and which is not really adequate.[37]

The structural similarities between Minimal Art and Pop Art were indeed noticed at the time. In contemporaneous reviews, formal aspects of the works of Warhol and Lichtenstein were discussed alongside those of Stella and Flavin, and a series of exhibitions (at the Green Gallery in New York, for instance) showed works of George Segal and Claes Oldenburg alongside those of Donald Judd. Judd appreciated the Pop Art of Claes Oldenburg; Robert Morris, like Oldenburg, aligned himself with Duchamp, while Dan Flavin, like the Pop Art artists, was also influenced by Dada and assemblage. None of these artists, incidentally, ever referred to themselves as Minimalists, just as the composers who are now attributed to Minimal Music never identified themselves with this term. The term "Minimal Art" only came into being in the mid-1960s, *post factum*. Before that, the terms "ABC Art", "Primary Structures Specific Objects" – and even "Cool Art" – circulated. Minimal Music was known as "Meditative Music", "Repetitive Music", "Ac' Art" and "Trance Music".

If one looks for similarities rather than differences between Pop Art and Minimal Art, one quickly finds them. In the same way that Donald Judd or Carl Andre subjected nonrepresentational, sculptural elements to a rigid order, Warhol formed individual pictures into rows, into surfaces without centre or hierarchy. The fact that no element is privileged over another has also been interpreted in Minimal Art as a sign of the non-hierarchical, quasi-"democratic" structure of Minimal Art works. The same could be said to apply to Warhol. In the context of my examination, however, this technique can also be described as a method of stripping images of their significance, degrading them to pure ornament. By repeating these images so often that they lose all meaning, they virtually invite a "cool" approach. It is not for nothing that the concept of the cliché, i.e. an empty, hollow commonplace, originated in the jargon of printmakers, can be applied to such print templates as those Warhol used for his silk screens. Through repetition, the term suggests, they become stereotypes that no longer convey any content. To view them with an attitude of inner distance, that is, with a cool stance, is appropriate. La Monte Young likewise suggests detachment from the world when he describes the effect that drones can have on the listener. "Once the so-called drone state of mind is reached, the mind should be able to make very special explorations and set off in new directions, because you always have a fixed point of reference to which you can return and to which you can refer."[38] Young here describes an immersion in things, which differs from Warhol's reflective process of eliminating the world. Warhol's distancing is devoid of any desire for transcendental exploration or mystical immersion. And yet, like Young's slow-motion music, both his art and films take a detached view of things. It seems as if Warhol had wanted to gain an inaccessible box seat from which he could coolly register the existence and passing of reality without being drawn into it himself.

From this point of view, one of Warhol's famous bon mots appears in a new light: "I want to be a machine." This quotation, like the name "Factory" for Warhol's studio, has been understood as an ironic justification for his industrial-style production methods. In the context of my argument, however, the machine appears more like a metaphor for an actual process of de-individualization or dehumanization, a process of "cooling".

But what was it that made Warhol so cool? Hans-Christian Dany points out that the combination of cool distance and seemingly inexhaustible physical energy, which distinguished Warhol in those years, bore a strong resemblance to the effects caused by amphetamines.[39] Speed, the slang term for amphetamines, was indeed the Factory's in-house drug, and Warhol admitted to its use quite frankly.

I could never finally figure out if more things happened in the sixties because there was more awake time for them to happen in (since so many people were on amphetamine), or if people started taking amphetamine because there were so many things to do that they needed to have more awake time to do them in. It was probably both. I was taking only a small amount of Obetrol for weight loss that my doctor prescribed, but even that much was enough to give you that wired, happy go-go-go feeling in your stomach that made you want to work-work-work, so I could just imagine how incredibly high people who took the straight stuff felt. I only slept two or three hours a night from '65 through '67, but I used to see people who hadn't slept for days at a time and they'd say things like "I'm hitting my ninth day and it's glorious!"[40]

Dany notes about the effect of amphetamines on Warhol, "There are…statements [of Warhol's], in which he describes a sense of his own absence, which was due to the effect of amphetamines… Warhol cultivated that sense of absence and created the mystique of a man behind a mask, whose expressionlessness suggested non-participation…"[41]

Those who do not participate in the world expend less energy, and have more energy to make pictures, pictures, pictures. The increased productive energy triggered by amphetamines also includes a manic need to repeat, to expand one's activities into infinity through ritualistic repetition. The euphoria about the increased, machine-like creative power can be seen in Warhol's paintings from this period – fifty Marilyns, a hundred Elvises, canvases full of Coke bottles, walls stacked with soup cans, stacks of washing powder cartons. *I just can't stop.* While painting at an assembly line pace, Warhol listened to pop singles. To the same piece, over and over again. Ivan Karp remembers that on his first visit to Warhol's studio in 1963, the same song was playing non-stop at top volume: *I saw Linda yesterday* by Dickey Lee as a continuous loop. In an article in *Time*, published 2 years later, the reporter also observes that in [Warhol's] studio, a single pop tune may blare from his phonograph over and over again."[42]

For his second exhibition at the Fergus Gallery in Los Angeles, Warhol sent the Elvis pictures to be shown there in a roll and asked the owner to cut them up himself and mount them on stretcher frames. He added that he was *too busy* – probably with more and more manic repetition. In a grotesque hyper-adaptation to industrial society, Warhol transformed the artist's studio, one of the last frontiers of the handmade and the original in modern industrial society, into an assembly line.

His serial paintings utilize the methods of reproduction by technical media, but at the same time, they do offer one last, tiny refuge for human imperfection: Warhol is a bad machine. His repetitions are sloppy. No repeated image ever really looks exactly like another. One is richer in contrast than another, the next is darker. Here paint that has been applied too thickly runs down and could do with a touch-up. Warhol never achieved the perfection of a printing press and didn't aim to. He was more concerned with overriding the perfection of technology with the weakness of the human body.

The amphetamines pulled a kind of invisible screen between Warhol and the world. The silver paint which covered the Factory's walls and which appears in many of his pictures from that period, just like the pale, dull grey that also features on many of his paintings from that time, reflects this view of the world. Some of the paintings just consist of two equally large surfaces. One shows the picture motif, the other only the background colour of the first, as a monochrome area, often spray-painted silver.

The silver spray paint reminds of a mirror but it does not reflect. It seems to represent an insipid reflection of the world, as dull and empty as Warhol liked to describe himself as being.[43] In the mid-1960s, Warhol began to use sprayed-on silver excessively in his paintings. At the 1964 New York World Fair, he exhibited his work *Thirteen Most Wanted Men*, portraits of 13 wanted felons on a silver background, at a pavilion. But the work displeased New York Governor Nelson Rockefeller. World Expo curator Philip Johnson gave Warhol a deadline to remove the painting or replace it with another. With his characteristic mixture of provocative indifference and ironic humour, Warhol had the entire painting covered in silver, creating the largest monochrome painting of his artistic career in the process. Later on, Warhol, who had always suffered from his very white skin colour, began to wear silver wigs, making the colourlessness part of his image.

The silver colour feigns a reflection of the world, but it actually shows nothing. Elvis, Jackie Kennedy and others whom Warhol portrayed in this way become objects through repetitions of the subject. Against the silver or grey background, their contours look like black craters on the surface of the moon, which reflects the sunlight in a cold and dull way. They look like recesses on the canvas.

Warhol's most radical paintings from the 1960s turn the world into a surface, and people and things into schemes in a void. They freeze, immobilize, render expressionless and deprive their subject of corporeality and sensuality. They often depict disasters, accidents, death and disaster, victims of accidents, car crashes, attacks, suicides. Jackie Kennedy, whose husband was assassinated, Marilyn Monroe, who killed herself, two pensioners who died from a can of bad tuna. Warhol's silver-grey images neutralize these tragedies. And just as Warhol neutralized reality through repetition in his art, so he kept the world at bay through renunciation in his life. The amphetamine-containing Obetrol tablets he took were diet pills. His lovers often referred to his lack of interest in sex; acquaintances lamented his lack of compassion, his lack of concern for the fate of his superstars, which was the other side of his coolness. In interviews, Warhol himself mentioned his passivity and indifference time and again.

The cool stance which Warhol strove for also accounts for his strange affinity with recording and reproduction media, for which he has been dubbed a *recording angle*. The cassette recorder with which he recorded amphetamine-infused conversations at the Factory, which he published unedited as the "novel" *A, a novel*, and the indifferent film camera that recorded the goings- on of his superstars, worked as stoically and imperturbably as Warhol viewed the world. Or wanted to, anyway.

The silver screens may also seem like a pun, due to the double meaning of the term. In fact, Warhol turns the projection screen into another kind of "silver screen" that records reality without leaving a trace on it. No matter how his "superstars" behaved in front of the camera, the camera's eye recorded it impassively. The actors in his improvised films repeatedly tried to get Warhol to move the camera by displaying eccentric behaviour, but he never did.

At an exhibition in Paris in 1964, Warhol announced that he was going to give up painting in order to be able to concentrate fully on film-making. The silver screen was to replace the silver screens. To document his withdrawal from art in autumn 1966, in a kind of farewell exhibition at Leo Castelli's gallery, he showed a wallpaper printed with a cow's pattern and the *Silver Clouds* – silver cushions filled with helium, which Warhol had created with the help of engineer Billy Klüver, founder of EAT, and which apparently flew weightlessly around the space. Warhol had wanted them to fly out of the gallery windows to symbolize the act of his retreat from art. A nice metaphor, but the helium apparently did not carry them that far. Today, the *Silver Clouds* are on view at the Andy Warhol Museum in Pittsburgh.

Warhol found the film camera to be his ultimate challenge, and it was to be his exclusive focus from then on. Even with the help of amphetamines he hadn't been able to produce 24 images per second in the medium of screen printing. The *Screen Tests* he recorded in the mid-1960s were film portraits that at first glance hardly differed from his panel portraits. He used a static camera to take portraits of acquaintances from the Factory. One wants to hang them on the wall, and in fact, the *Screen Tests* have been shown in this way in recent years with the aid of large screens and video projection. (Incidentally, one of the *Screen Tests* features the artist Marian Zazeela, La Monte Young's partner).

Once more, these films at first glance seem to be a joke about the methods of "white-on-white" Hollywood. Screen tests were performed by the major Hollywood studios to test how photogenic the aspiring actors were. But the films which Warhol produced under these titles are, once more, closer to an exercise in disappearance than a criticism of the mechanisms of mass media. The *Screen Tests* were shot at 24 frames per second and shown at 16 frames per second. Film, a medium of movement and action, is arrested, turned into the opposite by Warhol. He uses motion to show motionlessness, to slow down reality, to deprive life of its vitality. And yet, most of the victims of Warhol's *Screen Tests* cannot sit still in front of the camera; they wobble, fidget and wink incessantly.

One almost gets the impression that some of them, in their uncomfortable fixation in front of the lifeless camera's eye, grind their jaws like speed users. *Sleep* (1963), which shows the poet John Giorno sleeping, was also shot at 24 frames per second and shown at 16 frames per second. Once more, Warhol reduces the specific qualities of the medium of film *ad absurdum*. Instead of showing something that moves, he shows a person immobilized by sleep and then slows this immobility down further. Giorno sleeps the sleep that Warhol himself had cut down to 2 to 3 hours per day with the help of his diet pills.

Giorno later reported that Warhol had got the idea for this film during a weekend trip to the countryside, before he had purchased a film camera. They were sharing a room and Warhol is said to have watched Giorno sleeping all night. When Giorno woke up in the middle of the night, he looked over, "and there was Andy in the bed next to me, his head propped up on his arm, wide-eyed from speed, looking at me".[44] Warhol himself remembers that when Giorno woke up he had complimented him, "you sleep so well".[45]

Sleep is often presented in secondary literature as a particularly extreme example of Warhol's real-time cinema, in which a process is filmed artlessly and shown unprocessed. Anyone who has the patience to actually watch the almost 6-hour-long film in its entirety notices, however, that *Sleep* is anything but that. In 2004, art historian Joseph W. Branden and Whitney Museum film curator Callie Angell discovered, in a meticulous analysis of the film, that *Sleep* actually consists of only 22 different close-ups that are repeated as a loop.[46]

The fact that Warhol had to assemble the film from individual shots was due to the technical limitations of his newly purchased Bolex camera, which could only hold 4-minute film rolls. Warhol managed to make *Sleep* 6 hours long by combining his film material, using loops. Almost one-and-a-half hours of the film consist of a single 4-minute shot, repeated 20 times, showing Giorno lying on his back. In relation to the whole film, Warhol repeats a relatively short passage before "moving on".

But in actuality, it doesn't move on, because the seemingly linear, sequential film images are not assembled in the order in which they were shot. They do not show a continuous sequence in the sense of the process of a night's rest from falling asleep to waking up. The loops feign continuity and refuse the linear order of the medium of film, and therefore deprive the subject of its temporality. At the installation at the Lincoln Center, Warhol was forced to use film loops for technical reasons. In *Sleep*, he made deliberate use of repetition. Unlike Peter Roehr, however, who developed a significant part of his work from film loops, Warhol never returned to this artistic medium in his other films.

There is a remarkable moment in the final interview with Warhol, before his sudden death in February 1987. Interviewer Paul Taylor asks him if he would do anything differently if he were able to start his life over again. Warhol replies, "I don't know. I just worked hard. It's all fantasy." Taylor: "Life is fantasy?" Warhol: "Yeah, it is." Taylor: "What's real?" Warhol: "Don't know." Taylor: "Do you really believe that, or will you say the opposite tomorrow?" Warhol: "I don't know. I like this idea that you can say the opposite." Taylor: "But you wouldn't in this case?" Warhol: "No."[47]

Andy Warhol actually said this a few weeks before he died. It sounds like a Zen master speaking. Life is just a fantasy. Almost always the opposite is also true. But not in this case. *Life is just a fantasy.*

It is not the intention here to establish any direct links between Warhol's work and similar concepts, like Zen Buddhism. Rather, the similarities are coincidental, like a kind of creative misunderstanding. An apt term was coined during this final interview. During the conversation, Paul Taylor uses the word "zennish" and Warhol jumps at it, saying "zennish. That's a good word. That's a good title for...my new book."[48]

Gallery owner Ileana Sonnabend remarked that, "for Andy, everything is equal".[49] That sounds *zennish*, too – *everything is equal for Andy.* Equally boring, one might be tempted to add. In his book *Popism*, Warhol says that:

> apparently, most people love watching the same basic thing, as long as the details are different. But I'm just the opposite: if I'm going to sit and watch the same thing I saw the night before, I don't want it to be essentially the same – I want it to be exactly the same...I've been quoted a lot as saying, "I like boring things." Well, I said it and I meant it. But that doesn't mean I'm not bored by them.[50]

Did Warhol get bored with Satie's *Vexations* or with La Monte Young's music? It's too late to ask him. Why didn't he continue to work with loops, which, by virtue of their stasis force the viewer to deal with him/herself? He had tested the method in *Sleep* and in the installation for the Lincoln Center. It would have been logical for him to use it in other films as well.

Perhaps he was suspicious of the vibrant pulsation of loops, which so fascinated other artists of that time, and which contradicted his aesthetic of immobilization. Or maybe he deliberately wanted to be a bad machine, and the closed film loops were too perfect for him. He may have been satisfied with his aesthetic as a way of making deceptive existence disappear, or he may have wanted to hold on to a tiny remnant of that existence. Andy Warhol was only interested in methods of media reproduction if he could remove their perfection.

Gilles Deleuze, who was familiar with both Warhol's and Young's work, notes in *Differenz und Wiederholung* [Difference and Repetition] that, "the more daily life seems standardized, stereotyped and subject to ever faster reproductions of consumer objects, the more art must commit itself [to life] and wrest those small differences from it which, additionally and simultaneously, also exist between other levels of repetition..."[51]

In Warhol's art, he himself is that "small difference" – the flaw in the execution of his pictures, the brief stutter in the otherwise flawless functioning of reproduction media. To him, loops were what Deleuze calls "raw and mechanical repetitions", that is, perfectly mechanical and monotonous repetitions. Warhol could not acknowledge them as his work without tiny imperfections. His early films – such as *Sleep*, or the *Screen Tests* – paradoxically live from their monotony, as well as from minimal interruptions. They fascinate through their monotony, yet the slightest movement of their subjects, the slightest flickering of the film are the anti-climaxes that make the monotony recognizable in the first place.

Around the time when Warhol was making these films, he began packing everything that passed through his hands on a daily basis into boxes – letters, brochures, invitations, gifts, bills, books. At his home in New York, several rooms were filled with these boxes. From these *Time Capsules*, which have not yet been fully explored, Warhol's biography could probably be reconstructed more thoroughly than from his diary (which he dictated to his recording angel, colleague Pat Hackett, night after night over the phone, for years on end). Akin to his films, the *Time Capsules* document the passing of time by capturing and enclosing it.

La Monte Young, like Warhol, is an obsessive archivist who not only keeps recordings of all his concerts and shelves full of materials about his work in his loft, but who even – again like Warhol – records conversations and interviews with himself.[52] In his music, too, Young, who rehearsed every day for a one- and-a-half years with his Theatre of Eternal Music until they had found the right interval for their improvisations, makes time stand still. Akin to Warhol's paintings, Young's music stretches time until it conveys a feeling of eternity, of infinity. After their brief collaboration, neither of them worked with loops again. Yet the idea of arresting time remains one of the most important themes in their work.

Warhol takes the individual and specific from his subjects with his sloppy, imperfect silk screens. Repetition robs them of their emotional impact. So, they act as an anesthetic for the wounds which time inflicts on anyone who does not know how to stop it.

The work of Andy Warhol and La Monte Young share common ground in their attempt to leave the world and the passing of time behind by means of art or music. Through the periodic humming and overlapping frequencies of drones (Young), through endlessly repeating images without contours on flat, matt backgrounds (Warhol), they created a method of making the world disappear without having to disappear completely from it themselves. Just as Warhol uses silver spray paint to turn the world into an empty screen, Marian Zazeela's purple light installations turn the places where La Monte Young's music is heard into non-physical, "virtual" spaces. But while Young's music is about the possibility of creating a meditative state and immersing oneself in pure sound, the goal of Warhol's art (and life) was no longer to have to surrender to the world.

In 1966, the art magazine *Aspen* (design by Andy Warhol) published a flexi disc, a single on flexible plastic that continuously roared when played. The magazine – a snapshot of the 1960s New York scene – consists of various sheets, prints and two flipbooks by Warhol and Jack Smith. They are placed in a box designed like a box of washing powder.[53] The thin plastic disc reads "Velvet Underground: Loop". But it was probably La Monte Young's temporary collaborator John Cale who recorded his electric, feedback-distorted guitar to the disc on his own, without the rest of the band – for 7 minutes. When the record needle runs into the discharge groove, the record player does not turn off. It continues to repeat the scrap of sound in the flexi disc's discharge groove. The piece *Loop* ends in a record loop, similar to the *sillons fermés*, from which Pierre Schaeffer had constructed his *Études de Bruits* almost 20 years earlier.

Drone – clack – drone – clack – drone – clack. If one does not look at the turntable, one might not even notice that the piece is over, since it previously consisted only of stasis. The trick of sending a piece of music into the record's discharge groove and allowing it still to be repeated over and over (which today cannot be reproduced with CDs, MP3 files or streams) was first introduced into mainstream pop by The Beatles. In 1967, they, similarly, completed their concept album *Sgt. Pepper's Lonely Hearts Club Band* with a loop in the run-out groove, which made the trick famous, and it was subsequently imitated on records by bands like The Who, Heaven 17, the Fehlfarben and many others.

Technical means immortalized the never-ending sound of La Monte Young on *Loops*. No other work of noise as monotonous, monumental and cold as this was published again in pop music until *Metal Machine Music* (1975) by Lou Reed, who had been another member of Velvet Underground.

ACCUMULATING SUSPENDED TIME: TERRY RILEY AND THE BIRTH OF MINIMAL MUSIC FROM THE IDEAS BEHIND THE TAPE LOOP

You can't get away from yourself. Wherever you look, there is your own body. This is what I look like, what I sound like. Terry Riley's Time Lag Accumulator installation is like an echo chamber of the self. Mirrors reflect your image all around you and each noise you make is copied by countless overlapping echoes from different directions.

With its corrugated walls, the octagonal pavilion reminds of a guardhouse or of one of the historic Berlin street urinals from the outside. When you enter through its only door, you find yourself in one of eight symmetrical chambers cut like pieces of cake. Their walls are covered with mirrored film, and openings in the walls allow you to move from one chamber to the next. Beneath the ceiling, there are microphones which record every sound, and this is played back with a slight delay (i.e. a time lag) in another chamber. If you shout something, you hear your own voice echoing back from different directions. If you shout loud enough, these echoes overlap to form a wall of sound that swells before slowly dying away. The repetitions smooth out any imperfections in your voice. In the end, all that remains of your shouts is a hissing sound.

All of a sudden, it sounds as if a school class of about a hundred pupils has entered the room. There is giggling, screeching, the sound of doors slamming throughout the octagon. Then just two children run past. Long after they have left, their calls resound and the fading echoes resemble the sounds of a distant outdoor pool or fairground. Alone once again with your own image and sound, you can sing a polyphonic canon with yourself. Interestingly the confrontation with one's own ego quickly leads to a decentring of perception, accompanied by impulses of oceanic feelings.

The composer Terry Riley developed this installation in 1968 for the exhibition *Magic Theater Show* in Kansas City. It is the only work of its kind by Riley, who is best known as one of the founders of Minimal Music and as a composer of works of strictly repetitive patterns. Today, the Time Lag Accumulator is located in the Musée d'art contemporain in Lyon. While the original version generated echoes by means of tape loops, the current installation uses computers.

The Time Lag Accumulator is reminiscent of the "philosophical toys" of the eighteenth and nineteenth centuries. At that time, devices such as the Wheel of Life or the Magic Lantern popularized the latest scientific findings in easily comprehensible forms. The installation is a feedback system as it was described in the then popular cybernetics world models, and the time-delay-accumulator is the prototype of the closed- circuit video installations with which artists such as Dan Graham or Bruce Nauman began their careers in the early 1970s.

But above all, the installation is a monument to the Now Generation of the swinging sixties, with their celebration of the here and now. The Time Lag Accumulator allows poignant moments to linger; unable to make them eternal, it at least stretches them out. By referring the viewer back on him/ herself, it is simultaneously a rejection of any kind of statement or of intentionality in art. The Time Lag Accumulator is the culmination of an art that – like Minimal Art or early Concept Art – renounces artistic self-expression and the production of meaning, preferring to confront viewers with themselves instead. This is you. It's all there is.

It is Terry Riley's tape compositions, which had launched his career in the 1960s, turned into one installation. These compositions have had a permanent influence on his work and were the starting point for music that consists of short, rhythmically repeated, barely varied sound modules, which today is commonly known as Minimal Music. It is not the Minimalism of the long-lasting tones of a La Monte Young, however. The minimalism that Terry Riley introduced with his tape compositions is a "motoric Minimalism", or pulse or trance music, or "stuck record player needle" music, in which tiny melodies are endlessly repeated with tiny variations.

Terry Riley derived this compositional technique directly from the potentials of the tape loop. Unlike Schaeffer or Stockhausen, he didn't seek to conceal its repetitive characteristics, but developed music from it. The Minimalism of Terry Riley – and later that of Steve Reich – is a direct result of working with tape loops and the minimal variations which the two composers elicited from the tape recorder.[1]

His early tape compositions not only make Riley the progenitor of Minimalism in music, they also made him an important reference point for the pop music of the 1960s and 1970s, which saw numerous musicians referring directly or indirectly to Riley. Of all the avant-garde composers, his work probably had the greatest influence on the pop music of his time. His experiments, further, anticipated the electronic dance music of the 1980s and 1990s, which developed from repeated sequences of short, recorded sound elements, or samples: Hip-Hop, House and Techno producers work with very similar methods as does Riley in his tape compositions.

The early compositions and loop experiments of Reich and Riley still sound striking and radical today. They allow an insight, at least to some extent, into what a shock Minimal Music must have been in the 1960s and 1970s for listeners trained in the European classical avant-garde. They lack the complacency that characterizes the compositions of the second generation of Minimalists, like Michael Nyman or John Adams. Many listeners can only bear to listen to them for a short period of time.

Great Minimalists like Terry Riley, Steve Reich, Philip Glass and, to a lesser extent, Young are now so well-known in the history of serious music, and elements of Minimal Music are so omnipresent and widely accepted, that it is difficult to appreciate what a provocation this music amounted to in the 1960s and 1970s. Minimalist composers were laughed at or booed off the stage. Especially in Germany, their music was disregarded as a source of inspiration for drug addicts and dropouts, and it was even accused of having crypto-fascist tendencies. In the spirit of Adorno, critics dismissed this music as empty and void of passion, as a fitting soundtrack for the machine age and the acoustic equivalent of life in a boring, perfectly organized consumer society.

However, the early works of Riley and Reich, and also those of La Monte Young, signalled a fundamentally new artistic attitude, which began to be articulated in the early 60s. In the works of Minimal Art, in the conceptual art that developed from it, in Minimal Music and in John Cage's random compositions, artistic self-expression is no longer foregrounded. Instead, these "non-intentional" works confront the viewer/listener with (often serial) structures that evolved from "objective" rules.

Minimal Music belongs to a "zero point" around 1960, when artistic subjectivity began to give way to the viewer's subjectivity. Some years later, Roland Barthes focused on the reader's subjectivity in the much-quoted essay *The Death of the Author*, published in 1968. Whereas according to Barthes' work the death enabled the birth of a reader, in Minimal Music, the death of the author leads to the birth of the listener. Tape loops played an important role in this.[2]

The following chapter will emphasize two aspects of Minimalist composition that are particularly relevant to Reich and Riley's work with tape loops: the early Minimalists' opposition to European avant-garde music and their reference to American popular music on the one hand, and their recourse to 'non-Western' music on the other. In the previous chapter on the collaboration between Andy Warhol and La Monte Young, I emphasized the significance which Cool Jazz had for the emergence of Minimal Music. The composers who developed Minimal Music were well acquainted with the popular music of their time, in addition to their training in classical and contemporary avant-garde music.

Like Young, Reich and Riley played in jazz bands in their youth. Riley had to earn a living as a bar pianist from time to time in the 1960s, and for a while played ragtime every night in a bar in San Francisco. Steve Reich emphasizes the importance which Soul songs like Junior Walker's *Shotgun* had for him in addition to the importance of John Coltrane's Jazz. "Between 1961 and 1964, there was African music, John Coltrane and Motown Soul, and it all came together on the west coast of the USA. Terry Riley heard this, I heard it…It was the cultural environment from which this music emerged."[3] Riley used *Shotgun*, which is based on a single, uninterrupted, continuous, that is, very minimalistic, bass line, and which therefore has a certain proximity to loop music, as the raw material for his loop composition *Bird of Paradise*. His later tape compositions *I can't stop no* and *You're no good* are also based on Soul pieces.

Minimal music has often been described as a reaction of American composers to the dominance of European serious music, as a kind of plebeian rebellion against a music that was no longer comprehensible to a musically untrained audience. The European avant-garde, namely the music of the Second Viennese School and Serialism, was something that all first-generation Minimalists encountered extensively during their studies, and some even tried their hand at it. Riley and La Monte Young composed serial music during their time at the University of Berkeley, where they also met, and Reich tried his hand at serial and atonal compositions as a student of Luciano Berio. For many, Minimal Music arose out of a protest against Schönberg's 12-tone music and Webern's serialism, which at that time had become a kind of academic dogma in the USA and Europe. Philip Glass could still get worked up in 1986 about this "wasteland dominated by these maniacs, these complete creeps, you know — who were trying to make everyone write this crazy, creepy music".[4] The same year, Reich told a *New York Times* reporter, "Don't get me wrong. Berg, Schönberg and Webern were very good composers. They gave expression to the emotional climate of their time. But it would be ridiculous if today's composers wanted to reconstruct the fear of *Pierrot Lunaire* in Ohio or in a back room at Burger King."[5]

The search for a genuine American musical idiom is evident from the material which Reich and Riley used for their tape loops. Riley "remixed" a series of Afro-American Soul pieces, as already alluded to. Steve Reich, likewise, used materials he considered to be American for his tape loops. In an interview he mentions that "in those days, I was very interested in American poetry" and emphasizes the importance which the poet William Carlos Williams had for his work. "The tape pieces, it seemed to me, were a way of taking Dr Williams' advice. Here's American speech rhythm, particularly in the case of the black Pentecostal preacher and later in the black kid who was arrested for murder, then presenting it just as it is and letting the actual rhythm and cadence of the voice form the music."[6]

Another thing the founders of Minimal Music have in common is their interest in non-Western music. In the 1960s, Terry Riley was interested in North African music and in 1970, he and La Monte Young travelled to India to study raga, a music that shares the additive structure and cyclical rhythms of Minimalist compositions. Steve Reich travelled to Africa in 1970 to study African percussion at the University of Ghana's Institute of African Studies. In 1973 and 1974 he studied Balinese Gamelan at the University of California's Center for World Music. As with

African percussion music, he was impressed by the different ways of organizing the Gamelan, mainly through rhythms, while the harmony usually remains constant – which is also a characteristic of his compositions from the 1970s. It encouraged him to pursue his work with repetitive elements.

For both composers, these influences were confirmation, rather than direct inspiration, especially since they were already composing in the minimalist style at the beginning of the 1970s, when they started to focus intensively on non-Western music. The tape compositions which Riley and Reich created in the 1960s were the starting points for their respective musical development. For Riley, they provided the model for his seminal work, *In C,* which forms the origin of the "motor" style of Minimal Music. Steve Reich developed his compositional technique of gradual shifts and resulting patterns from tape loops, which provided the structure of pieces like *Piano Phase* (1967) or *Violin Phase* (1967).

Not all of Terry Riley's tape compositions from this period have been preserved and most of his tape-loop works were only published in the late 1990s. In the 1960s, Riley and his family led a nomadic life, living in New York and travelling through Europe and North Africa while he worked as a pianist in the casinos of the American army. During these journeys, some of the works from this period were lost, along with a lot of other material. Even the loop compositions that appeared under the label Organ of Corti in the late 1990s were allegedly on their way to the tip when they were rescued in the nick of time by Riley's wife.[7]

Because of Riley's own careless handling of his work, it took a long time for his pioneering role in the history of Minimal Music to be fully recognized. Pieces like Riley's *Mescaline Mix* and *Music for The Gift,* which were not released until the late 1990s, are at least on a par with, if not superior to, the tape works of Steve Reich, which are more widely known. They make Terry Riley the forerunner of generations of sampling and looping musicians, anticipating the production methods that are now part of the basic vocabulary of electronic dance music.

The house in Potrero Hill, a suburb of San Francisco where Riley lived with his family in the early 1960s, "had a wonderful view of San Francisco Bay. It was a very romantic place, a very old cottage (which has since been demolished), with a very small garden and lots of wine bottles outside; all those tape loops went out of the studio door and were wound around the bottles before coming back into the studio."[8]

It was in this dreamy place that Riley began to assemble his first tape composition in 1960, using tape loops wrapped around wine bottles in the garden – *Mescaline Mix* (1960-62). At this time, Riley was also in contact with other young composers who, like him, were experimenting with tape and used loops in their music – Pauline Oliveros, Morton Subotnick and Ramon Sender, with whom he would later establish the San Francisco Tape Music Center.

This Tape Music Center was not only to become the most important focal point for electronic music on the American West Coast in the 1960s, but also a meeting place for San Francisco's experimental music and the psychedelic rock scene, which was developing at that time. It was in this environment that Steve Reich, who performed some of his early loop pieces in a concert at the Tape Music Center, played with Phil Lesh, who later became bassist for the Grateful Dead. Together they bought the two tape recorders with which Reich created his first tape loop compositions. In the spring of 1964, they played a quintet by Phil Lesh and *Piano Piece # 3* by Tom Constanten, who later became keyboard player for the Grateful Dead, which brought an element of avant-garde electronics to the band's first records.[9] The close contact between electronic and pop music in San Francisco in the 1960s led to numerous such cross-genre collaborations, and in a way, Terry Riley's tape compositions should be counted among them. His *Mescaline Mix* was initially created for Californian choreographer Ann Halprin's dance theatre performance *Three Legged Stool*. In many respects, Riley is still close to Pierre Schaeffer's *musique concrète* here, because the piece consists exclusively of natural sounds, which Riley had recorded on his Wollensack mono tape recorder. They include piano playing, laughter, explosions and other sound effects.

When the magnetic tape was wound through his garden, it dragged across the ground. The grains of sand and lumps of earth that got stuck to it influenced the recorded sounds – this was not an accident, but a part of the artistic method. Riley notes, "It's more like folk art. I was really interested in the tactile quality and the kind of low-fi nature of the material I was working with."[10] To modify the sound of the resulting recording further, he turned to composer Ramon Sender, who set up the Center for Electronic Music at the San Francisco Conservatory. He comments that "although Ramon's studio was modest, he had a lot more stuff than I had including an echoplex".[11] So, to edit his first tape montage, Riley used an effects unit that was more or less identical to the unit which Elvis' guitarist Scotty Moore used to transfer the echo sound of the Sun Sessions to the stage in 1956.

In contrast to Riley's later tape compositions, *Mescaline Mix* does not pulsate rhythmically; rather, it is mostly slow, even elegiac. The sustained piano passages remind of the ambient music of Brian Eno. Riley said at a later date, "when you listen to these tapes today they're like looking at some cloudy landscape. It puts you at ease."[12] As with the other tape compositions of that time, the rhythmic loops are hardly audible in *Mescaline Mix*, so that this piece appears almost without structure in some places. It was not until the subsequent tape pieces, created in the following year in Paris, that cyclical repetition became the main element of musical organization.

In 1962 Riley emigrated to Europe with his family and worked professionally as a musician there. He earned his money as a pianist in vaudeville and at the American army's casinos. After stopping off in Germany (where he took part in the Fluxus Festival in Wiesbaden in 1962) and in Scandinavia, he and his family also temporarily settled in France. There he became acquainted with the films and books of the French *nouveau roman* writer Alain Robbe-Grillet. Later on, he commented that:

what I was influenced by was the French writer Alain Robbe-Grillet, and his novels and films. The film that I was most impressed with, was *L'Immortelle*, where he had this repetition of scenes, which had different outcomes for each period. He would go through a scene, and have one outcome, and then he would rerun the scene, and it would have another outcome. And that kind of technique, I thought, was really very powerful, because it would give you different versions of reality.[13]

He wanted to make this repetition effect fruitful for his compositions because he had noticed that things didn't sound the same when they were listened to more than once. What fascinated him was that the more often they were heard, the more different they sounded. In Europe, he began to establish relationships between the repetitions and the different cycles of tape loops.[14]

His subsequent tape composition, in which he tested this method for the first time, was produced for Ken Dewey's play *The Gift*, commissioned by Paris Theatre of Nations. Through Dewey, who directed the play, Riley gained access to the French broadcasting company ORTF's *Sarah Bernhardt Theater*. (Although Pierre Schaeffer had developed *musique concrète* at this station, Riley later said that he was not familiar with his work. "I knew about Pierre Schaeffer just by reputation. I hadn't heard his work."[15])

There he explained to a radio technician, who was "an ordinary guy in a white coat",[16] how he had used the Echoplex effects device to process his tape music and achieved repetitive echo effects in the process. The technician "had never worked with contemporary music, or electronic music. So, when I described to him what I wanted, he thought up this idea, that you could have tape run between two machines."[17] The first tape recorder would record a signal, the second tape recorder would play it back. In this respect, the process was similar to the one Sam Phillips had used when recording Elvis. But unlike in the Sun Sessions, the first tape machine recorded what the second played back, and one soundtrack was laid over another. This procedure is more reminiscent of the converted tape recorder which Karlheinz Stockhausen had used to make his *Studie,* in 1953.

In contrast to Stockhausen, who assembled the sounds he had created with tape loops according to complicated serial principles, Riley just let his devices run and play a mechanical canon with each other. The result was an uninterrupted, self-perpetuating echo effect. Riley later explained that "by varying the intensity of the feedback you could form the sound either into a single image without any delay or increase the intensity until it became a dense chaotic kind of sound".[18] Riley called this construction *Time Lag Accumulator* and subsequently made it into the central aspect of his music. With this installation, Riley also regularly performed live from the late 1960s onwards, and, with this comparatively simple equipment, developed a completely independent compositional method and his version of Minimalism.

Riley was later to say that despite his previous experiments with the Echoplex, it was his work on *Music for The Gift*, "which really made me understand what repetition can mean for musical form. It was the precursor to *In* C."[19] *Music for the Gift* is based on an improvisation by Chet Baker's quintet, who were in Paris at the time. Riley got the ensemble to record *So What* by Miles Davis. "Then I had them all play solo with each one improvising on it, so that I had both the group and individual instruments. I took all that upstairs to the mixing booth and we started cutting it up into loops and re-orchestrating it, putting all these loops together."[20]

The most impressive of the various segments of *Music for the Gift* is "She moves, she", which was assembled from a sentence spoken by actor James Graham. The complete text read, "she moves, she follows". Riley replaced the last word with a snapping sound that sounds like an arrow flying off. These two sound fragments are repeated over and over, and soon the sentence fragments lose any of the semantic meaning they may have retained after Riley's "cut up". Soon they no longer sound like a human voice, but like a percussion instrument. The tape delays create a complex, contrapuntal effect, which, through further overlays achieved with the Time Lag Accumulator, finally condenses into oscillating sound textures.

Quite incidentally, Terry Riley here overrides one of the most fundamental characteristics of Western music – its linear-teleological orientation. In his book *American Minimal Music*, Belgian composer Wim Mertens describes the contrast between the purposeful structure of the majority of Western music and the patterns of Terry Riley's Minimalism.

> The music of the American composers of repetitive music can be described as non-narrative and ateleological. Their music discards the traditional harmonic functional schemes of tension and relaxation and (currently) disapproves of classical formal schemes and the musical narrative that goes with them (formalizing a tonal and/or thematic dialectic). Instead there appears nondirected evolution in which the listener is no longer submitted to the constraint of following the musical evolution.[21]

Riley's courageous act of simply leaving the machines and loops to themselves is a decisive point in the music of the postwar period. Unlike the European electronic avant-gardists of the 1950s, he let the machines repeat themselves. For him, these technical repetitions were not agents of Thanatos, the Freudian death instinct; on the contrary, they were a source of joy and therefore closer to Freud's life instinct, Eros. Beyond this, however, loops are the starting point for Riley's insights. They include an epistemological aspect, since only multiple repetitions make it possible to delve deeper into the sound elements. In *Music for the Gift*, as with all his subsequent tape compositions, Terry Riley suspends time and offers the listener short moments of sound for closer examination and immersion.

These experiments were "endlessly fascinating" to Riley in the 1960s, as he later emphasized on numerous occasions. "I was interested in the psychological effects of tape loops and their effects on consciousness," he says more than 40 years later in a telephone interview, in which his enthusiasm for the discovery is still evident.

> I was interested in the psychological effect of tape loops, and their effect on consciousness. That aspect attracted me. Tape loops could become like a Mantra. You had a fragment of sound, and as you repeated that over and over, you would start sensing the minute characteristics of that sound, that started appearing, and you became really familiar with them. So that was what attracted me to tape loops, that it gave you a chance to study a sound very deeply, very consciously.[22]

The next composition Riley wrote was *In C*, for which he transferred the repetitive pattern method to instrumental music. Before discussing this ground-breaking piece, however, it is worth considering the other tape compositions Riley produced in the 1960s. *Sweet Bird of Paradise*, created in 1964 after Riley returned to San Francisco, is particularly impressive. The piece is based on the previously referred-to Soul piece *Shotgun* by Junior Walker and his All-Stars, a largely instrumental Soulfunk number for dance, which builds on a single bass line. This allowed Riley to recombine different parts of the song without creating any dissonances. Again he uses random methods. Some of the selected fragments are carefully chosen, others were cut out and looped without looking at the tape. These random excerpts were akin "to wild cards; if he didn't like them, they were removed."[23]

Of all of Riley's tape compositions, this piece reminds most of a contemporary rap piece. Like a Hip-Hop DJ, he chose a funk track as the basis for his composition and repeats short passages from this *ad infinitum*. At some points he slows down the rotating fragments with his hand, creating a sound effect like a scratch. In some passages of this 25-minute-long piece, the raw material is clearly recognizable and – underlaid with a contemporary beat – would fit in at any contemporary House or Techno club. Other passages are so profoundly altered that one can hardly guess their source. Riley isolated and edited passages of the pounding piece in such a way that it sounds as if whistling, braking sounds, human screams, whip cracking and water bubbling were being heard. One loop which Riley reverses, brakes and accelerates with his hand has a whirring sound that made him think of a giant pterosaur, hence the title.[24]

The other tape composition from this time is likewise based on a Soul piece – *You're no good* by the now largely forgotten Rhythm'n'Blues singer Harvey Averne. This Motown-inspired piece is a duet between two singers who describe their love relationship. The title also appealed to Riley because his daughter called him "Poppy No-Good" in toddler language at the time – a title he also used ironically as a stage name.

The piece was commissioned by a discotheque in Philadelphia. The owner had seen Riley at one of his *All-Night Flight* concerts, of which more later. He hired him to write a theme song for his club. The result was one of the first remixes in music history. By then, Riley had bought two good-quality Revox tapes, which provided the sound required to make an impression in a discotheque. The piece is preceded by a synthesizer glissando before the original begins. Riley lets it play once before he starts to repeat single passages of the piece as a loop.

According to Riley's memory, this part was well received by the dancers in the discotheque for which the piece was created. It was not until the tape loops began to drift apart that they began to throw the dancers out of rhythm. Riley dissects the piece into smaller and smaller repeating fragments that are layered on top of each other, stretching the song's catchy refrain to extreme, hypnotic lengths. At some positions, a loop plays on the right stereo channel and is repeated on the other channel to create a call and response, a technique derived from Riley's experiments with the *Time Lag Accumulator*. Around the middle of the 20-minute piece, he adds the pulsating sound of the synthesizer to the maelstrom of the increasingly confusing tape loops. At the point of total deconstruction, he accelerates the loops further and further until no trace of the original song remains.

You're no good is flawless Minimalism and pure pop music at the same time. It speaks for Riley's modesty that he makes such a detailed reference to black soul with this piece, which was an important influence on Minimal Music. At the same time, the method he used to change his source material and stretch it to infinity is identical to the procedure used in most remixes of Disco or House tracks since then – Riley extends the piece by repeating passages of it. Further, the technique of superimposing sound elements as echoes has also been used time and again in Disco remixes and House tracks.[25]

It is partly due to Riley's careless handling of his own work that the musical and historical significance of his tape compositions has been underestimated or even unknown today. These compositions present a blueprint for almost everything that was experimented with in electronic dance music of the 1980s and 1990s. It is also of interest for those born since then how close Riley's contacts were to the club and discotheque scene of the American East Coast, which formed a fertile ground for the Disco culture that emerged a few years later. Not only *You're no good*, but also *I can't stop no*, a tape composition that unfortunately has not been re-released to this day, were written for a discotheque.[26]

All these works open up a space for the listener in which time seems to stand still or doesn't exist. In Riley's versions of Soul pieces like *Shotgun* or *You're no good*, he takes away their linear order and narrative structure, the flow involving a beginning, alternating verse, choruses, solo passages, etc., to a conclusion. Instead, he makes them run on in never-ending loops, which short-circuit the linear order of the piece, to replace any awareness of progression with a sense that one is revving in neutral. Riley also transferred this technique of linear suspension in instrumental music to his most important composition: *In C.*

In early 1964, Riley broke off his stay in Europe and returned to the USA. After the assassination of President John F. Kennedy, the army clubs where he had been playing were closed for an extended period of time. Since he had lost his source of income, he moved back to San Francisco and played piano in bars there again. He is said to have got his idea for *In C* on his way to work. "In those days, I was playing at the Gold Street Saloon every night. One evening I was taking the bus to work, and *In C* just came to me. The whole idea. I heard it. It just came to me. I didn't want to go to work that night. As soon as I had finished work, I went home and wrote it down in its entirety."[27]

The piece consists of 53 short melodic fragments, most of them no longer than a bar, all of them in C major. Instrumentation is optional, as is the size of the ensemble – Riley's brief playing instructions just say, "the more the merrier". Only the note C, to be sustained throughout the performance, "should be played on the high keys of the piano or on a tuned percussion instrument", to give the piece cohesion. Other than that, the musicians are free to play any one of the 53 figures after the other, for as long and as often as they wish. They can insert rests when they want, before resuming and repeating the next fragment. The performance is finished when all the musicians have played all the figures and can last anywhere between 45 minutes and 3 hours, depending on the mood of everyone involved.

There are three reasons why the piece does not produce chaos, as these playing instructions may seem to suggest: firstly, there is the pulse of the C, which is struck throughout the piece in 4/4 time. Secondly, there is its constant key signature. Thirdly, a kind of team spirit appears to develop when the musicians play together. The key of C prevents strong dissonances from arising, even when the performance is subject to multitudinous sounds. For the listener, the piece sounds harmonious almost throughout. This is what distinguishes it from the avant-garde atonal serious music of the twentieth century. Terry Riley had abandoned serial and 12-tone music.

The unusual freedom of interpretation seems still more important than the compositional technique, as this is rare in works of "serious" music. *In C* is effectively a functioning anarchy. A complex musical, as well as social, organism is created from a minimum of rules through the mutual interaction of all participants. The piece is an exercise in practical selforganization. Even if the individual musicians can do what they want within the framework of its few rules, the piece discourages excessive departures or intrusive virtuosity.

The melodic fragments are so simple that single musicians can hardly shine while playing. If individual instrumentalists were to push themselves into the limelight, the overall interaction and thus the performance as a whole would suffer. Instead, it encourages performers to listen to their fellow musicians and work together to create a musical unity in which the result is greater than the sum of its parts. In an interview, Terry Riley describes his intention: "I didn't want a conductor or anyone else telling the musicians what to do. I wanted them to make decisions based on what they were hearing."[28]

All the voices, all the instruments, all the musicians are equal. Each performance of the piece is a continuous negotiation process between all participating instrumentalists. Sometimes, passages of *In C* get boring or unfocused, just like every collective process, it has its low points. But just as often, the musicians achieve triumphant highlights. In this respect, *In C* also differs from rock music, which was developing at the same time. While the never-ending solo performances of rock guitarists, which were popular in the 1960s and 1970s, were a relatively unreflective celebration of the cult of musical genius, *In C* is a piece for a collective by a collective.

In this sense, *In C* is an expression of the social values of the 1960s and the hippie movement. Since there is no conductor, no soloists and no overall leader, it is anti-authoritarian. It is emancipatory because it gives musicians a maximum of freedom within the framework of its simple rules. It appeals to the togetherness and solidarity of all participants while discouraging unsociable behaviour (which in this case would be tantamount to unmusical behaviour). *In C* is basic democracy made into music.

Strickland observes that "today the work continues to sound as inseparably a product of its times as any of the Beatles albums, yet remains as fresh."[29] With its continuous, pumping 4/4 time, it even has an unmistakable proximity to pop music, especially to the Motown Soul of the time. *In C* is not only the defining work of "motoric Minimalism", but probably also *the* exemplar of serious music that expressed the "*zeitgeist*" of the 1960s.

Strickland even goes so far as to cite political events of the 1960s as reasons for the success of *In C.*

> The free-form communal exuberance of the work embodies the brighter side of the paranoiac and jubilant, lacerated and ecstatic sensibility of the 1960s, which has been simplified beyond recognition in the various mythologies of the era that have since proliferated. The extent to which the ecstasy and jubilation, induced chemically or otherwise, were an overcompensation, even a reaction-formation, in the context of the cultural ravages of riots, assassinations, and the Vietnam War, is still downplayed... The popularity of Columbia's *In C* is undoubtedly similarly linked to its sense of collective ecstasy, free-wheeling improvisation, and trancelike repetition unamenable to chemical alterations in consciousness. Its ebullience came as a much-needed lift in a year that witnessed the assassinations of Martin Luther King and Robert Kennedy, the siege of Chicago, and the election of Richard Nixon, none perhaps designed to fill one with longing for the latest experiment in academic Serialism.[30]

But *In C* should not be dismissed as escapism, as an attempt to avoid unpleasant reality. It may not be an explicitly political work, like Luigi Nono's *Non consumiano Marx,* which incorporates slogans from the 1968 Paris riots to create a sound collage. But perhaps this is precisely why it has survived better than most of the politically motivated serious music of the 1960s and early 1970s. In its non-hierarchical interaction and its focus on a collective process, *In C* ultimately portrays a community based on cooperation and solidarity, rather than on competition and domination.

In secondary literature, the influence of Jazz improvisation on this piece has been repeatedly emphasized. *In C* does indeed resist reliance on notation, which had dominated serious music of the twentieth century up to that point, as it leaves the final form of the piece to its interpreters. However, it is Riley's tape experiments that seem to me to be more important to the compositional method used for *In C* – the piece owes much more to these than it does to Jazz improvisation. The repetitions that make up the piece imitate the technical reproductions of the tape loops with which Riley was working at the time.

In C unmistakably mimics the delay effect of the *Time Lag Accumulator*, the tape recorder which the French technician at ORTF radio station in Paris had created for Riley from two tape machines. Just as the *Time Lag Accumulator* repeats everything that is played, each figure played by one instrument is repeated by all the other instruments at some point in the performance. In this way, when performing *In C,* the different melodies can be heard wandering from one instrument to the next – a kind of homage to tape delay, except that no tape recorder is involved.

The communal spirit that emerges therefore takes its cue directly from media machines. Just as the *Time Lag Accumulator* halts the passage of time by accumulating it, in *In C,* the linear progression of time seems to be suspended. Individual melodic patterns appear, disappear, return, the tempi of the various instruments diverge and move together again. The whole piece gives the impression of non-linear time, time in which everything can happen simultaneously, time that does not progress, but contracts and expands instead.

The premiere of *In C* was on 1 November 1964 – it was therefore "at virtually the mathematical center of the 1960s".[31] Ramon Sender had organized the concert at the San Francisco Tape Music Center under the title *oneyoungamerican*, and it was sold out. Riley describes the audience as "poets, artists, dancers and other bohemians" and believes they were to some extent identical to the clientèle that attended the first psychedelic events soon afterwards.

For composer Morton Subotnik, a member of the San Francisco Tape Center and one of the instrumentalists in the world premiere of *In C*, this concert was the beginning of psychedelic fashion: "I remember Terry wore a floppy purple bow tie and orange pants. The audience was also dressed very colorfully. It was sort of the beginning of the psychedelic dress-up era. [32]

Riley, too, describes these concerts in a way that reminds of the psychedelic dance parties and acid tests which began a year later in San Francisco. "*In C*'s initial concerts were communal events where many people came to listen or dance to the music, because the music sometimes became quite ecstatic with all the repetitive patterns."[33] Riley saw the concert as an underground event – "the audience consisted of poets, theatre people, dancers and avant-garde composers from San Francisco and brought together the underground scene of the city, as it was then."[34] Like the psychedelic parties of the years to come, the premiere of *In C* was accompanied by an elaborate light show. It was created by artist Anthony Martin, who created the light installations for almost all the concerts held at the Tape Music Center. Martin stood on stage with two projectors and showed a "light composition" of constantly changing colours and patterns as a visual realization of the music. The first part of the concert consisted of some of Riley's tape compositions, all of which are now lost, with the exception of *Music from The Gift*. *In C* was the last piece of the evening. The following Friday, the concert was repeated and received rave reviews in the *San Francisco Chronicle*. Music journalist Alfred Frankenstein published a particularly insightful description, entitled "Music Like None Other on Earth". He predicted that Riley:

> is bound to make a profound impression with it... This
> primitivistic music goes on and on. It is formidably
> repetitious, but harmonic changes are slowly introduced
> into it; there are melodic variations and contrasts of rhythm
> within a framework of relentless continuity, and climaxes of
> great sonority appear and are dissolved in the endlessness.

> At times you feel you have never done anything all your
> life long but listen to this music and as if that is all there is
> or ever will be, but it is altogether absorbing, exciting, and
> moving, too.[35]

If Riley had been a composer intent on a career and a coherent oeuvre, *In C* would have been the model from which he could have developed more and more pieces over the years to come to consolidate his reputation as a composer of periodic Minimalist Music. But in fact, he hardly followed up on his newly discovered successful model at all. Few of his works from the 1960s follow or develop the methods of a modular composition technique. Around 1970, he began to study Indian music and for a long time, turned away from "motoric Minimalism" completely.

Terry Riley has even claimed that for 3 years after *In C*, he composed nothing. But that's not quite true. In 1965, he created *Keyboard Studies,* in which the technique of *In C* is transferred to the piano. Once more, the piece consists of a series of short melodies to be played simultaneously, sometimes at different tempi – a method that also mimics the effect of tape loops. To emphasize the cyclical nature of this composition, Riley wrote the score with the staves arranged in circular fashion. In a synthesizer improvisation entitled *A Rainbow in Curved Air,* written in 1967, which became Terry Riley's second hit in the hippie scene after *In C,* repetitive figures are played in different metres, which reminds of unsynchronized tape loops running next to each other.

But Riley's main work during this period undoubtedly were his concerts, the so-called All-Night-Flights, in which he used tape loops for live improvisations. These events were concerts that lasted for nights on end, beginning at nine or ten o'clock in the evening and continuing until early morning. In an interview, Riley describes how the first all-nighter, entitled Poppy No-Good and the Phantom Band, was born at the Philadelphia Art Academy. He relates that, "the only component that was a little bit related was, that he would put up mirror-like screens around the stage where

I was playing, so you had multiple images and the audience got different points of view of the stage."[36]

The All-Night Flights that followed were often multimedia spectacles, accompanied by stroboscopic effects and projections. Artist Bob Whitman, another friend of Riley's, built mirrored screens, "around the stage where I was playing, so the audience saw me from different perspectives, and sometimes he would make projections, he would take polaroids of me as I was playing and would project these polaroids as soon as they were developing, so you'd get multiple images."[37] Riley's installation Time Lag Accumulator, which I described at the beginning of this chapter, also developed from these concerts. Riley notes about the audience's reaction, "This is the Sixties, so that was a time, where the audience as well as the artists, I think, were interested in a consciousness-expanding experience. And tape loops were certainly a part of it, because they changed the way that people were experiencing music."[38]

The music from Riley's All-Night-Flights usually consisted of long, sustained meditative improvisations on the soprano saxophone[39] or organ. The melodies were played back with a time lag by the Time Lag Accumulator, re-recorded together with Riley's live improvisations and then repeated again. So Riley played a canon with himself with the aid of the tape recorder; the phrases and figures overlapped and blended into ever-new combinations before fading away.

> I really didn't have a plan, I just went in and started playing. One of my specialties was to be able to play for a really long time without stopping and I would play these repeated patterns for hours and hours and I wouldn't seem to get tired. I guess I have a lot of energy. Throughout the evening I would be recording these long saxophone delays and about four hours into the concert, if I wanted to take a break I would just play back the saxophone. And a lot of people didn't even wake up to know the difference because a lot of people just slept all night.

"It was mostly improvisation," he says in an interview about the music that was created in this way.

> It was a lot of improvisations, but the patterns of course were always created with the time lag process, so no matter what I played it was put in a loop format. Whatever I played very freely, it would turn into loops. There are two performances on Corti, and I have some tapes that we did not put out. I think it was quite powerful, and there is no way to duplicate that today, if you did not use the same technique. If you would try to do it today with computers, it would come out differently. The tape machines had a very distinct sound and the noise aspect for instance was very important. The distortions were very important, because it would accumulate on magnetic tape, and it built up a sound, because it would overload the tape, and you would get these really grungy sounds – which a lot of people like today. I also liked it, because you could create some very dark, sonic imaginary with all this really dense sound. But it wasn't only noise, noise was only an aspect of it. It was a cosmic sound, of what the universe would sound like with all this vast workings of molecular activities. To me it had this cosmic aspect to it, that was bigger than life on earth.[40]

Riley continued performing these improvisations into the 1970s. Recordings of these concerts justify the view of Riley as the composer who succeeded, not only in performing live with electronic instruments, but also in entering into a musical dialogue with them to create a music that is generated both by him and by technology.

Before Riley, electronic music was generally recorded music. The tape recordings of Schaeffer, Stockhausen, Le Caine, Cage, Luening, Ussachevsky and Varèse were generally produced in the studio. Once the pieces were completed, they were played on tape recorders for concerts. The fact that during these concerts of electronic music, the stage was full of loudspeakers rather than musicians was an often-voiced criticism at that time. Concerts that combined electronic recorded music with orchestral music were unusual, and pieces like Cage's *Imaginary Landscape Number One* or Stockhausen's *Short Waves*, where electronic sounds were either brought to the stage with record players (Cage) or radios (Stockhausen), were rare.

It was Riley and his technically simple Time Lag Accumulator that made it possible to make live music with a machine. Almost a decade before the German electronic band Kraftwerk claimed that their synthesizers were equal partners in composition, Riley was looking for ways to make music together with media technology. In contrast to Kraftwerk, who staged themselves as "human machines" with short hair, uniform clothing and mechanical movements, however, Riley performed in Indian robes, wearing a long beard. By now, he has turned 80 and gives the impression of a hermit or guru, rather than a composer who sought to establish technology as an equal partner on stage. But he performed in front of audiences in the mid-1960s using his Time Lag Accumulator, making music with and against the apparatus, and, with the help of recording technology, was able to achieve effects that were as unpredictable as they were unplanned, frequently being amazed by the result himself.

Riley himself wryly referred to the aspects of deindividualization and devaluation of artistic subjectivity, which accompany all types of music created with the aid of media machines. In the 1960s, he often performed with the name Poppy No-Good and the Phantom Band. The Time Lag Accumulator, or the two tape recorders that repeated the music which he improvised on the organ or saxophone to create a counterpoint to his playing, were the phantom band. Riley would later also refer to his "alternative, multiple personality, which was being recycled electronically."[41]

Later, electronic musicians would hide behind pseudonyms like LFO, Kid 606, Modeselektor or Prototype 909, names that are derived from the technology they used to make their music.[42]

They are part of a music cottage industry that no longer produces music collaboratively in the studio, but alone and at home. Like Riley in the 1960s and 1970s, these musicians didn't travel to live performances with their band or ensemble, but rather, played on their own with the aid of electronic equipment such as samplers and laptops, which can fit into a bag.

These practices developed from the late 1980s onwards and are a contemporary legacy of Riley and his two main musical achievements of the 1960s. Firstly, making music using tape loops while focusing on their repetitive properties and transferring the repetitions that resulted back into the instrumental music. Secondly, using the devices that produce loops to make music, not only in the studio (like Stockhausen, Schaeffer and other avant-garde composers did), but in live performances.

"IT IS ALL VERY CLEAR WHAT'S HAPPENING, BUT I STILL CAN'T FOLLOW IT."

Steve Reich's Early Tape Compositions and the Autonomous Functioning of Technology

Terry Riley's influence on Steve Reich has been the subject of long disputes that led to a falling out between the two composers. These disputes will not be recounted in detail here. Both Riley and Reich acknowledge that they were friends in the mid-1960s and that Reich was familiar with Riley's tape works before he began working with loops himself. Reich had played in the world premiere of *In C* and had even made the decisive suggestion that the piece should be given rhythmic coherence by playing a pulse on the high C of the piano. Reich also recounts that Riley had played *She said she* and another tape composition to him in late 1964 or early 1965. And even if Reich says that *In C* had a greater influence on him than those tape compositions, he'd also been familiar with the method of creating compositions from spoken text using loops through superimposition and phase shifting when he began working on his own first important tape work, *It's Gonna Rain*, which utilized similar effects.

Reich later always played down the influence which Riley's tape compositions had on his work. And yet *It's Gonna Rain* was originally called *It's Gonna Rain, or: Meet Brother Walter in Union Square after listening to Terry Riley.* But as much as Riley's and Reich's tape loops are similar in technical terms, there are distinct differences between the free and undogmatic way in which Terry Riley used tape loops and Reich's more disciplined and conceptual approach.

Born in New York, Reich had made initial attempts with tape during his university studies at Mills College in 1962. Like Riley, Reich had created some compositions for one of the alternative theatre groups that played such a major role in the San Francisco cultural scene of that time, and which provided an important impetus for the development of the Californian psychedelia scene. While Riley created tape compositions for Ann Halprin's dance company, Reich's early compositions were written for the San Francisco Mime Troupe. His first completed electronic composition, likewise, was a soundtrack. He processed excerpts from a record into loops and first played separately before "superimposing them to create noise" for Robert Nelson's short film *Plastic Haircut.* The result was "a kind of surrealistic rondo in which very different elements were repeated".[1]

Shortly afterwards, Reich went in search of acoustically interesting source material for his tape compositions in order to process these with his "Uher Recorder". Following a friend's tip, he discovered a black Pentecostal preacher who regularly performed on Union Square in San Francisco. He recorded a passionate sermon in which Brother Walter vividly described the horrors of the Flood and survival in Noah's Ark. This resulted in the tape composition *It's Gonna Rain*, which remains one of the most impressive works of American minimal music. Unlike Riley, Reich knew the French *musique concrète* and acknowledges that this style had an influence on his own compositions: "I had listened to a lot of electronic music and a lot of *musique concrete*. The bone I had to pick with (Pierre) Schaeffer and that bunch was that if they were using the sound of a car crash, they had to lower it by an octave or speed it up by an octave, run it through a ring modulator or play it backwards. Why not hear that it's a car crash! These sounds that you're using in the original state have some kind of emotional resonance. We relate to them in various ways. If you bring them into the music, that brings in an emotional, theatrical meaning which is useful. It's worthwhile maintaining and building upon...My idea was that I always wanted you to hear what the original sounds were. For *It's Gonna Rain* and *Come Out*, that meant what the people were saying. Because *It's Gonna Rain* was vocal music."[2] In his work with tape loops, Reich used material that presented the genuine American vernacular for him. In *It's Gonna Rain*, it's the ecstatic staccato speech of the lay preacher, in *Come out*, the slang of a black teenager. Reich further comments that, "I was interested in using comprehensible sounds, so that this documentary aspect would become part of the piece."[3] He had originally planned to disassemble and reassemble Brother Walter's sermon in a collage-like fashion. But after encountering Riley's *In C* and its use of repetitive sound modules, he decided in early January 1965 to reduce his material to a few short segments and to repeat this several hundred times.

In order to find the key passages of the sermon, Reich first wrote out the entire text and then isolated the passages that seemed to have musical potential, including the short fragment "It's gonna rain", which became the title of the piece. He was aided by the fact that the sermon was delivered in the excited chant that is typical of the performance style of African-American Pentecostal preachers. The passage which Reich selected for further development can even be notated. It involves a major third, increasing from C to E. (Curiously, Terry Riley's *In C* begins with a pattern based on exactly the same interval.) The fluttering of a dove in the background, which Reich had unintentionally recorded alongside, provided a real background rhythm. He composed the 17-minute-long composition, which is made up of two distinct parts, from four such vocal "samples". While the first part consists only of the looped phrase "It's gonna rain", Reich assembled several sentence fragments for the second part and closed them into a loop.

The phased effect, which was to characterize Reich's 1960s compositions, resulted from the technical inadequacies of the tape recorders he used. Their running speed was subject to slight fluctuations, and so they could not be synchronized exactly – Reich was using tape recorders that cost only a hundred dollars. He himself suspected that the devices did not run completely synchronously "because of the different tensions of the drive belts, or simply because of dirt".[4]

"I tinkered with the tape loops of the preacher's voice, and I was still influenced by *In C*," Reich said later in an interview. "I wanted to get a certain relationship going: I wanted the word *rain* to lie over the *it's*, so that the end result would be *rain, rain, rain, rain* as one voice of counterpoint, with the other voice saying, *it's gonna, it's gonna, it's gonna*."[5]

To test this method, Reich made two identical tape loops with the "It's gonna rain" fragment from the sermon and inserted them into two separate tape recorders, which he turned on and ran simultaneously. In his first attempt using two tape recorders, the two loops, which initially ran synchronously, began to drift apart after a short time. Reich's breakthrough while working on *It's Gonna Rain* was that he did not regard the irregularities that occurred during the operation of the tape recorders as a problem, but as an opportunity, turning the "malfunction" into a strength.

Reich put on the headphones he was using in the absence of a mixing console in order to hear the two loops running simultaneously on the tape recorders. Each of the two sockets of his stereo headphones was plugged into the output of one of the two mono tape recorders. Reich later said that:

> the effect of this was that I could hear the sound bouncing
> back and forth in my head between my right and left ear
> when one or the other machine was running out of sync.

Instead of immediately re-syncing, I waited...I did nothing. One of the machines ran a little faster and the sound moved to the left side of my head, went down my leg, then across the floor and started to reverberate because the left channel had overtaken the right. I let this go on and eventually, it acquired exactly the relationship I had imagined. But what struck me was that instead of creating a canon-like relationship that was a small part of a longer composition, I had produced a series of rhythmically flexible canons which...ended up running together in rhythmic unison. That struck me right away. It was an accidental discovery, but many people hearing the same phenomenon might have said, "the machines should be synced!" I had the feeling that I had discovered something that was more important than what I was actually trying to do, however. Suddenly I had the idea of making a tape piece that would be a kind of process.[6]

The effect of the two voices drifting apart and coming back together is uncanny; many listeners find it unbearable. From a relatively simple technical arrangement, an "infernal" auditory impression is created. Reich lets the passage from Brother Walter's sermon, in which the sentence fragment "gonna rain" occurs, run once before he sets the two loops in motion. Then, for over 7 minutes, the fragment is doubled, diverging and merging in turn while Reich piles up more and more "voices" from looped "gonna rain" excerpts. In the second part, he uses another passage from the sermon, which is subjected to complicated combinations and phase shifts. In some places he makes up to eight voices run against each other, creating a kind of technological canon.

The piece demonstrates in an almost textbook-style manner some typical features of loop-based compositions. The repetition of the short sample removes all humanity from the preacher's words. The uninterrupted staccato repetitions signal a kind of stamina that exceeds the limits of human capacity. By the time one sample emerges out of another, it becomes clear that it is no longer a person speaking and that the act of speaking has been taken over by repetitive media.

Simultaneously, the listener's attention gradually shifts from what is being said to the acoustic properties. *It's Gonna Rain* corroborates Pierre Schaeffer's insight that every sound becomes music if it is repeated often enough. The composition effectively reduces the semantic meaning of the material to its rhythmic and melodic properties. Steve Reich repeatedly said in interviews that tape repetitions increased the meaning and power of the spoken word: "the strength and content of the words are intensified by repetition and phase shifting".[7] However, this assessment probably results more from Reich's desire to inscribe artistic subjectivity into the mechanical functioning of the piece than from an actual listening impression. In fact, it is only the first repetitions at the beginning of the piece that intensify the emphasis of the words. Thereafter, the phase shifting makes the speech appear increasingly insignificant.

Brother Walter's words delivered the raw material for a musical process. As the piece progresses, one forgets that the sentence "it's gonna rain" has any specific meaning. It's no longer the content of Brother Walter's sermon but the process and sound phenomena resulting from the phasing that occupy the attention. Reich describes the psycho-acoustic phenomena as "resulting patterns". The different elements of a sentence reinforce or neutralize each other by overlapping. Additionally, elements are heard which are not on the tape, but which develop in the perception of the listener during focused listening. Using a switch on the amplifier, Reich intensifies this impression by switching between the two sound sources. In many of the variations that result from fragments drifting apart, the initial sentence can therefore hardly be discerned any longer. He is right when he comments on the complex results that result from a simple method, "The mystery is not in what I do but in the result. It is all very clear what's happening, but I still can't follow it."[8]

At other times, however, Reich comments on the piece in a way that foregrounds the intentionality of the composer. Time and again, he mentions that when he created the piece during his stay in San Francisco, he was feeling "very disturbed"[9] and that his condition had been a contributory factor. He did not even want to perform the second part of the piece because "he didn't want to impose his neurosis on his listeners".[10] A composition that is largely the result of two unsynchronized tape machines therefore unexpectedly becomes an expression of the composer's state of mind.

Yet evidently, for Reich, the piece is also much more than a psychogram of its creator – it is the depiction of an apocalypse.

> *It's gonna rain* is about the end of world. It was done in 1964 and in 1962 was the Cuban missile crisis. Living in San Francisco we felt that it was possible that we might all go up in radioactive smoke...It was terrifying, a very scary situation. So when everybody who was listening to it in that period of time, the Noah story and the story of Kennedy and Chruschov [Khrushchev] is one story, really. The second part of *It's gonna rain*, which is even more frightening, it is about trying to get into the arc and knowing that it was sealed by the hand of God...People say the tape pieces are just about pure sound, but that's not true. It is about taking something that means something and intensifying it through the repetition and the out-of-phase shifting, and of course you get lost, but the meaning hovers over it like a cloud.[11]

Even some 40 years after recording the piece, Reich still gets incensed when his work is primarily taken as the result of two diverging tape loops. "Loops in themselves are nothing," he says indignantly and straightens up in the armchair of the hotel lobby where I interview him and his wife, video artist Beryl Korot.

Loops by themselves are a stupid effect, and unfortunately a lot of stupid effects came out of using loops: people getting high on dope, and saying, "hey man, that's cool". But it's not cool, it's just stupid...So loops by themselves are of no interest. It is what you do with them. Just to have something going over and over again – you're crazy, you're stoned out of your mind. If you want to do that, fine. But it is not art, it is not even interesting. It's really stupid. But it is a powerful ingredient, and you can make fantastic works with it.[12]

Reich's second loop piece was written a few months after moving to New York in the autumn of 1965. He was asked to participate in efforts to renew a lawsuit against six black youths. The "Harlem Six" had been convicted of killing the Jewish owner of a candy store during a raid. The police had mistreated them during their arrest and then refused to provide them with medical care, despite the fact that some of their injuries were serious. Supporters of the group had interviewed the Harlem Six, their relatives and eyewitnesses, and had recorded these conversations on tape. Truman Nelson, the civil rights activist who led the support campaign for the group, had heard that Reich was working with tape. He approached the composer and asked him to create a composition from the interview tape recordings, which would be performed during a benefit event.

While reviewing the 10 hours of material, Reich came across a passage that particularly shocked him. One of the youths described how he had scraped off the scab from a just dried wound that the police had inflicted in order to get taken to hospital. "I had to, like, open the bruise up and let some of the bruise blood come out to show them." This sentence by teenager David Hamm attracted Reich for two reasons. Firstly, it gave a vivid impression of the circumstances under which the arrest had taken place. Secondly, the boy's somewhat muffled speech quality suggested interesting effects for looping. He wanted to "find raw speech material with musical potential", Reich later said in an interview.[13]

Once more, Reich makes two recordings drift apart on two tape recorders, and once more, the two loops deconstruct each other. As with *It's Gonna Rain,* the short phrase which makes up the piece could be notated as a third. Reich himself said about the piece, "*come out* is a refinement of *It's Gonna Rain*…I had already taken the radical step, now it was time to fine-tune the idea a bit. *Come out* may not have the raw energy of *It's Gonna Rain* but it is more subtle and has more musical focus."[14]

At the beginning of the 13-minute piece, which consists of one sentence, Reich repeats the complete sentence three times before isolating the fragment "come out to show them", which is then repeated several hundred times. At first it seems to be a single sample that is repeated over and over again. It is only gradually that one of the passages, which runs slightly faster than the other, emerges as distinct from the other. It seems like a psycho-acoustic hallucination imagined by the listener at first, triggered by the constant repetitions. It is as if the short echo, which gradually emerges from the loops' divergence, causes the listener's perception to supplement the ever-same with variations. It is only from the second minute onwards that it becomes clear that there are in fact two asynchronously running versions of the same sentence. The inhuman, machinelike repetition appears in stark contrast to David Hamm's warm and smooth voice. The stuttering syllable "co" from "come" out and "sh" from "show", and the resulting patterns appear like percussive elements, giving the piece a kind of meandering 4/4 time signature.

Since one loop runs on the left stereo channel and the other on the right one, a short echo sweeps across the acoustic space – an effect that is both disconcerting and disorientating, especially when listening to the piece with headphones. (Some 10 years later, Giorgio Moroder used a similar technique when producing Donna Summer's *I Feel Love* to transform the simple 4/4 time into a confusing, polyrhythmic beat, as discussed in chapter 13.)

Come out begins with two parts that slowly drift apart from each other, and in the third minute, Reich doubles the number of voices by adding a recording of the two original voices to each channel. By the second phase shift, the tonal characteristics of the piece begin to separate themselves from its content. This phase shift begins to produce its own motifs; the timbre of the syllables intrudes into the linguistic meaning. Further resulting patterns emerge from the superimposed loops. First, *Co-Ma*, then, *Co-Ma-Ma* and finally, *Co-Ma-Ma-Ma*. The tape recorder starts to perform a technological canon without human participation. Word sense becomes machine sound, text becomes texture. Reich superimposes more and more voices until the piece concludes and it is no longer possible to tell the voices apart at all. The initial sentence has become a pulsating mess that no longer bears any resemblance to the original material. Its meaning gives way to pure sound devoid of referentiality. Keith Potter describes the result as "charged with frustration and repressed suppression, further intensified by the fact that this human outcry against injustice is channelled into the machine-like mercilessness of a power that is beyond human control".[15] Like Reich, he ascribes authorial intentionality to the media technology process which is taking place here.

Like *It's Gonna Rain*, *Come out* makes use of the compositional method which Reich describes in his essay *Music as a Gradual Process*. "Once the process is set up and loaded, it runs by itself." In his essay, Reich emphasizes that through repetition and phase shifting, "by a kind of complete control I mean that by running this material through the process I completely control all that results, but also that I accept all that results without changes."[16]

The contradiction between the construction of experimental musical arrangements, which, once triggered, on the one hand produce autonomous sound structures and on the other, the desire for artistic self-expression, is at the heart of Reich's tape compositions from the 1960s. Reich recognized this and over the years that followed developed compositional methods that do not rely on autonomously functioning technology. He did not return to working with recorded sound material until the 1980s, when the first digital samplers made it possible to manipulate sound material more precisely than tape recorders could. Compositions like *Different Trains* (1988) and *Three Tales* (2001) use looped original sounds, arranged in parts reminiscent of vocals written for traditional opera.

At the end of the 1960s, he developed a kind of sequencer which he called "Phase Shifting Pulse Gate" as a continuation of his work with tape loops. The compositions produced in this way (*Four Log Drums, Pulse Music*) eventually seemed to Reich to be "too stiff and too unmusical...The device went down to the basement and remains there to this day."[17] His catalogue of works doesn't even mention these compositions.

Ironically, it was technology that liberated Reich from technology. After reflecting on how the phase shifting technique could be transferred to more traditional music, he began to play against a tape loop which he had previously recorded. "Soon after *It's gonna rain* and *Come out*, I decided that if I could only achieve this technique by phase shifting tape loops with machines, then I didn't want to do it anymore. I wanted to do it together with other people but was afraid that it would be a purely mechanical effect – windscreen wipers on a bus, bells on a train, barriers and so on. So, I said to myself, all right, then I will be the other machine. I made a recording of myself playing a piano pattern and made a tape loop out of that. I put it in the tape recorder and sat down at the piano, closed my eyes and miraculously, was gradually able to play six-tenths of a note faster than the tape. So then I said, well, let's do it with two pianos and forget about the tape. Arthur Murphy and I did that together and – *look, Ma, no tape*! That was a huge breakthrough for me in 1967; *Piano Phase, Violin Phase* and eventually, *Drumming* came out of that."[18]

The principles which Reich developed through his work with tape loops form the basis for all of his further work. In *Four Musical Minimalists*, Keith Potter comments that, "the crucial role that tape technology played in Reich's development in the late 1960s and beyond remains one of the most important examples in music history of how electronic music has influenced instrumental music".[19]

However, it was Terry Riley who had been the first to spot the rhythmic, modular properties of tape recorders and to exploit them, both compositionally and in his improvised live performances. While Schaeffer, Stockhausen and other experimenters had previously created complicated sounds from tape loops that involved many steps, Riley simply let them run on. He turned his work with tape from a meticulously planned method into an improvisational process. Before him, only Pierre Schaeffer had worked in a similar way for his early *Études de Bruits*, creating these with the aid of record players. However, as soon as the newly invented tape recorder allowed him to do so, Schaeffer turned to controllable and complex assembly methods.

By contrast, Riley used the simple process of recording and playback for which tapes had been invented to create his music, so that his own musical input was one factor, and the autonomous functioning of technology was the other. Possibly unconsciously following John Cage's call to "release the music", he made the tape into a musical collaborator. This led to the composition *In C*, which music critic Robert Palmer deems the "most influential composition by an American after 1960", and which William Duckworth now views as the "hymn" of Minimal Music.

Music made of repeating patterns, such as those composed by Riley and, after him, Reich, forms the basis of what is known as Minimal Music today – a music that emerged from tape loops. Through Riley and Reich, the tapping, hammering, pounding and pumping of the unleashed tape loops became a compositional principle that was to shape entire musical genres in the decades that followed.

Minimalism, which either shocked or annoyed audiences in the 1960s and 1970s, is now part of the canon of contemporary music. Terry Riley and Steve Reich are among the established contemporary composers whose works are performed all over the world. The pop star of Minimal Music, Philip Glass, is one of the most productive and successful composers of contemporary music. His operas, such as *Einstein on the Beach* (1997) and *the CIVIL warS* (1984), are regularly performed in concert halls and opera houses and he has composed soundtracks for successful films, like *Koyaanisqatsi* (1982), *The Truman Show* (1998), *The Hours*

(2002) and *The Illusionist* (2006). Through film scores by Glass and Michael Nyman (e.g. *The Piano* (1993) and *Gattaca* (1997)), Minimal Music has become accessible to a broader public. The style of music that once began in Terry Riley's garden with tape loops wrapped around wine bottles has also become an established aspect of commercials and fashion shows. Second and third generation Minimalist composers, like Arvo Pärt, John Adams, Tom Johnson, Andrew Poppy and Rhys Chatham, have developed and popularized the style further.

Additionally, the impulses of Minimal Music arrived in the pop culture of the 1970s and 1980s, to establish musical genres and entire youth cultures – electronic Disco, Hip-Hop, House and Techno. For the most part, those who shaped these genres were not aware of Reich's or Riley's compositions (the latter not being above composing music for discotheques). The machines with which Riley, Reich and the producers of dance music created their compositions – record players, tape recorders, sequencers, samplers – are repeating machines. These machines have their own ways of inscribing repetitive structures.

The psychedelic culture that developed on the American West Coast and in Britain at a time when Riley and Reich were creating their tape compositions in San Francisco were ideal settings to continue such sound experiments. While Reich steered clear of San Francisco's hippie and rock scene, Riley felt connected to it, and no other avant-garde composer probably had a greater influence on the pop music of his time than he. Three years after Riley had created *Music for the Gift*, The Beatles became the first pop group to record a piece based largely on loops. And yet, in the creative turmoil that prevailed in San Francisco in the mid- 1960s, it was a writer, rather than a musician, who made loops into the central elements of his work, and who therefore came to have a particularly far-reaching impact on pop culture. For Ken Kesey, author of *One Flew Over the Cuckoo's Nest*, tape loops were nothing less than the means to overcome the limitations of literature and to break down the separation between art and life.

THIS MACHINE DESTROYS SUBJECTIVITY! KEN KESEY, PSYCHEDELIA AND LOOPS OF THE GREAT HERE AND NOW

In the summer of 1964, a brightly painted school bus set off on an epic journey through the USA. Its occupants wanted to travel from La Honda, California, all the way to New York. The experience of the journey was more important to them than the destination. To enhance and document the experience, they took books, musical instruments, costumes, masks and film cameras with them. The front of the 1939 International Harvester Bus featured the word "Furthur"; the back read "Caution – Weird Load". This group of young writers and leader boss bohemians called themselves *The Merry Pranksters*. Their leader, Ken Kesey, had become famous through his novel *One Flew Over the Cuckoo's Nest*. Tom Wolfe describes their travels across the USA in detail in the journey log *The Electric Kool-Aid Acid Test*.[1] This book made the small group of Pranksters into the most influential source of inspiration for the American counterculture and hippie movement. The fact that the Pranksters' journey has become a legend of American hippie folklore is mainly due to the special kinds of travel provisions stashed in the fridge of the bus – a canister full of pure liquid LSD. The drug was not yet banned in the USA. Nor had it yet become the subcultural sacrament it was to be not long after. At that time, LSD was only being used by a small group of *cognoscenti*,[2] and it was these travellers' aim to change this as soon as they could. For Kesey and the Pranksters, LSD was a way to break down social conditioning and learned inhibitions and to enable a new view of the here and now – the "expansion of consciousness" that was the central mission of the psychedelic movement. But for Kesey, LSD was only one of several means by which to reach this goal. Photos of the interior of the bus show a sound system in a corner, which looks a bit like a private altar[3] – there are two tape recorders, amplifiers, microphones and many loudspeakers. In one photo, Kesey is standing by the tape recorders, looking through sunglasses and bending over the reels, reminiscent of a contemporary DJ. The ceiling, painted with drug-inspired patterns, makes a colourful archway above him. The sound system was intended to create echoes with the aid of tape loops. The Merry Pranksters called this the "delay machine". Tape loops therefore played a central role in the development of the American counterculture. For Kesey, tape echoes were intended to help propel him into new forms of perception and spontaneous self-expression, alongside LSD. The Merry Pranksters are the link between the beatniks of the 1950s and the hippies of the 1960s. Their drug-fuelled trip across the States combined enthusiasm for mobility, which beatnik author Jack Kerouac had celebrated in his cult novel *On the Road,* and the search for an alternative way of living, which the hippie movement would experiment with in the years to come. Neal Cassady, who had been the inspiration for the protagonist of Kerouac's novel almost a decade earlier, was driving the bus.

Allen Ginsberg later wrote that, "Neal Cassady drove Jack Kerouac to Mexico in a prophetic automobile, the same…Cassady that one decade later drove Ken Kesey's Kosmos-patterned schoolbus on a Kafka-circus tour over the roads of an awakening nation."[4] None of the passengers had long hair and other insignia of the hippie movement were also missing. The Prankster group was a precursor of the communities that would come into fashion over the years that followed. Their bus was painted with the kinds of colourful patterns which, a year later, were called "psychedelic". The destination was the World Expo in Queens (where General Motors' "Futurama Ride" was accompanied by music composed by Raymond Scott, and where Andy Warhol had to paint over his picture of the "thirteen most wanted men in the USA" with silver paint). Also, Kesey's just- published second novel, *Sometimes a Great Notion*, was to be presented in New York. After completing this book, Kesey was tired of the lonely work of writing a literary text. The proto commune in which he was living with his family and a number of friends in a house in La Honda was an attempt to end his isolation as a writer.

The bus journey was meant to continue his literary work by other means. Or, in the words of a friend of Kesey's, writer Gurney Norman, he wanted to find a new artistic form in which "life itself is a novel".[5] The journey was actually meant to become the subject of a collectively produced documentary. It is ironic that Kesey and the Pranksters took the attempt to expand the scope of literature so far that they never actually ended up producing a finished work – it took over 40 years for Alison Ellwood and Alex Gibney's documentary film *Magic Trip* (2011) to be made,[6] and it contains only a fraction of the material the Pranksters had recorded. In a sense, it might be seen as inevitable that an artistic experiment entirely devoted to the celebration of the here and now stubbornly resists its own immortalization as a work of art. The notion of art in which the creative process is more important than the product (such as films or novels) is a legacy from the 1960s that continues to resonate today. In literature, on the other hand, this notion has played a less important role. It is art forms such as performance, video, action art and experimental music where it was taken most seriously. In an interview, Ken Kesey says critically:

> in fact, I haven't been reading a whole hell of a lot, to tell you the truth. I feel like if I were looking back from 500 years from this time, I wouldn't look at the literature that's being turned out to see what's happening, what's going on with the people. I'd listen to the Rock'n'Roll music. I'd go to the movies. I'd read the comic books and look at the papers. Painting and sculpture, music, all of these other things, are breaking out of their bounds. Writing has remained the same for a god-awful long time.[7]

Unfortunately, Kesey does not mention the names of the artists, musicians and composers he is referring to. He only speaks in general terms, of artists "whose names would be meaningless, either because they haven't made IT yet, or aren't working in a medium that has as its end an IT to make."[8] Kesey would join the ranks of artists without work over the years to come. His attempt to abandon literature in favour of life-as-art ended with a prison sentence for being found in possession of illegal drugs. It also made him a hero of American counterculture – a status he enjoys to this day, despite his death in 2001. Today's reader, who might associate the hippie movement with a "return to nature" and rejection of technology as well as other achievements of civilization, might be surprised by the media arsenal the Pranksters' coach was equipped with. Perry and Babbs observe that, "during the course of this trip, the Pranksters spent $70,000 on gasoline, food and on miles and miles of 16-mm film and tape. An estimated 45 hours of film and hundreds of hours of audio tape recorded literally every dramatic encounter, every chatter, every groan, every traffic sign on their immortal journey. The purpose of all this documentation was to make a film called *The Merry Pranksters' Search for a Cool Place*."[9]

The Pranksters' equipment is described in great detail by Tom Wolfe in his book *The Electric Kool-Aid Acid Test*, which is narrated in the breathless style of New Journalism. Sandy Lehman-Haupt, who was a sound engineer:

> went to work on the wiring and rigged up a system with which they could broadcast from inside the bus, with tapes or over microphones, and it would blast outside over powerful speakers on top of the bus. There were also microphones outside that would pick up sounds along the road and broadcast them inside the bus. There was also a sound system inside the bus so you could broadcast to one another over the roar of the engine and the road. You could also broadcast over a tape mechanism so that you said something, then heard your own voice a second later in variable lag and could rap off of that if you wanted to. Or you could put on earphones and rap simultaneously off sounds from outside, coming in one ear, and sounds from inside, your own sounds, coming in the other ear. There was going to be no goddamn sound on that whole trip, outside the bus, inside the bus, or inside your own freaking larynx, that you couldn't tune in on and rap off of.[10]

Today, the 60s are considered as an epoch in which, especially in the USA, an entire generation dived into drug-induced hallucinations. This idea is apparently supported by many visual relics from this period – the images of multimedia shows, like Andy Warhol's *Exploding Plastic Inevitable*, or the light shows at Fillmore West Music Club, the colourful covers of psychedelic rock bands with their kaleidoscopic swirls of colour, and the concert posters by graphic artists like Rick Griffin, Randy Tuten, Wes Wilson and Victor Moscoso, which are reminiscent of Op Art. These images, which show a distorted reality dissolving into colours and forms, are often seen as a reflection of drug experiences, and therefore as incarnations of an "authentic" 1960s spirit.

In fact, many of the protagonists from the 60s seem to have been less concerned with using drugs and new technologies to create sensory illusions than with their use as a means of liberating blocked perceptions and enabling a view of reality that is free from social conditioning. It was more about epiphanies than about hallucinations, as in the William Blake quote on which the title of Aldous Huxley's influential mescaline-inspired book *Doors of Perception*, which was mandatory reading in the hippie scene at the time, is based: "If the doors of perception were cleansed everything would appear to man as it is, infinite."11 This is also why psychedelic drawings and posters often show mandala-like spiral patterns that seem to wind endlessly inwards, as if wanting to draw the viewer towards the centre of perception. Perception and its preconditions were among the most important cultural themes of the 1960s. Like many other apostles of his time, Ken Kesey wanted to liberate perception – among other things, with the aid of tape loops.

> Paula Sundsten has gotten hold of a microphone with the variable-lag setup and has found out she can make weird radio-spook laughing ghoul sounds with it, wailing like a banshee and screaming "how was your stay-ay-ay-ay...in San Ho-zay-ay-ay-ay-ay," with the variable lag picking up the ay-ay-ay-ays and doubling them, quadrupling them, octupling them. An endless ricocheting echo—and all the while this weird, slightly hysterical laugh and a desperate little plunking mandolin sail through it all...12

This scene, which took place during the Merry Pranksters' journey, is described in Tom Wolfe's book *Electric Kool-Aid Acid Test* and it emphasizes the delay machine's effect on language. The tape loops capture parts of words, "double, quadruple, increase [them] eightfold"; they make them appear endless by extending their duration beyond the physical rules of sound perception. They change real time into reproduced media time; they arrange the linear course of time into a loop and let it revolve in front of the amazed audience.

The echoes in the Pranksters' bus resonate with one of the most important artistic themes of the 1960s. Many attempts to overcome the barriers between the arts focus directly on

temporality during this decade. This includes not only the experiments conducted using Kesey's delay machine, but also – as previously outlined in the chapter on Peter Roehr – visual art movements such as Minimal Art, Systems Art, Process and Conceptual Art and Video Art.

Kesey was not the only writer who tried to extend the scope of literature through the use of electronic media. Other writers, like William S Burroughs and Byron Gysin, also experimented with tape recordings, creating collages using the cut-up principle. But compared to visual artists, the involvement of writers in such experiments remained relatively limited. With a hint of self-irony, Prankster and author Ken Babbs describe a quarter of a century later how the ideas for their experiments had come about:

> Before the trip, we'd talked about rapping novels instead
> of writing them, because writing on a machine is so slow.
> We wanted to take acid and stay up all night long, rapping
> novels and recording them on tape. And to add to that, we
> were going to play them back and make music to that, and
> then we started to imagine how we were going to get a film
> camera and capture that right away. And so, we quickly
> progressed from novels printed on paper to novels on tape
> and novels on film.[13]

This comment is more complex than might appear at first glance. What Babbs describes is effectively an improvement on the obsessive staccato-like stream-of-consciousness writing employed by beatnik writers like Jack Kerouac, who is said to have written his novel *On the Road* within 3 weeks and with a continuous role of paper in his typewriter.[14] Yet at the same time, in this provisional aesthetic program, literature comes together with – as yet vague – ideas about "multimedia" art and notions of collaborative forms of creativity. It was with good reason that the starting point for these experiments was the notion that the traditional mechanics of writing were too time-consuming, and that the kind of literature the Pranksters were looking for was a spontaneous expression that becomes manifest in the moment it is created. It is also consequential that they opted for recording media as the appropriate means – i.e. tape and film. (Sometime later, it would probably have been video that would have been chosen as the more suitable medium for this purpose, since this allows the immediate reproduction of recorded images. But it was still a year before video was to appear on the consumer market in the USA. Later on, the Merry Pranksters were to conduct similar experiments with video feedback.) Although loops were a central element of the Pranksters' heuristic experiments, there are few audio recordings of them. In the discussion that follows, I will primarily refer to witness accounts quoted in *Electric Kool-Aid Acid Test*.[15] Wolfe describes Kesey's initial tape experiments, which do not make use of tape loops. "They would do something like...all lie on the floor and start rapping back and forth and Kesey puts a tape-recorder microphone up each sleeve and passes his hands through the air and over their heads, like a sorcerer making signs, and their voices cut in and out as the microphones sail over."[16]

Even here, the sound system was used to isolate specific elements from the jumbled chatter. Kesey moving the microphone around the room reminds of the random operations that have featured in modern art since Dadaism, and which were being developed into a compositional system by John Cage at that time. By amplifying specific sentence or word fragments, these moved into the foreground of (technologically augmented) perception, so that sensory impressions focused on the individual particles of the larger, acoustic whole.

Kesey was soon to leave the selection process entirely to his media equipment. Wolfe writes about these early experiments that:

> they grow out of...the experience, with LSD. The whole other world that LSD opened your mind to existed only in the moment itself—Now—and any attempt to plan, compose, orchestrate, write a script, only locked you out of the moment, back in the world of conditioning and training where the brain was a reducing valve.[17]

In order to lend duration to ephemeral perceptions, Ken Kesey and the Pranksters developed the so-called delay system,[18] using tape recorders that were intended to muddle the linear passing of time.

Tom Wolfe writes about an evening in the Merry Pranksters' commune where Kesey:

> starts talking about the lag systems he is trying to work out with tape recorders. Out in the back house he has variable-lag systems in which a microphone broadcasts over a speaker, and in front of the speaker is a second microphone. This microphone picks up what you just broadcast, but an instant later. If you wear earphones from the second speaker, you can play off against the sound of what you've just said, as in an echo. Or you can do the things with tapes, running the tape over the sound heads of two machines before it's wound on the take up reel, or you can use three microphones and three speakers, four tape recorders and four sound heads, and on and on, until you get a total sense of the lag.[19]

With this design, Kesey had created a veritable cybernetic feedback system in which identical sounds are not just repeatedly fed back, the signal also interacts with external sources at the same time. Apparently unaware of Terry Riley's live performance with tape loops, he had arrived at an amazingly similar method. All of these experiments produce a similar effect. They virtually arrest the passing of time and suspend the (audible) presence of the world for a brief moment before presenting it to subjective perception in an accentuated form. Although the sound fragments themselves have a certain duration, when they are repeated, they enable a kind of perception that is closer to spatial than to temporal experience. It becomes possible to "move in the sound". The process of arresting time is, of course, itself subject to temporality again – the tape echo recedes and ultimately ebbs away – yet for a brief period, time seems to stand still, akin to a sculpture, and can be "viewed" as such. Tom Wolfe, quoting Ken Kesey, places the experiments with the delay machine in a larger phenomenological context:

> A person has all sorts of lags built into him (…) One, the most basic is the sensory lag, the lag between the time your senses receive something and you are able to react…We are all of us doomed to spend our lives watching a movie of our lives – we are always acting on what has just finished happening. It happened at least 1/30th of a second ago. We think we're in the present, but we aren't. The present we know is only a movie of the past, and we will really never be able to control the present through ordinary means. That lag has to be overcome some other way, through some kind of total breakthrough. Nobody can be creative without overcoming all those lags first of all.[20]

Unfortunately, Wolfe does not mention where Kesey learned about delayed perception, which human consciousness is subject to. Recent neurophysiological research agrees with him, albeit with different time values. Paradoxically, for Kesey, this is precisely why delays are able to break through the delay mechanism of perception. It is by pinpointing and delaying the reproduction of what has already been perceived that they enable direct access.

His interest in the mechanisms of perception connects Kesey with two thinkers who have particular significance for my reading of 1960s culture in general and the psychedelic movement in particular. I have previously referred to them in the chapter on Peter Roehr: the psychologist Friedrich Perls and the philosopher Maurice Merleau-Ponty. Kesey was personally acquainted with Perls and his Gestalt therapy method, which was an important influence on the Merry Pranksters' group processes, and especially on Kesey's delay machine. Before dealing with these connections in more detail, however, it is useful to explore the relationship between Merleau- Ponty's phenomenology, 1960s Minimalism and Kesey's loop experiments in a little more detail.

Ken Kesey does not seem to have had any direct involvement with the phenomenology of Merleau-Ponty or Husserl, yet his activities in the 1960s seem, akin to Minimalist art, like an attempt to make phenomenological thinking comprehensible. Merleau-Ponty had replaced the diametric opposition of subject and object with a dynamic model of consciousness that was based on experience. He thereby calls into question the notion of a fixed and self-reliant subject, as postulated in Western rationalism since Descartes. A simplified formulation of phenomenology could be a reformulation of Descartes' famous formula "I think, therefore I am" into "I am, therefore I think". The self here does not constitute itself in some abstract realm of consciousness but arises from the relationship between mind, body and world.

This was the basic assumption that made phenomenology interesting for some Minimalist artists. Due to their regularity, strictly geometric forms and linearity, their works might appear like rationalism turned into sculpture. And yet, it was Descartes' dualism of matter and spirit that they actually set out to question. Art historian Rosalind Krauss observes that, "the Minimalist subject is neither the old Cartesian subject nor the traditional biographical subject...rather, it is radically dependent on spatial conditions, it is a subject that is constituted in the act of perception, but always only temporarily, from moment to moment".[21]

The Merry Pranksters' drug and media experiments similarly seem like an implementation of Merleau-Ponty's "body thinking", in which perception is dynamically constituted from moment to moment. Kesey's group engaged with the channels of perception that were at the heart of Merleau- Ponty's phenomenology to experience moments of heightened perception. The term "epiphany" has always involved the search for elevated experiences, in religion, literature and the arts alike. Umberto Eco writes in *The Open Work* that:

> reality is a sum of forces and elements that become and
> dissolve, which makes only the experience that remains
> on the surface appear physical and fixed in an obtrusive
> present...In the moment of epiphany, these impressions
> are shared as if by a magic stroke. We then find ourselves
> in a world of unstable, flashing, unconnected impressions;
> habit is broken, the familiar disappears, and beyond it
> remain individual moments that can be briefly grasped yet
> quickly pass.[22]

The purpose of the Pranksters' drug and media experiments was to make such moments of unrestricted perception possible. For them, the temporary destabilization of perception was a cognitive tool which frees the object from illusory components and removes all contexts from perception and comprehension. In contrast to traditional art, it was not the artist's subjectivity that made possible or characterized such epiphanies. With his tape echoes, Kesey made media technology the trigger of such experiences. His method therefore differs from the usual way of presenting epiphany in literature as described by Eco, using James Joyce as an example: "the poet is the one who, in a moment of grace, discovers the deep soul of things, and through the poetic word alone, he is also the one who brings this soul into existence. Epiphany is a mode of discovering the real and at the same time, of defining it through language."[23] Kesey, who had lost his faith in literature, rejected the possibility of words giving form to the experience of epiphany. Instead, he let the tape recorder foreground specific fragments of the world. The consequent repetition of sound particles allows anyone who listens to experience their own epiphany. Kesey's loop experiments coincide with the methods of Minimal Art when it comes to what Michael Fried terms the "special participation that the works demand of the viewer".[24] The "specific objects" of Minimal art are not representations of the world as designed by an artist, but rather, an opportunity for individual, subjective experience. They do not say or express anything – they *are*. If they have a meaning, it is to enable an act of perception. They do not express a moment of epiphany, but they provide an opportunity for it.[25] This is how Ken Kesey works when he suspends audible reality with his tape loops in order to hold on to what otherwise passes by unnoticed. It is a procedure that resembles the Minimalists' methods not only in the way that Kesey uses repetitions of echoes to expand perception. Like Minimalist sculptures, his tape experiments are not the *expression* of aesthetic experience but an impetus for the same. While art traditionally consists of shaping the real through the artist's subjectivity, Kesey's tape loops offer listeners a mode of experiencing reality that has not been artistically transformed, yet which nevertheless offers more than a piece of unprocessed reality. They can pick up the microphone and create sound sources for echoes. Since the delay machine allows the listener to interact directly with the technology, Kesey's construction goes beyond the works of Minimalist artists in terms of the freedom to participate. In a much-quoted passage, Roland Barthes proclaims the "death of the author" as a precondition for the "birth of the reader". Kesey's delay machine similarly gives birth to the "reader", the audience, as co-creator. The delay machine not only resembles Terry Riley's *Time Lag Generator* even down to the name, it also anticipates ideas of sonic artists like Bill Fontana, Max Neuhaus, Laurie Anderson, Bernhard Leitner and Anja Wiese, who would go on to create interactive sound sculptures.

While phenomenology and Minimal Art may not have been direct influences on Ken Kesey's work, the *Gestalt* therapy of Friedrich Perls certainly was. Kesey knew Perls personally and visited him repeatedly at his therapy centre in Esalen, Big Sur,

California. He describes one of these visits in the short story "Demon Box", in which a character called Dr Klaus Woofner, who resembles Perls, appears.[26] Perls had been a student of Wilhelm Reich. In 1933 he fled from the National Socialists, first to the Netherlands, then to South Africa. In 1946, he moved to the USA, where he successfully championed the *Gestalt* therapy method. The attempt to enable a perception of the moment is at the heart of this method. During therapy sessions, Perls asked his patients to narrate their perceptions as they saw, heard and felt them. In this kind of exercise, they were to begin every sentence with the word "now". This unfiltered, instant narration was intended to enable authentic experience, which according to Perls is usually blocked by convention and habits. Patients were to be absorbed in the "here and now", rather than being dominated by their past or afraid of the future. In this way, he aimed to break through psychological barriers, which according to him lead to neuroses and other disorders. This method made Perls into an important figure of 1960s counterculture on the American West Coast and his influence can be felt in many hippie practices. Tom Wolfe calls him "the father of the 'now trip'".[27] In one sense, Perls' patients were transformed into a human version of Kesey's tape delay machine. They narrated what they perceived with a minimal time difference. Perls speaks of a "fertile void". In contrast to familiar experiences, exposure to direct and unprocessed perceptions was intended to enable the patient to overcome ingrained blockages. Perls repeatedly polemicized against filling this void with any meaning. Rather, it was to be endured without "theorizing or deluding oneself, without fleeing into the past or expectations", and, by "jumping from experience to experience like a grasshopper...none of the experiences are being processed, they are only taken in like lightning".[28] Another central concept of Perls' thinking is *awareness*, a term he used to distance himself from traditional notions of attention and consciousness. Perls' influence on 1960s and 70s American art was significant. Bruce Nauman's videos and installations are clearly influenced by the *Gestalt* psychology.[29] His video installations of the early

1970s, such as *Live-Taped Video Corridor* (1970), implement the method of directly narrating reality with the aid of surveillance video cameras. Dan Graham's early performances, like *Intention Intentionality Sequence* (1972) and *Performer/Audience/ Mirror* (1974), in which he, as if he were a patient of Perls, describes his ongoing perceptions, are *Gestalt* psychological methods turned into art.[30] Graham was building his own "delay machine" at the time. In his video feedback installation entitled *Time Delay Room* (1974), he worked with a delay system for video tapes that was very similar to Kesey's tape loops. The parallels between Pearls' "phenomenology of awareness",[31] the aforementioned works of art and Kesey's tape echoes are unmistakable. In each case, impressions are narrated with a minimal time delay, in one context by a patient, in the other by a recording medium. This kind of reproduction produces the fertile void that Perls refers to. Just as in *Gestalt* therapy, the patient is supposed to get through to authentic perception by relating his/her observations, so Kesey's delay machine was supposed to allow sound to be removed from its context and simply perceived, beyond any habits, classifications, standards of value and systems of categories. Kesey's tape loops suspend auditory reality without stopping it altogether. They facilitate a focus on the smallest components of the Great Reality. In the same way that slow-motion film shots reveal processes that cannot be perceived by the naked eye,[32] these tape loops allow viewers to immerse themselves in nuances, semantic fields, potentials that would normally elude them. On the one hand, tape loops are metaphors for perceptual limits, on the other hand, they also offer a way of overcoming these limits. By merely repeating what they "hear", the tape machines leverage both the semantic meaning and the referential, representative property of the sounds, to lend them a new, autonomous meaning. Along with Terry Riley, who started his work around the same time, Ken Kesey is one of the first artists to use tape loops in live performances. Because they "retrieve" the reality that has just passed by and turn it into confusing sound labyrinths, they allow their listeners to hear something beyond their obvious meaning. With the aid of tape loops, Kesey liberated the sound by temporarily suspending it. His experiments with tape loops and drugs were to lead to a temporary expansion of consciousness (Perls' awareness), which also had political implications. Kesey held that the natural delay in perception "keeps us away from the present...from our own world, our own reality, and as long as we cannot enter to our own world, we also can't control it."[33] Such reflections prompted Kesey to pursue a practice that would eventually eject him from the world of high culture.[34] Together with the Merry Pranksters, he began to design processes in which audiences were assigned an active role in shaping the overall result. These processes involved the Pranksters replacing the traditional notion of individual creativity with actions requiring collective creativity. They created spontaneous and intense situations to counter the notion of "eternal works". Success was partly beyond their control, since it depended on audience participation. In other words, the Merry Pranksters began organizing parties. After their bus tour through the USA, they organized the Acid Tests in California – multimedia dance events where music, light shows, projections and LSD offered an interface intended to make liberated perceptions possible, where all participants contributed to the proceedings. Jerry Garcia, guitarist of the Grateful Dead, who performed at most of the *Acid Test* events, recalls that:

> Everybody there was entertaining. Everything there was entertaining; every event that happened. And you didn't need expertise. The musician's chauvinism – 'I can do something you can't do' – all that stuff went up in smoke, which I think was very good for everybody; everybody learned a lot from that process. I think everybody who ever went to an Acid Test came out a different person and loved it.[35]

On another occasion he observed, "the Kesey thing depended on who you were when you were there. It was open, a tapestry, a mandala – it was whatever you made it...It was everybody doing bits and pieces of something, the result of which was something else."[36] The *Acid Test* entry ticket included a cup of "electric" Kool-Aid, a fizzy drink mixed with LSD, which also became Tom Wolfe's book's title. The walls were decorated with psychedelic posters and illuminated with slides of blending oil colours and other colourful light sources. Like contemporary Techno parties, these events usually lasted all night and those who made it through the night had "passed" the *Acid Test*.

In addition to the music of the Grateful Dead, tape echoes were an important part of the acoustic environment of these events. "The Pranksters always commanded as much attention as the Dead at these affairs, with their piles of sound equipment, Roy Seburn's light show and the unholy triumvirate of Kesey, Babbs and Cassady always moving in three equally weird but compelling directions at once, doing strange things with microphones."[37] The microphones were, of course, connected to the delay machine, which Kesey and the other Pranksters used for a kind of media echolalia, "laying down a rap...or chanting nonsense or narrating the insane scene in the room, sometimes even while the Dead were playing."[38] In this way, Kesey and his group used tape echoes to realize their idea of a literature that was created live and only for the moment in front of an audience. In front of listeners who were open to such experiments, they competed with the confusing echoes of their own performance to arrive at spontaneous poetry that was free from inhibitions. Kesey also often wrote poetic fragments on a slide projector and projected these on the wall. "We mostly used the figure eight tape delay for effects at the Acid Tests," Ken Babbs recalls. This refers to a construction in which tapes run through two tape machines, making a figure eight.[39] Carolyn Adams Garcia, a Prankster member who went by the name "Mountain Girl", observes that, "the delay machine was also one of the most important things, because there was this short lag on your voice; it was just long enough to be really uncomfortable, and it would really fuck you up. It was exactly the length of time it would take you to form a thought, so just as your next thought was formed, you heard your voice speaking the previous thought. It was really hard to make progress through that."[40] Kesey and Babbs had got the idea of "rapping literature" from Jack Kerouac, as already mentioned. His method of spontaneously produced, unedited prose was itself strongly influenced by the rapping of his friend Neal Cassady – the same who drove the Prankster bus and who stood next to Babbs and Kesey during the Acid Tests behind the delay machine, microphone at the ready. Kerouac adopted the style of Cassady's unfiltered verbiage, dubbed "rapping", as a literary method in order to leave behind the formalism of modern literature and instead capture direct, pure experience.

But the attempt to narrate authentic experience by literary means also makes Kerouac's novels an uncritical celebration of a dubious aesthetics of genius. With this kind of writing, every flash of thought and every observation issuing from Kerouac's breathless stream of consciousness is thought worthy of being communicated to the reader unfiltered and unprocessed. In his books, both Kerouac and his protagonists consequently embody creative energy in an exemplary fashion, quite according to Kerouac's maxim that "you're a genius all the time!"

When Kesey, Babbs and Cassady rapped during the *Acid Tests*, the delay machine got between them and the audience. Whatever went through their heads, the figure eight tape loops made it into an extended state for the audience, while the media echo stretched and repeated their spontaneous flashes into a kind of semantic nirvana. As Carolyn Garcia says, it became difficult to formulate a clear thought. The edited stream-of-consciousness writing of an ingenious writer like Kerouac turned into an interplay between humans and machines. The stuttering sound fragments produced by the delay machine undermined the artistic genius who was incessantly emitting literature. This machine destroys the author's subjectivity! Like Terry Riley and his Time Lag Generator, Kesey, Babbs and Cassady themselves blended with their tape recorders, to turn into a kind of part-man machine that continuously produced loops and nonsense.

Terry Riley developed the composition *In C* from his experiments with loops, which I have previously referred to as a "functioning anarchy". On the one hand, performers have maximum freedom when playing its 53 short figures, on the other hand, the piece discourages individual solo performances. It sanctions "antisocial" behaviour, which is tantamount to unmusical behaviour in its context, and the ensemble coheres as an egalitarian community for the duration of the performance.

Structurally, the Acid Tests were similar. They were not subject to rules. Everyone could do as they pleased, which was readily embraced by the participants. Although each time the Acid Tests brought together several hundred people (who often took LSD for the first time and in a relatively strong dose, and who were additionally exposed to intense stimuli from the music, light effects, film projections and tape loops), the events seem to have been mostly peaceful and harmonious. While some participants remember there occasionally being a "dangerous" atmosphere,[41] most *Acid Test* veterans describe these events as an anarchic, yet collectively consensual process. Jerry Garcia of the Grateful Dead recalls that, "you could dig that there was something that it was getting toward, something like ordered chaos…"[42] The Grateful Dead's second guitarist, Bob Weir, observes that the band learned to engage with each other by performing in these chaotic situations and that this led to a style of group improvisation that would later shape the band's legendary live performances. The loops structured the audio-visual chaos of noise, lights and film projections at these events. They orchestrated the assault on the senses, which the Pranksters staged with the aid of the latest media technology. Just as Pierre Schaeffer had been the first to use loops to order the "noise of modernity" into a concerted whole, the delay machine helped to give the droning jumble of music, rapping and sheer noise a unifying element. Carolyn Garcia remembers that she, "did a lot of the light shows – they used various slide projectors and film loops, mostly Prankster material, the bus going down the street and so on".[43] The Merry Pranksters' Acid Tests culminated in a major psychedelic event in January 1966, which they organized together with activist Stewart Brand, who later published the *Whole Earth Catalogue* and co-founded the influential California online community WELL.[44] The event was called Trips Festival and lasted for several days. As with the Acid Tests, the audience was again an important contributor. The invitation read:

> the general tone of things has moved on from the
> selfconscious happening to a more JUBILANT occasion
> where the audience PARTICIPATES because it's more fun to
> do so than not. maybe this is the ROCK REVOLUTION.
> audience dancing is an assumed part of all the shows & the
> audience is invited to wear ECSTATIC DRESS & bring
> their own GADGETS (a. c. outlets will be provided)."[45]

This 3-day event took place at Fillmore East Concert Hall, the main venue for the dance parties of San Francisco's psychedelic bands. Charles Perry describes it as, "a large dance floor with balconies on two sides of the room…The floor was strewn with electronic boxes and strings of electric cables. [The Pranksters] had packed in so much electronic equipment that the entire hall reverberated with the deep, muffled hum."[46] The technical equipment included video feedback systems, which enabled the audience to see themselves live on the monitor, similar to the closed-circuit installations that became so popular in video art a few years later.[47] On this occasion, the pranksters had distributed the delay machine throughout the building. Perry relates that:

> the balconies were used partly as dressing rooms and partly
> as offices, so that the Pranksters could wire the whole room
> with microphones and speakers in unexpected places. So,
> you could watch somebody on one of the closed-circuit TVs
> making a fool of themselves downstairs and suddenly you'd
> hear something you had said a few minutes before on the
> balcony, and it would resound throughout the hall.[48]

In contrast to the Acid Tests, the Trips Festival offered a much more organized programme and was a kind of who's who of San Francisco's psychedelic scene, including rock groups such as the Grateful Dead, Big Brother, Loading Zone and Holding Company, with their singer Janis Joplin. The event flyer further promised a Chinese New Year's Parade, a light show by Henry Jacobs, various theatre groups and a "stroboscopic trampoline jumper".

The Trips Festival was also a gathering of some of the most important actors working with loops on the West Coast around that time. Terry Riley had left San Francisco by then and Steve Reich wanted nothing to do with the city's psychedelic scene. But the members of the San Francisco Tape Music Center were an important part of the Trips Festival. Composer Raymond Sender was one of the organizers and Pauline Oliveros, who composed music with a loop-based tape delay system, gave a performance. Dancer Ann Halprin, for whom Terry Riley had created his first loop composition *Mescaline Mix* in 1960, and whose drastically reduced choreographies had served as an impetus for artistic Minimalism, also performed.

Bruce Connor showed his loop-based film *A Movie* (1964), which repeated a scene from amateur footage of John F. Kennedy's assassination. Don Buchla, who was developing one of the first-ever sequencers at the time, sat in the middle of the hall on a high tower full of electrical equipment and generated electronic sounds on a synthesizer he named the "Buchla Box", showed slides and operated the light show, which was partly controlled by the synthesizer. During the festival, Ken Babbs was often seen standing next to him, rapping into a microphone connected to the Pranksters' delay machine.

Later, Buchla couldn't recall what exactly he had done during those 3 days.[49] But he was undoubtedly one of the first to try to control various sound and image sources with impulses from an electric device. The attempt to connect different media together eventually resulted in the MIDI standard (MIDI stands for Musical Instrument Digital Interface) in the late 1970s. MIDI makes it possible to control and synchronize electronic instruments, computers and other devices. This makes MIDI the technical prerequisite for the development of musical styles such as Techno, House and Hip-hop. The idea of bringing acoustic and visual data into rhythmic synchronicity began at the Trips Festival. In his book on the Merry Pranksters, Tom Wolfe repeatedly highlights moments that are experienced only by "lucky devils and Merry Pranksters"[50] – moments when everyone's experiences appear "synchronized", when everyone seems to perceive and feel the same thing. Wolfe uses a media metaphor for a state, that, in the case of the Pranksters, was usually triggered by shared consumption of LSD. At such moments, everyone was said to be in the "same movie". According to the invitation, the Trips Festival was an attempt to "recreate the psychedelic experience without drugs". The repeated images and sounds that bombarded visitors were an important part of the experiment, since they put everyone "in the same movie". These repetitions structured the stimulus overload in a way that everyone could follow. Courtesy of the Merry Pranksters' delay machine and Don Buchla's electronic control desk, the rhythms, colours, images and sounds could diverge but could also come together again, in a kind of medial and technical self-organization.

In the playing instructions for *In C*, Terry Riley emphasizes the importance of the interlocking of the various patterns and musical cells for the success of the performance. In the Acid Tests and Trips Festival, what Riley had envisaged happened at a technical and social level. The various sounds, bodies, images, colours and people interlocked and began to pulsate in a common beat and the repetitions of the loops no longer functioned as an echo of Thanatos's death instinct, as post-war cultural-critical thinkers saw it, and also no longer represented the stereotypical rattling and inhuman banging of the factory. Rather, they represented bliss, dance and Eros. Participants of events like the Acid Tests called them "rituals", "mysteries", "prayers" or "services".

Many Californian bohemians had their first experience of LSD during the Acid Tests or Trips Festival, and this contributed to spreading the drug in US counterculture. These events also shaped the Hellenistic and experimental style that was typical of the 1967 Summer of Love and the Haight-Ashbury scene; they marked the starting point of the hippie movement in the USA. The Acid Tests and the Trips Festival were also the forerunners of all the media and technological Saturnalia that emerged with the Summer of Love in San Francisco.

California's hippie movement developed in that city's ballrooms and dance halls, at dance events during which diverse technical and chemical means were used to trigger pure or enhanced experiences. The hippie movement began with dancing at concerts, the Acid Tests and at the Trips Festival, its invitations reading "dancedancedance".

In their book *Acid Dreams*, Martin A. Lee and Bruce Shlain describe that:

> thoroughly stoned on grass and acid and each other, they rediscovered the crushing joy of the dance, pouring it all out in a frenzy that frequently bordered on the religious. When rock music was performed with all its potential fury, a special kind of delirium took hold. Attending such performances amounted to a total assault on the senses: the electric sound washed in visceral waves over the dancers, unleashing intense psychic energies and driving the audience further and further toward public trance. Flashing strobes, light shows, body paint, outrageous getups—it was mass environmental theater, an oblivion of limbs and minds in motion. For a brief moment outside of time these young people lived out the implications of Andre Breton's surrealist invocation: "Beauty will be CONVULSIVE or will not be at all."[51]

The drug and dance experiences (and their background of repetitive music, lights flickering to the beat, strobe flashes and tape loops) were technologically updated versions of the kinds of festivities that have led people to dance and share experiences not possible in everyday life since antiquity: the mysteries of Elysium, of Orpheus and Dionysus.

In *The Birth of Tragedy from the Spirit of Music*, Nietzsche describes the Dionysian rites of ancient Greece in a way that Acid Tests participants would probably have recognized:

> Now the slave becomes a free man…Now, within the gospel of world harmony, each feels not only united, reconciled, merged with his neighbour, but at one, as if the veil of Maya had been rent and were mere fluttering shreds before the mysterious primordial One. Singing and dancing, man expresses himself as a member of a higher community – he has forgotten to walk and speak and is on his way to fly up into the air, dancing…Man is no longer an artist; he has become a work of art: the artistic power of all of nature…is revealed in the showers of intoxication.[52]

Subject to "showers of intoxication", Ken Kesey discovered how to turn a simple tape recorder into a machine that tears the "veil of Maya",[53] using technical manipulations and loops. He had ceased to be a writer who describes reality, or perceptions or epiphanies. Instead, he developed a media installation which, by means of repetition, was intended to enable everyone to experience "the artistic power of all of nature" directly and without making a detour into art.

The sober Apollonian sculptures of the Minimalists would have seemed to Nietzsche – had he known them – as "corpse-coloured and ghostly", as he described the European Enlightenment. Nevertheless, the experiments with tape loops and the *Acid Tests* share a common impulse with the Minimalists and their use of squares and boxes – the aim of liberated perception, which does not rely on artistic subjectivity or superimposition but allows the viewer (Minimalism) or the participant (*Acid Test*) to experience phenomena as they appear in a moment of epiphany. Ken Kesey had given up literature in order to live a life that was itself a work of art. For him, there was no way back to art or literature with all their sublimation. In 1966, he went to prison for 6 months for being found in possession of drugs, just as the psychedelic movement was gathering momentum and turning into a mass phenomenon. After that, he and his family moved to his home in Oregon, and, until his death in 2001, he did not publish anything of great literary importance. He did, however, publish a screenplay about the Pranksters' bus trip.[54] His former student Jeff Forester wrote in Kesey's obituary:

> The Acid Tests and Further were sublime, important art, stretching boundaries, continuing America's arrested westward expansion on highways, in literature, within individual biochemistries, creating a collective conscious, defining a historical context. It was serious work. It also exacted a physical price, consumed a lot of time, created a vortex of people and made impossible Kesey's earlier authorial voice. One art ruled the other.[55]

The Acid Tests organized by Kesey and the Merry Pranksters are among the most important original impulses for the future development of multimedia dance parties. The idea that a party should be a complete, sensual experience of music, dance and lighting effects[56] has been carried over to raves and other contemporary saturnalia. Over the years that followed, the interlocking or syncing of sound, images and participants' experience has been technically perfected. Tape loops, which Kesey used to create new possibilities of perception, were an important step on the way to such a synesthetic space of experience.

Loops emerged in pop music starting just a few months after the Trips Festival. The Beatles were the first pop group to use them in a way that anticipates the repetitions of contemporary dance music. They had been one of the Pranksters' favourite bands until they saw a live Beatles concert in San Francisco on 2 September 1965. Beatlemania was at its peak in the USA. The Merry Pranksters had intended to invite The Beatles into their commune as potentially like-minded people. A poster saying "The Merry Pranksters welcome the Beatles" had already been painted and hung up at the entrance to Kesey's house in La Honda.

But watching the teenage hysteria at the concert, Kesey changed his mind. Their performance in front of thousands of screaming female fans seemed to him the complete opposite of the emancipatory experience he was striving for with the Acid Tests. As Tom Wolfe observes in *The Electric Kool-Aid Acid Test*, under the influence of LSD, the audience seemed to him like a screeching, manipulated insect:

> "The Beatles could be miming it for all it matters. But something else...does...matter...and Kesey sees it. One of the Beatles, John, George, Paul, dips his long electric guitar handle in one direction and the whole teeny horde ripples precisely along the line of energy he set off—and then in the other direction, precisely along that line. It causes them to grin, John and Paul and George and Ringo, rippling the poor huge freaked teeny beast this way and that – Control – it is perfectly obvious – they have brought this whole mass of human beings to the point where they are one, out of their skulls, one psyche, and they have utter control over them – but they don't know what in the hell to do with it."[57]

So, the meeting between the Merry Pranksters and The Beatles never took place – Kesey and his group left the concert before it ended in a mass panic. The collective experience of repetitive rock music, which had led to moments of collective ecstasy and pure insight during the Acid Tests, had here become a form of mass manipulation that bore out Adorno in his warnings about the nature of capitalist entertainment. Thanatos had triumphed over Eros. To Kesey, the concert hall where The Beatles performed seemed like a prison, a slaughterhouse, a concentration camp.

This is why the Pranksters did not introduce The Beatles to psychedelic drugs, as they had originally planned. (John Lennon's dentist had in any case beaten them to it 6 months before.) The

Beatles drew their own conclusions from the hysterical scenes at their performances. Early in 1966, they announced that they would never again perform live and would instead concentrate on perfecting their studio productions. Their last live performance took place a year after the concert which the Merry Pranksters attended, and, coincidentally, it was again in San Francisco.

After the end of their live concerts, they produced the LP *Revolver*, which explores the possibilities of electronic studio production, and reflects their experiences with marijuana and LSD. It is The Beatles' first psychedelic LP. Most of the pieces on the album could theoretically have been performed live. Except for one. *Tomorrow Never Knows*, a composition based largely on tape loops.

CHAPTER 12
PAUL MCCARTNEY GOES TOO FAR. THE BEATLES AND LOOPS IN A PLASTIC BAG

I don't believe that it ends with our Western logical thought. It can't do, because that's so messed up anyway, most of it, that you've got to allow for the possibility of there being a lot, lot more than we know about. To bang one note on the piano, instead of trying to put millions of notes into it, and just to take the one note of the piano and listen to it, shows you what there is in one note. There's so much going on in one note, but you never listen to it.

Paul McCartney, 1967

Loops appeared in pop music kicking and screaming – almost as with a real birth. One critic thought he'd heard a "swarm of prehistoric birds" or "ghostly string music in the sky"[1]; another supposed it was the "screeching of mad seagulls, or the buzzing of angry wasps".[2] Most of their descriptions seem to anticipate an apocalypse; there is reference to destruction, extinction, *tabula rasa*. The lyrics instruct listeners to switch off all thoughts and surrender to the void, and likewise seem to support a doomsday mood.

The musical work in question is *Tomorrow Never Knows*, released by The Beatles in 1966 on the LP *Revolver*. This album introduced loops into pop music and The Beatles made them their own. They were the first pop musicians to work with tape loops, as has been shown. But while other producers, like Sam Phillips, used loops as a sound effect (for instance, on Elvis' Sun singles), *Tomorrow Never Knows* uses them as a structural element.

The track is more similar to compositions by "serious" composers, like Pierre Schaeffer's *Études de Bruits* or Terry Riley's *Mescaline Mix*, than to Elvis' Sun Sessions. Unlike these composers' experiments, however, *Tomorrow Never Knows* was heard by countless people all over the world. As part of EMI's marketing strategy, songs from the album were given to radio stations one by one before the album was released. *Tomorrow Never Knows* was the last to be pre-released in this way – perhaps to avoid scaring off regular fans with a bizarre piece. For millions of people, it was their first encounter with tape loops. Two years later, John Lennon's 8-minute piece *Revolution 9*, which was influenced by Stockhausen's *Hymnen* and is also based on loops, appeared on The Beatles' *White Album* and this is an even more radical sound collage. Beatles biographer Ian MacDonald notes that:

> around a million households owned copies of it within days
> of its release and, a quarter of a century later, its hearers
> numbered in the hundreds of millions. One of the most
> striking instances of the communicative power of pop,
> *Revolution 9* achieved a global exposure never imagined by
> the artists who pioneered its techniques. While the cut-up
> texts of Burroughs, the collages of Hamilton and the sonic
> experiments of Cage and Stockhausen have remained the
> preserve of the modernist intelligentsia, Lennon's sortie into

sonic chance was packaged for a mainstream audience which had never heard of its progenitors, let alone been confronted by their work.[3]

It's probable that quite as many people listened to *Tomorrow Never Knows* – and, since this piece is less of a noise marathon than *Revolution 9*, probably more than once. This fact alone justifies crediting The Beatles with a particularly important role when it comes to the dissemination and popularization of loop-based music. Paul McCartney knew Stockhausen's music and also that this composer had created his electronic compositions using tape loops.[4] In a kind of creative misunderstanding, McCartney used Stockhausen's method to emphasize the rhythmic qualities of his own work. *Tomorrow Never Knows* is the first track in pop music history to leave behind conventional song structure, such as verse, chorus, etc. and to develop an alternative structure from repetitive musical fragments. Since loops form the metric basis, the track is also a precursor to the dance music styles of the 1980s and 1990s, such as House, Techno and Hip-hop, which are likewise based on looped sound fragments.

The rhythmic use of loops in *Tomorrow Never Knows* doesn't amount to a few, simple repetitions. Rather, a whole repertoire of different looping methods comes together in this piece. It differs from the compositions of avant-garde composers like Stockhausen in that it doesn't employ a single compositional method but amalgamates various experimental approaches.

MacDonald observes that the piece was for pop music what "Berlioz's *Symphonie fantastique* was to 19th-century orchestral music".[5] If Elvis' Sun singles hinted at the possibility that pop music might come to be recorded in a studio rather than being performed live, then *Tomorrow Never Knows* proclaims it loudly. The piece unfolds a tapestry of alien sounds that lack any referentiality in the natural world. The Beatles, who had previously released innocent pop songs like *I Want To Hold Your Hand* and *Love Me Do*, had catapulted themselves into a sonic no-man's-land.

The piece was written after a 2-month creative break that followed several years of almost non-stop touring. Not long after, The Beatles announced that they would not perform live again and would only work in the studio from then on. By this time, they were so successful that they had no need to perform live, whether to promote their music or as a source of income. As Ken Kesey had observed about their San Francisco concert, their performances had turned into hysterical mass events where the fans' screaming drowned out their music. "We were really fed up with touring and the reason was that we were becoming worse and worse musicians," Ringo recalled. "The audience volume was always louder than ours. I couldn't play a drum roll because it would have been drowned out. So, I looked at the other guys' arses and tried to tell from their lip movements where we were in the song."[6]

They were also increasingly unable to reproduce the pieces they had created in the studio. George Harrison later recalled in an interview that "as time went by, the technology we were now using on records didn't allow us to play a lot of songs live on tour. In those days there was no technology on stage as there is now. There were two guitars, bass and drums, and that was it. If we did stuff in the studio with the aid of recording tricks, then we couldn't reproduce them on tour. You could do it now. You could do 'Tomorrow Never Knows' – have all the loops up there on the keyboards and emulators."[7]

John Lennon is generally regarded as the "intellectual Beatle" who was always ready with a cynical comment ("The Beatles are more popular than Jesus") and who, through his relationship with Fluxus artist Yoko Ono, established his connection to high culture. And yet it was Paul McCartney who had first developed an interest in compositional methods found in serious music. In his book *Summer of Love*, Beatles producer George Martin observed that, "Paul was very much into what we called the avant-garde in those days: modern literature, modem music by the likes of John Cage, Stockhausen."[8]

McCartney was also the one who suggested putting Karlheinz Stockhausen on the famous cover of the *Sgt Pepper* album.[9] He recalls that:

> people were starting to lose their pure-pop mentality and mingle with artists. We knew a few actors, a few painters; we'd go to galleries because we were living in London now. A kind of cross-fertilization was starting to happen. While the others had got married and moved out to suburbia, I had stayed in London and got into the arts scene through friends like Robert Fraser and Barry Miles and papers like the *International Times*. We opened the Indica gallery with John Dunbar, Peter Asher and people like that. I heard about people like John Cage, and that he'd just performed a piece of music called 4'33 (which is completely silent) during which if someone in the audience coughed he would say, "See?" Or someone would boo and he'd say, "See?" It's not silence – it's music. I was intrigued by all of that. So those things started to be part of my life. I was listening to Stockhausen; one piece was all little plink-plonks and interesting ideas. Perhaps our audience wouldn't mind a bit of change, we thought, and anyway, tough if they do! We only ever followed our own noses – most of the time, anyway. 'Tomorrow Never Knows' was one example of developing an idea. I always contend that I had quite a big period of this before John really got into it, because he was married to Cynthia at that time. It was only later when he went out with Yoko that he got back into London and visited all the galleries.[10]

In *Tomorrow Never Knows*, influences from the European avantgarde also merged with George Harrison's interest in Indian Raga. Harrison describes his fascination in an interview: "in Indian music, the key doesn't change. You pick a key and stay in it. I think that *Tomorrow Never Knows* was the first piece with that form; the whole song is based on a single chord."[11]

Paul McCartney recalls Lennon first playing the piece to them:

> I remember we were with [Beatles manager] Brian Epstein on Chapel Street in Belgravia. We'd met and John had written a song entirely in the key of C, which we thought was a very good idea. I wondered how [producer] George Martin would react to it, because it was a radical change; we had always had at least three chords and maybe a key change in the B part. And here was John, incessantly strumming the C chord – "Lay down your mind..." And the words were all very deep and meaningful – certainly not "Thank You Girl"; a bit of a change from all that. George Martin took it very well. He said, "Rather interesting, John. Jolly interesting!"[12]

Paul McCartney was already experimenting with tape loops at that time. The Beatles had all bought Grundig tape recorders so that they could play back their studio recordings at home. McCartney, who was impressed by Stockhausen's *Gesang der Jünglinge* (1955-56), used his machine to create tape loops. "I loved Stockhausen and was always tinkering with tape loops at home, which I sent to friends just as they were. I recall telling John that I wanted to make an album out of it, which I wanted to call 'Paul McCartney Goes Too Far'".[13] But in the end, McCartney didn't go that far, although he did produce a 13-minute sound collage consisting almost entirely of tape effects for the underground theatre production *Carnival of Lights Rave* while The Beatles were recording the *Sgt Pepper* album.[14]

George Martin recalls that, "it was Paul who was at home experimenting with his tape recorder, removing the erase head, inserting loops and recording the strangest sounds".[15] Resembling Stockhausen's early loop experiments, the tape machine would record a sound, play it back with a slight delay, simultaneously recording and then playing it back again, etc. Because none of these recordings were deleted, sounds overlapped à la Terry Riley, and a dense carpet of sound resulted, in which the original sounds were hardly discernible anymore. McCartney carried his tape loops to Abbey Road studio in a plastic bag.

George Martin recalls that Paul McCartney, "explained to the other boys how he had done this, and Ringo and George would do the same and bring me different loops of sounds." In an interview, George Harrison recalls, "everyone went home and created a tape loop. 'And now for the homework! Go home and bring your own tape loop to the studio tomorrow.'" Ringo recalls that, "I had my own little set-up to record them. As George says, we were 'drinking a lot of tea' in those days, and on all my tapes you can hear, 'Oh, I hope I've switched it on.' I'd get so deranged from strong tea. I'd sit there for hours making those noises."[16]

The acoustic raw material that was used in *Tomorrow Never Knows* includes loops of Paul McCartney laughing, the clink of wine glasses and guitar chords. None of these sounds are discernible on *Tomorrow Never Knows*, however. The associations they invite range from Indian songs to the chirping of birds and the humming of locusts. Paul McCartney observes that, "I always think of seagulls when I hear it. I used to get a lot of seagulls in my loops; a speeded-up shout, hah ha, goes squawk squawk. And I always get pictures of seasides, of Torquay, the Torbay Inn, fishing boats and puffins and deep purple mountains. These were the slowed-down ones."[17]

The sounds created with the aid of loops were played forwards and backwards, at different speeds, recorded again in the process, glued together into loops, then played back on different tape recorders. Producer George Martin remembers that:

what I had to do then was find eight tape-recorders that could each play a tape-loop. So I took over EMI. I went to every room in the Abbey Road building and said, "Look, I want a tape-machine, with a guy standing by it playing this loop of tape here continuously. And to keep it on the heads, the operator will need a pencil, to maintain his own particular loop of tape on tension." The tape-recording machines in those days were enormous, big BTR3s. Once one was in place, it could not easily be moved. So we had white-coated operatives standing all over Abbey Road, on every floor of the building, each in front of a BTR3 with a pencil stuck in a small loop of tape. Each continuous loop was fed through Abbey Road's internal jack plug patching system, down through the intervening walls and floors, out into our studio, and plugged into my mixing console. By raising a fader, I would hear a particular loop going round and round, held in position by a man in a while coat several floors away, playing its cacophony continuously for ever and ever. Talk about hi-tech![18]

The initial version of *Tomorrow Never Knows* had been entitled Mark 1 or The Void. It was eventually published in 2000 on the *Beatles Anthology* after having been in circulation as an illegal bootleg for decades and it reveals what the original experiment had sounded like. It lasts for about 3 minutes and features an electric guitar that seems to be playing backwards, a crashing drum set and John Lennon's nasal vocals. This recording sounds sluggish and has an indifferent, machine-like quality. That said, in his book *The Beatles Recording Sessions*, Mark Lewisohn refers to it as a "sensational, apocalyptic version...a heavy metal recording of immense proportions, with thunderous echoes and booms, and trembling, oceanic oscillations."[19]

Regardless of how one perceives the initial version of *Tomorrow Never Knows*, there is no doubt that The Beatles had discovered principles of Minimalist tape composition for themselves, probably without knowing of Terry Riley or Steve Reich's experiments. *Mark 1* consists of two continuously running tape loops with short patterns, one featuring the backwards guitar and the other, some indefinable rhythmic booming. These fuzzy-sounding experiments remind of the timbre and mood of those wrapped around wine bottles in Terry Riley's garden some 5 years earlier.

On 22 April 1966, The Beatles recorded the final version of the piece in under 5 hours. Compared to the first version, it has far more texture and harmonic movement, though it's still constructed around a single chord. It is based on the whirring sound of an Indian tambura, a string instrument that produces long-lasting ostinato tones and which resembles the sitar. The musical whirring conveys a sense of continuity and forms an interesting complement to the repetitiveness of the loops. An unearthly impression results and is augmented by a bourdon hum that periodically overlaps, sounding like a UFO coming in to land. This is produced by the Mellotron, a keyboard instrument based on tape loops that was launched in 1966. In *Tomorrow Never Knows*, it is initially the flute and then the string sound on this instrument that repeatedly blend into the song, to merge with the humming of the Indian tambura, which continues throughout. Using drones, The Beatles took up a compositional idea that was central to La Monte Young, probably without being aware of it. (Interestingly, in the early 1970s, Young was also to get involved with Indian music, as previously discussed. He would take lessons from Raga singer Pandit Pran Nath for many years. Like The Beatles, he became fascinated by the sense of timelessness and constancy in Indian music.)

The Beatles and George Martin used a random method reminiscent of John Cage's approach when they integrated tape loops into their songs and got Abbey Road Studio's sound engineers to keep them in position with the aid of ballpoint pens and tumblers.

Paul McCartney recalls that:

we ran the loops... and just before you could tell it was a loop, before it began to repeat a lot, I'd pull in one of the other faders, and so, using the other people, "You pull that in there," "You pull that in," we did a half random, half orchestrated playing of the things and recorded that to a track on the actual master tape, so that if we got a good one, that would be the solo. We played it through a few times and changed some of the tapes till we got what we thought was a real good one.[20]

Geoff Emerick, who made his debut as The Beatles' sound engineer in these sessions, remembers it slightly differently. According to him, only technical personnel were permitted to operate the equipment of EMI Studios, and so it was he and George Martin who were mixing the loop signals that were fed into the mixing console from the other studios. He recalls that:

> what followed next was a scene that could have come out of a science fiction movie – or a Monty Python sketch. Every tape machine in every studio was commandeered and every available EMI employee was given the task of holding a pencil or drinking glass to give the loops the proper tensioning. In many instances, this meant they had to be standing out in the hallway, looking quite sheepish. Most of those people didn't have a clue what we were doing; they probably thought we were daft. They certainly weren't pop people, and they weren't that young either. Add in the fact that all of the technical staff were required to wear white lab coats, and the whole thing became totally surreal. Meanwhile, back in the control room, George Martin and I huddled over the console, raising and lowering faders to shouted instructions from John, Paul, George and Ringo. ("Let's have that seagull sound now!" "More distorted wineglasses!") With each fader carrying a different loop, the mixing desk acted like a synthesizer, and we played it like a musical instrument, too, carefully overdubbing textures to the pre-recorded backing track. Finally, we completed the task to the band's satisfaction, the white-coated technicians were freed from their labors, and Paul's loops were retired back to the plastic bag, never to be played again.[21]

A comparison between the initial and eventually published versions of *Tomorrow Never Knows* shows that, within a very short space of time, The Beatles and their studio team had developed amazing virtuosity in playing the mixer like an instrument. The sluggish, clattering initial version had turned into a bewildering, iridescent piece of music that successfully conveys the ideas of death and extinction referred to in the lyrics. Somewhere between machines that simply play back the various tapes and the people who operate them, something "happened" – an example of the "interlocking" of people and technology, which was an aim of the Trips Festival and which was later to become the principle behind technologies like MIDI.

George Martin was fascinated by how looped sounds could be played "like an organ".[22] The random character of the piece had not escaped him, either, and he remarks that, "the mix was a random thing that could never be done again. Nobody else was doing records like that at that time – not as far as I knew."[23] The bizarre overall sound of the piece is heightened by a number of other effects. John Lennon wanted his voice to sound like that of the "Dalai Lama on a mountaintop". In order to achieve the desired "Dalai Lennon" effect, the singing was altered using the loudspeaker of a Leslie organ, which rotates at a high speed and distorts the voice. Ringo Starr's drum kit was muted with sweaters stuffed into the drums, and the guitar solo runs backwards.[24]

Accounts of how the piece was created vary far more than is the case with almost any other Beatles recording. But one thing is clear. *Tomorrow Never Knows* brings together different compositional approaches that had first emerged in post-war avant-garde music. It includes elements of tape composition as created by composers like Karlheinz Stockhausen, Otto Luening and Vladimir Ussachevsky in the 1950s; it includes John Cage's random operations and combines these with William Burroughs' and Brian Gysin's tape cut-ups. And it brings together two separate strands of Minimal Music, which had begun to diverge around that time – the Minimalism of La Monte Young, with its long ostinato tones, and the "modular Minimalism" of Terry Riley and Steve Reich, which introduces short, repeated sound sequences.

And yet, *Tomorrow Never Knows* is no mere showpiece for a series of new studio tricks. It is a unique, fascinating song that ventures into territories that no other pop musician had entered at that point. Ian MacDonald notes that, "when *Tomorrow Never Knows* appeared, drones [like those produced by the tambura and Mellotron] had been absent from Western music since the passing of the religious 'organum' style in the 12th century." Drawing comparisons with folk instruments like the hurdy- gurdy and with La Monte Young, MacDonald continues:

> serving notice that the ensuing music will contain no tonal "progress" – no change of key or chord...the Indian drone, as brought into First World culture by this track, challenges not only seven centuries of Western music, but the operating premise of Western civilization itself. When Lennon's voice rises out of the seething dazzle of churning loops, the first words it utters, "Turn off your mind", are a mystic negation of all progressive intellectual enterprise. The message: it is not the contents of one's mind which matter; rather, what counts is the quality of the containing mind itself – and the emptier, the better. This proposition, now a truism in Western fringe thinking, and happily travestied in the Ecstasy subculture of "psychedelic" dance music, was radically subversive in 1966. *Tomorrow never knows* launched the till-then elite-preserved concept of mind-expansion into pop, simultaneously drawing attention to consciousness-enhancing drugs and the ancient religious philosophies of the Orient, utterly alien to Western thought..."[25]

The piece was indeed inspired by Far Eastern mysticism. The lyrics of *Tomorrow Never Knows* are taken from the *Tibetan Book of the Dead*, a cult book of the hippie scene, which had been reissued by Timothy Leary and Richard Alpert in the early 1960s. Leary and Alpert wanted to place the LSD trip in a quasireligious, meditative context. While searching for some kind of spiritual manual for taking LSD, Timothy Leary had become aware of a remark by Aldous Huxley, who refers to the *Tibetan Book of the Dead* in his book *Doors of Perception*. The *Book of the Dead* contains verses intended to be read at wakes to help the deceased find their way in the afterlife. Leary found the lines about the "radiation of the clear light of pure reality" to describe the LSD experience very well. John Lennon had used the book as a guide in his own LSD experiments, since there was no psychedelic scene in England which could have offered him a conducive frame of reference for his trips.

Lines like "that you may see the meaning of within, it is being, it is being" were originally aimed at visions of people shortly before their death. In the context of LSD, however, they can also be taken as references to the drug's ability to free perception from acquired conditioning, as Ken Kesey and the Merry Pranksters had claimed. The Beatles, who were later to tell their own story of a psychedelic journey in a colourful painted bus in the film *Magical Mystery Tour*, gave no hint of drugs in *Tomorrow Never Knows*. Instead, the piece deals with heightened forms of perception and transcendental experiences in a general, abstract sense. Tape loops, which could turn clinking wine glasses and laughter into Indian chants or bird song, offered a perfect acoustic metaphor for this.

In contrast to the formal elegance of *Tomorrow Never Knows*, the other Beatles recording that is based on loops is a chaotic affair, devoid of any direction – and this was intentional: John Lennon recorded *Revolution 9* in June 1968 with the aid of Yoko Ono and George Harrison. The band was starting to show the first signs of disintegration around that time. And yet, the group had developed enormously in musical terms since recording *Revolver* and *Tomorrow Never Knows*. In the previous year, they had published *Sgt. Pepper's Lonely Hearts Club Band*, probably the most influential record of the 1960s. *Sgt. Pepper* was not just a musical breakthrough, it also demonstrated that The Beatles had finally found their way into the British art scene. For the famous cover of *Sgt Pepper*, they had worked with Pop Art artist Peter Blake, and the design of the – actually nameless – *White Album* also came from a well-known British artist – Richard Hamilton, who not only designed the minimalistic cover (featuring the band's name as the only design element), but also the collage for the enclosed poster.[26]

The Beatles were no longer the boy band they had been in the early 1960s and had found their connection to high culture. With their music (especially with pieces like *Tomorrow Never Knows*), they influenced the development of psychedelic rock music and were noticed by intellectuals. John Lennon, inspired by his wife Yoko Ono, began to take an interest in avantgarde art. He is said to have been in contact with Karlheinz Stockhausen – Michael Kurtz's Stockhausen biography refers to a meeting that was planned between them in New York, where a joint Beatles-Stockhausen concert was to be discussed. Apparently, the meeting had to be cancelled due to a blizzard.[27] (The various extensive, detailed and anecdotal biographies of Lennon, however, do not make any mention of such a meeting.) Stockhausen's *Hymnen* is frequently referred to as an important influence on *Revolution 9*. Another avant-garde piece that *Revolution 9* has been compared to is Luigi Nono's *Non consumiano Marx*, which uses slogans from Paris 1968 to create a sound collage. Together with Yoko Ono, Lennon had already recorded the experimental album *Two Virgins* by that time, which, with tape-loop experiments and free noise passages akin to *musique concrète*, anticipates *Revolution 9* in various ways.

Ian MacDonald calls *Revolution 9* a "sensory attack on the citadel of the intellect"[28] and draws attention to similarities between the compositional method of *Revolution 9* and aesthetic concepts of the French Situationist group of artists and intellectuals. Situationists criticized a society that had turned into a "spectacle", and above all, its media representations, which some members of the group used as the source material of their collages, anti-films, comics and photo novels. Lennon, similarly, almost exclusively used sound materials he had found and compiled in the EMI archives. He was working on a stage version for his book *In his own write* at that time, which was to be performed at the Old Vic. For the soundtrack, he searched through the Abbey Road Studio sound effect archives, and many of the sounds of *Revolution 9* also seem to have resulted from this research. The loop with the famous line "number nine, number nine" was a test tape recorded at Abbey Road Studios for the Royal Academy of Music.

Other "sound bites" that make up *Revolution 9* include conversations in the studio, water splashes, shouts from an American sporting event, the whistling of a shortwave transmitter (possibly a reference to Stockhausen's *Kontakte* [1958-60], which also contains shortwave radio sounds), roaring applause and screams from a huge crowd. Right at the end, Yoko Ono is heard saying, among other things, "you become naked". The final chord of Sibelius' *Seventh Symphony*, a fragment from Vaughan Williams' *O Clap Your Hands* and the finale of Schumann's *Symphonic Etudes* op. 13 run backwards. Various other orchestral fragments, some of which have not so far been identified, are used as loops, along with part of the orchestral arrangement for The Beatles song *A Day in the Life* from *Sgt. Pepper* as well as various Mellotrons and Hammond organs, again run backwards.

The production method is surprisingly similar to that of *Tomorrow Never Knows*, especially considering how different the end results are. Once more, sound engineers stood in different studios, holding tape loops taut with pencils and other implements. The signals were again fed into the central mixing console, where John Lennon sat, producing a mix from the cacophony flowing in. Lennon jumps hectically from sound fragment to sound fragment without any recognizable rhythm, never sticking with any one, and searching and searching, instead. The only thing that gives the acoustic tumult a degree of coherence is the enigmatic repetition of "number nine, number nine, number nine …". Other than that, *Revolution 9* sounds like an unstructured stringing together of hallucinatory sound fragments that pass by the listener with some strange form of dream logic. MacDonald notes that "on one level, *Revolution 9* is another Lennonian evocation of the domain between sleeping and waking, its wavelength-wandering radio babble resembling the sound an infant might have apprehended in a suburban garden during a typical post-war summer".[29]

Only very attentive listeners will notice that almost all of the sounds are looped and continuously repeated. Lennon ignores the rhythmic and structuring possibilities of loops, which Riley and Reich placed at the centre of their work. It is as if he had wanted to use loops to cancel out the structuring effects that had so fascinated the Minimalists. Lennon's loops neither invite the listener to immerse him/herself in a sound fragment, nor do they address the act of perception. Instead, they bombard the listener with a flood of disordered sounds. This brings his work in proximity to Pierre Schaeffer's *musique concrete*, where loops also work with noise without making it into a rhythmical element. Unlike in *Tomorrow Never Knows,* they no longer refer to transcendental ideas and block the listener's perception with a frontal noise attack instead. And yet, *Revolution 9* is about two central themes of 1960s counterculture – process and the quality of perception. If in *Tomorrow Never Knows* The Beatles conjured up a 1960s utopia of expanded perception, then *Revolution 9* declares this utopia void.

Other psychedelic bands of the late 1960s began to experiment with loops not long after The Beatles had done so and many of them were inspired by the music of Terry Riley. One of these bands was called Soft Machine. Their guitarist, David Allen, had met Riley in Paris in the mid-1960s. On some of the band's recordings, Riley's influence is obvious – the ultra-monotonous, self-referential piece *We did it again* is an example and as the title suggests, it unceasingly repeats a single line. The modular keyboard figures on the album *Third* (1970) and the composition *The Soft Weed Factor* on the album *Six* (1973) are also influenced by Riley. The music for the multimedia spectacle *Spaced*, which British artist Peter Dockley organized in 1969 at the UFO Club in London's Roundhouse, is particularly close to Riley's methods. *Spaced* was an event similar to the Merry Pranksters' *Acid Tests* and also resembled *Carnival of Lights Rave*, which had taken place the previous year at the same venue, and for which Paul McCartney had created a sound collage made of loops. Soft Machine produced an hour-long soundtrack, for which sound engineer Bob Woolford had created loops in his living room.[30] (Incidentally, on this occasion, the loops were wound around milk bottles on the stairs).

Riley's influence on Soft Machine was also an indirect factor in the first international hit that incorporated elements of Minimalism. In 1969, bassist Kevin Ayers left Soft Machine to form a band called The Whole World, which included a young musician named Mike Oldfield. The latter's *Tubular Bells*, which became newly founded Virgin label's first-ever LP in 1973, was the first international pop hit to incorporate elements of Minimal Music. Oldfield, just 20 years old at the time, recorded the piece almost entirely on his own, and it took up the entire LP. In Britain, *Tubular Bells* remained in the album charts for 5 years and became internationally known as the soundtrack to the horror film *The Exorcist* (1973). In spite of its length and repetitive character, the composition is not a Minimalist creation as such – it includes numerous chord changes, melodic motifs and thematic development. Nevertheless, it was the first time that an international audience was confronted with a kind of pop music that was characterized by repetitions made of short melodic motifs.

Oldfield also experimented with tape loops. In an interview in 1998, he observed that the repetitions in *Tubular Bellsi*:

> are my trademark, but I discovered them by chance. I was 16 and had just left Kevin Ayers' band. Kevin gave me his tape recorder, a very early Bang & Olufsen. By soldering some wires together and blocking off the tape with bits of cigarette packets, I was able to multi-track on it. I took the insides out and started making tape loops. A few alternative musicians around that time were experimenting with repetitive pianos and synthesizers, like a mantra.[31]

Working with Kevin Ayers, Oldfield also became interested in repetitive music: "repetition, that's something Kevin taught me. There was this bit we used to play in *The Whole World* that went on and on and on, and I said, why does it go on and on and on? and he said, because it does."[32]

Through Ayers, Oldfield also heard of Terry Riley's music. He recalls that:

> I learned how to play that Terry Riley style from his album "A Rainbow In Curved Air", which was very complicated because one hand had to start – a bit like a round – with the other one starting a few moments later. A bit like rubbing your tummy and patting your head. It was also fashionable to use odd time signatures, so I made one bar seven beats and one bar eight and only later realized that it had the complexity of Eastern music, the repetitiveness of Terry Riley and the technique of Bach. It's still cropping up everywhere. Recently Janet Jackson used it in a single and rap stars like Ice-T take samples from it.[33]

Other rock musicians, too, acknowledge Riley's music. The band Curved Air was named after Riley's composition of the same title, while the piece *Baba O'Riley* (aka *Teenage Wasteland*) on the Who's album *Who's Next* (1971) pays tribute to the composer. The song begins with a synthesizer solo that reminds of Riley's composition *Rainbow in Curved Air*. Similarly, *We Won't Get Fooled Again* includes a minimalistic synthesizer passage.[34] Since the complete score of Terry Riley's *In C* was printed on the cover of the first LP version, it had become quasi-freeware and was being played by numerous rock groups. The Swedish band International Harvester and their keyboard player Bo Anders Persson, who, together with Terry Riley, had recorded *In C* for Swedish radio in 1967, made the piece famous in Scandinavia. In Germany, Berlin-based band Agitation Free and Manuel Göttsching of Ash Ra Tempel were influenced by Terry Riley's Minimalism[35] and in the German electronic band Kraftwerk it is particularly evident. Kraftwerk founders Florian Schneider and Ralf Hütter often listened to *In C* while driving and their first international hit, *Autobahn* (1974), clearly shows Riley's influence.[36] Their synthesizer music is composed of Minimalist patterns and electronic musical instruments designed to repeat musical passages as precisely as possible, which made them an important inspiration for early Hip-hop and Techno. There is therefore a direct connection between Riley's modular works and contemporary dance music.

Numerous musicians who superimposed sounds onto tape loops akin to the *Time Lag Generator* also pay testimony to Terry Riley. In serious music, these include Alvin Lucier, whose "I am sitting in a room" consists of a few sentences that were recorded, played and re-recorded on a tape recorder until the sentences, clear and comprehensible at the outset, become a dull and hissing distorted spatial sound through the superimposition.[37] The *Frippertronics* technique developed by Robert Fripp and Brian Eno is based on similar sound delays and overlays, which blur Fripp's guitar solos into iridescent sound surfaces. Eno knew of Riley's *Time Lag Generator*, and his first album in collaboration with Robert Fripp, *No Pussyfooting* (1973), is one of the first ambient albums that was recorded using a similar tape installation. David Bowie's hit *Heroes*, likewise, features this sound.

The phase shifts which Steve Reich added to the repertoire of Minimal Music, on the other hand, had far less impact on popular music. Techno, and especially Minimal Techno, occasionally includes rhythmic phase shifts and loops that diverge and converge, but to this day, such "doublings" are a DJ trick that only experts can use effectively. The electronic experimental band The Orb sampled a passage from Reich's *Electronic Counterpoint* (1987) for their piece *Fluffy Little Cloud* (1991) and the CD *Reich Remixed* (1999) features arrangements by internationally renowned DJs and producers, like Ken Ishii, Coldcut and Andrea Parker.

La Monte Young's Minimalism of drones entered the formal language of rock music via John Cale and Velvet Underground, as previously discussed. Another band, which developed its own version of punk rock from repetitive synthesizer patterns, was also influenced by La Monte Young – Suicide. In an interview, Suicide singer Alan Vega recalls how he produced his own version of drones in the early 1970s:

I used to have a keyboard in my pad, and I would tape down one key, and just let it go for hours and hours...Nothing was changing, but it WAS changing, if you listened for long enough. That was probably more outrageous than what La Monte Young was doing, it was just one-note things. I was just sitting there, and I was amazed how much it changed in the course of time.[38]

That Alan Vega also admits that he had never actually heard the music of La Monte Young – unlike that of Steve Reich and Philip Glass – speaks for the suggestive power which the legend of the Minimalist hermit must have had in New York at that time.

Suicide's electro-punk rock, with its monotonously repeating keyboard figures, reminds of the motoric Minimalism of Riley, Reich and Glass. The patterns of Minimal Music are structurally very similar to the riffs which rock music had taken from African-American folk music, which is one of the reasons why it was relatively easy to bring Minimal Music and rock music to a common denominator.

Suicide keyboard player Martin Rev emphasizes that the group's minimalistic electro-rock, when reduced to its basic structures, is derived from the simple riffs of classical Blues and Rock'n'Roll. He notes that:

my basic loop influence was Rock'n'Roll. That was the first great loops there were. Little Richard – that is loop music. That's what I have been brought up on, that's my mother's milk. Suicide is basically a Rhythm'n'Blues band. An urban Rhythm'n'Blues band. Anything more intellectual than that, like La Monte Young or Philip Glass, came much later. And by that time I had heard so much repetition, it wasn't anything new at all...The reality was that Rock'n'Roll and the Blues of course, had influenced the times to such an extent, that even the classical composers, like Steve Reich or Phil Glass, had to make their peace with Rock'n'Roll.[39]

The combination of African-American musical influences and repetitive, hammering electronics influenced not only Suicide's electronic punk rock in the 1970s, but also the electronic Disco music that was developing around the same time. The song *I Feel Love* by Donna Summer and producer Giorgio Moroder was to be simultaneously the pinnacle of electronic Disco and the first-ever Techno track. It introduces minimalistic, monotonous patterns and phase shifts into electronic dance music.

Disco and Minimal Music are more similar than the critical literature on these two musical styles generally cares to acknowledge. But there is one composer from the academic field who did notice the similarities – Philip Glass. In an interview in 1997 he observes that, "when I first heard Donna Summer, I just had to laugh. I said, 'it's just the same as we're doing!' How could you miss that?"[40]

TURNING THE MACHINE INTO A SLOPPY MACHINE: DONNA SUMMER, GIORGIO MORODER AND *I FEEL LOVE*

Donna Summer's *I Feel Love* still seems to come from another world. Created over 3 decades ago, it still sounds strange and futuristic. And the world from which *I Feel Love* emerges is made of nothing but loops. They fire off like a machine gun. At first glance, these loops seem deceptively simple. *I Feel Love* is based on the electronic pounding of a pattern comprising a few synthesizer notes, which the sequencer repeats again and again, and transposes intermittently. But while the song starts from this initial ultra-minimalistic condition, it goes on to encompass variations, deviations and shifts with the aid of additional loops. The dull mechanical pounding of a machine turns into complex polyrhythmic beats; the rigid rule turns into confusing diversity, an organism composed of repetitions. At one point, Donna Summer herself wasn't able to find her way through the bewildering rhythmic labyrinth of *I Feel Love* anymore. With the aid of a relatively simple production trick, producer Giorgio Moroder succeeded in transforming the quickfire synthesizer loops in *I Feel Love* into vibrant pulsations. The piece systematically dissolves pairs of opposites – which lends an organic quality to the mechanical loops, and amalgamates nature and technology on a musical level. The binary oppositions of discipline and freedom, self-determination and coercion, repetition and variation, Eros and Thanatos are all effectively suspended in *I Feel Love*. British rock journalist Jon Savage notes that the piece, "ends the tyranny of the clock – the everyday world of work, responsibility, money – and creates its own time, a moment of pleasure, ecstasy and movement that seems infinitely expandable".[1] And it does so, one should add, with the mechanical precision of a clockwork.

I Feel Love – text and vocals by Donna Summer, composition and production by Giorgio Moroder – is considered to be the first Disco song to be produced entirely by electronic means, excepting the vocals and the bass drum. This makes the song the "primordial plant",[2] the blueprint of Techno, House and other forms of electronic dance music. *I Feel Love* was a number-one-hit around the globe. And it has lost nothing of its potency to this day. Its meandering loops continue to make people dance at birthday and wedding parties, as well as at Techno raves. Musicians, from Blondie to Kylie Minogue, from the Red Hot Chili Peppers to Madonna, from Vanessa Mae to the Blue Men Group, and from Bronski Beat and Marc Almond to Curve have all tried their hand at a version of the song, while others, like Divine or Madonna, produced songs that more or less clumsily imitate the feel of *I Feel Love*. The sound has been recreated by producers such as Faithless, Masters at Work, Plump DJs, Fat Boy Slim, Danny Howells, DJ Sneak and Simon Harris, and the list of artists who have sampled the song ranges from Underworld to the Venga Boys. In Mash-Ups, *I Feel Love* has been crossed with songs from all genres under the sun, from *Highway to Hell* to *Blue Monday* to *Rolling in the Deep.*

The revolution that was *I Feel Love* was triggered by one of the strangest performer-producer duos in the history of pop music. The singer Donna Summer was a black American who had come to Munich from the USA in 1968 to play a role in the German version of the hippie musical *Hair.* Giorgio Moroder was a pop singer and composer from South Tyrol who had made the transition to successful producer of pop hits in Munich at the end of the 1960s. In 1974 this singer-producer pair had their first international hit with *Love to Love You Baby. Love to Love You Baby* was recorded exclusively with traditional instruments. But due to its musical structure, in which a few musical *patterns* are combined over and over in new configurations, this song does anticipate *I Feel Love.*

Love to Love You Baby is a kind of disco version of the scandalous hit *Je t'aime...moi non plus* by Jane Birkin and Serge Gainsbourg, which, with its rather blatant musical simulation of coitus, was popular in 1969. Like *Je t'aime...moi non plus, Love to Love You Baby* was banned by many radio stations when it was released in 1974 because of Donna Summer's lascivious moaning – in the 17-minute extended version, a journalist from *Time Magazine* claims to have counted 22 orgasms.[3] In spite, or perhaps because of this, the song made it into the charts in several European countries as well as the USA.

Another Donna, Donna Haraway, describes the figure of the cyborg as a model for liberating women from essentialist attributions of their "natural" role in her Cyborg Manifesto. For her, the cyborg is a creature of a "post-gendered world". As an "unnatural", technologically created creature, it has left behind the "natural" dualisms of gender and race in favour of a hybridized form of existence. And the fictional character who lent Donna Summer a siren-like voice in *I Feel Love* is a cyborg in just this sense. She systematically refuses the attributions that were commonly applied to black entertainers at the time. In *I Feel Love* she doesn't portray the Blues mama or soul diva, and with her angelic singing enters a terrain that is usually reserved for white singers. The anti-essentialist attitude expressed in this performance also fits in with the fact that, as Peter Shapiro notes, "I Feel Love once and for all cut all ties with the naturalism of black dance music. Moroder and Bellotte...made the African- American Summer play the Teutonic ice queen with the heart of a machine and let her sing about the most fundamental act of biology, while at the same time surrounding her with the most synthetic textures ever heard on a record."

At that time, rock music was just beginning to turn away from the 3-minute single and was starting to fill entire LPs with a single track. In black pop music, too, the songs were becoming ever more extended. Maxi singles came into use in discotheques. On these, songs were prolonged, often by using tape loops, to create remixes that could be played for longer periods of time in the clubs. When Moroder created the 17-minute version of *Love to Love You Baby* in the mid-1970s, it was therefore in keeping with an existing pop music trend. This version took up the entire A-side of the album of the same name, which was released in the USA by Casablanca and which became Donna Summer's first international hit – and it was also a remarkable success for a European producer working in the field of Disco, originally an African-Americangenre.

Love to Love You Baby was a Disco composition in the style of its time; opulent string arrangements, hissing hi-hats, elegant piano dabs, wah-wah guitar – all elements that are reminiscent of the Disco operas of those years, like Van McCoy's *The Hustle* (1975) or Barry White's *Love's Theme* (1974). At the same time, however, *Love to Love You Baby* is a piece of flawless minimalism. American musicologist Robert Fink compares the structure of this song with Steve Reich's *Music for Eighteen Musicians* (1974-1976),[4] which was composed around the same time. In respect of the structural similarities of the two compositions, he notes:

> the overall structure of the seventeen-minute version of *Love to Love You Baby* corresponds exactly with that of *Music for Eighteen Musicians:* the original three-minute version of the

song corresponds with the beginning and end of the "pulse section", while the ten minutes in-between are filled with passages of "variations" of the song's basic groove, melodic material and harmonic progressions.[5]

So, with this song, Summer and Moroder (as Philip Glass had already observed) came close to minimalistic art music – or perhaps art music resembled the repetitions of Disco to begin with? The next international hit that the duo produced was *I Feel Love*, an electronic Disco composition that, in terms of minimalism, left not only *Love to Love You Baby*, but every other pop song of its time far behind.

It was written for the concept album *I Remember Yesterday*, which Moroder produced with Pete Bellotte for Donna Summer. Published in 1977, it was the third album which Moroder, Bellotte and Summer released together. On *I Remember Yesterday*, each song was a reference to the music of a decade of the twentieth century. After songs that evoked the swing of the 1930s and Motown soul of the 1960s, *I Feel Love* was intended to represent the music of the 1990s, a music still a decade-and-a-half in the future. In retrospect, it was an astonishingly prophetic musical prognosis, since Techno, for which *I Feel Love* provided the initial impetus, came into its own in the 1990s.

The basic principle of *I Feel Love* is an absolute reduction of structural elements, which goes even beyond *Love to Love You Baby*. The basis of the piece is a single synthesizer riff consisting of four notes that are transposed up and down. The harmonic framework is also extremely simple – it consists of just four chords. In accordance with the minimalistic compositional elements, the text also consists of just a few phrases, which are repeated over and over again. In the shorter single version, Donna Summer repeats the line "I Feel Love" 25 times in verse and chorus, while in the 8-minute-long original version it is more than twice that. The other six phrases which make up the remaining lyrics are repeated five times each. If one takes the driving sequencer beat away, a short minimalist poem remains, which in its uniformity and symmetry corresponds entirely with art music's Minimalism.

In his search for a futuristic sound, producer Giorgio Moroder initially did little more than *use a sequencer*, which he had borrowed from Munich composer Eberhard Schoener[6] for the recording. As per the instructions, he played a short sequence of four notes, which the sequencer then repeated at the push of a button. Using the keyboard, he was able to increase and decrease the intervals at will.[7] Moroder let the four notes of the riff wander from A to C to D to E, giving *I Feel Love* a melodic basis that makes most children's songs seem compositionally and harmonically refined by comparison.

The sequencer loop is so dominant that the inattentive listener barely notices that the song also includes other elements – a rhythm machine and a kick drum accompany the sequencer, and sustained synthesizer tones support the harmonic structure of the piece. If the throbbing sequencer brings to mind pulsating Minimalist Music à la Terry Riley, the synthesizer loops remind of La Monte Young's minimalistic *drones*. Combined with the elongated vocal passages, they form a marked counterpoint to the sequencer's hammering beat. A further subtle counterweight to the pulsating synthesizer rhythm appears in some echo effects, which briefly turn the synthesizer sounds into distant thunder. They are reminiscent of effects used in Jamaican dub reggae, where the faster and slower reverberations of a rhythmic element create syncopations that supplement the main rhythm of the piece. Terry Riley's tape-loop compositions partly operate with similar retarding effects.

It is another production trick, however, with which Moroder transforms the *four-on-the-floor* four-four-time of the sequencer into a bewildering polyrhythm. Giorgio Moroder later recalled that this dazzling effect, which set the piece apart from other electronic disco productions, was actually the result of an oversight in the studio. "I put a delay [a digital echo] on the bass track purely by chance and – wow! It sounded fantastic when the delay doubled the bass line."[8] In the mix, Moroder put the original synthesizer bass on the left stereo channel and the digital echo on the right, so that the original bass could be separated from its echo on any home stereo system.

Used in clubs, this mix could create problems across the whole stereo spectrum. Moroder comments that, "if you were on the left-hand side [of the dance floor], you could hear the downbeat and on the right-hand side you could hear the upbeat. Even Donna herself, dancing to the song one evening, said, 'what's going on with the rhythm?'"[9] It's been suggested that this echo was created with a ribbon loop effect, similar to what Sam Phillips had created during the Sun Sessions, or Terry Riley with his *Time Lag Accumulator*. But in fact, it's an electronic delay effect that produces the dizzying result. It doubles the beat and lets the beats jump from speaker to speaker.

I Feel Love makes little secret of the fact that it's about sexual desire. Donna Summer's few breathed lines – as in *Love to Love You Baby* – have an unmistakable erotic undertone. Donna Summer, who demonstrates a powerful alto voice in other songs such as *Bad Girls* or *On the Radio*, here sings in a luxuriant falsetto, and succeeds in making the vocal part sound ethereal and physical at the same time. Her lines seem to flow straight from a halfconscious daydreaming into this world.[10] The contrast between dreamy, sensual singing and a strident, synthetic beat is one of the paradoxes that has kept the song vibrant to this day.

The repetition of a few sentences like "it's so good", which all deal with love and desire, combined with the driving sequencer beat, make the piece seem like a hymn to sex and erotic desire. Peter Shapiro writes that the piece is, "the epitome of the cocaine chills and metallic shine of the 1970s (after hearing it, your teeth ache), and *I Feel Love* could only have bettered its embodiment of the decade's obsession with the detachment of anonymous sex if it had been wrapped in latex".[11] But in the case of this complex and paradoxical piece of music, the opposite of such assertions is also correct. If one imagines Summer's sustained lines without the hammering of the sequencer, they are reminiscent of Gregorian chants. The vocal part then appears intimate and full of devotion, intimating a perfect merging into love that goes as far as self-abandonment. Summer seems oblivious of herself and absorbed in the glories she tries to relate in sentence fragments. One might ask whether she is really singing to a lover – or perhaps to the repetitive technology that accompanies her and which triggers such oceanic states of mind. As if the merciless sequencer rhythms of *I Feel Love* hadn't sufficiently drawn attention to the song's technological means of production and synthetic production methods, Donna Summer's singing is processed in a way that contributes to the clean-room impression of the overall song. Her voice sounds as though processed by the sequencer and it is multiplied during the course of the song until it finally appears as a three-part choir. This manipulation of a human voice shows more clearly than anything else that this music is "not quite right", that it is no longer "of natural origin", and made with media machines instead. What's more, *I Feel Love* basks in its "unnaturalness", in the negation of the human element.

I Feel Love is the ultimate pairing of organism and machine. In *I Feel Love*, under the drum-fire of the loops, Donna Summer presents herself as half human being and half machine, as a cyborg who is connected to the endless, throbbing stimulation of the machine and obviously enjoying it. The choreography with which Donna Summer presented *I Feel Love* at live performances underscored the fusion of man and machine, which the piece evokes at a musical level. During her stage dance, Summer alternates between seductive *diseuse* and robot. Flowing dance movements and lascivious hip swings are followed by choppy, mechanical movements reminiscent of the electro-boogie of Hip-Hop breakdancing. At such moments, Donna Summer seems like the artificial Maria from Fritz Lang's *Metropolis* – a robot that looks like a woman – before turning back into the provocative seductress two dance-steps later.[12]

In *I Feel Love*, technology and body, the human being and the media apparatus enter into a symbiosis that had never before existed in pop music. Although, in one of the previous chapters, I referred to Elvis as a technically enhanced "prosthetic god" who found the way to his artistic persona through tape echoes, and although James Brown described himself as a *sex machine*, neither of them wanted to turn into a machine for all that.

Disco, however, is full of organic-technical hybrids, some of whom emerged from the musical empire of Giorgio Moroder, who himself had made music under the pseudonym *Munich Machine*. These hybrids include the Jackson Five's *Dancing Machine*, Moroder's Munich Disco rival Supermax's *Love Machine*, Moroder's ex-protégé Dee D. Jackson's *Automatic Lover* and Kraftwerk's *Menschmaschinen*.

These disco cyborgs use pop music to pose the question of what people might look like in a world dominated by technology after the "end of man" and the "death of the subject" (Michel Foucault). The idea of a fusion of man and machine is here no longer the horror vision from films such as *Metropolis* or *Terminator*, but part of a redefinition of what the human being is. Disco, as discourse, gave such "post-human" ideas a face long before they were thematized in the critical theory of the 1980s and 1990s.

Donna Haraway describes the figure of the cyborg as a model for liberating women from essentialist attributions of their "natural" role in her Cyborg Manifesto. For her, the cyborg is a creature of a "post-gendered world". As an "unnatural", technologically-created creature, it has left behind the "natural" dualisms of gender and race in favour of a hybridized form of existence. And the fictional character who lent Donna Summer a siren-like voice in *I Feel Love* is a cyborg in just this sense. She systematically refuses the attributions that were commonly applied to black entertainers at the time. In *I Feel Love* she doesn't portray the Blues mama or soul diva, and with her angelic singing enters a terrain that is usually reserved for white singers. The anti-essentialist attitude expressed in this performance also fits in with the fact that, as Peter Shapiro notes:

I Feel Love once and for all cut all ties with the naturalism of black dance music. Moroder and Bellotte...made the African-American Summer play the Teutonic ice queen with the heart of a machine and let her sing about the most fundamental act of biology, while at the same time surrounding her with the most synthetic textures ever heard on a record.

With *I Feel Love*, Donna Summer celebrated the "unnaturalness" of her new role with such gusto that the audience became suspicious. If a black artist could turn away from the qualities usually attributed to her race, might not the same be the case with her gender? – a train of thought that Donna Haraway might approve of. Rumours began that Donna Summer had to be a transvestite!

It is one of the paradoxes of this piece that it opens a space for difference precisely through its rigid, mechanical order. Despite its driving beat, *I Feel Love* is of an extraordinary rhythmic complexity, thanks to Giorgio Moroder's echo on the sequencer. The piece therefore contradicts clichéd ideas about Disco and Techno music as an uninterrupted boom-boom-boom in four-four time. Through the echo effect, which obscures the bass riff, Moroder managed to get precisely-repeating machines out of time and turn the strict four-four time of the sequencer into a bewildering polyrhythm – he turned the machine into a sloppy machine. It no longer repeats like a machine, but like a living being, with small inaccuracies and minimal shifts. If the dissolution of the contrast between technology and organic nature is one of the themes of *I Feel Love*, then its polyrhythmic synthesizer riff is the musical realization of this idea.

Moroder's production trick with the echo delay is very similar to Steve Reich's minimalist method of *phase shifting*. As in Reich's *It's Gonna Rain*, with its two tape loops running apart and back together, Moroder's delay effect does not produce an exact and synchronous double of the synthesizer riff. Those who listen carefully will perceive how the echo plays a kind of acoustic catch with the riff that triggered it. Sometimes it is almost synchronized with the riff, then it pushes on ahead or falls behind. The result is a tremendously complex polyrhythm that could hardly be replicated by traditional instruments (and cannot be written down in the traditional way). The intricate electronic beat that fills the dance floors to this day is a *resulting pattern* in the sense that Steve Reich used it. It comes about because two loops overlap, and new rhythmic patterns emerge from this overlapping.

In his book *Unlocking the Groove,* American musicologist Mark J. Butler argues that such experiments with seemingly straight bars are one of the most important characteristics of electronic dance music. Butler calls rhythmic shifts such as those in the spooling bass line of *I Feel Love* "metric dissonances", a notable characteristic of electronic musical styles such as Techno. He initially observes that, "the repetitive nature of electronic dance music, along with the almost uninterrupted presence of a loud, emphatic bass line, might lead one to believe that its use of rhythm is homogeneous and simple".[13] However, Butler goes on to provide numerous detailed analyses of Techno tracks, to show how loops can be used to create highly complex and rhythmically ambivalent structures from seemingly simple patterns. For Butler, the contrast between simple four-four time, which seems to dominate most Techno pieces, and metric dissonances that contrast the simple pulse, is a central characteristic of Techno.

It is almost as if the producers of such tracks had wanted to translate Deleuze's dictum, that difference dwells in repetition, into music. When Deleuze writes about the meaning of repetition in art, it almost sounds as if he is describing the echo delay in *I Feel Love,* which produces diverse metric variations from the simple sequencer beat: "it is perhaps the highest object of art simultaneously to set in motion all these repetitions with their essential and rhythmic differences, their mutual displacement and disguise, their divergences and decentrations, to intertwine and envelop them...in illusions, the 'effect' of which changes each time..."[14] I *Feel Love* does just that. The song transforms a hammering machine beat into an organic-sounding rhythm (paradoxically with the aid of another technical device!) and opens it up to shifts and decentrations.

The metric subtleties of this song are probably not consciously perceived by many of its listeners. But there is no doubt that the tension between rigid beat and natural-sounding rhythm is what makes not only this song, but electronic dance music in general so appealing. The experience that a rigid, straight beat can lead to an endless feeling of freedom has apparently been intensely perceived in Disco's gay subculture. American author Walter Hughes argues, for instance, that:

Disco is not so much a decadent pleasure as a disciplining, regulative discourse that paradoxically allows, or even creates, a sense of freedom. If Disco is a form of discipline, then it resembles many other notable aspects of urban gay culture, such as body-building, fashion, sadomasochism and safer sex…Gay male identity is largely defined by a series of practices that combine pleasure with self-discipline. The realization that the control and regulation to which homosexuality is subjected in our society can themselves be erotic practices, practices that are better turned into sources of pleasure than left in the hands of parents, policemen, psychiatrists, homophobic individuals, priests or senators from North Carolina, may therefore be an important moment in gay self-perception. This moment, which involves snatching this power from others, is staged nightly at the disco. By submitting to the urgent, disciplining beat, one discovers through Disco how to be a certain type of gay man. Acceptance of the attribution of a version of gay identity is achieved through pleasure, rather than suffering."[15]

Musical styles such as High-NRG and Techno, which were to develop out of the pounding sequencer loops of *I Feel Love*, invite to turn domination and disciplining repetition into such "techniques of the self" (Foucault). In this way, Disco has succeeded in snatching machine repetitions from Thanatos' domain and in turning them into a medium of Eros.

Through its rhythmic ambivalence, *I Feel Love* leaves listeners free in their perception of the meter, and thus in their entire interpretation of the piece. Through its specific metric characteristics, electronic dance music opens up new possibilities for the interpretation and experience of music where dancing plays a particularly important role. The experiences that can be triggered by songs like *I Feel Love*, which are simultaneously monotonous and complex, are surprisingly similar to those which minimalist artists and composers wanted to trigger. What Rosalind Krauss observes about the "minimalist subject" (the viewer of Minimalist Art) also applies to the "Disco subject". The disco dancer moving to *I Feel Love* is likewise "a subject who is radically dependent on the conditions of the spatial field, a subject that constitutes itself in the act of perception, but always only temporarily, from moment to moment".[16] Krauss here refers to Merleau-Ponty's phenomenology, where there is no "pure" perception or experience, but only a bodily one that results from a dynamic interrelation between the perceiving subject and that which is perceived. Nothing illustrates this insight better than the anecdote about Donna Summer when she heard her own song in a discotheque and was puzzled by its rhythm. With their unreal spaces of dry ice mists, flickering lights and colours as "total environments"[17] that appeal to all the senses, discotheques and clubs aim precisely at this physical aspect of perception. At the same time, the loud hammering of the sequencers and loops confronts the listeners with themselves through the incessant repetitions, and this monotony throws them back entirely on their own perceptions. Through the metric dissonances and their *resulting patterns*, *I Feel Love* makes the "phenomenological" potential of electronic dance music particularly perceptible. Basically, this song can be seen as a pop version of La Monte Young's *Dream House*, which I referred to in an earlier chapter. In *Dream House*, the electronic buzzing that fills the entire installation sounds different to each visitor, depending on where they are in the room. In *I Feel Love*, too, the perception of the polyrhythmic electro-beat depends on whether

the dancer is closer to the right-hand or the left-hand speaker. In
I Feel Love, everyone moves to a rhythm that only they themselves
can hear, until, like Donna Summer, they repeat, self-forgetful and
ecstatic at the same time, *Ooh, it's so good, it's so good, it's so good, it's
so good, it's so good…*

CHAPTER 14

STAYING IN THE RHYTHM LOOPS AND THE HOMEOSTASIS OF MODERNITY

Einatmen, ausatmen, einatmen, ausatmen
Einatmen, ausatmen, einatmen, ausatmen
Einatmen, ausatmen, einatmen, ausatmen
Einatmen, ausatmen, einatmen, ausatmen
Im Rhythmus bleiben, im Rhythmus bleiben
Im Rhythmus bleiben, im Rhythmus bleiben
Was soll ich tun?
Im Rhythmus bleiben, im Rhythmen bleiben
Im Rhythmus bleiben, im Rhythmus bleiben
Front 242: Im Rhythmus bleiben

*I realize that when I was at [DJ Africa] Bambaataa's parties, I
was one of those guys who would never say anything, I would
just stay in the back and dance. I would close my eyes and
go off. I didn't know shit about African culture, but for some
strange reason, when we heard those beats and those rhythms
something happened. Bambaataa was the Mecca of the energy
source, Bambaataa was the witch doctor...there would be certain
moments when the records would play. At that point it would*

*be this tribal thing and everybody would just do it. That's some
deep shit. What was that? How can I use that information to
grow? That's the true purpose of what we have to do.*

Grandmixer DST[1]

It's evening. The bangka boat is chugging slowly up the Donsol
River and the orange light of the sunset, which is coming from the
direction of the ocean, is creating ever darker shades. The further
we get from the beach, the darker it gets. We pass by a tropical
mangrove forest of coconut trees and nipa palms, and rampantly
abundant ferns, grasses and creepers on the shore. The only sounds
that are heard are the quiet chugging of the engine and the chirps
of the crickets.

By degrees, it gets completely dark, the inky black of a place with
no artificial light for miles around. The moon lends the tree-tops
and the waves a touch of silver. If the boatman hadn't lit a small
kerosene lamp, we wouldn't be able to see our hands in front of
our eyes.

We're gliding ever deeper into the darkness. Suddenly the
boatman points ahead to a tiny spot of light on the shore. As we
approach it, it turns into individual spots of light. The *bangkero*
turns off the engine as we glide towards them. The closer we get,
the more these light spots appear like a spiral cosmic nebula within
the mangroves. We are just a few metres away now; the cloud of
light is hanging above us, suspended in the palm trees. It pulses
with a steady rhythm, as if in response to some secret signal that we
cannot perceive. The black river water reflects the movement.

The source of the light is thousands of fireflies, each one blinking
with a slow, steady rhythm. "Firefly watching" is a popular tourist
attraction at the beach resort of Donsol in the Philippines.
But on this evening, we can only hear the other tourist groups'

"aahs" and "oohs" faintly in the distance. After a few attempts at photographing the spectacle, we give up – it shows up as a mere collection of yellow dots before a black background. The only thing left to do is lean back and watch the blinking of the fireflies while slowly succumbing to a gentle trance.

Scientists assume that the luminous signals of the fireflies serve to entice potential mates. Some of the flashing rhythms produced by males are said to be more attractive than others to females. But that pulsating light show in the palm trees above our heads seemed to serve a different purpose altogether. Like the electric Christmas tree lights that are so popular in Southeast Asia, all the insects flash in a constant rhythm. It does not appear like a mating ritual in which the male fireflies try to outshine each other, rather, like a kind of celebration by the entire swarm. Not all species of firefly produce a pulse in the process of flashing their lights. It's only some species that occur in South East Asia which combine into a "mass symphony". For a long time, it was unclear how they achieved a unified rhythm. At the end of the 1960s, having conducted studies in Thailand, biologist John Buck concluded that there is no "central impulse". Rather, the insects organize in a spontaneous, quasi-collective manner. Each firefly sends light impulses at a particular pace, and at the same time responds to the blinking of the others. At first, the impulses are random, but after a while they synchronize so that all the insects assume the same interval – like an orchestra that coheres in the absence of a conductor, as Terry Riley envisaged for his Minimalist signature piece, *In C*.

In his book *Sync – How Order Emerges from Chaos in the Universe, Nature, and Daily Life*,[2] Steven Strogatz describes how metric processes structure phenomena, from biological cells to the orbits of planets. His book shows how nature, left to itself, can organize itself into rhythmic structures to create order. He observes that:

> at the heart of the universe is a steady, insistent beat: the
> sound of cycles in sync. It pervades nature at every scale
> from the nucleus to the cosmos. Every night along the

tidal rivers of Malaysia, thousands of fireflies congregate in the mangroves and flash in unison, without any leader or cue from the environment. Trillions of electrons march in lockstep in a superconductor, enabling electricity to flow through it with zero resistance. In the solar system, gravitational synchrony can eject huge boulders out of the asteroid belt and towards the Earth; the cataclysmic impact of one such meteor is thought to have killed the dinosaurs. Even our bodies are symphonies of rhythm, kept alive by the relentless, coordinated firing of thousands of pacemaker cells in our hearts. In every case, these feats of synchrony occur spontaneously, almost as if nature has an eerie yearning for order.

Loops, as outlined in this book, seem to follow a similar process at an aesthetic level. They synchronize sounds, machines and people. Like the fireflies of South East Asia or the cells of our bodies, loops tend towards the temporary, organic synchronization of disparate elements. Music created using loops transforms technical repetition into organic rhythms. Terry Riley's *In C*, Donna Summer's *I Feel Love* and many of the Hip-hop and Techno tracks of the past few decades show how rhythmically organized coherence, or a groove, can emerge from small, disparate elements, and how this can be a doorway to ecstatic experience and/or to excess. In *On Repeat*, Elizabeth Hellmuth Margulis' excellent study on the meaning of repetition in music, she observes that "repetition lays bare the fine line between the inside and outside, human and mechanical, private and public, in a way that can be considered both sublime and degenerate".[4]

In the tape compositions of early Minimal Music, as also in electronic dance music, musical patterns created with the aid of media machines acquire a pulsating harmony. The fact that these musical styles are based on machines rather than on the work of human composers seems crucial to an understanding of them. At a symbolic level, this kind of music is also about what a more constructively informed relationship between humans and machines might look like. The artists and composers whose work I have presented in this book expended their efforts to transcend the mechanical precision of machines and the rhythms of machines came to be coordinated with those of humans. The precise hammering produced by technology is transformed into "metric dissonances" (Mark J. Butler) by deliberately introducing inaccuracies to arrive at an organic, natural-sounding pulse, as heard in Donna Summer's *I Feel Love*. Gilles Deleuze's aim inaudibly to wrest away "mechanical" and "stereotypical" repetition through "small differences, variations and modifications" finds artistic expression here.

German philosopher Ludwig Klages provides useful definitions for such a process. In *Vom Wesen des Rhythmus* [On the Nature of Rhythm] (1934), he makes a distinction between repetitions occurring in nature (which occur as approximations and with minimal variations) and machine-made repetition (which is mechanically precise). He distinguishes the constricting monotony of a "soulless" beat from "natural rhythm" and sees both the beat, or pulse, and rhythm as subject to repetition. A pulse, when produced by a sequencer, sampler or tape loop, repeats exactly the same thing. By contrast, rhythm is the repetition of similar sequences that can be experienced over and over afresh. Human consciousness desires and expects the repetition of familiar things at regular intervals and experiences this as pleasing. Unlike a pulse, rhythm does not cause a sense of compulsion from an external source. Rather, experiencing rhythm can engender a sense of liberation, with the recurrence of the same amounting to the start of something new. Rhythm, therefore, can be experienced as revitalization; "the pulse merely repeats, while rhythm renews itself".[5] What makes rhythm enjoyable is that sequences and phrases move smoothly, unlike in technologically produced repetition. Klages observes that, "each bar has a beginning and an end, but a wave neither begins nor ends. It is therefore quite literally something infinite."[6] According to him, the strict linear arrangement of bars therefore tends to lead to rigid succession. When it comes to rhythm, on the other hand, succession is experienced as wavelike oscillation between two poles that function as an overarching, timeless principle.

In his book *Die Zeit, mit der wir leben* [The time with which we live], Rudolf Wendorff notes in respect of rhythm that:

> what fascinates is that, while repeating the same thing, rhythm doesn't remain exactly the same, but rather, like some mysterious power, leads to the repetition of similar elements as a living event...The elementary experience of rhythm is psychologically beneficial because, while time continues to pass by, it does not instantly disappear into the boundless and unknown but, as if checked by a ghostly hand, moves on the spot through the repetition of the similar...The concept "organic" rather than "mechanical" underlines the value of cyclical time.[7]

Compositions as diverse as Steve Reich's minimalistic tape composition *It's Gonna Rain* and Donna Summer's *I Feel Love,* Peter Roehr's films and Andy Warhol's silkscreens embody a desire to turn the mechanical pulse of their respective media into an organic rhythm. The "resulting patterns" of Steve Reich's tape compositions and Donna Summer's *I Feel Love* are examples of how the rigid functioning of machines – the pulse in Klages' terminology – can be turned into a natural rhythm.

When it comes to traditional music that has not been produced with the aid of technical media, it is particularly in the South East Asian Gamelan and West African percussion music that small differences make an existing dominant pattern more complex. Music from the Caribbean and from North and Latin America, which has been influenced by the folklore of the West African slaves who were deported there, is also based on a dominance of rhythms kept vibrant through tiny variations. The various forms of Jazz, Reggae, Calypso and Samba also form rhythmic variations that are so minimal they cannot be captured using traditional methods of Western notation. They swing, or have got the groove, to use two expressions that originated in musicians' slang and found their way into music ethnology and theory.

In their best work, the musicians and composers who work with the repetitive properties of recording media succeed in producing differences and minimal variations that are actually alien to the machines. This type of art or music transforms a machine-made pulse into an organic rhythm. In this context, artistic work with loops appears as an attempt to extract an element of difference from repetitions produced by technical media (such as tape, film, sampler, video, sequencer or computer), to endow them with an element of difference in Deleuze's sense, and to extract a groove from the predictable and error-free running of machines.

I call this procedure the homeostasis of modernity. Walter Cannon uses the term homeostasis (or self-regulation) to describe the ability of a system to maintain itself in a stable condition within certain parameters. Artistic work with tape loops, film loops and sequencers can be seen as symbolizing the possibility of transforming the violence of the mechanical beat of modern machines into a more natural rhythm, in some way to rebalance the interaction between people and technology. Working with loops is a way of organizing technologically reproduced words, images and sounds into a form accessible to human reflection. Instead of dramatizing the shock experience which mass media and other modern technologies represent to human perception, as was common practice in Modernist art forms, by using loops, materials are reassembled into an organic unity.

This potential also distinguishes the use of loops from the collages of Cubism, Dadaism and Constructivism in the 1910s and 1920s, the Pop Art of Robert Rauschenberg and the cutups of William Burroughs in the 1960s. All these approaches put found audio-visual and acoustic material into new contexts in order to create new structures. But in Modernist art, the collage technique was used to emphasize the chaos of modernity or fight it with its own weapons. The loops of post-modernity, on the other hand, create coherence from the chaos and noise of modernity. The collages present confrontation, conflicts and divergence. The loop unites, mediates and rebalances.

In an interview, Berlin DJ Jane Ellen Allien vividly illustrates this potential by describing her own first encounter with Techno music. Before this, her experience of the city of Berlin had been of, "living in a squat from 1990 to 1995. I was really in crisis back then. I was paranoid – the noise of the city, the dirt, cars, the reflections from the windows. It all drove me crazy. I ran through the streets and almost snapped; I couldn't get clear in my head."[8] It almost sounds like expressionist prose from the 1920s. When she first heard Techno in Berlin's nightclubs, it released her from her horrors.

> Through Techno music, I lost my fear and rediscovered a love for the city I lived in. For me, the sounds of Techno were the same sounds I heard while I was walking around the streets. The city, the madness of the great city resonated in these sounds. Whenever I used the subway, I got paranoid. I thought all the strange noises would make me scream. Through Techno, I learned to like those sounds… After listening to Techno, I'd sit on the subway, the doors would open and I would hear tracks.[9]

While Allien does not explicitly mention the repetition of mechanical sounds in Techno, it is repetition of such sounds which makes the noise of modernity more bearable and accessible. For Techno DJ and producer Richie Hawtin, too, Techno music, with its minimalistic repetitions, is a method of achieving inner balance in a media-driven world. In an interview, Hawtin, who is familiar with 1960s Minimalist art, observes that:

> for me, Minimalism just means balance, balance in music and in life; it's an understanding of what exactly is needed to make yourself understood. In the world in which we live, with so much crazy stuff going on and all that information

overload, the idea of balance and minimalism become more attractive every day.[10]

It is no coincidence that many people feel like they have been transported to a huge production hall when they visit a Techno party for the first time. Many of these events indeed take place in factory halls that were abandoned when Western Europe turned from an industrial to a post-industrial society. The areas where Techno first thrived were those that had been particularly affected by industrial deaths and factory closures – Berlin, the former GDR, and, internationally, the areas around Manchester as well as Detroit, the industrial rustbelt of the USA. It almost seems as if those who had been betrayed by industrialism wanted to confront the noise of industry one more time and overcome it with their music.

The aim of several twentieth-century musical genres – the Futurists' *Arte dei Rumori*, Edgar Varèse, Heavy Metal and drone music, for instance – was to find artistic expression for industrial noise. By contrast, loop-based music like Techno is about getting noise back under control, and, on a cultural level, finding a new balance between machine noise and human receptivity. It's often the sounds that evoke the noise of machines – motors, sirens, white noise, explosions, crashes – that are used in Industrial Music and Techno.

The Industrial Music of the 1970s and 80s still used throbbing noise to formulate a critique of prevailing socio-economic conditions. In an interview, Genesis P-Orridge of the Industrial band Throbbing Gristle explains that:

> one of the original intentions of Throbbing Gristle was to make a different kind of Muzak for factories, by using the sounds of the factory themselves...I'm in a huge concrete box with barred windows. And I'm a creature, I don't like this. It was not so much that we wanted to attack people with noise. We wanted to show up what was already there.[11]

In another interview, he describes the experience of living in the industrial East End of London; he was:

> walking down the street and a car goes by, a train goes by, or you work in a factory or walk alongside one, just that kind of industrial life…When we made our first record, we went outside and suddenly we'd hear a train and the small workshops under the railway arches, the lathes and electric saws running, and we suddenly thought, "we haven't done anything new, we only subconsciously took up what was already there and reorganized it".[12]

Other bands belonging to the Industrial Music and Electronic Body Music genres of the 1980s were also interested in finding artistic expression for unleashed technology in their noise-saturated music. Gabi Delgado of the band Deutsch-Amerikanische Freundschaft [German-American Friendship] observes that:

> we always wanted to have a kind of endangered music that was about to crash…Bands like Kraftwerk surrounded themselves with cleanliness, it was a case of anything rather than sweat. That's a concept in itself, but we didn't want that. We wanted a spaceship that was about to crash. Look, the wing is burning! I hope we'll make it![13]

This combination of fetishizing and demonizing technology is a characteristic element of Electronic Body Music and Industrial Music of the 1980s. It often expressed an unmitigated cultural pessimism. Jean-Luc de Meyer, for instance, describes the music of his band Front 242 by making comparisons to post-industrial apocalyptic narratives from films like *Mad Max* (1979) and *Blade Runner* (1982). "Imagine taking your camera across the country, past a burning city, a pile up on the motorway, scenes of looting, normal people going shopping, soldiers and helicopters, a mob gathering in an old factory building…"[14]

Technology, as implemented in the electronic music of the 1980s, is both messenger and trigger of catastrophe. It was the Techno music of the 1990s, which had developed from Industrial and Electronic Body Music, that assumed a more positive and even sensual attitude towards technology. Techno, according to DJ Juan Atkins' definition "music that sounds like a machine, not a machine that sounds like music", organized the noise of modernity into a party soundtrack.

Anyone who has ever walked along the walls of a disused factory building looking for the entrance to a party at night may remember how the blanked-out, partially broken window panes trembled and clanked with the hammering Techno beat booming from inside the hall. Whoever heard this clanking from the outside may well have believed that inside, machinery was unleashed and raging, as imagined by the Futurists, or as bands like Throbbing Gristle, Deutsch-Amerikanische Freundschaft and Front 242 wanted to achieve.

The Industrial bands had released noise in order to surrender to it. After a period of throbbing and rumbling, the performances of Throbbing Gristle regularly led to unleashed noise orgies full of feedback, amounting to an acoustic frontal attack, the dynamics of which were often beyond the control of the musicians. By contrast, Techno has always tended to control and reorganize noise with the aid of loops. While the initial experience at a Techno party can be that of a disorientating and chaotic flood of noise, this cannot be said to apply to the structure of this music. While Industrial bands intensified the feeling of being exposed to out-of-control technology to the point that it became unbearable and therefore also visible, Techno does not aim to achieve alienation. Rather, it neutralizes the origin of this sense with the aid of repetition.

The impulse to make noise, which nobody enjoys hearing in its raw state, acceptable through repetition was present from the very beginning of loop-based music. In his early *Noise Etudes* of 1948, Pierre Schaeffer used the pounding of a locomotive as musical material – another sound that exemplifies industrial society. His

Étude Pathétique combines the chugging of a boat engine, the rattling of metal cans and various musical fragments. Since these are looped, they do not simply clash, as they would in a collage, and Schaeffer is able to combine them into a comparatively organic, musical unity in keeping with his brilliant realization that "if you repeat the same thing twice it becomes music".

In this context, it is important to note that Techno and other electronic music styles are usually dance music that can only be "properly understood" on the dance floor. The dialectic between the machine-like regularity and listeners' individual experience of freedom comes into its own only there. This is why Hillegonda Rietveld argues in *This Is Our House* that electronic music only makes sense in a live DJ mix.

> It is only when played to and interacted with a dancing crowd, that house music, as a medium, is complete. In addition, a dance record is also pretty meaningless when it is separated from other dance records. One should look at dance singles as words which are looking for a sentence; they need to be combined to create a soundscape.[15]

The "metric dissonances" (Mark J. Butler) described in the chapter on Donna Summer's *I Feel Love* have been shown to be an important element of dance music, since they introduce an initial element of difference to the relentless throbbing of the sequencers. When such music is played for dancers at a rave or in a nightclub, the repetitive beats also become the means of highly individual self-expression on the dance floor. The dancers themselves interpret the rhythm through their movements and thereby introduce another level of difference. There are no set steps, nor is there any choreography. Each dancer physically interprets the music in their own way. Through their rhythmic movements, the dancers add a counterpoint to the patterns of the music.

Techno dancers are not passive victims of a tyrannical pulse. They actively contribute to the shaping of their musical experience and create a physical interpretation of the music. In the dancers' experience, therefore, the mechanical repetitions of sequencer and loop can paradoxically facilitate an experience of liberation and become a source of pleasure. The ambience of most clubs is conducive to such experiences – they create a space designed to enable expansive experiences by adding flashing lights, fog, stroboscopic effects and projections, legacies of the Merry Pranksters' Acid Tests.

Simon Reynolds observes that at a rave:

> it became even more crystal clear that the audience was the star: that bloke over there doing fishy-finger dancing was as much a part of the entertainment, the tableau, as the DJs or bands. Dance moves spread through the crowd like superfast viruses. I was instantly entrained in a new kind of dancing – tics and spasms, twitches and jerks, the agitation of bodies broken down into separate components, then reintegrated at the level of the dancefloor as a whole. Each sub-individual part (a limb, a hand cocked like a pistol) was a cog in a collective "desiring machine", interlocking with the sound system's bass-throbs and sequencer riffs. Unity and selfexpression fused in a forcefield of pulsating, undulating euphoria.[16]

Even though dancing constitutes the real experience of Techno and other electronic music, this has rarely been discussed in detail. The experience is probably too fleeting and individual to lend itself easily to description, let alone the formulation of theories. Nevertheless, it remains the centre of Techno music and culture, which cannot be understood without having had such experiences at first hand – the *jouissance*, which paradoxically arises when the music becomes very monotonous and regular.

Pop music scholar Simon Frith has belittled such moments as "routine transcendence". But those who become part of the great engine room of a dance floor experience how a heterogeneity of the smallest elements run parallel, diverge, converge, to form uniformity and harmony in the whole. It is precisely because these media machines do nothing more than function as machines that they allow the listener moments of free and unconditioned perception, as the proponents of Minimal Art, Minimalist Music and the propagandists of psychedelic culture had wanted to achieve in their turn.

It is one of the paradoxes of this type of music that experiences such as those outlined above are achieved by means which twentieth-century cultural criticism viewed as the epitome of stereotype and objectification. At the beginning of this book, I referred to the reservations which some of the leading thinkers of modernity – Canetti, Spengler, Anders, Eli, Huxley, Ortega y Gasset and Adorno – had in respect of media reproduction in art and music. Adorno's sarcastic remark that "what is repeated is healthy" referred both to the stereotypes introduced by mass media and to mindless technical repetition achieved with the aid of recording media.

Jacques Attali notes in *Noise: The Political Economy of Music* that through notation, music had become a monologue of power, while its media reproduction served to silence people by means of replication.[17] Music thus no longer functions as a form of "sociality, an opportunity for spectators to meet and communicate, but rather a tool making the individualized stockpiling of music possible on a huge scale".[18] Turned into a commodity through recording, it enables the acquisition of rights without ever using it, its endless exchange without deriving pleasure from it, without ever experiencing its original function. The possibility of recording and reproducing music leads to its joyless gathering and it is ultimately the "threat of death".[19]

Yet the contemporary Techno party does, of course, serve the purpose of drawing pleasure from recorded music. At such parties, music is produced with just the kind of recording media that embodies Thanatos, the death drive, for Attali. And in its best moments, community arises through the opportunity for the audience to meet and communicate, which Attali ascribes to shared musical experiences before technical reproduction was an option. Through its staging by a DJ, and through the performative interpretation of bodies on the dance floor, "dead" music stored on vinyl or digital data carriers takes on a new life.

In his famous essay, Walter Benjamin argues that art loses its aura through technical reproduction. Yet at Techno parties, such a process is suspended and reversed – stored, commodified music once again becomes an occasion of collective, ecstatic experience, similar to the religious cult objects which for Benjamin represent the origin of all art. But Benjamin also hoped that media reproduction would put an end to the cult status of art, to replace it with more democratic forms of access, and this has happened. Over the past 40 years, media culture has found ways of returning a kind of aura to technically reproduced music and to make it into a catalyst for collective, liberating experiences.

Through reproduction media, including records, CDs, computers, samplers and MP3 players, a new kind of hightech popular culture has emerged. Weekend after weekend, DJs pack vinyl records or hard drives full of loops into their cases in order to make people dance. Musicians who are able to keep their equipment in a backpack or a sports bag are travelling around the globe to bring dormant digital data to life at clubs and parties.

Usually, this type of music and the required devices function on the basis of loops, which allow a solo performer to make music for large audiences. This is also how an entire homebased industry provides an income for thousands – from DJs to record labels and retailers, and from discotheque owners to doormen. This culture sustains a substantial number of people and it entertains millions. From its origins in the USA, this type of music has spread all over the world. Today, Techno rocks crowds in Brazil, the Philippines, Japan and Israel.

From simple technical tricks and Pierre Schaeffer's and Raymond Scott's music machines, an entire industry which makes use of instruments and programs based on loops has developed. It began with analogue sequencers such as the Moog 960, which became a style-defining element for the sound of the Berlin school around

Tangerine Dream and Klaus Schulze, as well as for Vangelis and John-Michel Jarre, while loop-based rhythm machines, such as the Roland TB-303 and Roland TR-909 have defined musical genres like Acid und Techno. Software like Ableton's *Live* contains sequencers and the development of such programs has become a full-blown industry with innovations that continue to inspire new varieties of electronic dance music.

It seems as if the history of electronic music produced with such devices pursues a dialectic of more or less repetitive modes of music. Techno music of the early 1990s was followed by the more song-based Electro-clash, the renaissance of Minimal Techno around 2000 and the dubstep of the present. In an interview, Brostep stadium rocker Skrillex says about his "Post-Hardcore" style that he merely combines the usual elements of loop-based electronic dance music with approaches he considers progressive. "Traditional dance music consists of many loops that go on for five minutes, and this works really well on the dance floor!"[20]

Guitarist Robert Fripp who, with his Frippertronics, was one of the first to work with tape loops in pop music, has consistently referred to "small intelligent units" since the mid-1970s.[21] By this he means musicians who make music on their own and with minimal equipment, unlike the "rock dinosaurs" of that era, who, like Pink Floyd, Tangerine Dream and Yes, could only realize their musical ideas using huge equipment parks. In 1979, Fripp undertook a solo world tour to demonstrate this idea. He performed solo on an electric guitar alongside an installation of two tape recorders, an exact copy of Terry Riley's Time Lag Generator. By creating loops, he was able to perform rampant and complex solos with neither band nor a machine arsenal in evidence.

Nowadays "small intelligent units" are at work around the globe on any given day of the week. They no longer use tape recorders, but rather, laptops, small handy devices like the Kaoss Pad or other digital devices for their performances. When they perform, their equipment often looks no different than that of an average office – a computer and a few peripherals. The electronic dance music propagated in this way has been declared dead time and again, and it hardly ever appears in the charts anymore. And yet compared to other movements in popular music, Techno and the electronic dance music that was to follow some 40 years after its first emergence in Donna Summer's *I Feel Love* (which still fills dance floors without sounding dated), and 20 years after its codification in the rave movement, are still astonishingly vital and present. To this day, this music fills clubs, sells records, CDs, MP3s as well as subscriptions to streaming services, and is part of a lifestyle.

Other important popular-cultural movements, such as Rock'n'Roll, psychedelic rock and Punk lost their creative impetus after just a few years. Especially in psychedelic rock, some of the most important protagonists (like Jim Morrison, Jimi Hendrix and Janis Joplin) survived their success only a short time. It is a different story with loop-based dance music and with present-day DJs and producers like Francois Kevorkian, Nicky Siano, Afrika Bambaataa and Grandmaster Flash, who have been in the business for over 40 years. It may seem far-fetched to attribute this longevity to the homeostatic effects of loops. But it is remarkable that a scene whose declared intentions include excess, self-dissolution and all-night dancing has claimed far fewer victims than the traditional Rock'n'Roll lifestyle did, and that it continues to exist in a time of its own.

Staying in the rhythm – in the postmodern era, this paradigm seems more suited to survival than to an insistence on exalted self-expression, or an original artistic will and genius cult, which characterized rock music. Media repetition, notwithstanding its rejection by Modernist cultural criticism, has proven surprisingly enduring. It seems as though Adorno's mocking statement was confirmed in the artistic use of loops, and that repetition might actually be healthy after all.

In the end, loops have merged into a huge apparatus that ticks, knocks and pumps incessantly. The combination of these elements creates a metre. But not all parts of this machinery are in sync. Some of the cogs move apart and back together at regular intervals.

Others move in shifting cycles that never coincide. Yet all of them form a rhythm together. They do what the previously quoted Electro band Front 242 chants: *stay in the rhythm.* The natural physical inhalation and exhalation, in combination with a strict electronic beat, make up the paradoxical tension that can emerge through the use of loops.

Ernst Bloch observes that "not everyone is present in the same Now. It only appears that way, in that they can be seen together. But this doesn't mean that they are synchronously present."[22] When one is exposed to media repetitions, or loops, which seem to have neither originator nor external source and are devoid of direction or aim, it sometimes seems as if Bloch was wrong, and as if everyone were indeed present in the same Now, 'with the others, at the same time'. Loops pulsate. They beat like a heart. They never stop.

When one drops out, others take over. They drift apart, then come back together. Like life itself, they go on and on. On a clear day – or a booming wild party night – you can sense eternity.

ENDNOTES

Chapter 1

1. The only books I know of that deal with a similar subject are Michael Glasmeier's *Loop* and, to some extent, Robert Fink's *Repeating Ourselves*, which have been a great help while writing my book
2. Cf. also Anz/Walder 1999, 226-233
3. Horkheimer/Adorno 2002, 119
4. Handke 2000, 36
5. Cf. Gould 1987
6. Horkheimer/Adorno 1999, 3
7. Landwehr 2014
8. Cf. for instance, Brewster/Broughton 2000, Lawrence 2003, Shapiro 2000, Shapiro 2005, Denk/Thülen 2012. My personal favourites are the interview volumes Fleming 1995 and Huegli 2002, as well as Mesterharm/Amaretto/Brückner 1997 and Bublitz 1999, and Denk/Thülen's *Klang der Familie*
9. Deleuze 2004, 97
10. Cf. Fisher 2014
11. Diederichsen 2008, 37. Cf. also Schumacher 2015
12. Kierkegaard 2009, 34
13. MEW, Vol. 23, 445
14. Eisenberg 1999
15. Foucault 1979, 62

16. Hoffmann 1994, 33
17. Felix / Pine / Marshall 2001, 11

Chapter 2

1. Los Angeles Times, 7 July 1896. Quoted in Musser 2005, 104
2. Horton/Hoxtor 2014, 14
3. Around the same time, the German film pioneers Max and Emil Skladanowsky developed the *Bioscop*, which is also based on film loops. But since Edison is internationally more well-known, and since his *May Irwin Kiss* clip offers richer material, I have centralized him in this chapter
4. Bazin 2009, 21
5. Bergson 2005
6. Another method from the early days of cinema that extracted a comic element from captured time was the Lumière film *La démolition du mur*, which shows the demolition of a wall, and which was first shown forwards and then backwards – the wall first collapsed, and then re-erected by itself as if by magic
7. Bergson 2005, 17
8. *Ibid*, 17
9. Musser 2005. This essay made me aware of much of the information about the *May Irwin Kiss* and its amazing history, and also made me realize that the early Edison films were shown as loops
10. Quoted in Musser 2005, 99
11. *Ibid* 100
12. *Ibid 104*
13. Birnbaum 1987, 86
14. "Art in the 21st Century" 2005
15. In the visual arts and experimental film, it was not until the 1960s that artists and filmmakers began to use loops as an aesthetic means. In *The Language of New* Media, Lev Manovich cites a passage from Vertov's *Man with Camera* in which a loop appears, but technically it's not a loop
16. Huegli 2003, 67

Chapter 3

1. Prieberg 1960, 78
2. Schaeffer 1948, 28
3. Schaeffer 1974, 25. Cf. Dack / North 2006 on Schaeffer's written style
4. Schaeffer 1987, http://paul.mycpanel.princeton.edu/music242/shaefferinterview.html
5. Schaeffer 2012, 4
6. *Ibid*
7. Schaeffer undated., 51-60, here 51
8. Frisius, undated
9. Quoted from *ibid*
10. Cf. also Demers 2010
11. Lévi-Strauss 1983, 23
12. Frisius, undated c. (unpaginated)
13. Schaeffer 2012, 3
14. De la Motte 1999, 12
15. Schaeffer 2012, 4
16. *Ibid*
17. He realized this idea later, when he had studio engineer Jacques Poullin build the *phonogène* for him, an instrument that – similar to the Mellotron, which will be described in detail in the chapter on Raymond Scott – works on the basis of tape loops
18. Schaeffer, 2012, 7
19. *Ibid*
20. Schaeffer 1987, http://paul.mycpanel.princeton.edu/music242/shaefferinterview.html
21. Schaeffer 2012, 9
22. Cf. Prieberg 1960, 82; Schenk 1996; Elste 1996
23. Cf. Holmes 2008, 153-157. After moving to the USA, he also worked with tape loops at the Columbia-Princeton Electronic Music Center, cf. Seachrist 2003, 59
24. Adorno 2003, Vol. 14, 230
25. Adorno 2002, 461. It is interesting to note that Adorno adopts Marx's term for the worker as "appendages of the machine" here
26. *Ibid*

27. Adorno 2003, Vol. 14, 233-234
28. Adorno 2003, Vol. 14, 233-234
29. *Ibid*, 126
30. *Ibid*, 115
31. *Ibid*, 118
32. Anders 1956, 84. A detailed exposition of such viewpoints can be found in Holert 1998
33. Theobald 1956, 24
34. Quoted in Holert 1998, 220
35. Seibt 1997, 23. Ehrenreich expresses a far more positive view of instances of "collective joy". Cf. Ehrenreich 2007
36. The attitude of the National Socialists to Jazz was remarkably similar to that of West German cultural critics, who would certainly not have been happy about this parallel had they been aware of it. Under National Socialism, Jazz was undesirable, especially in its then current form of swing. The Nazis furnished detailed playing instructions for dance orchestras, which on the one hand warned against the "hysterical" rhythms of non-Aryan "barbarians", and on the other, set out apodictic instructions to play no more than 10 percent syncopated Jazz rhythms in any one performance
37. http://www.andreas.de/aphextwin/articles/interview2.html
38. Schaeffer 2002, 11
39. *Ibid*, 12
40. *Ibid*, 13
41. *Ibid*, 11
42. I am indebted to Bernard Bruges Renard and François Delalande from the *Groupe de Recherches Musicales* (Paris) for making available to me an unpublished interview with sound engineer Jacques Poullin, who worked with Schaeffer at the ORTF for a long time. This interview, in which Poullin explains some of the *musique concrète* techniques, finally enabled me, after a great deal of research, to understand how Schaeffer had come up with the idea of *sillons fermé*
43. Schaeffer 1974, 23
44. Schaeffer 1950, 41
45. Ibid, 42

46. *Ibid*, 39. Here Schaeffer also mentions a "famous chanson" by Edith Piaf, most likely "Le Disque Usé" [The Worn-out Record], 1943, which "illustrates" the principle of *sillon fermé*
47. Ulmer 1983, 84
48. Benjamin 2006, 176
49. Cf. de la Motte 1999, 11-13
50. Schivelbusch 1989, 53
51. Schaeffer 2002, 13
52. *Ibid*
53. *Ibid*, 12
54. Schaeffer 1950, 39
55. Schaeffer 1948, 28
56. Nevertheless, it is interesting to compare Schaeffer's *Pathétique* with the classic record player *tour de force* of, for instance, *Grandmaster Flash at the Wheels of Steel* by rap DJ Grandmaster Flash, which integrates some very similar sound fragments.
57. Stockhausen 1971, 243 [my italics]
58. Prieberg 1960, 93
59. *Ibid*, 92. A detailed technical representation of a *phonogène* and a *morphophone* can be found in Poullin 1955
60. Schaeffer 1974, 23
61. *Ibid*
62. Schaeffer 1950, 47
63. http://paul.mycpanel.princeton.edu/music242/shaefferinterview.html

Chapter 4

1. Frisius, undated b. (unpaginated)
2. Thornton 2001, 53
3. Cf. for instance, Ruschkowski 1998, 234
4. Ruschkowski 1998, 233
5. Prieberg 1960, 160
6. A detailed account of the history of this studio can be found in Morawska-Büngeler 1988
7. Kurtz 1988, 82

8. Stockhausen 1963, 42, *sic.*

9. Sabbe 1981, 42

10. The *Konkrete Etüde* was long considered lost but was rediscovered in 1992. It was re-released on the CD *Elektronische Musik* together with other early electronic compositions by Stockhausen

11. Quoted from the supplement to the CD *Elektronische Musik* by Karlheinz Stockhausen, 5-7

12. Kurtz 1988, 83f

13. Sabbe 1981, 42

14. *Ibid*

15. Kurtz 1988, 85; cf. also Frisius 2008, 61-64

16. Stockhausen 1963, 141

17. *Ibid*, 142

18. Translator's note: the German term is *Schwebungssummer*, which consists of two high frequency oscillators with constant and variable frequencies respectively

19. Morawska-Büngeler 1988, 33

20. Normally, the tape in a tape recorder first passes the erase head when recording, which removes previously recorded sounds from the tape. The tape then passes the recording head, which records the new sounds, and finally the playback head, which can be used to monitor the recording if desired

21. Sabbe 1981, 44

22. *Ibid*, 45

23. Ruschkowski 1998, 239

24. Many thanks to Holger Czukay for the concise explanation he provided in an interview I conducted with him for this book

25. Morawska-Büngeler 1988, 43

26. Stockhausen 1978, 365

27. Interview with the author

28. Stockhausen 1963, 144

29. Mießgang 1997, 72

30. Young, R. 1995

31. All citations from *ibid*, 20

32. *Ibid* Stockhausen's contemporary Pierre Boulez saw it in a very similar light. He told the *New York Review of Books* in 1984, "today's type of minimalist and repetitive music appeals to an extremely primitive reception...If an audience wants to get high with this kind of music rather than with another product, that's OK by me. But I don't consider that a very high level of enjoyment." (Boulez 1984, 14)

33. Cott 1973, 28. Cf. also Hewett 2007

Chapter 5

1. Guralnick 1994, 63. This chapter is indebted to the meticulous research which Peter Guralnick did for his two-volume biography of Elvis Presley. Other important sources were Marsh 1982, Floyd 1992, Escott/ Hawkins 1992

2. Guralnick 1994, 63

3. See Alsmann 1985

4. Kennedy/McNutt 1999, 20

5. Alsmann 1985, 26

6. Escott/Hawkins 1992, 134

7. Guralnick 1994, 5

8. Guralnick 1994, 7

9. Quote from Escott/Hawkins 1992, 84

10. Guralnick 1994, 64

11. Goldman 1981, 114

12. I have Scotty Moore to thank for this information, sent to me in an email dated 20 March 2004. His manager, James V. Roy, had been kind enough to put me in touch with Mr Moore

13. Guralnick 1994, 103

14. Goldman 1981, 115

15. Marcus 1990, 149

16. Guralnick 1994, 96

17. Cf. Shaughnessy 1993. Other production methods that Les Paul used for the first time included speeded-up and slowed-down tape speeds, and – long before multi-tracking – numerous "layered" guitar tracks.

18. Waksman 1999, 61
19. Bosseur, Jean-Yves: Concrete music and the visual arts, in: Beirer 1999, 76
20. Escott/Hawkins 1992, 156
21. *Blue Moon of Kentucky* is not to be confused with the Rogers/ Hardt ballad *Blue Moon*, which Elvis recorded later at Sun Studio. However, on *Blue Moon* one can hear the echo of the Echoplex-amplifier, which I will come back to at the end of this chapter.
22. Escott/Hawkins 1992, 64
23. Lévi-Strauss 1983, 339-40
24. Atkins uses the Echosonic on his version of *Mr Sandman*.
25. Details on how Moore got his Echosonic-amplifier are given on his website, www.scottymoore.net
26. Atkins uses the Echosonic on his version of *Mr Sandman*
27. Moore used the amplifier for another 50 years. When he toured England to play for Elvis' fan clubs, he took the Echosonic with him. But subsequently, he decided not to take it on the road anymore since he was afraid that it might break
28. Gracyk 1996, 7 (*sic.*)
29. Marsh 1982, 28
30. Floyd 1998, 29
31. Marcus 1990, 132f
32. Interview with The Cramps in Vale/Juno 1993, 6 – 27, here: 12

Chapter 6

1. This interview is cited on various fan websites on the Internet, but unfortunately never with a reference
2. For a history of the mellotron, cf. Samagaio 2002
3. Wakeman, who disposed of his mellotrons in such a dramatic way, subsequently had engineer David Biro build him a tape keyboard that was to overcome the technical problems. It functioned with closed tape loops mounted on cassettes. However, this instrument, named Birotron after its builder, was apparently as error-prone as the mellotron. Wakeman even founded the company Birotronics Inc. to market the instrument, but only 35 units were ever sold

4. In addition to instruments based on tape loops, such as the mellotron, still more obscure keyboard instruments, which also retrieved recorded sounds from analogue recording media, came onto the market in the 1970s. These included the Optigan by Matell, whose sounds came from celluloid records (!). All these instruments were unreliable and therefore not very successful. Today, however, they have become collectors' items and command sums far in excess of their original price

5. The Dutch label Basta Music has released CDs of Raymond Scott's electronic music and Jazz compositions. His experiments with the *Electronium* are available on the CDs entitled *Manhattan Research Inc.* and *Soothing Sounds for Baby*

6. Carl W. Stalling, Warner Brothers' in-house composer, used Scott's piece *Powerhouse* time and again in soundtracks for cartoons

7. Cited from the CD booklet about Raymond Scott: Manhattan Research Inc., 9-12

8. Interview with Herb Deutsch in the CD booklet about Raymond Scott: Manhattan Research Inc., 57

9. Winner/Chusid 2002

10. Ruschkowski 1998, 87

11. CD Manhattan Research Inc. CD booklet, 111

12. Chadabe 1997, 149

13. Pinch/Trocco 2002, 40

14. CD booklet about Raymond Scott: Manhattan Research Inc., 97

15. For an overview of the connection between developments in electronic music in the USA and new technologies, and their promotion and application by the American government, cf. Taylor 2001, 72-95

16. I am indebted to Dana Countryman (San Francisco), who provided me with material on Jean-Jacques Perrey's biography. His book offers a detailed account of how Perrey developed a signature way of using loops in his music (cf. pp 63-70), as well as a series of photos showing the preparation of tape loops, step-by-step

17. It was the same world exhibition where Andy Warhol's mural *Thirteen Most Wanted Men* was censored (cf. chapter on Warhol and La Monte Young in this book)

18. Over 30 years later, Matt Groening, creator of the animated series *The Simpsons*, was to use the name *Futurama* for an animated science-fiction series which plundered the arsenal of space-age motifs with post-modernistic verve

19. In the 1960s, the artists and writers of the Stuttgart School experimented with texts and drawings generated with the help of the first large computer systems. They gathered around philosopher and scientist Max Bense, professor at the Technical University of Stuttgart at that time

20. CD booklet about Raymond Scott: Manhattan Research Inc., 92

21. Interview with Herb Deutsch in CD booklet about Raymond Scott: Manhattan Research Inc., 55

22. Scott, Raymond: Unaddressed Letter, probably written at the end of the 1970s. CD booklet about Raymond Scott, Manhattan Research Inc., 57f

23. On the history of the *Sideman* and other early rhythm machines, cf. Schmitz 1987

24. CD booklet about Raymond Scott: Manhattan Research Inc., 57f. A thyratron is a gas-filled tube similar in construction to an amplifier tube, such as those used in tube amplifiers

25. Winner/Chusid 2002

26. CD booklet about Raymond Scott: Manhattan Research Inc., 92

27. *Ibid*, 124

28. www.raymondscott.com/1946.htm

29. Winner/Chusid 2002

30. Supplement to the CD box *Soothing sounds for Baby*, Aalsmeer 1996 (Basta Music). [Based on my own experience, *Soothing Sounds for Baby* does indeed have a calming effect on screaming infants.]

31. Winner/Chusid 2002

32. Lev Manovich calls the loop "a new narrative form appropriate to the computer age". Cf. Manovich 2001, 264-269

33. CD booklet about Raymond Scott: Manhattan Research Inc., 124

Chapter 7

1. Quoted from Lippert/Maenz 1991, 72. Roehr's sound montages were published as CDs in 2002 by Supposé, (Cologne)

2. Telephone interview with photographer Günther Guben. The photos therefore do not show "Roehr producing sound montages", as is often stated in catalogues and books

3. Fuchs 1977, 25

4. In an excellent essay on Peter Roehr, Gerda Wedermann provides a comprehensive overview of similar approaches to Western post-war art. Cf. Wendermann 2000, 10-70

5. Note in Roehr's estate, Berlin, November 1964

6. Among other things, they have been shown in the exhibitions and touring exhibition of *Photography in Contemporary German Art*, which was staged at the Guggenheim Museum in New York and the Walker Art Center in Minneapolis

7. This took place in the spring of 1967 at Frankfurt University's *Studio-Galerie*. Frank Stella, Hans Haacke, Christo, Jan Dibbets, Thomas Bayrle, Markus Raetz, and Charlotte Posenenske. Agnes Martin was among the participants

8. In Germany, Roehr recently featured in an exhibition at the Städel Museum and the Museum of Modern Art in Frankfurt/Main. Roehr 2010

9. Notes on a lecture, in Roehr's estate, Berlin

10. Stemmrich 1995, 18

11. Notes on a lecture, undated, in Roehr's estate, Berlin

12. *Ibid*

13. *Ibid*

14. Glasmeier 2002, 20

15. Sitney 2002, 348

16. Cited in: Fuchs 1977, 25

17. Note in Roehr's estate, Berlin

18. *Ibid*

19. With the title *Zen for Film*, Nam June Paik also emphasizes the connection between loop technique and Buddhism

20. Autobiographical note in Roehr's estate, Berlin. Roehr was not the only one who came to make use of monotony, sequences and series after studying non-European cultures. The Minimal Music of composers like La Monte Young, Terry Riley and Steve Reich also drew their inspiration

from sources such as the Indonesian gamelan, West African percussion music, Japanese gagaku and Indian raga. Cf. also the following two chapters on the development of Minimal Music.

21. Messler 1988, unpaginated
22. Note in Roehr's estate, Berlin
23. *Ibid*
24. *Ibid*
25. Wendermann 2000, 127
26. Deleuze und Guattari 1997, I
27. *Ibid*
28. Diederichsen 2004, unpaginated
29. Potter 2000, 170
30. Duckworth 1995, 269
31. Dibelius 1988, 176f.
32. In: Stemmrich 1995, 444-470
33. In some cases, such as those of Donald Judd and Frank Stella, avowals of this method have been made with unpleasant nationalistic undertones. Cf. for instance, Stemmrich 1995, 35-57
34. Osswald 2004, 100
35. Lee 2004
36. Lessing, 1962, 91
37. Perry/Babbs 1990, XIX
38. On the Arts and Technology movement of the 1960s, cf. Davis 1975, esp. 33-66 and 83-103; Tuchman 1971; Dinkla 1997, 33-42
39. Although – often ritual-like – repetitions also had a central role as an aesthetic method in Happening, Performance, body art and Yvonne Rainer's structuralist dance. They are not discussed here because they are not the result of media manipulations. The many examples of repetitions that border on the manic in the then new areas of art, however, do underscore the importance which repetition acquired in 1960s art forms, and it is no coincidence that composers like Terry Riley and Steve Reich created their first tape compositions for such dance companies
40. In: Hyssen/Scherpe 1986, 64
41. Bromell 2000, 2-3
42. Fried 1996, 36-38

43. Stemmrich 1995, 365
44. Forster 1995, 591f. Cf. also Osswald 2004, 100ff
45. Diederichsen 2004, unpaginated
46. Huegli 2002, 21
47. Fuchs 1977, 11

Chapter 8

1. Cage 1987, IX
2. This was a circumstance that still enraged Warhol some 20 years later. Cf. Warhol/ Hackett 1980, 211
3. This form of presentation was taken up again in 2003 at an exhibition of his *Screen Tests* at *Berlin Kunstwerke*
4. Quoted from Joseph 2003, 17. The essay offers an excellent overview of Warhol's multimedia experiments, such as the light show entitled *Plastic Exploding Inevitable* and his collaboration with the group Velvet Underground
5. In 2012, the *Dream House* was installed at the *März Musik Festival* in Berlin for a few days.
6. Duckworth 1995, 251
7. The full title of this composition, in the best Fluxus and Conceptual Art tradition, is purely descriptive and reads *The Base 9:7:4 Symmetry in Prime Time When Centered above and below The Lowest Term Primes in The Range 288 to 224 with The Addition of 279 and 261 in Which The Half of The Symmetric Division Mapped above and Including 288 Consists of The Powers of 2 Multiplied by The Primes within The Ranges of 144 to 128, 72 to 64 and 36 to 32 Which Are Symmetrical to Those Primes in Lowest Terms in The Half of The Symmetric Division Mapped below and Including 224 within The Ranges 126 to 112, 63 to 56 and 31.5 to 28 with The Addition of 119*
8. According to an email interview I conducted with Young and Zazeela in June 2004, they are not familiar with Merleau-Ponty's phenomenology.
9. My account owes much to Strickland 1993, Duckworth 1995, Schwarz 1996, Gann 1997, Potter 2000, Zuckermann 2002 a, Duckworth/ Fleming 2002 and Oteri 2003. After La Monte Young himself criticized

Jeremy Grimshaw's biography *Draw a Straight Line and Follow it* (Grimshaw 2012) with Old Testament furore, I have refrained from referring to it in this book

10. Holger Czukay, Can's bassist, used an organum-style piece as one of two looped elements for his piece *Boat-Woman-Song* (1969), one of the earliest and most intriguing loop compositions in pop music to this day

11. It should be mentioned, at least in passing, that the *Walls of Sound* created by pop artist Phil Spector in the early 1960s also bear a striking conceptual and sonic resemblance to the sound monuments of La Monte Young

12. That sentence sums up a very productive time in Young's biography. In fact, he not only organized a number of important performances and concerts from Yoko Ono's loft, but also edited the Fluxus reader *An Anthology*. His compositions from this period consist largely of instructions for action such as "Draw a Straight Line and Follow it", which anticipated Conceptual Art instructions by almost a decade

13. Cale 2000, 60

14. *Ibid*, 61

15. Quoted from Strickland 1991, 160

16. Cardew 1971, XIV

17. The play was premiered in Britain by John Cale, who later became violist for Velvet Underground and who performed the piece at Goldsmiths College in 1964 before moving to the United States to join La Monte Young's Theatre of Eternal Music

18. Bangs 2003, unpaginated

19. Young 2001, unpaginated

20. Cale 2000, 57

21. *Ibid*, 61

22. Quoted from Joseph 2005, 38

23. Cale 2000, 57

24. Plimpton 2002. For the sake of historical accuracy, it should be noted that Plimpton's memory is misleading in two details. The premiere of *Vexations* was not at Carnegie Hall, but at the small, independent Pocket Theatre, and Andy Warhol's *Empire* lasts 8 hours rather than 24, while *Sleep* lasts only five-and-a-half hours.

25. Stein/Plimpton 1982, 235
26. Cage *et al.* 1982, 24
27. Crone 1976, 143
28. Quoted from *ibid* 158
29. Wehmeyer 1997, 106
30. *Ibid* He was referring to the composition *Socrate*
31. Warhol/Hackett 1980, 51f
32. In some of paintings, which are sprinkled with diamond dust, and in one of his re-interpretations of da Vinci's *Last Supper*, he came very close to the idea of white-on-white pictures without slipping into monochrome abstraction
33. Booklet accompanying the CD *Tony Conrad: Early Minimalism*, 16
34. Cf. Ferris 1966
35. Jones 1963, 213. Another account of the principle of coolness, which, however, hardly touches on the African-American roots of the concept, is provided by Poschardt 2002
36. Booklet accompanying the CD *Tony Conrad: Early Minimalism*, 16
37. Some recent works, such as Bippus 2003 or Meyer 2003, have disregarded the traditional antinomy
38. Young 2001, unpaginated
39. Dany 2004
40. Warhol/Hackett 1980, 33
41. Dany 2004, unpaginated. Cf. Dany 2007, 109-125 on Warhol's consumption of diet pills and its influence on his life and work
42. Both quoted from Joseph 2005, 42
43. It is perhaps not by chance that the mirror metaphor is found on Velvet Underground's first record, on which Nico sings and which Warhol had produced. "I'll be your mirror. Reflect what you are, in case you don't know."
44. Quoted from Joseph 2005, 27
45. Warhol/Hackett 1980, 33
46. A detailed analysis of *Sleep's* montage and loop techniques can be found in Joseph 2005. Cf. also Crimp 2006 on Warhol's films
47. Young 1987, unpaginated
48. *Ibid*

49. *Ibid*

50. Warhol/Hackett 1980, 50

51. Deleuze 1992, 364

52. Duckworth 1995, 214

53. *Aspen* has now been documented with great attention to detail by Ubuweb (http://www.ubu.com/aspen/aspen3), but the documentation of the record loop inevitably fails due to the nature of the digital medium.

Chapter 9

1. Some readers may wonder why Philip Glass, the most famous Minimalist composer, does not feature in this chapter (or indeed elsewhere in this book). This is, firstly, because Glass' compositional technique did not develop directly from his work with tape recorders or other media. Secondly, it seems to me that his importance lies less in his compositional method than in his popularization of techniques that Riley and Reich had developed before him

2. In this chapter, I will refer to the best available contemporary representation of the parallel development of artistic and musical Minimalism in Strickland 1993, as well as to the most detailed publication on Young, Riley, Reich and Glass – Potter 2000.

3. Author's interview with Steve Reich and Beryl Korot on 12 December 2002 in Berlin

4. Garratt 1986, 37

5. Page 1986, 23

6. Gross undated, unpaginated

7. Mostrom 2001

8. Gagne 1993, 238

9. Cf. Bernstein undated, Bernstein 2008, Smith undated, Ruschkowski 1998, 120-135, Pinch/Trocco 2002, 89-106 on the history of the San Francisco Tape Music Center

10. Interview reproduced on the CD cover of *Music for the Gift*, Organ of Corti

11. *Ibid*

12. *Ibid*

13. Author's telephone interview with Terry Riley on 10 August 2004

14. Cf. Potter 2000, 105

15. Interview with the author

16. Strickland 1991, 112

17. Interview with the author

18. Interview reproduced on the CD cover of *Music for the Gift*

19. Strickland 1991, 113

20. Interview reproduced on the CD cover of *Music for the Gift*

21. Mertens 1983, 17

22. Interview with the author

23. Cf. Potter 2000, 118

24. *Ibid*

25. Cf. Larry Levan's remixes of songs from the 1980s, such as Inner Life's *Ain't No Mountain High Enough*, Taana Gardner's *Work That Body* and, especially, *Don't Make me Wait* by the New York Peech Boys, where echoes act as a polyrhythmic accompaniment to the beat of the song.

26. The title *I Can't Stop No* is not only a neat reference to the compositional method of the piece, but also sounds like the title of a typical Garage House track.

27. Duckworth 1995, 277

28. Oteri 2001, 6

29. Strickland 1993, 176

30. Strickland 1991, 175

31. *Ibid*, 146

32. Anonymous 1989, unpaginated

33. Riley, undated, unpaginated

34. Duckworth 1995, 271

35. Quoted from Strickland 1991, 174

36. Duckworth 1995, 278

37. Interview with the author

38. *Ibid*

39. A recording of the first-ever *All-Night-Flights* was made together with *You're No Good* and published by the label Organ of Corti. Another recording of Riley's solo concerts appeared as *Poppy No-Good and the Phantom Band Purple Modal Strobe Ecstasy with the Daughters of*

Destruction, which was also published by Corti and didn't appear until the 1990s. This CD features an extract of the 6-hour-long concerts which Riley gave in 1968 as part of the concert series Intermedia III in various cities of New York state

40. Interview with the author
41. Potter 2000, 128
42. LFO stands for "low frequency oscillation", one of the electronic methods of sound processing that is common in Techno. The numbers 606 and 909 refer to two rhythm machines produced by Roland, which are also important in Techno: the TR606 and the TR909. "Modeselektor" is a function of Roland's effects pedal RE 201, which, with the aid of tape loops, produces a "space echo" that sounds similar to the guitar effects pedal Echoplex, described in the chapter on Elvis Presley.

Chapter 10

1. Potter 2000, 162
2. Gross undated, unpaginated
3. Duckworth 1995, 296
4. Henahan 1971, 26
5. Interview with the author
6. Duckworth 1995, 196f
7. Lovisa 1996, 66
8. Interview with the author
9. *Ibid*
10. *Ibid*
11. *Ibid*
12. *Ibid*
13. *Ibid*
14. Duckworth 1995, 297f
15. Potter 2000, 178
16. Battock 1981, 152
17. Duckworth 1995, 302
18. Interview with the author
19. Potter 2000, 177f

Chapter 11

1. This book was an important source for this chapter, and I also found a lot of important material in Perry/Babbs 1990 and Kesey 1990. For a different interpretation of the journey, cf. Diederichsen 2006

2. On the history of LSD, cf. Lee/Shlain 1992

3. Cf. for instance Perry/Babbs 1990

4. Lee/Shlain 1992, 122

5. Perry 1990, 36

6. Not only Kesey and the Pranksters, but several other editors and directors failed in their attempt to create a coherent film from the extensive footage (which was largely out of focus and had numerous other technical issues). Ken Kesey's son, Zane Kesey, published parts of the material on video tape. He also provided me with video material from his archive for this book. He was kind enough to answer a number of questions by email about the Merry Pranksters' journey, which he himself had been part of as a child

7. Perry/Babbs 1990, 50

8. *Ibid*

9. Perry/Babbs 1990, 45. In fact it was Ken Kesey himself who paid for the entire trip

10. Wolfe 1968, 61

11. Huxley 1970, 9

12. Wolfe 1968, 85f. In the film *Magic Trip*, there is a shot in which Paula Sundstren describes the same scene

13. Perry/Babbs 1990, 89f

14. This may be seen as part of Kerouac's self-mystification. The part with the manuscript of the novel on telex paper does exist, but much of the text comes from Kerouac's notebooks, which he preserved for years

15. The best source for the Merry Pranksters' tape loop experiments is the bootleg *The Grateful Dead & The Merry Pranksters 65'-67' Acid Tests*. On the video tape *Acid Test*, which Zane Kesey published after his father's death, tape echoes can be heard at the beginning. In several places, the Pranksters' tape recorder can be seen in the film, but, because no sound was recorded with the pictures, no tape echo is heard. According to Ken Babbs, tape echoes were mainly used live on the bus or as sound effects

at the Merry Pranksters' *Acid Test* parties later on; they were hardly ever recorded. (Cf. email interview with the author.) The Pranksters did experiment with different tape echo effects, but the technical setup – with recorded sounds being played back immediately and re-recorded through the loudspeaker – made it impossible to record the echo on the same tape. If one had wanted to record audible echoes, they had had to be recorded with a second tape recorder, or, depending on the setup used, even with a third

16. Wolfe 1968, 69f
17. *Ibid*, 70
18. Terry Riley used almost exactly the same term for his audiotape experiments. As outlined in the chapter on musical Minimalism, he called his tape installation *Time Lag Generator*
19. Wolfe 1968, 164f
20. *Ibid* (According to brain physiologist Ernst Pöppel, incoming stimulus in the brain triggers a neuronal oscillation within a certain conversion time. Different stimuli are subject to different conversion times. A light stimulus needs at least 25 milliseconds to be converted into "brain language", whereas an acoustic stimulus needs only one millisecond)
21. Krauss 1992, 136
22. Eco 1977, 32
23. *Ibid*, 331
24. Stemmrich 1995, 345
25. In the context of my argument I am obliged to give a very truncated account of the concerns of the various artists considered to be part of Minimal Art today. In fact, their motifs vary greatly – while the 'literary' approach can be said to apply to Stella, Andre, and Judd, Morris was at times strongly orientated towards *Gestalt* theory. For a detailed account of the differences and conflicts that arose from them, cf. Meyer 2003
26. Kesey 1988, 172-241
27. Wolfe 1968, 106. Friedrich Perls was not the only "father of the 'now trip'", since religions like Hinduism and Buddhism incorporate similar ideas which found their way into hippy ideology, as did books like Richard Alpert's *Be Here Now* (1971)
28. Perls 1969, 30

29. Detailed accounts of Perls' influence on Bruce Nauman can be found in Osswald 2004 and Engelbach 1998, among others. Nauman mentions Perls' influence on his early works in Livingston/Tucker 1972, 13 and Bruggen 1988, 9. Cf. also Kacunko 2004

30. Interview with Dan Graham by the author

31. Perls 1979, 11

32. It is therefore no coincidence that slow-motion films played an important role in Expanded Cinema and Fluxus films, e.g. *Film No. 5 (Smile)* (1968) by Yoko Ono, *Smoking* (1966) by Joe Jones and *Crossroads* (1976) by Bruce Connor

33. Wolfe 1968, 169

34. Unless you agree with Ken Babbs' joke that the tape echo experiments were "high art, some of the highest going". (Email interview, August 29, 2004)

35. Jackson 1999, 89

36. *Ibid*, 92

37. *Ibid*, 89

38. *Ibid*

39. Email interview with Ken Babbs, 29 August 2004

40. Jackson, undated, unpaginated. Interestingly, her description strongly reminds of *Boomerang* (1974), a video by Nancy Holt and Richard Serra, which is based on an echo effect that was also created with two tape recorders and a tape loop.

41. Richard Alpert, who together with Timothy Leary experimented with LSD on the American East Coast, attached great importance to a calm, meditative setting when experimenting with drugs, and found the acid tests too wild. "I call them scary because there were clearly bad trips going on within the framework of the Tests...The Acid Tests...had an incredibly strong sensual immediacy. They turned people inside out into the moment, in a way that they felt extremely alive. These events were crowded, wild and confusing; they almost demanded surrender. For some the surrender was great; but others didn't like the feeling of having no safe ground." Jackson, undated, unpaginated

42. Lee/Shlain 1992, 143f

43. Jackson 1999, 91

44. On Steward Brand cf. Turner 2006, Diederichsen/Franke 2013
45. Lee/Shlain 1992, 143
46. Perry 1985, 181
47. In addition to the previously mentioned works by Bruce Nauman and Dan Graham, well-known projects include Les Levine's *Iris* (1968), *Contact: A Cybernetic Sculpture* (1969) and *Wipe Cycle* (1969) by Ira Schneider and Frank Gillette. On the history of closed-circuit installations cf. Kacunko 2004
48. Perry 1985, 181
49. Pinch/Trocco 2002, 97
50. Wolfe 1968, 163
51. Lee/Shlain 1992, 142f.
52. Nietzsche undated, Vol. 1, 596
53. Maya (In Hinduism a goddess representing a state of spiritual blindness) covers the original unity of the world with her veil of diversity
54. Kesey 1990
55. Cf. Forester 2003, E1
56. Andy Warhol's *Exploding Plastic Inevitable* was another precursor. Cf. the corresponding chapter
57. Wolfe 1968, 183f

Chapter 12

1. Robertson 1992, 81
2. Hertsgaard 1995, 125
3. MacDonald 1995, 230
4. It is not clear if he also knew of Terry Riley's loop compositions
5. MacDonald 1995, 152
6. Martin 1994, 10
7. Roylance *et al* 2000, 214
8. Martin 1994, 79
9. Stockhausen is the fifth person from the left in the top row, half covered by W. C. Fields
10. Roylance *et al* 2000, 212

11. George Harrison later wrote *Within You and Without You,* another piece based on a single chord
12. Roylance *et al* 2000, 210
13. Benson 1992, 198
14. The recording has not been released to this day and belongs to the great myths of pop music. Paul McCartney had wanted to release it on the *Beatles Anthology* CD series, but allegedly, the late George Harrison had voted against it. McCartney has since repeatedly announced its release.
15. Roylance *et al* 2000, 210
16. All Beatles quotes: *ibid*
17. Miles 1999, 337
18. Martin 1994, 80f
19. Lewisohn 1988, 70
20. Miles 1997, 292
21. Emerick 2007, 112
22. Roylance *et al* 2000, 210
23. *Ibid*
24. Emerick 2007, 8-14; 111-113
25. MacDonald 2005, 192
26. On their collaboration with Blake and Hamilton cf. Grasskamp 2004
27. Kurtz 1988, 226f
28. MacDonald 1995, 231
29. *Ibid*, 232
30. A more detailed description can be found in the booklet of the CD *Spaced*, which was released almost 3 decades later (Cuneiform Records 1996) and which features excerpts of the stage music.
31. Oldfield 1998, unpaginated
32. Gill 1999, unpaginated
33. Oldfield 1998, unpaginated
34. The title is composed of Riley's surname and the first name of Meher Baba, who was Who guitarist Pete Townsend's guru at the time. The piece, which was later also covered by Nirvana and Pearl Jam, was an early pop song that uses a repetitive synthesizer figure for the basis of the piece. Townsend had composed *Baba O'Riley* for the never-to-be-completed

Lifehouse project, where the band's music emerges from the musicians' interaction with fans. Their personal information – size, age, etc. – was to be used to programme a synthesizer, while the synthesizer figure at the beginning of *Baba O'Riley* allegedly uses Meher Baba's data.

35. However, there is no proof that Agitation Free actually played Riley's *In C*, as is often claimed. Cf. also Baumgärtel 2006

36. Flür 1999, 148; oral statement by Richard Castelli. Kraftwerk members also seem to have been well informed about other developments in Minimal Music. The inspiration for the piece *Numbers / Numbers*, for instance, clearly stems from *Knee Play 1* from Philip Glass' opera *Einstein on the Beach*

37. Cf. also Cramer 2005

38. Interview of the author with Martin Rev and Alan Vega

39. *Ibid*

40. Fink 2005, 25. Fink's *Repeating Ourselves*, which this quote is taken from, was the first academic study that deals extensively with parallels between Disco and Minimal Music

Chapter 13

1. Savage 2012 [no page numbers]

2. Fink 2006, 61

3. Moroder 2012 [no page numbers]

4. Cf. Fink 2005, 31-61

5. *Ibid*, 55

6. Kedves 2012

7. For a detailed production history, cf. Buskin 2009, which includes many new original statements by Moroder and Bellotte. For the functioning of a sequencer cf. Kneif 1978, 186. The synthesizer riff strongly reminds of the bass riff of *Do What You Wanna Do* by the black disco formation T-Connection

8. Chin 1999, 44

9. *Ibid*

10. Summer had, in fact, extemporized the melody and lyrics in the studio while listening to the song, which her producers Giorgio Moroder and

Pete Bellotte had already recorded. The lyrics of the finished song were inspired by the hypnotic hammering of the sequencer loops, and were intended merely as placeholders that were later to be replaced by "real" lyrics. Cf. Howard 2003, Summer 2003

11. Shapiro 2005, 109
12. It fits into this cyborg universe that early in the 1980s, Giorgio Moroder produced his own version of *Metropolis* with an original electronic soundtrack
13. Butler 2006, 137
14. Deleuze 1997, 364
15. Hughes 1994, 148
16. Krauss 1992, 136
17. Thornton 1996, 57

Chapter 14

1. Fricke/Ahearn 2002, 336 (author's italics)
2. Strogatz 2003
3. *Ibid*
4. Margulis 2014, 83
5. Klages 1934, 32
6. *Ibid*, 35
7. Wendorff 1991, 184
8. Baumgärtel/Lenz 2002, 4
9. *Ibid*
10. Huegli 2002, 21
11. Kessen, undated, unpaginated
12. Re/Search 4/5, 11
13. Baumgärtel 2002, unpaginated. DAF, who also described Donna Summer's *I Feel Love* as their most important influence in this interview, had their own method of depriving their sequencers of their stiff, mechanical beat. Band member Chrislo Haas had the idea of playing the synthesizers through bass speakers, which gave them a fat, organic sound that made the pulse seem metrically more flexible
14. Wirtz 2003, unpaginated

15. Rietveld 1998, 107
16. Reynolds 1998, XVI
17. Attali 1985, 121
18. *Ibid*, 32
19. *Ibid*, 126
20. Florino 2010, unpaginated
21. Cf. Tamm 1990, Tamm 1995
22. Bloch 1962, 104

BIBLIOGRAPHY

Adorno 1941

Adorno, Theodor W.: On Popular Music, in: Studies in Philosophy and Social Science/ Zeitschrift für Sozialforschung, Vol. IX, No. 1, 17ff.

Adorno 1991

Adorno, Theodor W.: Dissonanzen. Musik in der verwalteten Welt, Göttingen 1991 (Kleine Vandenhoeck Reihe)

Adorno 1969

Adorno, Theodor W.: Nervenpunkte der Neuen Musik, Reinbek bei Hamburg 1969 (rowohlt)

Adorno 2002

Adorno, Theodor W.: Essays on Music, California 2002 (University of California Press)

Adorno 2003

Adorno, Theodor W.: Gesammelte Schriften, edited by Rolf Tiedemann with Gretel Adorno, Susan Buck-Morss, Klaus Schulze, revised and expanded electronic edition on CD-ROM, Berlin 2003 (Digitale Bibliothek)

Aikin 1986

Aikin, Jim; Joel Rothstein: Der Komponist von "In C" erforscht indische Quellen und Synthesizer Solo-Spiele, in: Begleitheft zu Pro Musica Nova, Bremen 1986 (Pro Music Nova), unpaginated

Alsmann 1985

Alsmann, Götz: Nichts als Krach, Drensteinfurt 1985 (Huba) Anders 1956

Anders, Günther: Die Antiquiertheit des Menschen, Munich 1956 (Beck

Anonym 1989

Anonym: A 25th Year Celebration of *In C.* Programm Notes, o. O. 1989, unpaginated

Anz 1999

Anz, Philipp, Patrick Walder (eds.): techno, Hamburg 1999 (Verlag Ricco Bilger)

Art in the 21. century 2005

Website der PBS-Serie "Art in the 21st Century" www.pbs.org/art21/

Attali 1985

Attali, Jacques: Noise – The Political Economy of Music, Minneapolis/ London 1985 (University of Minnesota)

Bachtin 1998

Bachtin, Michail: Rabelais und seine Welt – Volkskultur als Gegenkultur, Frankfurt/ Main 1998 (Suhrkamp)

Baker 1988

Baker, Kenneth: Minimalism: Art of Circumstance, New York 1988 (Abbeville Press)

Bangs 2003

Bangs, Lester: Brian Eno. A Sandbox in Alphaville Perfect Sound 2003 http:// www.furious.com/perfect/bangseno.html

Barthes 1980

Barthes, Roland: Der entgegenkommende und der stumpfe Sinn, Essays III, Frankfurt/ Main 1980 (Suhrkamp)

Battock 1981

Battock, Gregory: Breaking the sound barrier. A Critical Anthology of the new music, New York 1981 (E. P. Dutton)

Baudrillard 1995

Baudrillard, Jean: Von der absoluten Ware, in: Schwander; Martin (ed.): Andy Warhol. Paintings 1960-1986, Stuttgart 1995 (Hatje Cantz), 20-29

Baumgärtel 2002

Baumgärtel, Tilman: "Bildung ersetzt keinen Rhythmus", Interview with Gabi Delgado and Robert Görl of Deutsch-Amerikanische Freundschaft (DAF), die tageszeitung, 12 July 2002

Baumgärtel 2006

Baumgärtel, Tilman: Ganz simpel. Interview with Manuel Goettsching, die tageszeitung, 12 December 2006

Baumgärtel/lenz 2002

Baumgärtel, Tilman; Susanne Lenz: Augen zu und die Freiheit genießen. Interview with DJane Ellen Allien, Berliner Zeitung, 9.2.2002, magazine supplement 4

Bazin 2009

Bazin, Andre: *What is Cinema?* Montreal 2009 (Caboose)

Beirer 1999

Beirer, Ingrid (ed.): 50 Jahre musique concrete, Saarbrücken 1999 (Pfau)

Benjamin 1978

Benjamin, Walter: Über einige Motive bei Baudelaire, in: Gesammelte Schriften I.2, Frankfurt/Main 1978 (Suhrkamp)

Benjamin 1980

Benjamin, Walter: Das Kunstwerk im Zeitalter seiner technischen Reproduzierbarkeit, in: Gesammelte Schriften I, 2, Frankfurt/ Main 1980 (Suhrkamp)

Benjamin 2006

Benjamin, Walter: The Writer of Modern Life: Essays on Charles Baudelaire, Harvard 2006 (Harvard University Press)

Benson 1992

Benson, Ross: Paul McCartney – Die Biografie, Munich 1992 (Goldmann)

Berg 1989

Berg, Gretchen: "Nothing to lose: An Interview with Andy Warhol", in: O'Pray, Michael: Andy Warhol: Film Factory, London 1989 (British Film Institute), 58-60

Bergson 2005

Bergson, Henri: Laughter: An Essay on the Meaning of the Comic, New York 2005, (Dover Publications)

Bernstein undated

Bernstein, David W.: Thirty Years of Non-Stop Flight: A Brief History of the Center for Contemporary Music http://www.mins.edu/campus_life/center_for_contemporary_music/archives.php

Bernstein 2008

San Francisco Tape Music Center: 1960s Counterculture and the Avant-Garde, Berkeley 2008 (University of California Press)

Beyer undated

Beyer, Robert: Elektronische Musik, in Melos 21, 35-39 Beyer 1955

Beyer, Robert: Zur Situation der elektronischen Musik, in: Zeitschrift für Musik, 1955, No. 8/9, 452-456

Biesenbach 2001

Biesenbach, Klaus: Magazine 03/01: Special Issue Loop – Alles auf Anfang, Munich 2001 (Kunsthalle der Hypo-Vereinsstiftung)

Bippus 2003

Bippus, Elke: Serielle Verfahren. Pop Art, Minimal Art, Conceptual Art und Postminimalismus, Berlin 2003

Birnbaum 1987

Birnbaum, Dara: Rough edits. Popular Image Video, Halifax 1987 (The Novia Scotia Pamphlets)

Björk 1996

Anonym: Compose yourself – Björk meets Karlheinz Stockhausen, Dazed & Confused No. 23, August 1996, o. P.

Bloch 1962

Bloch, Ernst: Erbschaft dieser Zeit, erweiterte Ausgabe, Frankfurt/ Main 1962 (Suhrkamp)

Bockris 1999

Bockris, Victor; John Cale: What's Welsh for Zen – The Autobiography of John Cale, London 1999 (Bloomsbury)

Bolte 1935

Bolte, Johannes: Das Echo in Volksglaube und Dichtung, Berlin 1935 (Verlag der Akademie der Wissenschaften)

Boulez 1963

Boulez, Pierre: Musikdenken heute I, Mainz 1963 (Schott, Darmstädter Beiträge zur neuen Musik No. 5)

Boulez 1984

Boulez, Pierre: On New Music, The New York Review of Books, 28 June 1984, 14-15

Breyer 2003

Breyer, Nike: "Das ist alles wirklich Plastik, haha", die tageszeitung/taz mag, 8/9 November 2003, 1-3 (Interview with Gabi Delgado-Lopez)

Brewster/Broughton 2000

Brewster, Bill; Frank Broughton: Last Night a DJ saved my Life, London 2000 (Headline)

Bromell 2000

Bromell, Nick: Tomorrow Never Knows. Rock and Psychedelics in the 1960s, Chicago 2000 (Chicago University Press)

Bublitz 1999

Bublitz, Ilona: Love Parade Story 89-99. O-Töne einer Bewegung, Hamburg 1999 (S- and L-Mediencontor)

Bühler 1965

Bühler, Karl: Die Krise der Psychologie, Stuttgart 1965 (G. Fischer) Buskin 2009

Buskin, Richard: Donna Summer >I Feel Love<, Sound on Sound, October 2009 http://www.soundonsound.com/sos/oct09/articles/classictracks_1009.htm Bussy 2001

Bussy, Pascal: Kraftwerk. Man, Machine and Music, London 2001 (SAF Publishing)

Butler 2006

Butler, Mark J.: Unlocking the Groove. Rhythm, Meter, and Musical Design in Electronic Dance Music, Bloomington/ Indianapolis 2006 (Indiana University Press)

Cage 1987

Cage, John: Silence. Lectures and writings by John Cage. London 1987 (Marion Boyars)

Cage et al 1982

John Cage, Roger Shattuck, and Alan Gillmor: Erik Satie. A Conversation, in: Contact: A Journal of Contemporary Music, No. 25, Herbst, 1982, 20-24

Cale 2000

Cale, John: What's Welsh for Zen, London 2000 (Bloomsbury)

Cardew 1971

Cardew, Cornelius: On the role of the instructions in the interpretation of indeterminate music, Treatise Handbook, London 1971 (Peters)

Chin 1999

Chin, Brian: The Disco Beatmasters: From the Studio to the Dance Floor, Leaflet in the CD compilation The Disco Box, Rhino Records 1999, 28-41

Chadabe 1997

Chadabe, Joel: Electric Sound. The Past and Promise of Electronic Music, Prentice Hall 1997 (Upper Saddle River)

Chernoff 1979

Chernoff, John Miller: African Rhythm and African Sensibility: Aesthetics and Social Action in African Musical Idioms, Chicago 1979 (University of Chicago Press)

Claisse 2002

Claisse, Frédéric: Industrial Rock: Elektronische Brücken zwischen Pop, Rock und Neuer Musik, in: Ungeheuer, Elena (ed.): Elektroakustische Musik, Laaber 2002 (Laaber Verlag), 111-132

Cogan 2004

Cogan, Jim; William Clark: Temples of Sound. Inside the Great Recording Studios, San Francisco 2004 (Chronicle Books)

Collins 1998

Collins, John: The Story of Chess Records, New York 1998 (Bloomsbury)

Cope 1996

Cope, Julian: KrautRockSampler – One Heads Guide To The Grosse Kosmische Musik, Löhrbach 1996 (Der Grüne Zweig)

Coomaraswamy 1995

Coomaraswamy, Ananda K.: The Dance of Siva, New York 1995 (Dover)

Cott 1973

Cott, Jonathan: Stockhausen. Conversations with the Composer, New York 1973 (Simon and Schuster)

Countryman 2011

Countryman, Dana: Passport to the Future. The Amazing Life and Music of Electronic Pop Music Pioneer Jean-Jacques Perrey, Everett, WA 2011 (Sterling Swan Press)

Cramer 2005

Cramer, Florian: With Perhaps the Exception of Rhythm: Sprechen, Stottern und Schleifen in Alvin Luciers I am Sitting in a Room, in: Naumann,

Barbara: Rhythmus: Spuren eines Wechselspiels in Künsten und Wissenschaften, Würzburg 2005 (Königshausen & Neumann)

Crimp 2006

Crimp, Douglas: Our Kind of Movie: The Films of Andy Warhol Paperback, Cambridge 2006 (MIT Press)

Cromelin 2012

Cromelin, Richard: Donna Summer: "The audience was groaning worse than I was", The Guardian, 15 May 2012 http://www.guardian.co.uk/music/2012/may/17/donna-summer-classic-interview

Crone 1976

Crone, Hans-Rainer: Das bildnerische Werk Andy Warhols, Berlin 1976 (Komissions- vertrieb Wasmuth)

Cunningham 1996

Cunningham, Marc: Good Vibrations, New York 1996 (Sanctuary Publishing)

Czukay, undated

Czukay, Holger: Karlheinz Stockhausen's Influence on Today's Electronic Music http://www.furious.com/perfect/stockhausen.html

Dack/North 2006

Dack, John; Christine North: Translating Pierre Schaeffer: Symbolism, Literature and Music, EMS: Electroacoustic Music Studies Network, Beijing 2006 (unpublished manuscript)

Dany 2004

Dany, Hans-Christian: Mechnical Boy, Manuskript, 2004

Dany 2007

Dany, Hans-Christian. Speed. Eine Gesellschaft auf Droge, Hamburg 2007 (Edition Nautilus)

de la motte 1999

de la Motte, Helga: 50 Jahre Musique Concrète, in: Beirer 1999, 11-13

Deleuze 2004

Deleuze, Gilles: Difference and Repetition. London 2004 (A&C Black)

Deleuze/Guattari 1997

Deleuze, Gilles/Guattari, Felix: Anti-Ödipus. Frankfurt am Main 1997 (Suhrkamp)

Denk/Thülen 2012

Denk, Felix, Sven von Thülen: Der Klang der Familie – Berlin, Techno und die Wende, Frankfurt/Main 2012 (Suhrkamp)

Demers 2010

Demers, Joanna: Listening Through the Noise: The Aesthetics of Experimental Electronic Music, New York 2010 (Oxford University Press)

Dibelius 1988

Dibelius, Ulrich: Moderne Musik II, Munich 1988 (Piper)

Diederichsen 1993

Diederichsen, Diedrich: Freiheit macht arm. Das Leben nach Rock'n'Roll 1990-1993, Cologne 1993 (Kiepenheuer & Witsch)

Diederichsen 2004

Diederichsen, Diedrich: The Primary: Political and Anti-Political Continuities between Minimal Music and Minimal Art, in: Goldstein, Ann (ed.): A Minimal Future? Art as Object 1958-1968, Cambridge/London 2004 (MIT Press), 111-131 (zitiert nach dem unveröffentlichten, deutschsprachigen Originalmanuskript)

Diederichsen 2006

Diederichsen, Diedrich: Higher and Higher. Aufbruch, Geschichte, Loop, in: Menke, Christoph; Juliane Rebentisch (eds.): Kunst, Fortschritt, Geschichte. Berlin 2006 (Kadmos)

Diederichsen 2008

Diederichsen, Diedrich: Eigenblut-Doping. Selbstverwertung, Künstlerromantik, Partizipation, Cologne 2008 (Kiepenheuer & Witsch)

Diederichsen/Franke 2013

Diederichsen, Diedrich; Anselm Franke (eds.): The Whole Earth. Kalifornien und das Verschwinden des Außen, New York 2013 (Sternberg Press)

Dinkla 1997

Dinkla, Söke: Pioniere interaktiver Medienkunst, Ostfildern 1997 (Hatje Cantz)

Duckworth 1995

Duckworth, William: Talking music. Conversations with John Cage, Philip Glass, Laurie Anderson and Five Generations of American Experimental Composers, New York 1995 (Schirmer Books)

Duckworth/Fleming 2002

Duckworth, William; Richard Fleming (eds.): Sound & Light: La Monte Young Marian Zazeela (Bucknell Review), Plainsboro, NJ 2002 (Associated Univ. Presses)

Doyle 2005

Doyle, Peter: Echo and Reverb: Fabricating Space in Popular Music Recording, 1900-1960, Boston 2005 (Wesleyan)

Dyer 1990

Dyer, Richard: In Defense of Disco, in: Simon Frith and Andrew Goodwin (eds.): On Record: Rock, Pop, and the Written Word, New York 1990 (Pantheon Books), 410-418

Eco 1977

Eco, Umberto: Das offene Kunstwerk, Frankfurt/Main 1977 (Suhrkamp)

Ehrenreich 2007

Ehrenreich, Barbara: Dancing in the Streets: A History of Collective Joy, New York 2007

Eisenberg 1999

Eisenberg, Götz: "Wer nicht arbeitet, soll auch nicht essen". Zur Sub- und inneren Kolonialgeschichte der Arbeitsgesellschaft, in: krisis. Beiträge zur Kritik der Waren- gesellschaft, 31/12/1999 http://www.krisis.org/1999/wer-nicht-arbeitet-soll-auch-nicht-essen

Elste 1996

Elste, Martin: Hindemiths Versuche "grammophonplatteneigner Stücke im Kontext einer Ideengeschichte der Mechanischen Musik im 20. Jahrhundert", in: Hindemith-Jahrbuch, Vol. 25, Mainz 1996 (Schott), 195-221

Emerick 2007

Emerick, Geoff; Howard Massay: Here, There and Everywhere. My Life Recording The Music of The Beatles, New York 2007 (Gotham)

Engelbach 1998

Engelbach, Barbara: Der Künstler als Versuchsobjekt, in: Bruce Nauman. Versuchs- anordnungen. Werke 1965-1994, Hamburg 1998 (Christians), 37-44

Eno 1976

Eno, Brian: Generating and Organizing Variety in the Arts, Studio International, November-December 1976), 279-283

Ermilio/Levine 2015

Ermilio, Brett; Josh Levine: Going Platinum: KISS, Donna Summer, and How Neil Bogart Built Casablanca Records, Guilford, CT 2015 (Lyons Press)

Escott/hawkins 1992

Escott, Colin; Martin Hawkins: Good Rockin' Tonight. Sun Records and the Birth of Rock'n'Roll, New York 1992 (St. Martin's)

Felix/Kiefer/Marshall 2001

Felix, Jürgen; Bernd Kiefer; Susanne Marshall; Marcus Stiglegger (eds.): Die Wiederholung. Festschrift für Thomas Koebner zum 60. Geburtstag, Marburg 2001 (Schüren)

Fikentscher 2000

Fikentscher, Kai: "You better work!" Underground Dance Music in New York City, Hanover/London 2000 (Wesleyan University Press)

Fink 2005

Fink, Robert: Repeating Ourselves. American Minimal Music as Cultural Practice, Berkeley 2005 (University of California Press)

Fisher 2014

Fisher, Mark: Ghosts of My Life. Writings on Depression, Hauntology and Lost Futures, London 2014 (Zero Books)

Fleming 1995

Fleming, Jonathan: What Kind of House Party is this?, Slough 1995 (MIY Publishing)

Florino 2010

Florino, Rick: Interview: Skrillex, Artist Direct, 2 August 2010 http://www.artistdirect.com/entertainment-news/article/ interview-skrillex/7350623

Floyd 1998

Floyd, John: Sun Records – An Oral History, New York 1998 (Avon Books)

Flür 1999

Flür, Wolfgang: Kraftwerk – Ich war ein Roboter, St Andrä-Wördern 1999 (Hannibal)

Forester 2003

Forester, Jeff: Sparks fly upwards – Remembering Ken Kesey, San Francisco Chronicle, 30 November, 2003, E1

Forster 1995

Forster, Hal: Die Crux des Minimalismus, in: Stemmrich, Gregor (ed.): Minimalismus.

Eine kritische Retrospektive, Dresden/Basel 1995 (Verlag der Kunst), 589-633

Foucault 1976 a

Foucault, Michel: Mikrophysik der Macht. Über Strafjustiz, Psychiatrie und Medizin, Berlin 1976 (Merve)

Foucault 1979

Foucault, Michel: Power, Truth, Strategy. Sydney, 1979 (Feral Publications)

Freud 1959

Freud, Sigmund: Jenseits des Lustprinzips, in: Studienausgabe, Vol. 3, Frankfurt/ Main (1959)

Fricke/ahearn 2002

Fricke, Jim; Charlie Ahearn: Yes yes y'all. Oral History of Hip-Hops First Decade, Cambridge 2002 (Da Capo Press)

Fried 1996

Fried, Michael: The Return of the Real, Cambridge 1996 (MIT Press)

Frisius 2008

Frisius, Rudolf: Karlheinz Stockhausen II: Die Werke 1950-1977, Mainz 2008 (Schott)

Frisius undated, a

Frisius, Rudolf: Experimentelle Musik in Frankreich: Tendenzen und Studios der Elektroakustischen Musik, undated

http://www.frisius.de/rudolf/texte/tx682.htm

Frisius, undated, b

Frisius, Rudolf: Pierre Schaeffer – Pionier der akustischen Kunst, undated http://www.frisius.de/rudolf/texte/tx395.htm

Frisius, undated, c

Frisius, Rudolf: Schaeffer: Rundfunkpionier und Musiker wider Willen, undated http://www.frisius.de/rudolf/texte/tx580.htm

frith 1990

Frith, Simon and Andrew Goodwin (eds.): On Record, London 1990 (Routledge)

Fuchs 1977

Fuchs, Rudi; Werner Lippert; Paul Maenz; Charlotte Posenenske/Burkhard Brunn (eds.): Peter Roehr, Cologne 1977 (DuMont)

Gagne 1993

Gagne, Cole: Soundpieces 2. Interviews wich American Composers, Metuchen, N. J./ London 1993 (The Scarecrow Press)

Gann 1997

Gann, Kyle: American Music in the Twentieth Century, New York 1997 (Schirmer)

Garcia 2005

Garcia, Luis-Manuel: On and On. Repetition as Process and Pleasure in Electronic Dance Music, Music Theory Online, Vol. 11, No. 4, October 2005 http://mto.societymusictheory.org/issues/mto.05.11.4/ mto.05.11.4.garcia.html

Garratt 1986

Garratt, Sheryl: Fun with Monotony, The Face 75 (July 1986), 37

Gates 1988

Gates, Henry Louis: The Signifying Monkey. A Theory of African-American Literary Criticism, New York 1988 (Oxford University Press)

Geslin 2002

Geslin, Yann: Digital Sound and Music Transformation Environments: A Twenty-Year Experiment at the "Groupe de Recherches Musicales", Journal of New Music Research 2002, Vol. 31. No. 2, 99-107

Giese 1925

Giese, Fritz: Girlkultur. Vergleich zwischen amerikanischem und europäischem Rhythmus und Lebensgefühl, Munich 1925 (Delfin)

Gill 1999

Gill, Andy: Mad? Us?, Q Magazin, October 1999, unpaginated

Glasmeier 2002

Glasmeier, Michael: Loop. Zur Geschichte und Theorie der Endlosschleife am Beispiel Rodney Graham, Cologne 2002 (Salon Verlag / édition questions)

Goldman 1981

Goldman, Albert: Elvis, London 1981 (Penguin)

Goodwin 1990

Goodwin, Andrew: Sample and Hold. Pop Music in the Digital Age of Reproduction, in: Frith, Simon and Andrew Goodwin (eds.): On Record London 1990 (Routledge), 258-273

Grasskamp 2004

Grasskamp, Walter: Das Cover von Sgt. Pepper. Eine Momentaufnahme der Popkultur, Berlin 2004 (Verlag Klaus Wagenbach)

Gracyk 1996

Gracyk, Theodore: Rhythm and Noise, An Aethetics of Rock, Durham 1996 (Duke University Press)

Grimshaw 2012

Grimshaw, Jeremy: Draw a Straight Line and Follow It: The Music and Mysticism of La Monte Young, New York 2012 (Oxford University Press)

Gross/Gorschlüter/Teipel 2002

Groos, Ulrike; Peter Gorschlüter; Jürgen Teipel (eds.): Zurück zum Beton. Die Anfänge von Punk und New Wave, Cologne 2002

Gross undated

Gross, Jason: Interview with Steve Reich, www.furious.com/perfect/ohm/reich2.html, undated

Großklaus 1995

Großklaus, Götz: Medien-Zeit, Medien-Raum, Frankfurt/Main 1995 (Suhrkamp)

Gruhn 1981

Gruhn, Wilfried (ed.): Reflexionen über Musik heute, Mainz 1981 (Schott)

Gould 1987

Gould, Stephen Jay: Time's arrow, time's cycle. Myth and Metaphor in the Discovery of Geological Time, Cambridge 1987 (Harvard University Press)

Guralnick 1979

Guralnick, Peter: Feel like I am going home, London 1979 (Penguin)

Guralnick 1994

Guralnick, Peter: Last Train to Memphis. The Rise of Elvis Presley, Boston 1994 (Little Brown and Company)

Handke 1986

Handke, Peter: *Der Chinese des Schmerzes*, Frankfurt/Main 1986 (Suhrkamp)

Handke 2000
Peter Handke. *Across: a Novel*. New York 2000 (Farrar, Straus and Giroux)
Haraway 1991
Haraway, Donna J.: Simians, Cyborgs and Women: The Reinvention of Nature. New York 1991 (Routledge)
Harris/Gooch/Suhs 2009
Harris, Larry Harris; Curt Gooch; Jeff Suhs: And Party Every Day: The Inside Story Of Casablanca Records, Milwaukee, WI 2009 (Backbeat)
Hegel 1952
Hegel, G. W. F.: Vorlesungen über die Philosophie der Weltgeschichte, Vol. I: Die Vernunft der Geschichte, Hamburg 1952 (Felix Meiner)
Henahan 1971
Henahan, Donal: Reich? Philharmonic? Paradiddling? New York Times, 24 October 1971, Section II, 13, 26
Hertsgaard 1995
Hertsgaard, Mark: The Beatles. Die Geschichte ihrer Musik, Munich 1995 (Hanser)
Hewett 2007
Hewett, Ivan: Obituary Karlheinz Stockhausen, The Guardian, 7 December 2007, unpaginated
Hilmes/mathy 1998
Hilmes, Carola; Dietrich Mathy (eds.): Dasselbe noch einmal. Die Ästhetik der Wie- derholung, Wiesbaden 1998 (Westdeutscher Verlag)
Hodgkinson 1987
Hodgkinson, Tim: Pierre Schaeffer Interview, Recommended Records Quarterly, Vol 2, No. 1 (1987), unpaginated
Hoffmann 1994
Hoffmann, E. T. A.: Der Sandmann, Erläuterungen und Dokumente, by Rudolf Drux, Philipp Reclam jun. Stuttgart 1994
Holert 1998
Holert, Tom: "...repetitious, though not necessarily boringly so". Notizen zur schwankenden Reputation der Repetition: Jazz. Techno etc., in: Hilmes/ Mathy 1998, 215-228
Holmes 2008

Holmes, Thom: *Electronic and Experimental Music: Technology, Music, and Culture*, New York 2008 (Routledge Chapman & Hall)

Horkheimer/Adorno 2002

Horkheimer, Max; Theodor W. Adorno: *Dialectic of the Enlightenment.* Stanford University Press 2002

Howard 2003

Howard, Josiah: *Donna Summer – Her Life and Music*, Cranberry Township 2003

Howell 1981

Howell, Mark: *From a Strangers Evening with Brian Eno*, Another Room, June/July 1981, unpaginated

Huegli 2002

Huegli, Walter (ed.): *Raw Music Material – Electronic Music DJs today*, Zürich 2002 (Scalo)

Hughes 1994

Hughes, Walter: In the Empire of the Beat, Discipline and Disco, in: Ross, Andrew and Tricia Rose (eds.): *Microphone Fiends. Youth Music and Youth Culture*, London/ New York 1994 (Routledge), 147-157

Hufschmid 1981

Hufschmid, Wolfgang: Musik als Wiederholung – Anmerkungen zur periodischen Musik, in: Gruhn, Wilfried (ed.): Reflexionen über Musik heute, Mainz 1981 (Schott), 148-168

Huxley 1970

Huxley, Aldous: Die Pforten der Wahrnehmung. Himmel und Hölle, Munich 1970 (Piper)

Huyssen/Scherpe 1986

Huyssen, Andreas; Klaus R. Scherpe (eds.): Postmoderne. Zeichen eines kulturellen Wandels, Reinbek bei Hamburg 1986 (rowohlts enzyklopädie)

Jackson undated

Jackson, Blair: Chapter Five Additions, blairjackson.com, undated http:// www.blairjackson.com/chapter_five_additions.htm

Jackson, blair 1999

Jackson, Blair: Garcia. An American Life, London 1999 (Penguin)

Jacob 1993

Jacob, Günther: Agit-Pop. Schwarze Musik und weiße Hörer, Berlin 1993 (edition ID-Archiv)

Jensen 1985

Jensen, Alan: The Sound of Silence: A Thursday Afternoon with Brian Eno, Electronics/ Music Maker (December 1985), 20-25

Jones/Kantonen 1999

Jones, Alan; Jussi Kantonen: Saturday Night Forever. The Story of Disco, Edinburgh/ London 1999 (Mainstream Publishing)

Jones 1963

Jones, LeRoi: Blues People. The Negro Experience in White America and the Music that developed from it, New York 1963 (Quill)

Joseph 2003

Joseph, Branden W.: "My Mind Split Open" – Andy Warhols "Exploding Plastic Inevitable", in: Michalke, Matthias (ed.): X-Screen – Filmische Installationen und Aktionen der Sechziger-und Siebzigerjahre, Cologne 2003 (Verlag der Buchhandlung Walther König), 14-32

Joseph 2005

Joseph, Branden W.: The Play of Repetition, Grey Room 19 (Spring 2005), 22-53

Kacunko 2004

Kacunko, Slavko: Closed Circuit Videoinstallationen. Ein Leitfaden zur Geschichte und Theorie der Medienkunst mit Bausteinen eines Künstlerlexikons, Berlin 2004 (Logos)

Kedves 2012

Kedves, Jan: "Die Torte flog erster Klasse!" Interview with Disco legend Giorgio Moroder, Spiegel Online, 30 June 2012 http://www.spiegel.de/kultur/musik/giorgio-moroder-disco-legende-spricht-ueber-donna-summer-und-daft- punk-a-841166.html

kennedy/mcnutt 1999

Kennedy, Rick; Randy McNutt: Little Labels – Big Sound, Bloomington/ Indianapolis 1999 (Indiana University Press)

Kesey 1988

Kesey, Ken: Die Dämonenkiste, Munich 1988 (Goldmann)

Kesey 1990

Kesey, Ken: The Further Inquiry, New York 1990 (Viking Adult)

Kessen, undated

Kessen, Peter: Politics of Sound; Digital Hardcore – Eine gesampelte Höllenfahrt, Manuskript einer Radio-Sendung für WDR/Eins Live

Kierkegaard 2009

Kierkegaard, Sören: *Repetition and Philosophical Crumbs.* Oxford 2009 (OUP)

Kittler 1986

Kittler, Friedrich: Grammophon, Film, Typewriter, Berlin 1986 (Brinkmann & Bose)

Kittler 2002

Kittler, Friedrich: Short Cuts, Frankfurt/M.2002 (Zweitausendeins)

Klages 1934

Klages, Ludwig: Vom Wesen des Rhythmus, Kampen auf Sylt 1934 (Niels Kampmann Verlag)

Klanten 1995

Klanten, Robert & Elsa for Toys: Localizer 1.0. The Techno House Book. Berlin 1995 (Die Gestalten)

Kneif 1978

Kneif, Tibor (ed.): Sachlexikon Rockmusik, Reinbek bei Hamburg 1978 (rowohlt)

Koch 2003

Koch, Albert: Kraftwerk, Höfen 2003 (Hannibal)

Krauss 1992

Krauss, Rosalind; Die Logik des spätkapitalistischen Museums, in Texte zur Kunst 6 (1992), 131-145

Kurtz 1988

Kurtz, Michael: Stockhausen. Eine Biographie, Kassel/Basel 1988 (Bärenreiter)

Kyle, undated

Kyle, Dave: An Interview with Ray Butts. undated http://www.scottymoore. net/Ray_Butts_interview.html

Landwehr 2014

Landwehr, Achim: Geburt der Gegenwart. Eine Geschichte der Zeit im 17. Jahrhundert, Frankfurt/Main 2014 (S. Fischer)

Lawrence 2003

Lawrence, Tim: Love saves the day. A History of American Dance Music, 1970-1979, Durham/London 2003 (Duke University Press)

Le Caine 1966
Le Caine, Hugh: A Tape Recorder for the Use in electronic music studios and related equipment, Journal of Music Theory 7 (1966), 82-97

Lee/Shlain 1992
Lee, Martin A.; Bruce Shlain: Acid Dreams. The complete social history of LSD: the CIA, the sitxies, and beyond, New York 1992 (Grove Press)

Lee 2004
Lee, Pamela M.: Chronophobia. On time in the art of the 1960s, Cambridge/London 2004 (MIT Press)

Lessing 1962
Lessing, Ephraim Gotthold: Laocoon, Indianapolis 1962 (Bobbs-Merrill)

Lévi-Strauss 1983
Lévi-Strauss, Claude: The Raw and the Cooked, Chicago 1983 (University of Chicago Press)

Lewisohn 1988
Lewisohn, Mark: The Beatles: Recording Sessions, New York 1988 (Harmony Books)

Linke 1997
Linke, Ulrich: Minimal Music – Dimensionen eines Begriffs, Essen 1997 (Verlag Die Blaue Eule)

Lippert/Maenz 1991
Lippert, Werner; Paul Maenz (eds.): Peter Roehr, Frankfurt/Main 1991 (Museum für Moderne Kunst)

Livingston/Tucker 1972
Livingston, Jane; Marcia Tucker: Bruce Nauman. Works from 1965 to 1972, Los Angeles 1972 (Los Angeles County Museum of Art)

Lovisa 1996
Lovisa, Fabian R.: Minimal Music. Entwicklung, Komponisten, Werke, Darmstadt 1996 (Wissenschaftliche Buchgesellschaft)

Macdonald 1995
MacDonald, Ian: Revolution in the Head, London 1995 (Pimlico)

Macdonald 2005
MacDonald, Ian: Revolution in the Head, London 2005 (Pimlico)

Maenz, undated

Paul Maenz: Wiederholungen, unveröffentlichtes Manuskript, undated

Maenz 1988

Maenz, Paul: Peter Roehr zum 20. Todestag, Cologne 1988 (Galerie Paul Maenz)

Manovich 2001

Manovich, Lev: The Language of New Media, Cambridge 2001 (MIT Press)

Marcus 1990

Marcus, Greil: Mystery Train. Images of America in Rock'n'Roll Music, New York 1990 (Dutton Obelisk)

Margulis 2014

Margulis, Elizabeth Hellmuth: On Repeat. How Music plays the Mind, New York 2014 (Oxford University Press)

Marsh 1982

Marsh, Dave: Elvis, New York 1982 (Rolling Stone Press)

Martin 1994

Martin, George: Summer of Love. The Making of Sgt. Pepper, London 1994 (Pan Books)

Marx 1998

Marx, Karl: Das Kapital, Kritik der politischen Ökonomie, Werke Vol. 23, Berlin 1956-1990

McClary 1998

McClary, Susan: Rap, Minimalism, and the Structures of Time in Late Twentieth-Century Culture, Lincoln 1998 (University of Nebraska)

Mertens 1983

Mertens, Wim: American Minimal Music. La Monte Young, Terry Riley, Steve Reich, Philip Glass, London 1983 (Kahn & Averill)

Messler 1988

Messler, Norbert: Peter Roehr, in Noema No. 2, Nov./Dez. 1988, unpaginated

Mesterharm/Amaretto/Brückner 1997

Mesterharm, Nico; Joel Amaretto; Wolfgang Brückner (eds.): Berlin Techno/ logy (Technology) 1. Clubland und Leute, Berlin 1997 (A-Verbal Verlag)

Metzger 1981

Metzger, Heinz-Klaus; Rainer Riehn (eds): Karlheinz Stockhausen...wie die zeit verging..., Munich 1981 (edition text + kritik: Musik-Konzepte 19)

Meyer 2003

Meyer, James: Minimalism. Art and Polemics in the Sixties. New Haven 2003 (Yale University Press)

Meyer-Eppler 1949

Meyer-Eppler, Werner: Elektronische Klangerzeugung, Bonn 1949 (Ferd. Dümmlers Verlag)

Michalka 2003

Michalka, Matthias (ed.): X-Screen. Filmische Installationen und Aktionen der Sechziger- und Siebzigerjahre, Cologne 2003 (Verlag der Buchhandlung Walter König)

Middleton 1990

Middleton, Richard: Studying Popular Music, Philadelphia 1990 (Open University Press)

Mießgang 1997

Mießgang, Thomas: Schlagsahne, Irrengesang, Kirmesgeister. Karlheinz Stockhausen testet Krautrock, Die Zeit No. 17, 18 April 1997, 72

Miles 1997

Miles, Barry: Paul McCartney – Many Years from Now, New York 1997 (Henry Holt & Co)

Mitchell 2003

Mitchell, Tim: Sedition and Alchemy – A Biography of John Cale, London 2003 (Peter Owen)

Morawska-Büngeler 1988

Morawska-Büngeler, Marietta: Schwingende Elektronen. Eine Dokumentation über das Studio für Elektronische Musik des Westdeutschen Rundfunks in Cologne 1951-1986, Cologne-Rodenkirchen 1988 (P. J. Tonger Musikverlag)

Moroder 2012

Moroder, Giorgio: Tributes To Those We Lost in 2012: Donna Summer, Time Magazine, 19 December 2012 http://poy.time.com/2012/12/19/tributes-to-those-we-lost-in-2012/slide/donna-summer/

Morton 2000

Off the Record: The Technology & Culture of Sound Recording in America: The Technology and Culture of Sound Recording in America, New Brunswick, NJ 2000 (Rutgers University Press)

Morton 2006

Morton, David L. Jr

Sound Recording: The Life Story of a Technology, Baltimore 2006 (Johns Hopkins University Press)

Mostrom 2001

Mostrom, Tony: Noise Ecstasy, LA Weekly, 2-8 November 2001 http://www.laweekly.com/ink/01/50/music-mostrom.php

Musser 1990

Musser, Charles: The Emergence of Cinema: The American Scene to 1907, New York 1990 (Scribners)

Musser 1991

Musser, Charles: Before the Nickelodeon: Edwin S. Porter and the Edison Manufacturing Company, Los Angeles 1991 (University of California Press)

Musser 1998

Edison Motion Pictures, 1890-1900: An Annotated Filmography, Washington 1998 (Smithsonian Studies in the History of Film & Television)

Musser 2005

Musser, Charles: The May Irwin Kiss: Performance and the Beginnings of Cinema, in: Toulmine, Vanessa; Simon Popple (eds.): Visual Delights Vol. II. Audience and Recep- tion, Eastleigh 2005 (John Libby), 96-115

Neal 1987

Neal, Charles: Tape Dealy – Confessions from the Eighties Underground, London 1987 (SAF Publishing Ltd.)

Niemczyk/Schmidt 2000

Niemczyk, Ralf; Torsten Schmidt: From Scratch. Das DJ- Handbuch, Cologne 2000 (Kiepenheuer & Witsch)

Nietzsche 1967

Nietzsche, Friedrich: Die fröhliche Wissenschaft. La gaya scienzia. Werke, Kritische Gesamtausgabe, edited by Giorgio Colli und Mazzino Montinari, Berlin 1967ff, Vol. V 2

Oldfield 1998

Mike Oldfield, Mojo, November 1998, zitiert nach: http://tubular.net/articles/98_11.shtml

O'pray 1989

O'Pray, Michael: Andy Warhol: Film Factory, London 1989 (British Film Institute)

Osswald 2004

Osswald, Anja: Sexy Lies in Videotapes. Künstlerische Selbstinszenierung im Video um 1970 – Bruce Nauman, Vito Acconci, Joan Jonas, Berlin 2004 (Gebr. Mann)

Oteri 2001

Oteri, Frank: Obsessed and passionate about music, Terry Riley in conversation with Frank Oteri, New Music Box, 2001 http://www.newmusicbox.org/26/riley_interview.pdf

Oteri 2003

Oteri, Frank: La Monte Young and Marian Zazeela at the Dream House New Music Box, 2003 www.newmusicbox.org/assets/54/interview_young.pdf

Ovid 1992

Ovid: Metamorphosen, Frankfurt/Main 1992 (Fischer)

Page 1986

Page, Tim: Steve Reich, a Former Young Turk, wird 50, New York Times, 1 June 1986, Section 2, 23

Partridge 1974

Partridge, Robert: An Interview with Robert Fripp, Melody Maker, 5 October 1974

Perls 1992

Perls, Fritz: Grundlagen der Gestalt-Therapie, Munich 1992 (Verlag J. Pfeiffer)

Perls 1979

Perls, Fritz: Gestalt-Therapie. Wiederbelebung des Selbst, Stuttgart 1979 (Klett)

Perls 1969

Perls, Fritz: Gestalttherapie Verbatim, John O. Stephens, Moab Utah (eds.) 1969 (Real People Press)

Perls 1990

Perls, Frederick: Das Vermächtnis der Gestalttherapie, edited by Patricia Baumgardner, Stuttgart 1990 (Klett-Cotta)

Perry 1985

Perry, Charles: The Haight-Ashbury. A History, New York 1985 (Vintage Books)

Perry/Babbs 1990

Perry, Paul; Ken Babbs: On The Bus. The Complete Guide to the Legendary Trip of Ken Kesey and the Merry Pranksters and the Birth of Counterculture, New York 1990 (Thunder's Mouth Press)

Pinch/Trocco 2002

Pinch, Trevor; Frank Trocco: Analog Days – The Invention and Impact of the Moog Synthesizer, Cambridge/London 2002 (Harvard University Press)

Plimpton 2002

Plimpton, George: He put the camp into Campbell's, The Observer, 27 January 2002, unpaginated

P-Orridge 1986

P-Orridge, Genesis: The Industrial Records Story, Booklet-Text zu der CD TBCD1, London 1986 (Mute Records)

Poschardt 1997

Poschardt, Ulf: DJ Culture, Hamburg 1997 (rowohlt)

Poschardt 2002

Poschardt, Ulf: Cool, Reinbek bei Hamburg 2002 (rowohlt)

Potter 2000

Potter, Keith: Four Musical Minimalists, Cambridge 2000 (Cambridge University Press)

Poullin 1955

Poullin, Jacques: Musique Concrete. Aufnahmetechnik bei der Verarbeitung von Klangmaterial und neuer musikalischer Form, in: Winckel, Fritz: Klangstruktur der Musik. Neue Erkenntnisse musik-elektronischer Forschung, Berlin 1955 (Verlag für radio-foto-kinotechnik)

Prieberg 1960

Prieberg, Fred K.: Musica ex Machina, Berlin 1960 (Verlag Ullstein)

Raab 1981

Raab, Claus: Musik der Allmählichkeit und des Präsenz, in: Gruhn, Wilfried (ed.):

Reflexionen über Musik heute, Mainz 1981 (Schott), 169-181

Reich 1974

Reich, Steve: Writings about music, Halifax/New York 1974 (Press of Nova Scotia College of Art and Design/New York University Press)

Re/Search 1982

Throbbing Gristle, in: A Special Book Issue. W. S. Burroughs, Brion Gysin and Throbbing Gristle, Re/Search 4/5, San Francisco 1982 (Research)

Reynolds 1998

Reynolds, Simon: Energy Flash. A Journey through Rave Music and Dance Culture. London 1998 (Picador)

Rietveld 1998

Rietveld, Hillegonda: This Is Our House, Brookfield, VT. 1998 (Ashgate)

Riley undated

Interview with Terry Riley, undated https://qaswa.com/reference/qaswa1/rhythmos/terry.html Roehr 2010

Peter Roehr: Ausstellung from 28 November 2009 to 7 March 2010, Petersberg (Imhof)

Robertson 1992

Robertson, John: John Lennon – Rocklegenden, Königswinter 1992 (Heel)

Roylance et al 2000

Roylance, Brian et al (eds.): The Beatles Anthology, London 2000 (Cassell & Co)

Rose 1994 a

Rose, Tricia: A Style Nobody Can Deal With – Politics, Style and the Postindustrial City in Hip Hop, in: Ross, Andrew; Tricia Rose (eds.): Microphone fiends: youth music and youth culture, London 1994 (Routledge), 71-88

Rose 1994 b

Rose, Tricia: Black Noise. Rap Music and Black Culture in Contemporary America, Hanover 1994 (University Press of New England)

Ross/Rose 1994

Ross, Andrew; Tricia Rose (eds.): Microphone Fiends. Youth Music and Youth Culture, London/ New York 1994 (Routledge)

Roylance 2000

Roylance, Brian (ed.): The Beatles Anthology, Munich 2000 (Ullstein)

Rule 1999

Rule, Greg: Electro Shock! Groundbreakers of Synth Music, San Francisco 1999 (Miller Freeman Books)

Ruschkowski 1998

Ruschkowski, André: Elektronische Klänge und musikalische Entdeckungen, Stuttgart 1998 (Reclam)

Sabbe 1981

Sabbe, Herman: Die Einheit der Stockhausen-Zeit. Neue Erkenntnismöglichkeiten der seriellen Entwicklung anhand des frühen Wirkens von Stockhausen ud Goeyvaerts. Dargestellt aufgrund der Briefe Stockhausens an Goeyvaerts, in: Metzger, Heinz-Klaus; Rainer Riehn (eds.): Karlheinz

Stockhausen...wie die zeit verging..., Munich 1981 (edition text + kritik: Musik-Konzepte 19), 6-71

Samagaio 2002

Samagaio, Frank: The Mellotron Book, Vallejo 2002 (ProMusic Press)

Savage 2012

Savage, Jon: How Donna Summer's *I Feel Love* changed pop, The Guardian, 18 May 2012 http://www.guardian.co.uk/music/musicblog/2012/may/18/donna-summer-i-feel-love

Schaeffer 1950

Schaeffer, Pierre: Introductions a la musique concrète, in: *La musique mecanisée: Polyphonie 6*, Paris 1950 (Richard-Mass), 30-52

Schaeffer 1974

Schaeffer, Pierre: Musique Concrete. Von den Pariser Anfängen um 1948 bis zur elektro- akustischen Musik heute, Stuttgart 1974 (Ernst Klett)

Schaeffer 1987

http://paul.mycpanel.princeton.edu/music242/shaefferinterview.html

Schaeffer 1998

Schaeffer, Pierre: A la recherche d'une musique concrète, Paris 1998 (Editions Du Seuil)

Schaeffer 2012

Schaeffer, Pierre: *In Search of a Concrete Music*, California 2012 (University of California Press)

Schaeffer (undated)

Schaeffer, Pierre: Wechselwirkung zwischen Musik und Akustik, in: Gravesaner Blätter 14, 51-60

Schenk 1996

Schenk, Dietmar: Paul Hindemith und die Rundfunkversuchsstelle der Berliner Musikhochschule, in: Hindemith-Jahrbuch, Vol. 25, Mainz 1996 (Schott), 179-194

Schivelbusch 1989

Schivelbusch, Wolfgang: Geschichte der Eisenbahnreise, Frankfurt/Main 1989 (Fischer)

Schmitz 1987

Schmitz, Reinhard: Der trommelnde Roboter. Geschichte des automatischen Schlagzeugs, Keyboard 11/1987, 38-42

Schnebel 1972

Schnebel, Dieter: Denkbare Musik. Schriften 1952-1972, hg. v. Hans Rudolf Zeller, Cologne 1972 (DuMont)

Schönberg/stephan 1979

Schönberg, Arnold; Rudolf Stephan: Die Grundlagen der musikalischen Komposition, Wien 1979 (Universal Edition)

Schreiber 1981

Schreiber, Ulrich: Die wiedergewonnene Fülle des Wohllauts, Merkur 4/1981, 407

Schuller 1968

Schuller, Gunter: The History of Jazz, Vol. 1: Early Jazz. Its Roots and Musical Development, New York 1968 (Oxford University Press)

Schumacher 2015

Schumacher, Eckhard: Popkolumne. Vergangene Zukunft. Repetition, Rekonstruktion, Retrospektion, Merkur 788 (January 2015), 51-57

Schwartz 2000

Schwartz, Hillel: Déjà Vu. Die Welt im Zeitalter ihrer tatsächlichen Reproduzierbarkeit, Berlin 2000 (Aufbau Verlag)

Schwarz 1996

Schwarz, Robert: Minimalists. London 1996 (Phaidon Press)

Scott 2000

Scott, Raymond: Unadressed Letter, in: Blom, Gert-Jan, Jeff Winner, Irwin Chusid (eds.): Manhattan Research Inc., New Plastic Sounds and

Electronic Abstractions, Composed and Performed by Ramond Scott, Aalsmeer 2000 (Basta Music), 15f.

Seachrist 2003

Seachrist, Denis: The Musical World of Halim El-Dabh, Kent 2003 (Kent State University Press)

Seibt 1997

Seibt, Gustav: Der Aufstand der Massen. Zu Risiken und Nebenwirkungen der Love Parade: Nachfrage bei Freud, Canetti und anderen, Berliner Zeitung, 12 July 1997, 23

Shapiro 2000

Shapiro, Peter (ed.): Modulations. A History of Electronic Music. Throbbing Words on Sound, New York 2000 (Distributed Art Publishers)

Shapiro 2005

Shapiro, Peter: Turn the Beat Around. The Secret History of Disco, New York 2005 (Faber & Faber)

Sidran 1993

Sidran, Ben: Black Talk, Schwarze Kultur – die andere Kultur im weißen Amerika, Hofheim 1993 (Wolke Verlag)

Sitney 2002

Sitney, P. Adams: Visionary Film: The American Avant-Garde in the 20th Century, New York 2002 (Oxford University Press)

Small 1977

Small, Christopher: Music, Society, Education: An Examination of the Function of Music in Western, Eastern and African Cultures with its Impact on Society and Its Use in Education, New York 1977 (Schirmer)

Smith 1977/78

Smith, David: Following a Straight Line: La Monte Young, Contact No. 18 (Winter 1977-78), 4-9

Smith, undated

Smith, Geoff: The History of Live Looping, *Live Looping* web site http://livelooping.org/researchpapers/geoffsmith/index.htm

Snead 1984

Snead, James: Repetition as a figure of black culture, in: Gates Jr., Henry Louis (eds.): Black Literature and Literary Theory, New York 1984 (Methuen), 59-79

Stein/Plimpton 1982
Stein, Jean; George Plimpton: Edie. An American Autobiography, New York
    1982 (Alfred A. Knopf)
Stemmrich 1995
Stemmrich, Gregor (ed.): Minimal Art. Eine kritische Retrospektive,
    Dresden/Basel 1995 (Verlag der Kunst)
Stockhausen 1963
Stockhausen, Karlheinz: Texte zur elektronischen und instrumentalen Musik.
    Aufsätze 1952-1962 zur Theorie des Komponierens. Vol. 1, Cologne
    1963 (DuMont)
Stockhausen 1964
Stockhausen, Karlheinz: Texte zu eigenen Werken, zur Kunst Anderer,
    Aktuelles. Vol. 2: Aufsätze 1952-1962 zur musikalischen Praxis, Cologne
    1964 (DuMont)
Stockhausen 1971
Stockhausen, Karlheinz: Texte zur Musik 1963-1970, Vol. 3: Einführungen
    und Projekte, Cologne 1971 (DuMont)
Stockhausen 1978
Stockhausen, Karlheinz: Texte zur Musik 1970-1977 Vol. 4, Cologne 1978
    (DuMont)
Stockhausen 1995
Article from "The Wire", http://www.andreas.de/aphextwin/articles/
    interview2.html
Strawinsky 1929
Strawinsky, Igor: Meine Stellung zur Schallplatte, in: Kultur und Schallplatte
    No. 9, 1929, 65
Strickland 1991
Strickland, Edward: American Composers. Dialogues on Contemporary
    Music, Bloomington 1991 (Indiana University Press)
Strickland 1993
Strickland, Edward: Minimalism: Origins, Bloomington 1993 (Indiana
    University Press)
Strogatz 2003
Strogatz, Steven: Sync. How Order emerges from the Universe, Nature, and
    Daily Life, New York 2003 (Theia)

Stroh 1994

Stroh, Wolfgang Martin: Handbuch New Age Musik. Auf der Suche nach neuen musi- kalischen Erfahrungen, Regensburg 1994 (ConBrio Verlagsgesellschaft)

Summer 2003

Summer, Donna (with Marc Eliot): Ordinary Girl – The Journey, New York 2003 (Villard)

Tamm 1995

Tamm, Eric: Brian Eno – His Music, Ideas, and the Vertical Color of Sound, ursprünglich: Boston & London 1995 (Faber & Faber), quoted from version published on www.erictamm.com/tammeno.html

Tamm 1990

Tamm, Eric: Robert Fripp – From Crimson King to crafty master, Boston/London 1990 (Faber & Faber), zitiert nach der im Internet veröffentlichten Version www.progressiveears.com/frippbook/

Tannenbaum 1985

Tannenbaum, Rob: A Meeting of Sound Minds: John Cage and Brian Eno, Musician 83 (September 1985), 68

Taylor 1987

Taylor, Paul. Final Interview with Andy Warhol, Flash Art, April 1987, zitiert nach: http://www.warholstars.org/warhol/warhol1/warhol1n/last.html

Taylor 2001

Taylor, Timothy: Strange Sounds. Music, Technology and Culture, New York/London 2001 (Routledge)

Teipel 2001

Teipel, Jürgen: Verschwende Deine Jugend. Ein Doku-Roman über den deutschen Punk und New Wave, Frankfurt/Main (2001)

Theobald 1956

Theobald, Adolf: Der schwarze und der weiße Jazz. Jazz wurde exportiert und verfälscht, in Rheinischer Merkur, No. 15, 13 April 1956, 24

Thompson 1966

Thompson, Robert Farris: An Aesthetic of the Cool: West African Dance, in: African Forum, Vol. 2, No. 2 (Herbst 1966), 85-102

Thompson 1983

Thompson, Robert Farris: Flash of the Spirit. African & Afro-American Art & Philosophy, New York 1983 (Vintage Books)

Thornton 1996

Thornton, Sarah: Club Cultures. Music, Media and Subcultural Capital, Middletown 1996 (Wesleyan University Press)

Toop 1994

Toop, David: Rap Attack. African Jive bis Global HipHop, Munich 1994 (Wilhelm Heyne Verlag)

Toop 1995

Toop, David: Ocean of Sound. Aether Talk, Ambient Sound and Imaginary Worlds, London 1995 (Serpent's Tail)

Turner 2006

Turner, Fred: From Counterculture to Cyberculture. Stewart Brand, the Whole Earth Network, and the Rise of Digital Utopianism, Chicago 2006 (University of Chicago Press)

Ulmer 1983

Ulmer, Gregory: The object of Post-Criticism, in: Foster, Hal (ed.): The anti-aesthetic: essays on postmodern culture, Seattle 1983 (Bay Press)

Ungeheuer 2002

Ungeheuer, Elena (ed.): Elektroakustische Musik, Laaber 2002 (Laaber Verlag)

Vail 2000

Vail, Mark: Vintage Synthesizer, San Francisco 2000 (Miller Freeman Books)

Vale/Juno 1993

Vale, V.; Andrea Juno (eds.): Incredibly Strange Music, Vol. 1, San Francisco 1993 (Re/Search Publications)

Van Bruggen 1988

Van Bruggen, Coosje: Bruce Nauman, New York 1988 (Rizzoli)

Varela 1994

Varela, Francisco: Der kreative Zirkel – Skizzen zur Naturgeschichte der Rückbezüglichkeit, in: Watzlawick, Paul (ed.): Die erfundene Wirklichkeit, Munich 1994 (Piper), 294-309

Waksman 1999

Waksman, Steve: Instruments of Desire. The Electric Guitar and the Shaping of Musical Experience, Cambridge 1999 (Harvard University Press)

Warhol/Hackett 1980

Warhol, Andy; Pat Hackett: POPism. The Warhol Sixties, New York 1980 (Harcourt)

Wehmeyer 1997

Wehmeyer, Grete: Erik Satie, Kassel 1997 (Gustav Bosse)

Wehmeyer 1998

Wehmeyer, Grete: Erik Satie, Reinbek bei Hamburg 1998 (rowohlts monographien)

Wendermann 2000

Wendermann, Gerda: Peter Roehr 1944-1968, Ostfildern 2000 (Hatje Cantz)

Wendorff 1991

Wendorff, Rudolf: Die Zeit, mit der wir leben, Herne 1991 (Heitkamp Edition)

wicke 1993

Wicke, Peter: Popmusik. Vom Umgang mit Popmusik, Berlin 1993 (Volk und Wissen)

Wicke 1987

Wicke, Peter: Rockmusik. Zur Ästhetik und Soziologie eines Massenmediums, Leipzig 1987 (Verlag Philipp Reclam jun.)

Wicke 1998

Wicke, Peter: Von Mozart zu Madonna. Eine Kulturgeschichte der Popmusik, Leipzig 1998 (Suhrkamp)

Wicke/Zeigenrücker 1997

Wicke, Peter; Kai-Erik und Wieland Zeigenrücker: Handbuch der populären Musik, Mainz 1997 (Schott/Atlantis)

Williams 1961

Williams, Raymond: The Long Revolution, New York 1961 (Columbia Press)

Williamson undated

Williamson, Clive: Digital DIY. Interview with Bob Moog, undated www. symbiosis-music.com/moog.html

Winkler 2002

Winkler, Thomas: Amerikas schmutzigste Wäsche, taz – die tageszeitung, 5 November 2002, 15

Winner/Chusid 2009

Winner, Jeff; Irwin Chusid: "Circle Machines and Sequencers". The Untold History of Raymond Scott's Pioneering Instruments, Electronic Musician https://beatpatrol. wordpress.com/2009/10/25/jeff-e-winner-irwin-d-chusid-circle-machines-and sequencers-the-untold-history-of-raymond-scotts-pioneering-instruments/

Wirtz 2003

Wirtz, Markus: Front 242. The Legend Returns, 2003 http://www.ikonenmagazin.de/interview/Front242.htm

Wolfe 1968

Wolfe, Tom: The Electric Kool-Aid Acid Test, New York 1968 (Farrar, Straus & Giraux)

Young, G. 1989

Young, Gayle: The Sackbut Blues. Hugh Le Caine: Pioneer in Electronic Music, Ottawa 1989 (National Museum of Science and Technology)

Young, G. 1999

Young, Gayle: Begleit-Buch zu der CD "Hugh Le Caine: Compositions. Demonstrations 1946-1974", JWD Music 1999

Young, l. m. 2001

Young, La Monte: Program Notes for Composition 1960 #7, performed by a Theatre of Eternal Music String Ensemble, Diapson Gallery, 20 June, 2001 http://diapasongallery.org/archive/01_06_20.html

Young, r. 1995

Young, Rob: Advice to clever children, The Wire, November 1995, 20-24

Zglinicki 1979

Zglinicki, Friedrich von: Der Weg des Films. Textband, Hildesheim/New York 1979 (Olms Presse)

Zuckermann 2002 a

Zuckermann, Gabriele: American Mavericks: An Interview wich La Monte Young and

Marian Zazeela, American Public Media 2002 http://musicmavericks.publicradio.org/features/interview_young.html

Zuckermann 2002 b

Zuckermann, Gabriele: American Mavericks: An interview with Steve Reich, American Public Media 2002

http://musicmavericks.publicradio.org/features/interview_reich.html

DISCOGRAPHY

Cale, John: Stainless Gamelan: Inside the Dream Syndicate, Table of the Elements (1997)

Cale, John; Tony Conrad; Angus MacLise; La Monte Young; Marian Zazeela: Inside the Dream Syndicate Volume I: Day Of Niagara, Table of Elements (2000)

The Grateful Dead & The Merry Pranksters 65-67 Acid Tests, Bootleg

Conrad, Tony: Early Minimalism Volume One, Table of the Elements (1997) Conrad, Tony; Early Minimalism, Volume Two, Table of the Elements (1997) The Disco Box, Rhino Records (1999)

Le Caine, Hugh: Compositions. Demonstrations 1946-1974, JWD Music (1999) Presley, Elvis: Sun Sessions, RCA (1990)

Reich, Steve: Sextet/Six Marimbas, Nonesuch (1986)

Reich, Steve: Drumming, Nonesuch (1987)

Reich, Steve: Early Works, Nonesuch (1987) Reich, Steve: Music For 18 Musicians (1989)

Reich, Steve: Different Trains/Electric Counterpoint, Nonesuch (1989)

Reich, Steve: The Four Sections/Music for Mallet Instruments, Voices and Organ, Nonesuch (1990)

Reich, Steve: Proverb/Nagoya Marimbas/City Life (1996)

Reich, Steve: Steve Reich 1965-1995, Nonesuch (1996)

Reich, Steve: Phase Patterns/Pendulum Music/Piano Phase/Four Organs, Wergo (1999)

Reich, Steve: City Life/New York Counterpoint/Eight Lines/ Violin Phase, RCA Red Seal (2002)

Riley, Terry: Happy Ending, Warner (1972) Riley, Terry: Le Secret De La Vie, Philips (1975) Riley, Terry: In C, CBS (1988)

Riley, Terry: Poppy Nogood and the Phantom Band, All Night Flight Vol. 1, organ of Corti 4 (1996)

Riley, Terry: Reed Streams / In C (Mantra), Organ of Corti Riley, Terry: A Rainbow in Curved Air, Columbia Masterworks (1999) Riley, Terry: Olson III, organ of Corti (1999)

Riley, Terry: Music for the Gift, organ of Corti (2000)

Riley, Terry: You're No Good, Organ of Corti (2000)

Roehr, Peter: Tonmontagen I + II, supposé (2002)

Schaeffer, Pierre: L' Œuvre Musicale, L'Institut National de l'Audiovisuel & Electronic Music Foundation (1998)

Scott, Raymond: Soothing Sounds for Baby, Basta Music (1997) Scott, Raymond: Manhattan Research Inc., Basta Music (2000) Summer, Donna: Love to Love You Baby, Oasis (1975)

Summer, Donna: I Remember Yesterday, Casablanca (1977) Young, La Monte: Black Album, Bootleg, undated

Young, La Monte: Trio for Strings, Bootleg, undated

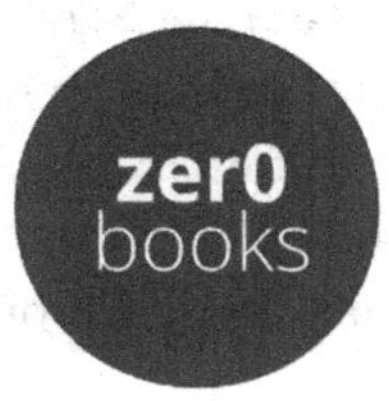

CULTURE, SOCIETY & POLITICS

Contemporary culture has eliminated the concept and public figure of the intellectual. A cretinous anti-intellectualism presides, cheer-led by hacks in the pay of multinational corporations who reassure their bored readers that there is no need to rouse themselves from their stupor. Zer0 Books knows that another kind of discourse – intellectual without being academic, popular without being populist – is not only possible: it is already flourishing. Zer0 is convinced that in the unthinking, blandly consensual culture in which we live, critical and engaged theoretical reflection is more important than ever before.

If you have enjoyed this book, why not tell other readers by posting a review on your preferred book site.

You may also wish to subscribe to our Zer0 Books YouTube Channel.

Sweetening the Pill

or How We Got Hooked on Hormonal Birth Control
Holly Grigg-Spall
Has contraception liberated or oppressed women?
Sweetening the Pill breaks the silence on the dark side of hormonal
contraception.
Paperback: 978-1-78099-607-3 ebook: 978-1-78099-608-0

Why Are We The Good Guys?

Reclaiming Your Mind from the Delusions of Propaganda
David Cromwell
A provocative challenge to the standard ideology that Western
power is a benevolent force in the world.
Paperback: 978-1-78099-365-2 ebook: 978-1-78099-366-9

The Writing on the Wall

On the Decomposition of Capitalism and its Critics
Anselm Jappe, Alastair Hemmens
A new approach to the meaning of social emancipation.
Paperback: 978-1-78535-581-3 ebook: 978-1-78535-582-0

Neglected or Misunderstood

The Radical Feminism of Shulamith Firestone
Victoria Margree
An interrogation of issues surrounding gender, biology,
sexuality, work and technology, and the ways in which our
imaginations continue to be in thrall to ideologies of maternity
and the nuclear family.
Paperback: 978-1-78535-539-4 ebook: 978-1-78535-540-0